THE LIFE OF
WILLIAM BRANHAM

VOLUME II
BOOKS 4 & 5

1951 - 1960

O W E N   J O R G E N S E N

SUPERNATURAL
CHRISTIAN BOOKS

Supernatural:
The Life of William Branham

Volume II
Books Four and Five
(1951–1960)

Copyright © 2011
By Owen Jorgensen

ISBN Soft Cover 978-0-9828616-1-5
ISBN Hard Cover 978-0-9828616-4-6

Published by:
Supernatural Christian Books
P.O. Box 695
Coulee City, Washington 99115 USA
supernaturalchristianbooks.com

Distributed by:
Believers Christian Fellowship
1695 Stewart Road,
Lima, OH 45801-3209 U.S.A.
bcfellowship.org
(419) 221-0085

Acknowledgments

In a project of this magnitude, it is understandable that I should owe many people a debt of gratitude for their help. First I want to thank Pearry Green for his initial encouragement and support. I also want to thank David Buckley, Jinjoo Kim, Anton Liachovic, Saundra Miles, Jay Weber, and all the other people who spent many hours editing and proofreading the six manuscripts in this series. Incorporating their suggestions into the text improved the accuracy of this biography and made it a better book. Also, I want to thank Steven and Kathie Strooh, who recorded this biography for all those people who would rather listen than read. I must certainly thank those people who have translated this biography into Chinese, Finnish, French, German, Hindi, Korean, Norwegian, Portuguese, Russian, Spanish, Vietnamese, and other languages. Finally, my thanks to the Lord Jesus Christ for His never-failing love and care through the 23 years it took me to finish this biography of William Branham.

—Owen Jorgensen, 2011

Now thanks be to God who always leads us in triumph in Christ, and through us diffuses the fragrance of His knowledge in every place.

—2 Corinthians 2:14 (NKJV)

Contents

Introduction

The subtitle for *Supernatural: Book Four* is *The Evangelist and His Acclamation* because it covers the four years of William Branham's life when his worldwide popularity reached its zenith. Thousands of ministers wanted him to hold faith-healing campaigns in their areas. When he went to large cities, hundreds of local pastors would cooperate with him in huge interdenominational gatherings. Between 1951 and 1954 he conducted the largest Christian meetings ever held up to that time. Fifty thousand people came to one meeting in Durban, South Africa, and 300,000 attended a meeting in Bombay, India.

Remarkably, the size of his crowds did not impress William Branham. He would preach to 25 people just as willingly as he would to 25,000. In 1953, he said, "Tonight I know of places that's calling me where they've got 15,000 people that can be there the first night. I know of many places where at least a 150,000 will be gathered on the first night. But it isn't crowds that I'm thinking about. The Gospel must be preached in this city, and that city, and to all the world for a witness, then the Lord shall come. Not theology must be preached, but the power and demonstration of the Holy Ghost must be preached in all the world for a witness. Then the time shall come. God bless you. It's your hour. Receive ye Him."

William Branham's entire ministry was a spectacular display of God's power. Although *The Evangelist and His Acclamation* describes many miracles and other phenomenon, these are just representative of the thousands of supernatural things that took place in his ministry during these four years. After telling about the miraculous healing of former Congressman Upshaw, William Branham said, "Concerning this type of testimony, I believe I could stand here for the next 500 hours (if that were possible) and give testimonies about things I have seen our Lord do, and it wouldn't cover it... thousands of volumes of books wouldn't cover in detail all the things I've seen our Lord Jesus do. Friends, it's just been hundreds times hundreds times hundreds... You say, 'Why didn't I hear about it?' That's the same thing many Jews thought after Jesus was crucified. Many of them said, 'Why didn't I hear about the miracles before?' It's your privilege to hear about it now, and to accept it. This is your day."

Having done exhaustive research into William Branham's life, I agree with his assessment—it would take thousands of volumes to cover all the details of the visions, miracles, healings, and other supernatural phenomenon that have taken place in and around his ministry.

The subtitle for *Supernatural: Book Five* is *The Teacher and His Rejection* because in one sense it accurately describes the next period of William Branham's life. At the end of 1954 he felt the Holy Spirit was leading him to teach people about the deeper things of God during his faith-healing campaigns. Consequently, he began to offend people when his sound teachings exposed many fallacies and misconceptions Christians had about the Bible. In a few years he had offended enough people so that the demand for his services dropped noticeably.

Jesus Christ had the same thing happen in his ministry. Thousands of people loved Jesus when He was healing the sick, feeding everyone fish and bread, and teaching them in parables. Eventually, Jesus put away the baby bottle and taught them the meat of the Gospel. Jesus said, "Blessed is he who is not offended in Me."[1] But many people were offended when they heard him

---

[1] Matthew 11:6; Luke 7:23

teach deep truths. For example, Jesus said, "Unless you eat the flesh of the Son of Man and drink His blood, you have no life in you." After hearing this, the crowds thinned drastically until even 70 of His closest followers left Him. Jesus turned to His 12 disciples and asked, "Do you also want to go away?" Simon Peter answered Him, "Lord, to whom shall we go? You have the words of eternal life. Also we have come to believe and know that You are the Christ, the Son of the living God."[2] After that day, Jesus never again enjoyed widespread popularity in Israel. A critic might argue that His ministry went downhill from there, until on the cross even Jesus Himself cried out, "My God, My God, why have You forsaken Me?"[3] But remember, widespread public opinion is not the same thing as truth. Although His popularity with the masses dwindled, Jesus fulfilled the purpose for which His Father put Him on earth—the salvation of all those who will believe on His name.

I mention this to show that the decline in William Branham's popularity during the late 1950's has a Scriptural precedent in Jesus Christ. While the crowds at William Branham's faith-healing campaigns were getting smaller and the invitations for him to speak were getting fewer, God was preparing him for the final stage of his ministry which would surpass everything that happened earlier. This would be his "third pull" (a term you will understand later).

To be fair, my subtitle, *The Teacher and His Rejection*, is only referring to how the denominational church leadership viewed William Branham during the latter half of the 1950's. There were still people all over the world who appreciated the gift God had given him. What is equally important, God had not rejected him—that was soon to become abundantly clear.

–Owen Jorgensen 2011

---

[2] John 6:47-71
[3] Matthew 27:46; Mark 15:34

Jesus said, "Believe Me that I am in the Father, and the Father in Me, or else believe Me for the sake of the works themselves. Most assuredly, I say to you, he who believes in Me, the works that I do he will do also; and greater works than these he will do, because I go to My Father."

—John 14:11, 12 (NKJV)

Book Four:
The Evangelist and His Acclamation

(1951 — 1954)

Chapter 53
Miracles in Black and White
1951

WILLIE UPSHAW had been waiting 66 years for this night. "It's now or never," he thought anxiously. "If I can only get there in time..." He wanted the taxi to move faster, but rush-hour traffic was forcing the driver to go slower. Willie glanced at his watch. William Branham's meeting would start soon. If he didn't arrive early enough to get a prayer-card, this trip might be in vain. Without a prayer-card, he couldn't get into the prayer-line; and if he didn't get in the prayer-line, how could he ever realize his dream?

For more than half a century he had kept a fantastic dream smoldering in his heart, a tiny glowing ember of desire that he would not let die. Willie Upshaw wanted to walk without help. It was that simple – and that complicated. The last time he had walked on his own was back when he was 18 years old, before he had broken his back in a farming accident. Through all the difficult years that followed, he struggled to live up to his motto, "*Let nothing discourage you, and never give up.*" Believing in a God of unlimited power, Willie had prayed earnestly to walk again. God had healed him of various ailments, including an inoperable cancer on his face. Despite the many years he had prayed for appropriate faith, somehow he had never been able to reach the level of faith he needed to rise and walk, until now—maybe...

The day before, Willie Upshaw and his wife Lily were at a convention of Baptist ministers near his home in Santa Monica, California. There they met Dr. Roy Davis, the minister who had ordained William Branham in 1932. Willie Upshaw asked Dr. Davis if all the phenomenal reports he was hearing about William Branham were true. Roy Davis told him about one miracle which he had seen firsthand. A deacon in his church named Frank Shoemaker had lost the use of his legs when he had broken his back ten years earlier. Confined to a wheelchair, he made himself useful by working in the church office. The previous year Shoemaker attended a Branham faith-healing campaign, and that night William Branham said he saw a vision of Frank Shoemaker walking. Shoemaker immediately stood up and walked away from his wheelchair. Dr. Davis told Willie Upshaw that Frank Shoemaker had walked just fine ever since.

That story fanned the ember of Willie's dream until it was glowing red and smoking. If he could ever get William Branham to pray for him, maybe he too could walk again. Then he learned that William Branham was about to finish a healing campaign in Los Angeles. Suddenly Willie's old dream started burning again. He went straight home, packed his bags, and booked the next flight to Los Angeles. This was it! This was probably his last chance! That is why he had to get to Branham's meeting early enough to get a prayer-card.

Unfortunately, traffic was now getting heavier, slowing his taxi even more. Nervously, he picked at a rivet of his back brace.

"Willie," said his wife, "keep your eyes on the Lord Jesus. God has already brought you victoriously through so many trials. Think how much more it will honor Him for you to cross the continent and witness for Him without crutches, declaring Him the Savior of your soul, but also as the Great Physician who has healed your body."

Willie knew she was right, but a blanket of doubt was still trying to smother his fire. He thought about how long it had been since he had last walked without crutches. His accident happened in 1884. It was now 1951, sixty-six years later.

So much had happened since that fateful summer day in 1884. The seven years he spent in bed seemed like a nightmare, yet those same agonizing years drew him closer to God. From his bed of suffering, he wrote an inspirational book, *Earnest Willie, or Echoes From a Recluse*. This book started his long career in public service. Sales of *Earnest Willie* gave him enough money to attend college. Later he founded *The Golden Age* magazine, which he edited for 13 years.

Then he plowed into politics. In 1919 he won a seat in the United States Congress, elected by the people of Georgia. Willie was especially proud of the eight years he had served in the United States House of Representatives. Many of his friends still referred to him as Congressman Upshaw. In 1932 he campaigned for president of the United States, running as the candidate for the Prohibition Party.

After his presidential defeat, he worked without pay in Christian education, helping disadvantaged children go to college. He traveled to schools in 42 states, lecturing to tens of thousands of students, encouraging them to have a purpose linked to God. In 1938, at the age of 72, he was ordained as a Baptist minister and later served two terms as vice-president of the Southern Baptist Convention. He even worked for a time as vice-president of Linda Vista Baptist College and Seminary in San Diego, California.

Now, at age 84, Willie Upshaw felt proud of his distinguished career, especially considering his disability. Through all those difficult years he never lost his dream that someday he would again walk as freely as other men. He always believed if he could just take hold of the appropriate faith, anything was possible.

As the taxi driver struggled to make progress in the heavy traffic, Willie took a newspaper clipping from his pocket and read it again for encouragement. The article told about a miracle that happened last year to Florence Nightingale Shirlaw, a relative of Florence Nightingale, the famous nineteenth-century English nurse. Florence Shirlaw lived in South Africa. Although she was only in her thirties, her life was being strangled by a malignant cancer that had grown over the duodenum of her stomach, preventing her from digesting her food. Because the cancer was inoperable, her condition seemed hopeless. Her doctors fed her intravenously for several months, while her muscles shriveled and her skin shrank back to the bones. Eventually her weight dropped to 50 pounds, making her look like skin stretched over a skeleton. Those around her believed she was going to die, but Florence Nightingale Shirlaw had not yet given up hope.

She had read about William Branham and the amazing success he was having praying for the sick. In 1946, William Branham said an angel brought him a commission from God to take a gift of divine healing to the peoples of the world. The angel told him that if he would be sincere and could get people to believe him when he prayed, nothing would stand before his prayer, not even cancer. Miss Shirlaw sent William Branham an airplane ticket and begged him to fly to South Africa to pray for her. Unfortunately the evangelist was already scheduled to go to Sweden, Finland, and Norway. When Florence Shirlaw learned that Brother Branham would be stopping in England to pray for King George VI, she chartered an airplane to London. Her plane landed just minutes behind the plane carrying the famous American evangelist. By now, Florence was almost dead. Her veins had collapsed, meaning her nurse could no longer insert a needle for intravenous feeding.

Her voice was a whisper; her breathing was shallow; her pulse was slow and faint. William Branham asked God to heal her in the name of Jesus Christ, and then he prophesied, "Thus saith the Lord, 'You will live and not die'." As incredible as that prophecy sounded, it came true. The article included a current picture of Florence Nightingale Shirlaw, showing her standing on a sidewalk wearing a plaid dress and holding a large purse. The article said she now weighed 155 pounds.

Willie Upshaw put the newspaper clipping back in the pocket of his blue suit coat. His faith was burning like a brush fire fanned by a hot California wind. Just let him get in that prayer-line now! He was ready to believe all the way.

But even as he thought this, his taxi slowed to a stop in the jam of traffic, making that prayer-card look a long ways off. Willie muttered to himself, "Let nothing discourage you, and never give up."

HOWARD BRANHAM knocked lightly on the door of his brother's hotel room. "Billy," he said softly, "the meeting is about to start. If we don't get going, we're going to be late."

He listened for an answer. None came. Howard raised his hand to knock louder, but decided against it. This was their fourth day in Los Angeles and he could tell his brother was feeling the strain of praying for the sick. Still, Howard had never known his brother to fall asleep before a meeting. More than likely he was deep in prayer. Howard walked downstairs to a restaurant, ordered a malted milkshake, and sipped it slowly through a straw. Finishing the malt, he went back upstairs to knock again. This time the door was ajar.

William Branham didn't speak to his brother as they drove to Calvary Temple. His thoughts were centered on the Holy Spirit. In his hotel room the angel of the Lord had visited him. Even when Bill could not see the angel, he could always tell when the angel came near. A pressure would touch his skin, like a breeze that was charged with static electricity. In the presence of this supernatural being, Bill would grow numb with awe and fear. Although the angel had met him hundreds of times, Bill always felt apprehensive at his coming. However, this fear would diminish when the angel spoke. Often visions followed. Bill had no control over these visions. At such times he couldn't even control his own voice. That is why he said nothing to his brother Howard on the way to church; he didn't want to disturb the anointing of the Holy Spirit that was upon him, because he knew his gift would automatically operate under that anointing, draining his energy, and he needed to save his strength for tonight's meeting.

Since they arrived at Calvary Temple later than scheduled, Bill was not surprised to find his manager, W. J. Ern Baxter, behind the pulpit, preaching. On seeing Bill, Ern Baxter immediately ended his sermonette and led the people in singing the Branham Campaign's theme song:

> Only believe, only believe,
> All things are possible, only believe...

After greeting his audience, Bill asked if those in the back could hear him. Not enough hands went up to satisfy him, so he asked the man who was running the public address system to increase its volume. This was a common adjustment, caused by the difference in size between Bill and his manager. Although the two men were close to the same age, they were opposites in look and manner. Ern Baxter was a big bear of a man, standing over six feet tall, with a huge rib cage that produced his booming baritone sermons. Baxter's hair grew thick and coarse on top of a squarish head, set off with wire-rimmed glasses. In contrast, William Branham stood only five feet seven inches tall and weighed 153 pounds. At 42, Bill's hair had thinned on top and receded at the temples, accentuating his high, sloping forehead. He had deep-set eyes which gave the impression of intense concentration, like an eagle on a high cliff searching the valley below, letting no movement escape his notice.

From the beginning of his national ministry in June 1946 to this Los Angeles meeting in February 1951, William Branham had focused most of his energy on praying for sick people. If he preached before calling a prayer-line, it was usually a short sermon on the Biblical basis for divine healing. Even if he did not preach, he would always take a few minutes to explain his unusual ministry. He would say things like:

"Dear Christian friends, before we start the prayer-line, I want everyone to understand clearly that I do not claim to be a divine healer. The only thing I can do for you is pray for you. No man can heal. God alone is the healer.

"I am just a man, your brother, with a ministry vindicated by a supernatural being, the angel of the Lord that has come from God to minister these blessings to you. Does the electrical wire going to that light say, 'Look what a great wire I am?' No, the wire has nothing to do with making the light. It's the current in the wire that makes the light. I am like that electrical wire. I have no light of my own until it is turned on from somewhere else. Do you see that I give praise to Jesus Christ? It's not of myself; it's from Him.

"Some people think angels aren't in the New Testament and that only the Holy Ghost led the early church. It is true that the Holy Ghost led the church, but angels are always ministering spirits in every age. Remember in Acts chapter 8, the angel of the Lord appeared to Philip and told him to go to the Gaza desert and witness to that eunuch from Ethiopia. And when Peter was in prison, the angel of the Lord shined like a light over him, touched him, broke loose his shackles, and led him out.[4] And don't forget St. Paul. After 14 days and nights on the ocean in that storm, all hope gone of being saved, Paul said, 'Sirs, be of good cheer; for the angel of God, whose servant I am, stood by me last night and told me there would be no loss of life; wherefore, I believe God, that it will be just as it was shown to me.'[5] John the Revelator wrote in the last chapter of the Bible, "*I, Jesus, have sent mine angel to testify unto you these things in the churches.*"[6] See, the book of Revelation was shown John by the angel of the Lord. And John fell down to worship that angel and the angel stopped him, saying, 'See thou do it not, for I am thy fellow servant and of thy brethren the prophets.'[7] The prophetic spirit that has been on the prophets down through the ages was there prophesying through John, showing him the future by an angel. That same Spirit is here in this building tonight. He's the same yesterday, today, and forever. Don't try to figure it out; just accept it."

On this night in February 1951, while Bill was explaining his ministry to his audience in Los Angeles, he felt the angel of the Lord leave his side and move out over the audience. That in itself was not uncommon in his meetings, except that the angel usually didn't do this until after the prayer-line had started and faith was generally higher. Perhaps there was someone here who already had tremendous faith. Bill studied the crowd while he talked. Then he saw it—a Pillar of Fire burning as brightly as a camera flash. It hung over a thin old man who was sitting toward the rear of the sanctuary next to an aisle.

Bill watched that supernatural light until it became a vision. Although his eyes remained wide open, he could no longer see the crowded sanctuary of Calvary Temple. Instead he saw a boy pulling a wagon up to a haystack on a summer day. The boy

---

[4]   Acts 12
[5]   Acts 27
[6]   Revelation 22:16
[7]   Revelation 19:10

climbed to the top of the haystack and started pitching hay down into the wagon box. One part of Bill's mind was dimly aware that he was still at Calvary Temple in Los Angeles, talking to thousands of people; but the active part of his mind was there at that haystack, watching a drama unfold. It felt like being in two places at once.

As he watched, he continued to speak into the microphone. "I see a boy playing on top of a haystack. He's dressed very odd. Oh! He fell off the haystack and struck his back on the wagon. I see a man pick him up and take him to a doctor. The doctor's got a white mustache and is wearing glasses that slip down to the end of his nose. I see the doctor working on the boy, but it's no use. Nothing can be done. The doctor sends him home to bed. The boy gets so bad that he can't even stand the vibration of someone walking across his bedroom floor. I see them boring holes in the wooden floor to reduce the vibrations. Now the boy is doing some kind of work... oh, he's writing. Now he becomes a great man. I can see them rolling him around in a wheelchair, and he can even walk if he uses crutches and a back brace. I see him sitting at a bench and people are applauding his speeches. And folks, I don't know why, but I see the White House in Washington D.C. Now it's left me."

The rapid succession of scenes faded away and Bill was again looking at the people in Calvary Temple. He could no longer see the light of the angel at the back of the sanctuary, so he studied the faces of those who were sitting near where that light had been. "There he is," said Bill, pointing. "It's the old man sitting back there with that pair of crutches laying in the aisle next to his seat."

While everyone turned to look, Bill asked Howard how many prayer-cards he had given out. Typically Howard passed out 100 new cards each night of a campaign. Every card had a letter and a number printed on it. Bill would pick a number at random, like

85, and then he would ask for those who had numbers 85 through 100 to assemble for the prayer-line. Because a different letter of the alphabet was used nightly, each number 85 was good for only one service. This kept the selection processes fair; everyone who wanted prayer had the same chance to get in the prayer-line every night.

As Howard lined the people up on the side aisle, Ern Baxter came to Bill and said, "Brother Branham, do you know who that man is you saw a vision of?"

"No, sir, I don't."

"It's William Upshaw, a former congressman of the United States. He wants to talk to you, so I ran the extension mike back there."

An usher plugged the extension microphone into the public address system. Mr. Upshaw's voice came through the loudspeakers. "My son, how did you know that I fell and hurt myself when I was a boy?"

"Sir," Bill answered, "I've never heard of you before. The only thing I can say is what I seen in the vision."

"Well, that's exactly what happened. My name is William Upshaw and for eight years I was a congressman from Georgia. I ran for President of the United States in 1932, but I was defeated because I stood against legalizing whiskey. I still stand against it today. I was 18 years old when I got hurt. I have been an invalid for 66 years—seven years in bed and 59 years using wheelchairs and crutches. I have been prayed for dozens of times, without success. Just a few days ago Dr. Roy Davis advised me to come over here and have you intercede to God for me. My son, will I ever be healed?"

"I cannot tell you, my brother. I do not know. The only thing I can tell you is what I seen in the vision. And now it's gone from me."

Bill looked over to the side aisle. Howard nodded that the prayer-line was ready to begin.

Although the sanctuary was crowded, few people were allowed to sit behind Bill on the platform. He had learned from experience this was best. Under the anointing he became extremely sensitive to spirits. If the platform was full of people, he could feel every skeptic among them, and their doubt made it harder for him to focus his attention on the needs in the prayer-line. This was not just his own idea; he had Scriptural precedents. Before Jesus raised Jairus' daughter from the dead, He made every doubter leave the room. Peter did the same thing before he prayed for Dorcas.[8] But there was another reason Bill didn't want skeptics behind him: whenever a person with epilepsy came near the angel of the Lord, the demon of epilepsy would throw a tantrum. If there were skeptics nearby, their unbelief would feed that demon, making it more difficult for Bill to control. Sometimes Bill did let ministers sit behind him on the platform if he was sure they believed in his gift. He could feel their faith, and it helped him.

When the first person in a prayer-line came before him, Bill would talk to him or her for a while in order to contact that person's spirit, just like Jesus did when he talked to the Samaritan woman at Jacob's well.[9] If the person was a Christian, Bill could feel a warm spirit of welcome. Often he would see a glow of light around a Christian's head. It didn't take much conversation before Bill would feel the anointing drop down on him. That is when a vision would usually appear. He would see the patient rise in the air and shrink, almost as though the person was moving away from him at supersonic speed. A scene would then form in

---

[8]   Mark 5:35-48; Acts 9:36-42
[9]   John 4:6-19

miniature, often showing something revealing from the person's past, and always showing something specific about the person's problem. These visions were similar to dreams, except that Bill was wide-awake, and the scenes he watched were clear and distinct. He might see the person's address on the side of a house or a name on a mailbox. Many times he would know what was wrong with a patient by listening to a doctor making a diagnosis. While he watched each vision, he would tell the audience what he was seeing, but these words did not come from his own will. When the vision left him, he might retain a faint memory of what he had seen, and little about what he had said. But those in the line always confirmed that what he told them under the anointing was true. If Bill saw a bright light swirling around a patient's head, he knew a miracle had taken place. At other times, Bill would see people healed in the vision. It never failed to be the truth.

There was a distinct difference between the anointing to preach and the anointing to see visions. The first gave Bill strength; the second exhausted him. Bill was not a weak man. When hunting, (which he did often) he could easily walk 20 miles a day over rugged country, then get up and do it again the next day... but seeing one vision tired him more than if he was swinging a sledgehammer for an hour. During these prayer-lines, the visions came one right after another. When each vision ended, the anointing would leave him temporarily, hovering above him like a dove, waiting for the next patient to come forward. If it did not do this, Bill would have collapsed in minutes. His body could not have stood the strain. As it was, he could last 20 minutes, maybe 30, before exhaustion numbed him nearly senseless.

That night in Calvary Temple, the 15 people chosen for the prayer-line came forward one by one, each with his or her own unique problem, which the visions discerned with precision. When the time came for the last person in line to approach him,

Bill staggered like he might fall. Ern Baxter stepped forward to catch him, but Bill regained his balance. He rubbed his face. His lips felt thick and his skin tingled as though lacking circulation.

Suddenly another vision appeared. Bill looked at a young doctor in a white medical coat. The doctor wore glasses with thick lenses and he had a round reflector strapped to his forehead. Folding his arms, the doctor looked down and shook his head in discouragement. Bill followed the doctor's gaze, and said, "I see a young doctor, thin and tall; he's got orange-rimmed glasses on. He's operating on a little colored girl about five or six years old. He took her tonsils out, but something went wrong and now she's paralyzed from the shoulders down."

The same moment the vision left him, Bill heard a woman scream. From way back in the sanctuary, a large black woman had started for the front. She was pulling a stretcher on wheels and she kept shouting, "Lord, have mercy! That was my baby!" Several ushers tried to stop her. Like a football player stiff-arming tacklers, this big woman knocked the ushers aside and kept coming. Finally enough men formed a line in front of her that she had to stop, but she kept shouting, "Parson, that was my baby! And that is the way the doctor looked. It happened two years ago and she hasn't walked since. Is she healed?"

"I don't know, auntie. Like I told the congressman earlier, the only thing I can say is what I see in a vision. Is that your girl on the stretcher?"

"Yes. I've prayed and I've prayed for her healing."

"Well, auntie, I can pray for her and maybe the Lord Jesus will heal her; but to say it will be, that I can't do on my own." He looked at his brother. "Howard, is that the last person in the line?"

Howard nodded and signaled for the last patient to go forward. Bill noticed what looked like a dark streak moving just above the heads of the people. As he watched, the streak expanded into a city street. Then he saw a little black girl skipping down the street rocking a doll in her arms.

Bill said to the mother, "Auntie, Jesus Christ has rewarded you for your faith. Your little girl is healed."

Quivering with emotion, the mother stooped over the stretcher and kissed her daughter. Then she looked up and asked, "Parson, when will my baby get well?"

"She's well now, auntie."

While the mother was looking at the evangelist, her daughter had quietly slipped off the stretcher. As soon as the girl was sure her legs would support her, she screamed. Spinning around to look, her mother screamed too, and then fell backwards into the arms of the ushers. A minute later, mother and daughter marched hand in hand up the center aisle, praising God. The crowd enthusiastically added their approval.

Bill watched them until the mother and daughter had gone out the door. "See what the Lord Jesus can do," he said, his words slurring because he felt so weak. He was about to turn to speak to the last woman in the prayer-line when he again caught a movement out of the corner of his eye. Looking closely, Bill saw the former congressman strolling down the same street above the audience. Congressman Upshaw was dressed in a chocolate brown suit with white pinstripes and he was wearing a southern Stetson hat. He smiled cordially and tipped his hat to people as he walked.

Bill glanced down at where Mr. Upshaw sat in a chair next to the center aisle. Here in church the elderly statesman was wearing a blue suit with a red tie.

"Congressman, have you got a dark brown suit with thin, white stripes?"

The old gentleman still held the extension microphone. "Yes, my son. I bought one the day before yesterday."

Now Bill knew what was going to happen. "My brother, you have been a reverent man and have honored God all these years. God is rewarding you now by making your last days happy. You can walk now, congressman. The Lord Jesus Christ has healed you."

Mr. Upshaw did not know what to do. He said, "God be praised. My son, if Jesus Christ will let me walk without crutches, I'll spend the rest of my days for his glory."

"Congressman..." Bill paused, and staggered. He felt his strength ebbing fast. Ern Baxter and Leroy Kopp supported him and began to lead him away. Bill whispered, "Congressman, in the name of Jesus Christ, stand up on your feet and walk. God has healed you. That is, 'Thus saith the Lord'!"

Pastor Leroy Kopp returned to the microphone and said, "Brother Branham says the congressman is healed!"

Willie Upshaw felt his heart leap. He said to himself, "Brother Branham knows the mind of God, so I must step out in faith and accept Jesus Christ as my Healer."

He felt something cool sweep down through his body. Kicking aside his crutches, he stood and stepped into the aisle. Nerves in his legs, long dead, suddenly tingled with life. Blood filled his shriveled muscles. Miraculously, his legs supported him. He took another step, then another. He was doing it! He was walking without help!

While the audience worshiped God enthusiastically, Willie Upshaw walked down the aisle to the front and shook hands with a stunned Leroy Kopp. Then, standing where everyone could see him, Willie Upshaw reached down and touched his toes.[10]

---

[10] The miracle William Upshaw experienced in Los Angeles was permanent. He walked normally from that night in February 1951 until his death on November 21, 1952, at the age of 86.

Chapter 54
Looking Back
From 1951

O**N A WARM** June morning in 1951, William Branham arrived home in Jeffersonville, Indiana, hoping to get some rest before tackling his next series of faith-healing campaigns. In July he was scheduled for two straight weeks of meetings—first a week in Toledo, Ohio; then two nights in Zion, Illinois; then four nights in Erie, Pennsylvania. He knew it would be strenuous. Since he was already exhausted from his last campaign, taking a break now was important to preserve his health.

Finding time to relax and unwind was not easy for him, not even at home. As soon as people found out he was back in town, visitors would start ringing his doorbell, and by noon his living room would be crowded with strangers wanting personal interviews and prayer. It had been this way ever since God had given him his commission in 1946. Usually Bill did not mind this constant intrusion into his privacy. He loved people and wanted to help them. But right now he was too tired to help anyone. If he gave personal interviews today, the visions (and there were always visions during the interviews) would tear him apart.

Meda said, "Bill, before the crowds gather in, let me take you somewhere."

They drove out to the Tunnel Mill area, 15 miles northeast of Jeffersonville. Into these woodlands he had often retreated during times of trouble, finding peace in this quiet, green wilderness. Hidden among these hills lay a cave where he sometimes went to rest and pray. But today that was not his destination. It was a strenuous hike to his secret cave. Bill had taken Meda there once, shortly after their marriage in 1941. Once had been enough for her.

On their way back to Jeffersonville, Bill felt an urge to stop at the spot where he had gone to school as a boy. He turned the car into a meadow and parked. Rebekah ran off to gather wild flowers. Meda wandered after her. Bill strolled over to the old well pump and, working the handle up and down, pumped himself a drink of water. The one-room schoolhouse used to sit not far from the well. Nothing was left of the schoolhouse now, not even a stone to mark its foundation. Leaning against a wooden fence, Bill gazed across the valley to the place where he had grown up. Then it had been sparsely populated; now well-built homes covered the hillside. How different they looked from the two-room log cabin he had lived in as a boy. How drastically the world had changed in 30 years.

Bill remembered how big the logs of his cabin had looked to him when he was a small boy. Behind the cabin stood a giant apple tree that he once thought would live forever. Now it was gone. He remembered the wash bench his father built under that apple tree, and the broken mirror tacked to its trunk. How many times had he watched his father shaving under that tree? Charles Branham had been a short, wiry man with powerful muscles. When he took off his shirt to wash and shave, those muscles seemed to ripple under his skin. Bill remembered thinking, "My! Look how strong my daddy is. He's going to live 100 years!" But he didn't. He died in 1936 at the age of 52, having destroyed himself by drinking too much whiskey.

There used to be a spring in front of the cabin. Bill thought about how many times he had lugged a heavy cedar bucket down to that spring for water. It had been hard being the oldest of ten children. His parents had expected so much of him. He used to get his brother Edward to do chores for him in exchange for candy. Now the spring was gone, no doubt filled in by a bulldozer. Edward was gone too.

Bill choked back tears at the thought of Edward. Although Edward was a year younger than he was, they had started school together. Those were difficult years. His family was so poor that neither he nor Edward had enough clothes. That fall of 1917 Bill had gone to school without a shirt. When it snowed, a neighbor lady felt sorry for him and gave him a coat. All that winter Bill wore his coat every minute he sat in school so the other children wouldn't know he wasn't wearing a shirt. During recess the other children went sledding with their store-bought sleds. Bill and Edward salvaged an old dishpan from the dump and used it as a sled until the rusty bottom wore out. At noon he and Edward would go down by the Ohio River to eat their meager lunch. They owned just one lunch bucket. Setting it on a log between them, they carefully divided their beans and cornbread into equal portions. Bill remembered the time his mother had packed them a treat of popcorn. Bill had slipped out of class early to sneak more than his share. Oh, how he regretted cheating on his brother!

That happened in 1917, during the First World War. The morning ritual never varied. After ringing the school bell, Mrs. Temple would round up her students in the schoolyard, forming them into a single line, using a willow switch to keep order. After pledging allegiance to the flag, they would turn to face the schoolhouse, put one arm on the shoulder of the pupil in front of them, and march inside. Each student had their assigned place in that line. Bill could still remember the order. First there was Roland Hollaway, redheaded and fierce-tempered. Roland shot a man in a dice game and died in prison. Next came Wilmer. He got into a knife fight and died with his throat slashed. And Willis Paul? He died from a disease that stripped his body. Howard Higgins died when the Colgate factory blew up. Ralph Fields and Willie Hinkle? —they were gone too. After Willie came Edward, Bill's younger brother. Edward always stood behind Bill in line, with his hand on Bill's shoulder as they marched into school. (Suddenly Bill's bittersweet nostalgia turned more bitter than sweet. In 1928 Edward Branham had died in Jeffersonville while Bill was punching cows in Arizona. That was before Bill was a Christian. Even so, when Edward was dying he said, "Tell Billy I'll see him someday in heaven.")

"Oh, God," Bill thought, "here I am alone left among them. Who am I to still be alive? How true is Your Word: *"For here have we no continuing city, but we seek one to come."*[11] Oh, Lord, I'd give the rest of my mortal life if You'd let me take some popcorn, walk up to them doors and say, 'Edward, buddy, here's that handful of popcorn I cheated you out of when we were boys.'" Suddenly Bill cried out loud, "Oh, God, let the angels come get my poor, tired soul and pack me away from here! This world is not my home any longer!"

This outburst brought Meda back to his side. Putting her arms around him, she said, "Honey, you came out here to rest and here you are crying like a baby. Don't do that."

"Sweetheart," Bill said, "if you only knew what was traveling through my heart. I remember standing right there at that house when little Sharon Rose took sick. Hope got sick right after that.[12] I

---

[11] John 4:6-19
[12] Hope was Bill's first wife. They had two children, Billy Paul and Sharon Rose. Hope died from tuberculosis in 1937 when she was only 24 years old. Sharon died a few days later from tubercular meningitis.

can understand why God took Hope, but I have never understood why He took Sharon Rose. She was only nine months old."

Meda hushed him. "You shouldn't think about such things, Bill. Not now."

But her admonition came too late. He was already remembering...

WILLIAM BRANHAM was born in a crude, one-room log cabin near Burkesville, Kentucky. His mother Ella was practically a child herself—only 15 years old. His father, Charles, was 18. Bill came into the world just before daybreak on April 6, 1909. According to those who were there—the midwife, a neighbor, the grandmother, Ella and Charles—a few minutes after his birth, an unnatural light darted into the cabin through the open window, hung for a moment over his bed, and then disappeared up through the roof. It was the first hint that his life was destined to be different.

In 1912 Charles moved his family to a farm near Jeffersonville, Indiana. In 1917, shortly after Bill started school, something happened that so terrified him, the experience became one of his most vivid childhood memories. It was during Prohibition and his father was making him haul buckets of water uphill to a moonshine still hidden in a shed behind the house. Halfway up the hill, seven-year-old Billy sat down beneath a poplar tree to rest. Soon he noticed a strange whirlwind caught in the upper branches—strange because it stayed in one place. Suddenly he heard a voice that sounded like it came from the whirlwind. The voice said, *"Don't ever drink, or smoke, or defile your body in any way. There will be a work for you to do when you get older."* Billy dropped his water buckets and sprinted to the house, screaming for his mother. He never forgot that voice; and when he tried to disobey its command, something beyond his understanding always prevented him.

In spite of these experiences, Bill grew up far from God. At the age of 23, while working for the New Albany Gas Company, gas fumes overcame him. This mishap seriously affected his health. His head and stomach ached constantly and he developed severe astigmatism. His doctor, searching for a diagnosis, was stumped. Finally he decided Bill's appendix was inflamed and must be removed.

Immediately following the operation, while Bill was lying in a hospital room, he felt his life slipping away. He tried to call for a nurse, but he could only whisper. As his heart rate dropped lower, the room changed. He thought he was walking in a dark, cold forest. Death was stalking him. In the distance he heard the sound of wind approaching. Terrified, he thought death was coming to get him. Suddenly he was standing again beneath that poplar tree of his boyhood, looking up at the same whirlwind stuck in its branches. Again he heard that deep voice speak to him, only this time the words ended differently. The voice said, *"Don't ever drink, or smoke, or defile your body in any way... I called you and you would not go."*

Bill cried out, "Jesus, if that is You, let me go back again to earth and I will preach Your Gospel from the housetops and street corners. I'll tell everyone about You."

Instantly the vision ended and Bill was back in his hospital room. Gradually his health returned.

He became a preacher in the Missionary Baptist Church, but soon he felt led to form an independent church of his own. On Sunday afternoon, June 11, 1933, he was finishing up two weeks of revival meetings by baptizing his converts in the Ohio River. Over a thousand people watched from the shore. After Bill baptized 16 people in the name of the Lord Jesus Christ, suddenly a ball of fire appeared in the sky directly over him and a voice said, "*As John the Baptist was sent to forerun the first coming of Jesus Christ, so are you sent with a message to forerun His second coming.*"

At the time, Bill did not understand what it meant. It seemed like just one more incident in a string of amazing events that had followed him all his life; only now that he was a Christian, such experiences were increasing. Once he even saw a vision of the Lord Jesus Christ standing in the air just a few feet off the ground. Puzzled by these happenings, he sought the advice of other ministers who lived in his area. They warned him to leave such things alone, suggesting that the devil was playing with his mind. That scared Bill and for years he resisted this unusual call of God in his life. Then in May of 1946, Bill's confusion reached its limit. Secluding himself in a cabin in the woods, he vowed not to come out of the wilderness until God met him and explained to him the meaning of his strange life.

For many hours he poured out his anguished feelings in prayer. Then he fell silent. Although the hour was past midnight, sleep was far from his mind. Bill sat in the total darkness, praying, thinking, and listening. Suddenly he saw a pinprick of light in the air, which grew into a ball of fire that illuminated the cabin. Then he heard footsteps. Out of that light stepped a barefoot man dressed in a white robe. The man stood 6 feet tall and must have weighed at least 200 pounds. Thick black hair hung to his shoulders, framing a beardless face with piercing eyes and a stern look.

Terror gripped Bill with strangling fingers. Then the man said, "*Fear not,*" and all Bill's terror disappeared. It was the same deep, resonating voice Bill had heard speaking to him from that poplar tree when he was a boy. The man continued, "*I am sent from the presence of Almighty God to tell you that your peculiar birth and misunderstood life have been to indicate that you are to take a gift of divine healing to the peoples of the world. If you will be sincere when you pray, and can get the people to believe you, nothing shall stand before your prayer, not even cancer. You will go into many parts of the earth and will pray for kings and rulers and potentates. You will preach to multitudes the world over and thousands will come to you for counsel. You must tell them that their thoughts speak louder in heaven than their words."*

Bill protested that he was too poor and uneducated to accomplish this feat, arguing that no one would believe him. The angel said, *"As the prophet Moses was given two signs to prove he was sent from God,[13] so you will be given two signs. First: when you take a person's right hand in your left hand, you will be able to detect the presence of any germ-caused disease by vibrations that will appear in your left hand. Then you must pray for the person. If your hand returns to normal, you can pronounce the person healed; if it doesn't, just ask a blessing and walk away. Under the anointing from God, do not try to think your own thoughts; it will be given you what to say. If you will stay humble and sincere, it will come to pass that you will be able to tell by vision the very secrets of their hearts. Then the people will have to believe you. This will initiate the Gospel in power that will bring on the second coming of Christ."*

Returning to Jeffersonville, Bill told his congregation about the angel's visit. One church member repeated the story at work. That brought it to the attention of William Morgan, whose wife was dying from cancer. Since the doctors had given up on his wife, Mr. Morgan figured he had nothing to lose by taking her to Billy Branham for prayer.

William Morgan brought his unconscious wife to church on a stretcher. When Bill held her right hand in his left, he felt the oddest sensation. His wrist and lower arm tingled fiercely, just as if he had touched a mild electric current. Vibrations moved up his

---

[13] Exodus 3

arm all the way to his heart. His wristwatch stopped. The skin on the back of his hand turned red and displayed a pattern of small white bumps. When he asked Jesus Christ to heal this dying woman, the vibrations stopped. Instantly Bill's hand returned to normal. That is when he realized those vibrations had come from the cancerous life of the demon that was ravaging the woman's body. Now the demon was gone. Without a speck of doubt in his mind, Bill declared, "Sir, don't you fear; for thus saith the Lord, 'Your wife will live!'"

Margie Morgan recovered so quickly that in a few days her astounded doctor released her from the hospital. She walked away in perfect health.

News of this miracle spread through Christian circles, prompting ministers as far away as St. Louis, Missouri, and Shreveport, Louisiana, to write Bill, asking him to come and hold revival meetings in their areas. Bill quit his job at the Indiana public service company and stepped aside from his position as pastor of Branham Tabernacle in Jeffersonville so that he could work full-time as an evangelist.

He traveled extensively, holding faith-healing campaigns throughout the United States and Canada. The sign in his hand, and the miracles that followed combined to draw increasingly larger crowds. Whenever Bill grasped the right hand of someone with his left hand, if that person was suffering from a germ or a viral-caused illness, Bill's own left hand would turn red and swell. He could identify any germ or viral disease by the pattern of white bumps that appeared on the back of his swollen left hand. People didn't even have to tell him what disease they had; he would tell *them*, and every time he was right. After he prayed for the patient, if the swelling in Bill's hand disappeared, he knew the demon had been cast out; the person was healed.

At every meeting thousands of people flocked to see this dramatic sign from God and hundreds clamored for prayer. Seeing the great need, Bill pushed himself mercilessly, praying for a line of sick people for three, four, five, and sometimes even six hours straight, night after night, month after month, with few breaks. After two years of this exhausting work he suffered a nervous breakdown, which forced him to leave the ministry for six months. When again he ventured out in the service of the Lord, he was a wiser, more cautious man.

In 1949 the second sign appeared in his ministry, just as the angel said it would. Bill was holding a prayer service in Regina, Saskatchewan. A middle-aged woman came forward in the prayer-line. Before Bill could take her hand for a diagnosis, he saw her in a vision as a young girl; he saw her problem and he knew why she had come for prayer. Then he saw her future, a future in which she was well. Beginning on that night this second sign, discernment by vision, superseded the first sign in every meeting.

Not that the sign in his hand ever left him; it didn't. He could use it anytime it seemed appropriate. Bill would never forget an incident that happened in 1949, when he was holding meetings in California. He and Meda were in their hotel room when a friend of his, Paul Malicki, called him to ask a favor. "Brother Branham, my wife just gave birth and now she's really sick. Her doctor can't figure out what's wrong. Can I bring her up to see you?"

"Sure, Brother Malicki," Bill answered, "but you'll have to bring her today. Tomorrow I'm going to Catalina."

Paul Malicki brought his wife right over. Bill could see at once that she was a very sick woman. He said, "Sister Malicki, put your hand on mine. We'll see if the Lord will tell us what it is." As soon as her right hand touched his left hand, Bill said, "Oh, its milk leg."

"That's strange," she said, "I don't seem to have any symptoms of a blood clot in my leg."

"You wait and see. It's milk leg all right. The gift is never wrong."

Mrs. Malicki looked at the back of Bill's swollen hand, which was mottled with little, white welts. "That is an amazing thing to watch, Brother Branham. Does that work on every hand you touch?"

"No," Bill answered, "it only works if there is something wrong with the person. Watch what happens when I take my wife's hand. There's nothing wrong with her."

The back of Bill's hand returned to normal as soon as he removed it from Mrs. Malicki's hand. Meda reached over and slipped her right hand into her husband's left. Bill was surprised. "Meda, you have female trouble. You have a cyst on your left ovary."

"I don't feel it," Meda said.

"But it's there, just the same."

Two days later Mrs. Malicki's doctor treated her for a blood clot in her leg.

Ever since then, Bill had been concerned about that cyst on his wife's ovary. Recently he had an opportunity to check on it. On March 19, 1951, he took Meda to the hospital for the birth of their second child, Sarah. Just as with Meda's first baby, this one also had to be delivered by Caesarean section. While she was being prepped for the operation, Bill said to Dr. Dillman, "When you have her open, look at her left ovary and remove that cyst if you find it."

Later Dr. Dillman reported, "There was nothing wrong with her ovary that I could see."

Hopeful, Bill grasped his wife's right hand with his left. Unfortunately he saw the back of his own hand turn puffy and red. He knew the cyst was still there.

A CLOUD covered the meadow with its shadow. Now the breeze coming off the river felt chilly. Bill's nostalgic reverie was interrupted when Meda, shivering a little, suggested it was time to go home.

Bill gazed into his wife's face, admiring her soft cheeks and gentle eyes. She was only 32 years old, but already her dark hair was streaked with gray. Bill attributed that graying to her efforts in protecting him from the public when he was home. How deeply he loved her. How terrible it would be to lose her like he lost his first wife, Hope. Surely the Lord would never let that happen. Or would He?

Bill picked up little Rebekah with her bouquet of wild flowers and carried her back to the car.

Chapter 55
The Hall Paradox
1951

BECAUSE HIS MINISTRY kept him traveling for weeks at a time, whenever William Branham came home from the field there was always lots of news to share. Meda was excited to hear that a date had finally been set for Bill's upcoming campaigns in South Africa. He would fly out of New York on October 1, 1951.

Bill harbored mixed emotions about this trip. Part of him shared Meda's excitement. This would be only the second time he had left North America. In the spring of 1950 his healing campaigns in Scandinavia had drawn huge crowds and had inspired astounding miracles, including a Finnish boy, dead for half an hour, who received back his life by the power of Jesus Christ. Bill expected similar results in South Africa, because God had specifically told him to go there.

In January of 1950, while Bill was holding a campaign in Houston, Texas, he received a letter from Florence Nightingale Shirlaw begging him to come to Durban, South Africa and pray for her. Stomach cancer was causing her to slowly starve to death. Along with her letter, Miss Shirlaw included an airplane ticket and picture of herself that showed a woman so thin she looked like an Egyptian mummy. Bill was sorry he could not fly to her. It was impossible because he was soon leaving for campaigns in Scandinavia. Her picture so filled him with pity that he prayed, "God, if You want me to go to South Africa, then please heal this woman." To Bill's surprise, Florence Shirlaw chartered a private airplane and flew to England to meet him. There, on a foggy April morning in 1950, God miraculously healed her. Consequently, Bill knew God wanted him to go to Durban, South Africa, and he was expecting God to do great things in that country.

At the same time he was apprehensive. Last fall when he was in Shreveport, Louisiana, the Holy Spirit fell on him and he prophesied that Satan was setting a trap for him in South Africa. Bill wondered what kind of trap it could be. His imagination conjured up thoughts about witch doctors challenging the power of Jesus Christ. That didn't seem like much of a trap. Was there another kind of trap waiting for him in Africa, one he couldn't imagine? Thinking about it made him uneasy.

Along with the good news, Meda had some bad news to share—Bill's friend William Hall was dying.

"Surely not Brother Hall," said Bill in surprise. William Hall had been his first convert at a revival campaign he had held in Milltown, Indiana, eleven years before. Later the man became the pastor of the Milltown Baptist Church.

"Yes," said Meda. "He's got cancer of the liver. Dr. Dillman said he couldn't live much longer. They brought him up to New Albany and he's lying at his sister's house. He's been calling for you."

"Well, let's go over and see him right now."

When they arrived at the house, Bill was startled to see how thin and ghastly his friend looked. The man's skin had turned as orange as a pumpkin. Bill asked, "What about it, Brother Hall?"

William Hall labored to speak. "Brother Branham, the doctors have done all they can do. I guess it's the end of the road for me, unless God does a miracle."

Bill prayed for his old friend. When Bill and Meda were leaving, Mrs. Hall followed them out of the house. She asked, "Brother Branham, isn't there something else you can do?"

"I'm sorry, Sister Hall, but the only thing I can do is pray."

She looked off into the distance and muttered, "Maybe there's another doctor..."

"Doctors are like ministers in that respect," Bill said. "You have to have confidence in them or they can't help you. Of course, there is my good buddy Dr. Sam Adair. As far as medical science goes, I think he's the best."

Mrs. Hall brought her eyes back to focus on Bill. "I wonder if your friend Dr. Adair would examine my husband."

Bill said, "I'll ask."

When Bill called him, Dr. Adair said, "Billy, I'll just go down to the hospital and read the lab reports. They will tell me what I need to know." Later that morning, Dr. Adair called back. "I read the lab reports. The man has cancer of the liver. That kind of cancer is inoperable and incurable. He's going to die."

"Isn't there a specialist you could send him to?" Bill asked.

"Well, we could send him to Dr. Able in Louisville. He's one of the best cancer specialists in the country."

Grasping at straws, Mrs. Hall hired an ambulance to take her husband across the Ohio River to Dr. Able's clinic.

THAT EVENING another longtime friend, Pastor Johnson of the Main Street Methodist Church in New Albany, telephoned

Bill to ask a favor. "Brother Branham, would you hold a service or two for me? It would make me so happy if you would."

"I don't want to pray for the sick, Brother Johnson. When I'm home I try to relax and keep away from that, because when the discernment comes, it just wears me down."

"Come and preach for me then. Just give me one night. I promise I won't ask you to pray for the sick."

"All right, Brother Johnson. What night would you like me to come?"

"Wednesday night would be perfect."

Because Reverend Johnson advertised this meeting on his Wednesday morning radio broadcast, that night over 500 people squeezed into the sanctuary of the Main Street Methodist Church, and as many more stood outside wishing they could get in. Because the church windows were positioned too high for the people on the sidewalk to see inside, a deacon placed loudspeakers in windows so they could at least hear the sermon. By the time Bill arrived at church, the crowd on the sidewalk was so thick he could not get to a door. A deacon directed him behind the building to the alley, where another man reached down from an open window, held on to Bill's wrists, and hoisted him inside.

While he was preaching that night, Bill said, "You don't go to hell because you get drunk. You don't go to hell because you smoke cigarettes or chew tobacco. You don't go to hell because you lie, cheat, or steal. You don't go to hell because you commit adultery—"

Suddenly a Methodist mother jumped to her feet and interrupted him. "Reverend Branham, I resent that. Those are sins! If you don't go to hell for those things, what do you go to hell for?"

"You go to hell because you don't believe the Word of God. The only sin God condemns is the sin of unbelief. These other things are just attributes of sin. You do them because you believe not. The strange thing of it is, you can sit in church all your life and still not believe God's Word! The Bible says that whoever believes in Jesus Christ and is baptized will be saved; but whoever believes not is condemned already![14] Jesus said, *"He that heareth my word, and believeth on him that sent me, hath everlasting life, and shall not come into condemnation."*[15] If you really believe that Jesus Christ is the Son of God, you won't live the same sinful life you lived before you met Him."

After the service ended, Reverend Johnson said, "Brother Branham, I know I promised you I wouldn't ask you to pray for anybody who was sick, but we've got a Sunday school teacher here who needs help. Her name is Mrs. Shane. She's a lovely woman, one of my most faithful members; but she's neurotic. She's been going to a psychiatrist in Louisville for the past ten years, but it hasn't helped a bit. Many faith-healers have prayed for her too, but nothing has helped. She's still in a terrible condition. Her nerves are a mess. Would you just lay your hands on her and ask God to bless her?"

"All right. Where will I find her?"

"I told her to wait for us at the bottom of the basement stairs."

By the way Reverend Johnson described her, Bill expected to find a woman who needed to be restrained by a straightjacket. Instead he met a pretty lady in her thirties who seemed at first glance to be normal.

"Hello, Brother Branham," she said.

"Howdy, ma'am. Are you the patient I'm supposed to pray for?"

"Yes. I'm Mrs. Shane."

---

[14]   Mark 16:16, John 3:18
[15]   John 5:24

"You don't look sick."

"I'm really not sick. I don't know what is the matter with me. I just can't hold myself together. Sometimes I wonder if I've lost my mind."

Now Bill noticed little signs of neurosis in the woman's actions: fidgeting with her fingers, a twitch at the corner of her mouth. Bill said, "I don't think you've lost your mind, sister? Let's take your problem to the Lord Jesus." He laid his hands on her and prayed for her, but at the end of the prayer, he had no assurance that she was healed.

Two days later Bill and Meda were shopping in New Albany when they met Mrs. Shane on the street. "Are you any better, sister?" Bill asked.

"No, I'm getting worse," she moaned. Her head made little bird-like jerks as her eyes darted back and forth between objects on the street. She seemed deathly afraid, as though she feared at any moment she might be mugged. "Brother Branham, I can't leave New Albany, because if I do, I know something will get me. I really think I've lost my mind."

"I don't think so, sister. Are you a Christian, living above sin?"

"Yes, I'm a sanctified Methodist, born again. I teach a young ladies Sunday school class every Sunday afternoon."

"Well, let's pray for you again." Bill bowed his head and prayed, "God, please have mercy on this poor little lady; in the name of Jesus Christ we pray. Amen." But when they parted, Bill felt the matter was still not settled.

The next day some of Mrs. Shane's friends brought her over to Bill's house. She struggled against them, screaming, "Take me home! I can't leave New Albany or I'll die!" When Bill tried to talk with her, she babbled on about how she must never leave New Albany or the earth might open and swallow her. Bill prayed for her again and she calmed down; but Bill held no delusions that she was healed. Something deeply hidden was troubling her.

Mrs. Shane knew it too. "Brother Branham, I believe if you pray for me when the anointing is on you, I'll be healed." Then she said to her friends, "The next time Brother Branham has a healing campaign close to New Albany, I'm telling you now that I want to go, even if you have to put me in a straightjacket and drag me there kicking and screaming."

LATER THAT DAY Bill received a call from Dr. Sam Adair. "Billy, Dr. Able gave me his conclusion about your friend. It might be best if you tell his wife. Mr. Hall is going to jump overboard in about four days."

"There's nothing that can be done?"

"Billy, the cancer is in the liver! You can't take his liver out and have him live. He's dying. I suppose he ought to be ready to go, since he's a preacher."

"Oh, his soul is right with God; but I hate to see him go. He's only 55 years old. There's plenty of work yet he can do for the Lord. Why God's taking him, I don't know."

"Yes, that's hard for anybody to understand. Sometimes we've just got to accept it."

Bill and Meda drove over to tell Mrs. Hall. With her last hope dashed against the rocks of reality, she crumpled in grief. Bill tried to comfort her. "Sister Hall, remember he's a Christian. He's ready to go. The apostle Paul said to the Christian, 'If this earthly tabernacle be dissolved, we have one already waiting.'[16] Brother Hall will be far better off where he's going. Of course at your age, with no children, you'll be lonely. But you must remember, God knows what's best and is working what is best."

---

[16] 2 Corinthians 5:1

"I just don't know what I'll do without him," she lamented.

"Let's go in and pray for him one more time," Bill suggested.

William Hall had been drifting in and out of consciousness for a week. Now he was unconscious. His orange skin looked like wax. Bill, Meda, and Mrs. Hall prayed again, asking God to have mercy and spare his life.

Before Bill left, Mrs. Hall asked, almost pleading, "Brother Branham, has God ever said one word to you about it in a vision?"

"I'm sorry, Sister Hall, but He hasn't said a thing. I've prayed with all my heart. Maybe God is just going to let Brother Hall die."

"Do you think he's going to die?"

"Yes, I believe he is, because all the evidence is against him. It must be the will of the Lord, but I couldn't say for sure."

Bill and Meda drove home. As usual, many cars were parked along the lane in front of his house. A dozen strangers waited to see him. He prayed for every one of them. The last person left shortly after midnight. Bill propped his squirrel-hunting rifle next to the bedroom door. Sitting on the edge of his bed, he set the alarm to ring at 4:00 a.m. Since he had so much trouble getting some rest at his own house, he liked to go into the woods early in the morning, hunt for several hours, then lay down under a tree and nap. At least no one could interrupt his sleep in the woods.

At 4:00 a.m. the alarm rang. Groggily, Bill rolled out of bed and fumbled with his clothes. Putting his fingers between the slats of the window blinds, he bent them open far enough to peek outside. Sometimes people showed up in the middle of the night and slept in their cars, waiting for morning so that he could pray for them. This morning the driveway was empty, which meant he could go hunting without being delayed.

Picking up his .22 rifle, he turned on the hall light and shuffled toward the bathroom, rubbing sleep out of his eyes. Halfway down the hall, he saw a little green apple, apparently hanging on the wall. Bill thought, "Why would my wife hang a knotty, worm-eaten apple on the wall?" He stepped closer to get a better look. Suddenly he realized his mistake. The apple wasn't pinned to the wall; it was hanging in midair!

Dropping to one knee and laying aside his rifle, Bill jerked off his hat and said, "What will my Heavenly Father have His servant to know?"

Another green apple, covered with scabs, appeared beside the first... then another and another until five knotty green apples floated in a cluster. While Bill watched in amazement, a large, unblemished, yellow apple dropped down on top of this cluster. Bill heard a crunching sound, the type of sound a man makes when he bites into crisp fruit. With five chomps the single yellow apple devoured all five green apples.

The vision disappeared, but that supernatural light lingered, rotating near the ceiling with a sound like a whirlwind. The light was not a vision. Bill said again, "What would my Lord have His servant to know?"

"*Stand upon your feet,*" the angel commanded. "*Go tell William Hall—thus saith the Lord, 'You will live and not die.'*"

The light vanished.

All thoughts of squirrel hunting left him. Running back to the bedroom, he woke up his wife to tell her the good news. She said, "Oh, can I go with you?"

Together they drove over to the house where William Hall lay dying. The sun was just peeking over the treetops when they arrived. Maggie Hall sat beside her husband's bed, looking tired and listless, rubbing her husband's hand.

"How is he doing?" Bill asked.

"He's not dead yet, Brother Branham, but he's going. Why are you looking so bright and cheerful?"

"Sister Hall, I have 'thus saith the Lord' on your husband."

She gasped. "Is it good?"

"Yes, Sister Hall." Then Bill turned and said, "Brother Hall, can you hear me?"

His eyelids fluttered, and his faint voice croaked, "Haven't I gone yet?"

"No, and you're not going—not yet. I have a word from the Lord for you. About two hours ago I saw a vision. Brother Hall, how long have you been sick?"

Too feeble to recall, William Hall rolled his eyes toward his wife and wheezed, "Magg, you tell him."

"It's been five months now."

Bill nodded. "That's what I thought. Earlier this morning I saw a vision where a large yellow apple swallowed up five little, green, worm-eaten apples. The green apples represented the months Brother Hall has been sick. From now on, he's going to start getting well. That is 'thus saith the Lord'!"

When Bill got home, he telephoned his friend Sam Adair. "Doc, you know that man you said was going to jump overboard in four days. The Lord just told me that he isn't going to die."

Sam Adair balked. "That's impossible. How's he going to live with that cancer in his liver?"

"I don't know, but he *is* going to live, because the Lord has done said so."

"Billy, I don't want to doubt you; I have seen so many amazing things happen around you that I should believe anything you tell me. But this old doctor will have to see that happen before I believe it."

"Well, you won't die from old age before you see it, because it's going to be."

Chapter 56
Life in a Shabby Cafe
1951

O N SATURDAY NIGHT, July 21, 1951, the auditorium in Toledo, Ohio, felt like an oven. Elevated on a platform in front of the audience, William Branham perspired under the bright lights. He had just finished his sermon and now Howard Branham was organizing ten people into a prayer-line. The first man in line came forward. Tape recorders continued to turn, capturing this meeting forever.

"Speaking shakes me up a little," Bill confessed. "I guess that's just human nerves. Now I've got to quiet myself down to the anointing of that angel of the Lord. I presume that we are strangers."

"Yes."

As soon as the man spoke, Bill saw him shrink to the size of a fist in the air. Then the vision revealed his problems. Bill said, "It looks like you have sinus headaches. I see you sitting like this, holding your head. You have weak spells come over you, too. Say, you're a minister of the Gospel. And you've got heart trouble. Isn't that right?"

"That's right."

Bill prayed, "Our Heavenly Father, I ask for mercy for my dear brother. And I pray that Your Spirit that is here now, will bless him and heal him, in the name of Jesus Christ. Amen. God bless you, brother. Go now. You are going to be well."

The next in line was a thin, elderly woman who looked very frail. Bill said, "You've had an operation. There were several people around the operating table. I see a blond nurse go back to one side. I see the surgeon as he turns—a tall, thin man wearing a white mask over his face. He removed seven ribs from your body. You've been weak and nervous ever since, haven't you, sister? You've been at a sanitarium, but nothing seems to help."

The vision faded and Bill shook his head slightly to reorient himself. "Was that true?" he asked.

"Every word of it," she replied.

Laying his hands upon her, Bill said, "Satan, as a believer in Jesus Christ, as representing Him in His vicarious suffering at Calvary, I adjure thee by Jesus Christ to leave the woman." Bill urged the woman to go home, eat whatever she wanted, weigh herself in a few days, and send him her testimony.

With his next patient, Bill demonstrated that sign in his hand still worked, revealing a cancerous tumor in the woman's throat. She too was healed in the name of Christ.

Then a girl came forward. Bill asked, "Where are you from?"

"Ontario."

"Ontario, Canada. So we're born many miles and many years apart. If there is anything in the world that I could know about you, it would certainly have to come through a supernatural power. Is that right?"

"Yes."

The vision came. "I see you have an asthmatic condition. you've been examined in a hospital for it; I see a doctor around you. Now I see something different. You were in an auto accident too." When the vision ended, the short burst of scenes also left his memory. But he knew from experience that whatever he had said under the anointing for discernment was right. Confidently he said, "Sister, do you believe me as God's prophet, that I've told the truth? You do? Good. I'm going to lay my hands upon you. When Jesus died at Calvary, He healed you. You're aware that a supernatural being is here now, which you believe to be His presence. Is that right? I bless thee, my sister, in the name of the Lord Jesus Christ, that He takes this asthma from you. May you go back to Ontario to be a well woman, and testify of God's grace to you all the days of your life."

Turning back to the audience, Bill asked "Are you in love with Jesus?"

The air vibrated with amens.

"If Jesus was standing right here, tonight, wearing my suit, He couldn't do any more for you than what He's doing right now. Jesus said, '*The Son can do nothing of Himself, but what he seeth the Father do...*'[17]. Jesus saw those things by visions from His Father. Jesus took no credit for what He did. Then the Spirit that was upon Him went away. He said, 'A little while and the world will see me no more, yet you shall see Me, for I will be with you, even in you, to the end of the world.'[18] Is that right? '*Jesus Christ the same yesterday, and today, and forever.*'[19]

"If I said I did these things, I'd be a liar. I do them not. Jesus Christ shows them to me through His sovereign grace and mercy. Not for my sake; it's for your healing. After God sent His Word, and then His ministers, now He sends His prophetic gift to increase the faith of His people, to get them to believe on Him. If that isn't mercy and grace, I don't know what is.

---

[17] John 5:19
[18] Matthew 28:20; John 14:16-20
[19] Hebrews 13:8

"God never takes His Spirit from the earth. God takes His man, but never His Spirit. When He took Elijah, a double portion of Elijah's spirit came upon Elisha.[20] Is that right? And several hundred years later it came out in John the Baptist.[21] And it is predicted to come out again in the last day.[22] God takes His man but not His Spirit. His Spirit remains here. When the Spirit is gone, the Church is gone too. There will be no more salvation then. When the Spirit is gone, mercy is over."

WHEN HE WOKE UP the next morning—Sunday July 22, 1951—Bill still felt tired. After preaching five consecutive nights in the humid July heat, his energy was badly depleted. Ern Baxter offered to preach the morning service, so that Bill could rest in his motel room. Bill gladly accepted this offer, using his free time to pray and prepare for the Sunday afternoon and evening meetings. Around noon he got hungry, so he stepped out to go get a sandwich.

He was staying at a motel several miles outside of Toledo. All that week he had been eating at a nice, clean restaurant near the motel, but this restaurant was closed on Sunday. Another restaurant was open on the other side of the road, so Bill walked over and went inside.

The door banged shut behind him. He looked around a dingy café, vibrating with western style honky-tonk music from a jukebox. To his left, he saw a policeman standing with one arm around a woman and his other hand feeding coins into a slot machine. That shocked Bill. He thought that gambling was illegal in Ohio, and here stood a representative of the law openly violating the law he had sworn to uphold. What kind of example did that set for the young people in this room? Bill noticed a girl

---

[20]   2 Kings 2:1-15
[21]   Luke 1:11-17
[22]   Malachi 4:5-6; Matthew 17:10-11

about 18 years old, sitting on the side of a table with a beer in her hand. She was indecently dressed in a short skirt, and she had two boys fawning over her. Bill felt disgusted. Then he looked to his right. There sat an elderly woman with two elderly men. All three were drinking beer. The woman looked horrible. Her short, kinky hair was tinted blue; she had blue eye-shadow smeared above her eyes, blue lipstick on her lips, and blue nail polish on her finger and toenails. She wore a sleeveless blouse that revealed the flab on her arms and she wore shorts that exposed the flab on her thighs. She was trying to light a cigarette, but she couldn't get the match to fire.

Bill sickened. In his mind he compared the awesome holiness of God, which he experienced each night in the meetings, with the worldliness he saw around him in this shabby cafe. He thought, "Oh, God, how can You look at it? Are my little Rebekah and Sarah going to have to be raised among such corruption as this? Why don't You just destroy the world and be done with it? Look at that teenage girl, carrying on so when she ought to be in church; and that woman with the policeman, gambling; and then that grandmother sitting there boozing. It looks like it's all gone corrupt: the youth of our nation, motherhood, the law, even the elderly. It's all gone."

While he stood there criticizing all of them in his heart, a strange feeling came over him. He walked back to a dimly lit corner and sat in an empty booth. Suddenly he saw the world spinning in space. Around the earth swirled a deep red streak, like a long, thin cloud. Bill could hear a voice explaining, "*That crimson cover is the blood of the Lord Jesus who died to save sinners. That is the reason God can't destroy these people. They still have a chance. Every mortal being has a right to accept their salvation, until the day they die and go beyond that blood. If they die without accepting it, they are already judged. But as long as they are alive, they have a right to the Tree of Life, if they will accept it."*

Rubbing his eyes, Bill thought, "What's going on? I know I didn't go to sleep. It must be a vision. I'm sure this is a vision."

He could see Jesus Christ standing above the world, gazing down on His creation. Jesus looked sorrowful and pathetic. Bill could see the crown of thorns on His head, the blood running down His temples and the spit of the soldier's mockery on His beard. Now and then Jesus would jerk His head as though something had struck Him in the face. Bill wondered about those jerks, until Jesus said, *"They are caused by the slaps from your sins."*

Stunned, Bill watched himself in the vision, doing things he shouldn't do and saying things he shouldn't say. Every time he sinned, he could see a dark blot sail up through the atmosphere toward God's throne. Instinctively he knew that if one of his sins ever reached the throne of God, his life would be over; God would kill him right then. But something blocked the way; that red cloud surrounding the earth acted like a bumper, deflecting his sins from the presence of a Holy God.

Now Bill noticed that the crimson stream around the world came from blood flowing out of a wound in Jesus' side. Another sin-blot flew upward. Jesus jerked when it struck Him and a drop of blood trickled down from His forehead. He raised His hand and said, *"Father, forgive him. He doesn't know what he's doing."*

Bill's heart wrenched in pain. He thought, "Oh, God, did I do that? Surely it wasn't me?"

But it was him. A book lay open near the throne of God. Bill could see his own name written on the front in large letters. Beneath his name was another word that he could not make out. The pages of the book were filled with writing, and every time a dark sin-blot came up from earth, another sentence was added. Trembling, Bill stepped up close enough to read the book. He gasped in horror. Beneath his name was written the chilling word, "*Condemned.*"

In the vision, Bill's strength left him and he collapsed. Weak and shaking, he crawled up to the feet of Jesus and begged, "Lord Jesus, I didn't know my sins hurt You like that. Will You please forgive me?"

Jesus dipped His finger into His wounded side, and, using His own blood for ink, He wrote with His finger across the cover of the book, "*Pardoned.*" Then He put the book behind Him, out of sight.

Never before in a vision had Bill seen anything so lovely, or felt such joy and relief. But before he could express his thanks, Jesus said, "*I forgave you, but you want to condemn these people.*"

Bill stiffened with realization. Yes, a minute ago he had wanted God to blow the whole place up. Now he saw the people in this cafe from a different perspective.

While the vision was fading, the voice said to Bill, "*You're forgiven, but what about her. She needs the Gospel too.*"

Looking around the cafe with fresh compassion, Bill thought, "Oh, God, how do I know who You've called and who You haven't called? It's my business to speak to everyone."

The two old men and the flabby woman were laughing uproariously. As Bill watched, the two men got up and headed toward the men's room, leaving the woman sitting alone. Walking over to her table, Bill said, "How do you do, lady. Could I sit down? I want to talk to you."

Giggling, she looked up at Bill, hiccuped, set down her beer, and said with a slur, "I've got company already."

"I didn't mean it that way, sister. I'm a minister and I want to talk to you about your soul."

When he called her "sister," her attitude changed. She said, "Help yourself to a seat."

Scooting his chair up to the table, Bill introduced himself. Then he told her about the vision he had just seen. "I stood there criticizing you in my heart. I felt that God should come down and tear this place up. But now I've changed my mind. Would you forgive me for condemning you like that? God forgave me my sins and I want Him to forgive you also."

"Branham," she muttered. "Branham... Are you the man who's holding a revival down here at the arena?"

"Yes, ma'am. That's me."

"I've been wanting to get down there, but I just couldn't bring myself to go. Mr. Branham, I was raised in a Christian family. I've got two girls who are Christians. I know just where I got off the right path and started down the wrong one." Briefly she told her story, touching on the wrong choices that led her over to life's darker side, with all its disappointments and pain.

When she finished, Bill said, "Sister, I don't care what you've done, the blood of Jesus Christ is still around you. This world is covered over with His blood and it's protecting you from the wrath of God. As long as you've got breath in your body, the blood has you covered. Someday when the breath leaves your body, your soul will go out and you'll go beyond this world to a place where that blood won't do you any good. There will be nothing there but judgment. While you've still got a chance for pardon, accept it. Ask Jesus for forgiveness and be saved."

She looked down at her beer. "Mr. Branham, I've been drinking."

Taking her hand, Bill said, "That doesn't matter. The Holy Spirit warned me to come and tell you this. Before the foundation of the world God called you, sister. You're doing wrong and you're only making it worse."

"Do you think God will have me?"

"Absolutely He'll have you."

Squeezing Bill's hand, she asked fervently, "Will you pray for me that I will be saved?"

They knelt on the floor of that cafe and prayed together until the woman accepted her salvation in Jesus Christ. When Bill stood up, he noticed that the policeman had removed his hat and bowed to one knee in respect.

As Bill walked away from the restaurant, he thought, "That's right. Don't condemn them; give them the Gospel."

ON AUGUST 26, 1951, after six weeks on the road, Bill returned to Jeffersonville, Indiana, thankful to spend a few weeks at home before flying to South Africa. That same night he delivered his last hometown sermon for 1951. Knowing that his own church building would not hold the crowd, he rented a local high-school auditorium that could seat 4,000. Unfortunately that was still not enough room. After all the seats were filled and the walls were lined with people standing, there were still several thousand people outside who could not get in.

While the audience sang sweetly: "Only believe, only believe, all things are possible, only believe," Bill walked out onto the stage. Looking up into the bleachers, he noticed Dr. Dillman. "Good evening, Dr. Dillman," he said into the microphone. Dillman returned his greeting with a nod. Bill continued to scan the crowd as he spoke. He saw his friend Sam Adair standing near the entrance. "Howdy, Dr. Adair. I'm sorry we haven't got a seat for you. May the Lord bless you." Then Bill noticed William Hall sitting in the bleachers, beaming a robust smile. Bill said,

"Dr. Dillman, do you remember a patient you had not long ago named William Hall? About six weeks ago he was almost dead from cancer of the liver."

Dr. Dillman nodded.

"Dr. Adair, do you remember telling me that William Hall was going to jump overboard in four days?"

Sam Adair nodded too.

Bill looked at William Hall and said, "Brother Hall, do you want to testify?"

William Hall sprang to his feet. "Do I want to testify? Praise the Lord, yes!"

After the meeting ended, Dr. Adair and Dr. Dillman took William Hall to the hospital for a thorough examination. Not a trace of cancer could they find.

ON SEPTEMBER 26, 1951, William Branham began a faith-healing campaign in New York City. The next five nights would be his last campaign in America before leaving for South Africa. On Friday, the first person to come up in the prayer-line was a middle-aged woman. Just by looking at her, Bill could tell she was suffering.

He said, "You're sick. Of course, Jesus healed you over nineteen hundred years ago. That's the Word of the Lord, isn't it?[23] And we must believe it. Now He didn't write that directly to you, using your name. He wrote it to the multitudes. But it's just the same as if He wrote it directly to you. Then God sent prophetic gifts into His church in these last days to stimulate the faith of His people. So if He would speak through me, that would be secondary, but it would be His Word just the same. To doubt this written Word would be sin, and to doubt His spoken Word would be sin.

[23]   Isaiah 53:5; 1 Peter 2:24

"All of you people in the prayer-line must be prepared to believe. If you don't believe, just step out of the line now, because you could end up worse off than ever. Jesus said to one man, *'Sin no more, lest a worse thing come unto thee.'*[24] When He said 'sin no more,' He wasn't talking about some immoral act. Sin is disbelieving God's Word. *'He that believeth not is condemned already.'*[25] See? It's your unbelief that will condemn you. God won't send you to hell for any specific thing that you did. He will send you to hell if you reject the provision He made for your salvation. If you just reject Jesus, just fail to believe His Word, that's all you have to do to be condemned to hell. Satan always puts a question mark across that, but it is 'Thus saith the Lord.'"

"I guess you wonder why I'm stalling. I've been waiting for the angel of the Lord, and now I feel Him moving down." To the woman beside him, Bill said, "You're aware of something going on. That's just the anointing. You feel it as a warm, welcome, sweet spirit. If that is right, raise your hand." Her hand sprang up. "The angel of the Lord is here on the platform, and your faith is beginning to pull Him this way. You are a stranger here in New York. You come from Pennsylvania. I see you're suffering in your lower organs. It's cancer on the bladder. You have other ailments too, like heart trouble. I see you in a checkered dress, smothering, trying to catch your breath."

He prayed, "Heavenly Father, be merciful to our sister, and heal her of this hideous demon that's trying to take her life. Satan, as Christian believers, we curse thee in the name of the Lord Jesus, that you depart from this woman, go into outer darkness, and bother her no more."

"Now, mother dear, it has left you. Go back to Pennsylvania and rejoice."

---

[24] John 5:14
[25] John 3:18

And so the evening progressed, from one precise diagnosis to another, from one healing to another miracle. Cancers, heart trouble, diabetes, neurosis, deafness, epilepsy, all these diseases succumbed to the healing power of Jesus Christ. After awhile the angel left the platform and moved out over the audience.

Bill said, "I keep seeing the Spirit of God hanging over that lady there with a red dress on. I don't know why. She's either been blessed, or healed, or something. Lady, are you a Christian?"

Ern Baxter said, "Brother Branham, she was healed in the meeting the night before last."

"Oh, that's what it is. I don't remember these things. They have to tell me what happens in the meetings. It seems to me like I dreamed it. If this audience could only know how I feel right now: my hands feel a bit larger; my lips feel thick. When the Spirit comes down, it's like I am listening to myself talk. He just takes hold of the subject. He does the talking, not me; I have nothing to do with it. All right, be reverent, everyone. Believe with all your heart. God will bring it to pass."

The meeting ended around 11:00 p.m., and it was nearly midnight before Bill and Meda got back to their hotel. When they entered the lobby, the night receptionist handed them a letter from home. The letter said that six-month-old Sarah was deathly sick. Frantically worried, Meda wanted to call home and find out how little Sarah was doing now. Bill wanted to wait. Sarah was staying with her grandmother Branham, who had no telephone. That meant Meda would have to call a neighbor, who would then have to walk across a field to reach Ella Branham's house and bring back news. Since it was so late, Bill convinced Meda that her call could wait until morning.

Bill lay in bed a long time, unable to fall asleep. He often had this trouble after meetings. Even though he felt exhausted, his tense nerves kept him awake. But tonight he had the additional concern about his sick daughter. He lay quietly until his wife's breathing dropped into the slow, steady rhythm of slumber. Then he slipped out of bed, went into the next room, knelt and prayed for Sarah.

About three o'clock in the morning, he saw his mother walking toward him, carrying his baby girl. Sarah was choking. Her little face flushed red as she gasped and struggled for breath. Grandma Ella handed the baby to Bill, who hugged Sarah to his chest and prayed, "Oh, God, don't let my baby die. Spare her life, will You, Lord Jesus?"

Sarah sucked in a draft of air, and then started breathing normally. Bill handed her back to her grandmother.

The angel of the Lord said, "*In the morning you will receive the news that your baby has been awfully sick, but she's all right now.*"

With his mind at peace, Bill went back to bed and fell asleep. He woke at 9:00 to the sound of Billy Paul knocking at his door. Meda was already dressed. After Billy Paul came in, Meda said, "I'm going to call home now and see about our baby."

"Honey, you don't have to call. But if you do, here is the message you're going to receive. When the neighbor lady goes over to find out about Sarah, she's going to come back and say, 'The baby has been awfully sick, but she's all right now.'" Meda looked puzzled, so Bill added, "God healed Sarah last night, then showed it to me in a vision."

As many times as Meda had watched her husband's visions come true, the mother in her had to call home anyway. As they waited by the phone for the neighbor to call back, Bill said, "Watch the wording, because her answer will be word for word the way the angel told me." The phone rang. Meda held the receiver a few inches away from her ear so that her husband and stepson could hear the neighbor lady say, "The baby has been awfully sick, but she's all right now. God healed her last night."

Bill nodded. By now, after five years of experience, he knew the angel of the Lord always told him the truth. But he did not yet realize how crucial it was to do exactly what the angel said. In South Africa he would soon learn.

Chapter 57
Tremors in Africa
1951

PULLING OFF his safari hat, Sidney Jackson wiped his brow. Today felt warmer than yesterday. It was September 1951; the beginning of summer in South Africa, and Jackson was repairing irrigation lines in his citrus grove. Leaving his shovel standing in the dirt, Jackson sat down with his back against a tree. From here on the hillside he could look out across the Highveld—that thinly wooded grassland that stretched west into Botswana and north into Southern Rhodesia.[26] To the east of him, between his farm and the Indian Ocean, ran the Transvaal Drakensberg, South Africa's largest mountain range. Although Sidney Jackson had lived in this country all his life, he never tired of its wild, arid beauty.

Idly he caressed his leopard-skin hatband, remembering the safari when he had shot this particular cat. That enterprise had been larger than most of his safaris. Since he had been after the king of beasts, he had employed a whole village of natives to beat the bush and flush lions out of hiding in the tall grass.

His thoughts turned naturally to the black skinned natives, many of whom were his friends. For years he had traveled the

---

[26] Today Southern Rhodesia is named Zimbabwe

Transvaal region doing part-time missionary work. By now he spoke several native dialects, in addition to English, Dutch, and Afrikaans. He loved the bush country and had developed a deep respect for the African natives who lived in it.

Sidney Jackson closed his eyes to pray about his own missionary work among the natives. Soon his prayer branched out to include all missionaries working in South Africa. As he forged deeper into the Spirit of the Lord, he suddenly heard himself say, "William Marrion Branham." That surprised him. Although he had read about William Branham, the American evangelist had not been on his mind. And who was Marrion Branham? He wondered if Marrion was William Branham's wife? If so, what did William and Marrion Branham have to do with missionaries in South Africa? Jackson knew God was trying to tell him something, but at the moment he didn't know what it was.

The following night he dreamed he saw William Branham sitting in a stadium seat, smoking a cigarette. That troubled Jackson. William Branham had a worldwide reputation as a man of God. Why had he dreamed that such a godly man was doing something as unhealthy and unholy as smoking? What was God trying to tell him?

A few weeks after this dream Sidney Jackson was startled to read in the newspaper that William Branham would be visiting South Africa in October. The National Committee—composed of church leaders from South Africa's three largest Christian denominations: the Dutch Reformed Church, the English Church, and the Apostolic Faith Mission—was sponsoring a two-month tour that would shuttle William Branham around to 11 African cities. The tour would begin in Johannesburg on October 3, 1951. Sidney Jackson remembered his odd dream about William and Marrion Branham. Jackson didn't know what God was trying to tell him, but he knew he had to be in Johannesburg when that famous American evangelist arrived.

TROUBLE BEGAN for William Branham even before he left New York. When he got to the international airport, he learned that he and Billy Paul could not board their scheduled flight because their visas were incomplete. They both lacked the required yellow fever shots. So, the rest of their party—Ern Baxter, Fred Bosworth, and Julius Stadsklev, an American army chaplain—boarded the plane and flew to South Africa ahead of them. Bill and Billy Paul got their shots at a clinic near the airport, but they had to wait three more days in New York before they could follow.

When they finally were able to make the trip, it was a long, turbulent, sleepless flight across the North Atlantic. Bill's plane began circling Johannesburg at 6:30 in the evening, October 6, 1951, but dense fog and malfunctioning instruments kept it from landing until nine o'clock. Ern Baxter was waiting for Bill at the arrival gate. Next to Baxter stood Reverend A. J. Schoeman, head of the National Committee that had approved Bill's trip to South Africa. By prior arrangement with the government, Bill was rushed to the head of the customs line. Unfortunately, his visa was still not valid because his yellow fever vaccination required a 12-day incubation period before he could enter the country. Reverend Schoeman pleaded with the authorities to make an exception, explaining that thousands of people were right now waiting to hear this man speak. Finally the South African Medical Association agreed to let Bill into the city, but they refused to let him travel anywhere else in South Africa for another ten days.

As soon as they left the airport, Ern Baxter told Bill what had happened in the past three days. When Baxter landed in South Africa, he found hundreds of people waiting at the airport to meet

Bill. Of course they were disappointed when they learned Bill had been delayed in New York. There was nothing else to do except go on without him, so Baxter and Bosworth held a meeting in one of the largest church buildings in the city. It could only fit a fraction of the people who came, so the next day they moved the campaign to Maranatha Park Tabernacle about 20 miles outside the city limits. Ern Baxter said, "The crowds have been averaging over 10,000 a night. Brother Bosworth and I have been taking turns preaching, laying a foundation of faith in the promises of God to heal. The people are very receptive and I think their faith is ripe. We'll get there tonight when the meeting is about over, but at least you can greet the people and say a few words to get them ready for tomorrow."

"That sounds fine," Bill said wearily. He was studying the buildings on the well-lighted streets. "I didn't realize Durban was such a modern city. I thought it would be more primitive."

"Oh, Brother Branham, you're mistaken," said Reverend Schoeman. "This isn't Durban. This is Johannesburg."

"Isn't this Southern Rhodesia?" asked Bill.

"No, this is South Africa," Mr. Schoeman replied.

"Well, what part of South Africa is Southern Rhodesia in?"

"Brother Branham, there is no Southern Rhodesia in South Africa."

"I'm confused. I told my wife to write to me in Durban, Southern Rhodesia, South Africa."

Reverend Schoeman chuckled. "Brother Branham, that would be like writing a letter to New York City, Canada. There is no New York City in Canada. Rhodesia is a different nation from South Africa."

"Then where is Durban?"

"It's over on the eastern coast, about 450 kilometers southeast of here."

"How many miles is that?"

"About 300 miles."

"Well, Durban is the place the Lord wants me to go. When will we be going there?"

Schoeman looked uncomfortable. "Oh, you will get there," he said evasively. "Don't worry about that." Then he changed the subject.

Maranatha Park Tabernacle was not really an auditorium; actually it was an enormous open-sided steel structure with a galvanized roof that had once been Johannesburg's railway station.

The William Branham party with the National Committee that was responsible for the arrangements of the campaign in Africa

FRONT ROW: A. W. Preller, F. F. Bosworth, A. J. Schoeman, William Branham, W. F. Mullan, and W. J. Ern Baxter

BACK ROW: H. C. Phillips, E. D. Pettenger, D. Freeman, E. King, G. Vermeulen, J. W. Gillingham, J. H. Saayman, Julius Stadsklev, Billy Paul Branham

The Apostolic Faith Mission, which is the largest Pentecostal denomination in South Africa, had purchased this park for a conference grounds. Now the Tabernacle covered part of a crowd numbering around 15,000 people.

The nationality of this crowd puzzled Bill because they all looked like light-skinned Europeans. "Are all these Africans?" he asked. "I thought Africans were black."

"Yes, these are Africans," Schoeman explained, "just like I'm an African. The Dutch, the French, and the English colonized South Africa. Altogether South Africa has about 3,000,000 people of European descent, and another 10,000,000 non-Europeans—, but also a large population of immigrants from India. In our country we have segregation, so in most of your meetings the two groups won't mix. But we have scheduled some of your meetings with the natives, so you will get to preach to them too."

The people stirred excitedly when they learned that the American evangelist had arrived. Bill mounted the platform and looked out at the huge throng. "Good evening, friends," he said into the microphone. Reverend Schoeman translated each sentence into Afrikaans, the official language of the Republic of South Africa.

Bill had been speaking only five minutes when he saw a blue bus roll out of the shadows and lumber through the air above the audience. The bus drove by the platform close enough for him to see the name "DURBAN" in the destination slot above its front windshield. Then it passed from his line of sight. He kept speaking, telling the audience about his trip. "So you see, friends, I'm really tired tonight, worn out from the flight." A few minutes later he saw that blue bus again driving through the air, coming from the back of the building. When it reached the middle of the auditorium, it stopped. A teenage boy on crutches boarded the bus. Bill could see that one of the boy's legs was at least six inches shorter than the other. The bus continued its journey, its wheels turning just a few feet above the crowd. It stopped again near the platform where Bill was speaking. The door opened and that same teenager stepped out, this time without crutches. He walked above the people until he was halfway to the back of the tabernacle, then he vanished in a flash of light. Directly under that light sat the same boy in reality.

Pointing at the young man, Bill said, "You, back there... the boy with the white shirt and black suspenders. Don't you come from Durban?"

Bill was not sure whether the boy would understand English; but he did, because he shouted back, "Yes, I do come from Durban."

"You're crippled, aren't you. One of your legs is shorter than the other and you have to walk on crutches."

"That's it exactly," the boy shouted.

"It isn't anymore," Bill said. "You're healed. Jesus Christ has healed you."

A stir of amazement rustled through the audience, but nothing happened right away. The boy was penned in so tightly that he could not test his legs. Several men picked him up, carried him through the crowd to the front, and left him standing on the elevated platform where everyone could see him. When the men let go, the boy broke out into a cold sweat. Cautiously he took one step, testing himself on his shriveled limb. It held. His next step was more reckless, and soon he was prancing about the stage without even a hint of a limp.

While the audience praised the Lord Jesus, Julius Stadsklev got the boy's story. His name was Ernest Blom. The youngest of ten children, he had been born crippled and had been under the care of a specialist since he was four years old. For two years he wore an iron leg-brace without any noticeable improvement. Later the specialist suggested an operation; but since there could be no guarantee of success, the family declined. When Ernest heard that William Branham would be in South Africa, he couldn't wait for the evangelist to get to Durban. He convinced his family to take him to Johannesburg. Ernest said that when William Branham spoke to him, he experienced a weird sensation, something like cold water was running through his body. He knew then that he was healed.

Meanwhile, Bill was challenging the audience to believe. "Do you see what faith in Jesus Christ can do? Now, I'm not against doctors. I'm for doctors. God bless them. Doctors are there to help you. But doctors don't claim to heal; they only claim to assist nature. God is the real healer. If you broke your arm, a doctor can set it, but who is the one who makes the bones grow back together? If you cut your hand, a doctor can sew it up, but only God can make the skin grow back together. And when a doctor has done all he can do for you, it is time to look in faith to the Lord Jesus Christ."

As he spoke, he saw a green car speeding in the air above the heads of the people. Going too fast into a turn, the car lost control, spinning around and slamming into a tree backwards. An ambulance drove up and a rescue team removed a blond teenage girl from the wreckage. Bill heard one of the rescuers say that the girl's back was broken in several places.

When the vision ended, he studied the crowd looking for this girl, but he couldn't find her. Then the Pillar of Fire flashed in front of him and hovered just a few feet away. Bill walked to the edge of the platform and looked down. There she lay on her back, her cot so close to the stage that he would not have seen her if he hadn't stepped forward. She looked like she was about fourteen years old. Bill pointed at her and said, "Young lady, didn't you have an accident recently?"

"Yes," she gasped, excitement flushing her cheeks.

"You were in a green car that spun around and hit a tree backwards, and you broke your back in three places." Then Bill saw her by vision, walking above the audience with her hands up, jumping and praising God. Without a grain of doubt he said, "In the name of Jesus Christ stand up, for thus saith the Lord, 'You're healed.'"

The girl's mother, sitting beside her daughter, jumped up and objected. "No! She can't! She hasn't moved since the accident! If she moves, the doctor said it could kill her!" But even while this mother was protesting, her daughter had already risen from her cot and had stepped to the floor, where she let out a squeal of joy. That turned her mother's head. When she saw her daughter standing beside her, the mother fainted, collapsing onto the same cot that her daughter had just vacated.

Spontaneously, the audience praised God. Sensing it was time to close the service with a general prayer for the sick, Bill asked everyone to lay their hands on one another and pray for those around them. While the audience was praying with fervent emotion, Bill saw a vision of a woman being healed of arthritis. When the vision passed, he saw her in the crowd and pointed her out. She waved that it was true. Feeling lightheaded, Bill almost collapsed from the strain. Vaguely, he was aware of strong arms supporting him, helping him out of Maranatha Park Tabernacle and into a car.

After the meeting, Reverend Schoeman took Ern Baxter and Bill home for a good night's sleep. On the way, Schoeman talked about how wonderful it was to see these miracles and how excited he was about the meetings. Bill was not deceived. He could see the man's skepticism as clearly as he could spot an elephant's trail through the grassy savanna. That skepticism did not surprise or discourage him. He had often run into the same attitude among educated Christians who wondered if his discernment might be some kind of elaborate trick—perhaps mental telepathy, or else mass psychology, like using the power of suggestion to manipulate audiences. Usually he didn't concern himself with skeptics. But this man chaired the committee in charge of all Bill's meetings in South Africa. If Reverend Schoeman remained skeptical, that might create problems.

ALTHOUGH four Pentecostal denominations were the main sponsors of William Branham's African campaigns—the Apostolic Faith Mission, the Assemblies of God, the Pentecostal Holiness, and the Full Gospel Church of God—many other denominations were cooperating in various degrees. One exception was the Dutch Reformed Church, which didn't believe in divine healing. But there was at least one elder in the Dutch Reformed Church who braved the criticism of his peers and sat in the audience that first night in Johannesburg. Throughout the meeting he studied the American evangelist with a critical eye. When he saw William Branham's gift of discernment reveal the problems of total strangers, he was convinced this was a supernatural move of God. On his way home he stopped to share his excitement with a friend who was a Dutch Reformed Church minister.

The minister scolded him for being so naive, saying, "Branham is inspired by the devil. He's nothing more than a polished up soothsayer. Stay away from him."

The elder left his friend's house in distress. Not far from the minister's door, he knelt under a peach tree and prayed, "God, I believe what I saw tonight is real and I believe that Brother Branham is telling us the truth, because nobody except You could do such miracles. I believe it, but my friend doesn't. How important is it that he sees this too?"

Suddenly he felt a hand grab the back of his shoulder with a grip that burned into him like a hot iron. Jumping to his feet, he turned to see who had touched him. No one was there—at least, no one like he expected to see. In the air hung a vertical strip of light about a foot long. As he watched, the light expanded, then split in two, and out from between these two halves stepped a large, white-robed man with dark, shoulder-length hair. The elder held his breath until the man spoke.

"*Go,*" said the man in white, "*Tell your friend he must not condemn that man, for this is the hour of your visitation.*" Then the robed figure vanished along with the light.

Running back to his friend's house, the elder burst through the door, shouting, "I just saw an angel! He met me outside and told me to tell you this is the hour of our visitation. He put his hand on my back and it burned me."

Of course the minister was skeptical. But when he looked on his friend's back, he was shocked to see the imprint of a man's hand scorched into the white fabric! That convinced him.

THE NEXT MORNING the three Americans met their host in his dining room. "Good morning, Brother Schoeman," Bill said cheerfully as he sat down at the breakfast table. "It certainly is beautiful weather we're having."

Mr. Schoeman was a tall, thin man with a bald forehead, a gray mustache, and thick plastic rims on his glasses. He adjusted his napkin on his lap and said, "Yes, it's fine weather. Remember this is the beginning of our summer. Our seasons are just the opposite of yours."

Sensing the doubt that still troubled Schoeman's thoughts, Bill prayed silently, "Lord, if You'll just help me shake him up a little and convince him, that will help, because he's the chairman of the committee that's sponsoring me here."

They continued with breakfast and small talk until presently Bill felt the anointing of the Holy Spirit. Soon a vision appeared. Like watching a miniature play, he saw Mr. Schoeman and a little girl sitting in a doctor's office listening to the doctor talk. On the wall behind them hung a calendar dated April 1951.

"Brother Schoeman, your little girl is named Andrea, isn't she."

Mr. Schoeman dropped his fork in surprise. It clattered off his plate and fell to the floor. "Yes, Brother Branham. How did you know?"

"About six months ago you almost lost her, didn't you. Something was wrong in her throat. They operated on her and took out her tonsils, but it wasn't very successful. She's had a hard time swallowing since then, hasn't she."

"Brother Branham, that is exactly right. Has the Lord showed you anything about her future?"

"Yes. Don't worry about her. She's going to be all right."

Schoeman's chair scraped against the floor as he reached under the table to get his fork. Then he said, "Brother Branham, I have a confession to make. Up until right now I was just a little bit skeptical of you. But now I know, it's true what I've heard."

When the morning paper arrived, Schoeman was surprised to read the story about the elder in the Dutch Reformed Church who claimed an angel had touched his back last night. The newspaper even printed a picture of the white shirt with the scorched imprint of a man's hand on the back shoulder. "Brother Branham, you have to read this!"

"I already know about it, Brother Schoeman. The Lord showed me a vision of the whole thing. If you'll bring that shirt here, you'll find that my left hand will fit that scorched imprint perfectly."

Reverend Schoeman contacted the newspaper and soon a reporter brought the shirt to his house. The burned outline of a hand was clearly visible on the back of the shirt. Bill laid his own left hand over the imprint, adjusting his fingers to match the outline. Just as he claimed it would, his hand matched the imprint exactly.

Chapter 58
Satan Springs His Trap
1951

JOHANNESBURG SHOOK under the seismic shock of William Branham's ministry, sending spiritual tremors across the entire southern tip of Africa. Those who attended the first meetings called their families and friends to tell them what they saw. Every night the crowds grew larger. By Tuesday night, October 8, 1951, (Bill's third night in the city) over 17,000 people jammed into Maranatha Park to see this amazing gift of supernatural discernment. Many who came in sick, went out healed. Almost everyone left excited, spreading the news that a prophet was visiting South Africa, that Jesus Christ was in this prophet doing the same works He did when He walked the roads of Palestine: healing the sick, the crippled, the deaf, the dumb, the blind, revealing the secrets of the heart. Nothing seemed impossible.

Wednesday morning the South African Medical Association invited Bill to have breakfast with them. Their spokesman said, "Reverend Branham, many doctors in South Africa are Christians. We became doctors because we wanted to help people. At first we were suspicious of you, thinking you might be preaching the Christian Science notion that doctors and medicine are bad and should be avoided. But now it's obvious to us that you support doctors. We believe in divine healing the way you preach it. Reverend Branham, even though the incubation period for your yellow fever shot is not yet over, we are giving you permission to travel in the country anyway. Not only that, we are opening the doors of our hospitals, and any of our patients who want to go to your meetings, we'll see that they get there."

After breakfast, Ern Baxter came to Bill and said, "Brother Branham, I've got some news for you. I know you want to go to Durban, but rather than going straight there from Johannesburg, the National Committee has set up an itinerary that will take us over 1,000 miles south to Capetown, then up the east coast to Durban. How does that sound?"

"It doesn't matter to me," said Bill, "just as long as we get to Durban, because that's where I feel led to go. When are we leaving?"

"The day after tomorrow."

That did strike Bill as peculiar, since they were just getting started in Johannesburg. Not only did they have the endorsement of the local medical association, they even had a favorable review by the press, which was something Bill did not always receive. The meetings were going tremendously well. Each night the size of the crowd increased, as did the number of healings and miracles. Why should they leave so soon? It did not make sense to Bill, but he didn't say anything about it. After all, he was a guest of the South African ministerial association, so it seemed only right that he should let them make all his arrangements.

That night after the meeting, Bill fell into a fitful sleep. About two o'clock in the morning, a strange screech woke him. He stumbled to his bedroom window to see what kind of bird made such an unusual sound. All he could see were reeds waving in a gentle breeze. Returning to bed, he tried to go back to sleep, but couldn't. Thinking that reading might make him drowsy, he switched on a lamp, sat back against the headboard, and opened his Bible.

Suddenly his skin began to tingle and the hair on the back of his neck bristled. Looking up from his Bible, he saw the angel of the Lord standing in the middle of the room, his white robe shining in the glow from the electric lamp. The breeze from the open window played with the angel's long, dark hair. Even in the natural, he was an imposing figure, standing six-feet tall and weighing at least 200 pounds. In the supernatural he was awesome, causing Bill's chest to constrict into a tight knot of fear.

The angel folded his arms across his chest, gazed sternly at Bill and said, *"Don't go with those men down to Capetown. Stay here in Johannesburg for two more weeks of meetings. Tomorrow you will meet a man..."*

While the angel spoke, the room blurred like a fresh painting in watercolors on which clear water had been spilled. When the colors jelled, Bill found himself looking at a Caucasian man, tanned and vigorous, looking perhaps 50 years old, judging by the wrinkles on his forehead and around the corners of his eyes. He had small ears and a large, flat nose. On his head was cocked a safari hat with a leopard-skin hatband. The vision showed this man dreaming a shocking dream.

The angel said, *"His name is Sidney Jackson and he runs a farm up north. He is a great hunter and he can take you on a safari. After two weeks in Johannesburg, you must take the next ten days and go hunting with Sidney Jackson. Then go straight to Durban and stay there until I call you. If you will do these things, I will give you the country."*

"But how am I going to convince these other men? They have my itinerary all set up."

"That they might know this is the will of the Lord, tomorrow Reverend Schoeman is going to take you into Johannesburg..." The

scene changed and Bill saw a street corner by a park. Bright flowers colored the banks of a ditch. A native woman dressed in purple stood near the corner. The angel said, *"Bring this to Reverend Schoeman's attention. After this they are going to take you to Pretoria..."* The scene shifted to a highway where a young native girl was selling beads by the side of the road. Her hair was scraped bare on one side of her forehead, revealing a nasty scar. While looking at her beads, Bill heard a squawk and saw a strange bird fly across the road. Here the angel said, *"Remind Ern Baxter that you told him this would happen, so that he will know this is 'thus saith the Lord.' When you get to Pretoria, they will take you to pray for a man who thinks he has cancer of the hip, but he is mistaken. He is suffering from a surgical error. During a recent operation, the surgeon's knife slipped, cutting the wrong thing. Don't pray for this man because he is going to die."*

The vision dissolved around him and Bill found himself back where he had started, sitting up in bed, his back propped against the headboard, his Bible in his lap, a trickle of sweat running down his temple. The angel of the Lord was gone.

Bill ran to the next room to tell his manager. "Brother Baxter, wake up. The angel of the Lord just met me and told me we can't take that itinerary the National Committee set up."

Sleepy-eyed, Ern Baxter nodded and mumbled, "Well, you'll have to tell Brother Schoeman tomorrow."

In the morning Bill went looking for Reverend Schoeman. He found the man just as he was leaving on an errand. Bill asked to go along. When they finished the errand and were heading back to the estate, Bill told his host about the angel's visit last night. "So you see, Brother Schoeman, you're going to have to cancel that itinerary."

Schoeman ran one hand up over his bald forehead. "Brother Branham, I can't do that. All the dates are set and the arrangements are made. We're leaving for Klerksdorp tomorrow morning. We can't just cancel out for no reason."

"But there is a reason, a good reason. The Lord's done told me I shouldn't go."

"I'm sorry, Brother Branham, but we've got to keep that itinerary. We've already spent thousands of dollars on advertising, and many people are expecting you to be there."

Bill insisted that their itinerary should be canceled, but Schoeman wouldn't budge. Back and forth they reasoned for and against. Finally, Bill grew quiet with frustration. At the moment he was getting nowhere, but he had not yet used his vindication. He would save that for the breakfast table.

Reaching his estate, Schoeman turned in through his gate and started down the long driveway. Before he reached his house, he passed a middle-aged man and woman walking the other direction. As soon as Schoeman's car drove by this couple on foot, Bill recognized the man. "Brother Schoeman, stop!"

Startled, Schoeman slammed on his brakes. Bill jumped out and introduced himself to the couple. "Hello, I'm Brother Branham."

"Brother Branham, I came here to meet you. My name is—"

"I know," Bill interrupted. "Your name is Sidney Jackson. The angel of the Lord told me that I was to come to your farm to rest. He also told me that you saw me in a dream, smoking a cigarette, but I want to tell you that I didn't smoke a cigarette. The Lord was showing you that I will be disobedient to Him if I do what the National Committee wants me to do. I'll tell you more about that later. Why don't you come back and have breakfast with us."

"I'd love to," said Jackson, a look of bewilderment on his face.

"Fine. By the way, Marrion is my middle name."

Sidney Jackson opened his mouth as though he was going to say something, but was too stunned to speak.

After breakfast, Bill declared, "I have an announcement to make. We must not take the itinerary to Klerksdorp and beyond. The Lord told me to stay here in Johannesburg for two more weeks, then go over to Mr. Jackson's farm and go hunting with him, so that I can rest up for ten days. Then I'm to go directly to Durban and stay there until He calls me. I suspect I'll be in Durban about a month."

It was an uncomfortable moment for everyone. Ern Baxter said, "Brother Branham, to me that's all right, but you'll have to okay it through the National Committee."

"Well, I've told Brother Schoeman, and he's the head of the committee. So now they know." Bill turned to Reverend Schoeman and added, "So that you will know this is the truth, today when we go into the city we will see a native woman wearing a purple shirt."

A disbelieving look spread over Schoeman's face. "Brother Branham, I've lived here all my life and I've never seen a native woman dressed in purple before."

"Well, you'll see one today. She'll be standing by a park where there are lots of benches, and people selling flowers."

Schoeman raised an eyebrow. "I know where that park is."

"We'll pass by there today," said Bill. "Later, Brother Baxter and I will be riding over to Pretoria and we'll stop to see a native girl selling beads. She has the side of her forehead shaved off where there's a big scar. While we are buying some of her beads, a funny looking bird will fly across the road. By these signs you will know that what I've told you is the truth. The Lord doesn't want us to take that itinerary south."

Reverend Schoeman hedged. "I'll talk it over with the other committee members and see what they say."

They got busy with other things. About ten o'clock Mr. Schoeman asked Bill to ride with him downtown. They stopped at Schoeman's office. On their way back to the estate, Bill noticed the park he had seen in last night's vision. Tapping Reverend Schoeman on the shoulder, Bill pointed out a native woman dressed in purple. All Mr. Schoeman said was, "Well, what do you know about that."

When they got back to the estate, Bill met Justus du Plessis, the man who would be his Afrikaans interpreter during the rest of his stay in South Africa. Du Plessis was smartly dressed in a three-piece business suit. With his bald forehead and thin cheeks, he looked a lot like Mr. Schoeman, minus the glasses and beard. Du Plessis and Schoeman were going to drive over to Pretoria (which was about 29 miles from Johannesburg) and pray for a man who was dying. They asked Bill if he wanted to come along. Of

Sidney Jackson and his wife.

course he did. Ern Baxter joined them. As they drove, Justus du Plessis explained to his American passengers tidbits about South Africa's native culture. "There are usually dozens of native vendors along this stretch of highway. They set up booths along the road, hoping to sell little things they've made to motorists. We'll stop and talk to some of them so you can see what sort of crafts they sell. You might want to buy something for a souvenir."

Playfully, Bill punched his manager in the side, but he didn't say anything to Justus du Plessis about last night's vision. Mile after mile rolled by and they didn't pass any vendors. "That's odd," said du Plessis. "Usually there are lots of salesmen along here." The conversation moved on to something else. After several more miles, they passed one lone girl sitting in a booth by the side of the highway. Du Plessis was so busy talking that he drove past her. Half a mile farther, he stopped talking long enough for Bill to mention the vendor they had passed. Remembering his promise, du Plessis turned the car around and drove back.

The native girl was selling hand-carved beads. She had a memorable face due to a scar that creased the side of her forehead. Ern Baxter snapped a picture of her. Hearing a squawk, he turned to see a large, many-colored bird flying across the highway. He said, "Look, Brother Branham. Isn't that a funny looking bird?"

"That's a wild peacock," said Schoeman.

Pointing back at the girl with the scar on her forehead, Bill asked his companions, "Do you remember the vision I told you about this morning?"

Baxter took off his glasses. His eyes had widened from amazement. "Brother Branham, this is exactly how you said it would be."

Looking directly at the chairman, Bill again declared, "Brother Schoeman, I can't take that itinerary tomorrow. I'm sorry if it interferes with your ministers and their plans, but the Lord told me not to take it."

Mr. Schoeman sputtered in exasperation. "Brother Branham, we have to take it."

"Oh, you may have to take it, but not me." Bill turned and walked back to the car.

Ern Baxter caught up with him and whispered, "Brother Branham, if this was America, I would have the authority as your manager to say no, we're not taking that itinerary south. But we're over here at the mercy of these ministers. They don't understand how the Lord leads you by visions. I am with you 100%; but to make these men understand it, that will be something different."

"Well, whether they understand it or not, I know what the Lord told me to do, and that is what I intend to do."

The next morning—Friday, October 12, 1951—Bill woke up to the sound of motors idling in the driveway. Still dressed in his pajamas, Bill wandered out to the foyer to see what was happening. He was surprised to learn that his escorts had arrived to drive him south.

Justus du Plessis was also surprised. "Aren't you ready to go yet, Brother Branham?"

"No, sir. I'm not even packed. I'm not planning on going anywhere."

"You had better get packed," said Reverend Schoeman. "We're leaving for Klerksdorp as soon as you're ready."

Bill stood firm in his resolve. "I won't need to pack for another two weeks, and then I'll be packing to go to Jackson's farm to hunt lions. Until then, I'll keep holding meetings here in Johannesburg."

Schoeman shook his head. "We have already closed the meetings here."

"You closed the meetings?" That stunned Bill. He had not foreseen this tactic and it threw him off guard. "That's ridiculous. The Lord has given us favor here and told us to stay. This is where we should be."

"It's too late to do anything about it now," du Plessis said. "All the people have gone home. But we have another crowd waiting for us in Klerksdorp."

"What size of a city is Klerksdorp?" Bill asked.

"It's a small town of about 30,000 people," answered Schoeman.

Bill's jaw sagged in amazement. How shortsighted could these men be? "Johannesburg has 500,000 people in it," he pointed out. "Why are we going to a dinky little place like Klerksdorp?"

"We promised Brother Fourie that we would bring you to his town," Reverend Schoeman explained, adding hastily, "but we're expecting between ten and fifteen thousand people to attend the meetings, most of them coming in from the surrounding countryside."

That staggered Bill even more. "Where are you going to put them all? How will they eat?"

Feet shuffled as the ministers sent embarrassed glances back and forth. Then Reverend Schoeman admitted, "We don't know, but we promised Brother Fourie we would be there by the 12th of October, so we've got to leave today. And since the meetings here are officially over, you might as well go with us."

Bill didn't know what else to do. What was the use of staying in Johannesburg now that the meetings were closed? Reluctantly he went to his bedroom and packed.

There were three cars making the 100-mile trek southwest to Klerksdorp. Ern Baxter, Fred Bosworth, Julius Stadsklev, and Billy Paul Branham rode in the second car. Bill rode in the lead car along with Justus du Plessis, Reverend Schoeman, and two other members of the National Committee. It was a beautiful, sunny summer day. Reverend Schoeman, Justus du Plessis, and the other committee members talked with animation about the marvelous things they had seen God do in Johannesburg. In contrast, Bill sat quietly, brooding about his disobedience to the will of the Lord. Silently he prayed, "Heavenly Father, I want to go to Durban like You told me to, but I'm at the mercy of these men. Will You forgive me for my disobedience?"

He didn't feel forgiven. Mile after mile he felt the condemnation getting worse until he could not stand it any longer. "Stop the car!" he ordered.

The driver pulled over and stopped. "What's the matter, Brother Branham?"

"I can't go any farther. Brother Schoeman, you're going to have to take me back to Johannesburg. The Lord is telling me to not go on."

The other two cars had driven up and stopped behind the lead car. Reverend Schoeman walked back to the second car and said to Baxter and Bosworth, "He refuses to go south. You two will have to go talk to him."

Ern Baxter and Fred Bosworth got out of their car and walked up to where Bill was standing. The other ministers gathered around them. Baxter asked, "Brother Branham, what's the matter?"

"Brother Baxter, I'm supposed to hold meetings in Johannesburg for two more weeks, then go hunting with Brother Jackson for ten days, and then go straight to Durban. If I go on to Klerksdorp, I'll be disobeying the Lord."

No one in this group believed in Bill's ministry more strongly than Fred Bosworth, a 74-year-old veteran minister who had himself held large divine healing campaigns in the 1920's and 1930's. After visiting one of Bill's meetings in 1948, Bosworth had been so impressed that he had come out of retirement to be one of Bill's managers. Now, uncharacteristically, he took the other side. "Brother Branham, you're wrong. If you go south with these men, I believe you're going to see exceedingly abundantly above all you could ask or think"—quoting Ephesians 3:20.

To Bill it felt like the knife of betrayal had stabbed him between his ribs. "Daddy Bosworth, I'm shocked at you! As many times as you've stood on the platform and heard me say, 'thus saith the Lord,' has it ever been wrong?"

Averting his eyes from Bill's accusing glare, Bosworth mumbled, "Well, this time I think you're wrong."

The South African ministers got huffy. One man said angrily, "Don't you think that God speaks to somebody else besides you?"

Bill answered dryly, "Korah had that idea one day and he told Moses the same thing, but the earth opened and swallowed Korah up.[27] I don't know what God has told you gentlemen. I can't judge that. All I know is what He has told me."

"God told us to make this itinerary," the minister snapped.

"And God told me not to take it," Bill countered.

The argument continued. Finally Ern Baxter pulled Bill aside and whispered, "Brother Branham, we're kind of in a bad spot here. We don't have any money or resources of our own, so we've got to handle this thing diplomatically. I wish you wouldn't say any more about a hunting trip, because they're going to think you really came to Africa for a safari. Half of these ministers don't believe it's right for a Christian to hunt anyway. When you mention hunting, they think about the thousands of people wanting prayer and they think you're wrong."

Bill answered in a voice loud enough for the others to overhear, "If I never hunt again in my life, it doesn't matter to me. I am

---

[27] Numbers 16

only wanting to do what God told me to do. Brother Baxter, you have been with me enough to know that when I see a vision and tell you something in the name of the Lord—"

Ern Baxter interrupted, "Brother Branham, if you're following a vision, then I won't interfere anymore. Whatever you decide to do, I'll stand by you." He glanced nervously back at the group of ministers standing by the lead car. "But since you're still hooked up with this National Committee and it is getting later in the afternoon, couldn't you go on into Klerksdorp and pray for those people there? Then we could go back to Johannesburg, if that's what you want."

A scattering of locust trees shaded this spot where the highway curved. Bill reached up and stripped the leaves off a low hanging branch, carried them in his fist back to the car and threw them on the ministers' feet. "All right," he said tearfully, "we'll drive on into Klerksdorp for the meeting tonight. But remember, thus saith the Lord, 'From this hour on, we're out of the will of God and there will be nothing but trouble until we return to Johannesburg.'"

As soon as they reached Klerksdorp, they saw how mightily Bill's Johannesburg campaign had stirred the rest of South Africa. Over 10,000 people (of European descent) had converged on this little provincial city, far outstripping its meager capacity to handle their needs. Looking at the hundreds of makeshift tents and little camps pitched on the hills and in the fields, Bill's driver commented excitedly, "Looks like we'll have a good meeting tonight." Bill shook his head, feeling sorry for these poor people, many of them sick, who were stranded in the open, helplessly exposed to the weather.

They drove to the home of Pastor P. F. Fourie, where they would be staying. That evening Brother Bosworth opened the Klerksdorp campaign. However, before Bill could leave Fourie's house to go to the meeting, a tropical storm blew in. Thunder boomed like cannon blasts, while heavy rain flattened the grass. Hastily the meeting was cancelled, but still it was midnight before Baxter, Bosworth, Schoeman, and the other ministers could get back to Fourie's house.

"Oh my, we tried tonight," said Fred Bosworth, shedding his drenched coat and hat.

"Didn't I tell you this would happen?" Bill said. "The Lord told me not to come down here. I am out of His will. I have to go back to Johannesburg."

The South African ministers disagreed. One of them said, "We can't go back. We've made these promises and we have to keep them."

"Besides," another added, "we have these storms all the time. This one will blow over tonight and tomorrow everything will be fine."

The thunderstorm did blow over during the night and Saturday morning dawned clear and warm with promise. But that evening, as they were getting ready to take Bill to the meetings, an unseasonable cold front moved in. The temperature dropped almost to freezing and the wind blew with shivering force. Again the meeting was canceled.

"Didn't I tell you," said Bill. "Now, tomorrow night we'll have an earthquake."

The members of the National Committee looked at each other nervously. They were finally giving serious consideration to the words of this unusual man who said an angel spoke to him. Justus du Plessis asked, "Do you really mean we'll have an earthquake tomorrow?"

"I don't know whether we will or not," Bill qualified. "I just said that as an illustration. But something bad has got to happen because we're out of the will of God."

Mrs. Fourie set some refreshments on the table, then sat down to listen to the conversation. Bill leaned forward in his chair and said that earlier in the afternoon he had seen a vision of Mrs. Fourie, but could not speak it until everyone was sitting at the table exactly as the vision had shown. He told Mrs. Fourie about things that happened in her childhood; then he told her she had heart disease and stomach trouble caused by nervousness, but not to worry because Jesus Christ had healed her.

Astonished phrases tumbled from the mouths of the South African ministers. Bill asked, "Now do you believe me? God has told me to go back to Johannesburg, stay there for two weeks, then go up to Brother Jackson's farm for a rest; and from there go straight to Durban. Then I'll go home."

Fred Bosworth said, "Brother Branham, if you go that route, you won't be able to minister to as many African natives as you could by traveling through these smaller places." (On this point the South African ministers kept quiet, knowing that the majority of meetings they had scheduled were for the European segment of the population. Bill did not learn until later that Durban was the only place in South Africa where native Africans would be allowed to attend the same meetings as the white Africans.) Bosworth continued, "Brother Branham, if you will follow this itinerary south, I still believe that you will see God do exceedingly abundantly above all we could ask or think."

Putting a weary hand on his friend's shoulder, Bill said, "Brother Bosworth, as many battles as we've been in together, and now you're doubting me? I tell you in the name of Jesus that we're out of His will, and it's going to be nothing but trouble from here on."

"Still," said Reverend Schoeman, "we have already committed ourselves to certain brothers, so we have to follow this itinerary through."

Since they would not accept the argument of supernatural guidance, Bill tried common sense. "Look at it logically for a minute. In Johannesburg we have the favor of the newspapers and the medical association; and there are hundreds of thousands of people there, with places to eat and sleep. But here the people are lying out in the open with no place to eat. Last night they almost drowned and tonight they're out there freezing. If you just look at it in the natural, doesn't it make sense to go back to Johannesburg?"

Some mumbling and coughing passed between the ministers before Schoeman responded, "Brother Branham, we have thousands of dollars invested in advertising on this tour. We have the buildings and grounds already rented. The dates are set; the times are set. People have made their plans and some have already traveled. We have made our promises and we can't go back on our word."

Bill said, "Well, I didn't promise anybody, and in the morning I'm going back to Johannesburg."

Justus du Plessis asked, "What are you going to do when you get there?"

They had him there. Bill didn't have any money and he couldn't do anything by himself. So even if he did go back to Johannesburg, he would have to have the cooperation of these same men who were now opposing such a move. He was in a terrible fix. As he sat there pondering his dilemma, suddenly he remembered the prophecy that had come to him in Shreveport, Louisiana, when the Lord warned him that Satan was going to lay a trap for him South Africa. Bill had assumed the trap would have something to do with witch doctors and demons. But that wasn't it at all. Here was the trap! Right here among his Christian brethren! The political jaws of their denominational systems had snapped closed around him, holding him firmly between their cold, unyielding teeth, keeping him from doing what the Lord had told him to do. His situation seemed hopeless.

Bill warned his sponsors, "As Paul said long ago, 'You should have listened to me and not have loosed from Crete, and caused all this trouble.'[28] Now brethren, God has a permissive will, but I never like to work in his permissive will. I want His perfect will."

The committee members liked the idea of God having a permissive will. One said, "I think this is a case where it would be good to operate in the permissive will of God. Brother Branham, why don't you ask the Lord if you can?"

By now it was two o'clock in the morning. They had been arguing since ten o'clock. Weary and discouraged, Bill said, "All right. I'll pray about it one more time."

Billy Paul Branham, who had been listening quietly through the four-hour argument, followed his father into the bedroom and shut the door. He watched his father cross the room and look out the window at the windstorm that was still blowing. His father stood with his shoulders hunched slightly, looking like a beaten man. Crossing the room, Billy Paul put one arm around his father's shoulder and said, "Daddy, don't you listen to that bunch of preachers. You do what God is telling you to do."

"Billy, I'm all tore up. I don't know how I can do what God wants me to do. I don't have any money. Even if I go back to Johannesburg now, I don't see how I could hold any meetings without the cooperation of these men. And you can see they won't cooperate. If ever I stood between a rock and a hard place, I'm there now."

"Daddy, if nobody else in the whole country stands by you, I'll stay by you."

Bill hugged his son. "Pray with me, Billy."

---

[28] Acts 27:21

They knelt between the twin beds and prayed together. But soon Billy Paul gave in to the late hour, crawled up on his bed, and fell asleep. Bill, on the other hand, was too troubled to sleep. His thoughts ricocheted back and forth between the rock and the hard place that had him trapped. Somehow he had to stand against the very people who had invited him to South Africa. How could he persuade them to listen? What if he couldn't persuade them? How could he do God's will in both Johannesburg and Durban without the cooperation of these men? His dilemma seemed insurmountable. The emotion in his head felt like a wet washrag being twisted tighter and tighter, slowly squeezing out the moisture; and that moisture was seeping from the inside corners of his eyes, tinged with salt.

Around three o'clock in the morning, Bill felt the presence of the angel of the Lord. In another moment a light formed in the air, then rose to the ceiling, leaving the angel of the Lord standing beneath its amber flame. Outside the wind blew, rising and falling in a wild pitch, rattling the windowpanes. Bill shivered in fear. Every time he met the angel of the Lord face to face, he felt the same paralyzing fear. The supernatural never became common to him. It was a dimension impossible to understand and difficult for his human senses to bear. But even as he trembled, he felt thankful that the angel had come. Perhaps now this deadlock could be broken.

Bill asked, "Who are these men and what do they mean?"

The angel stood with his arms folded. Although Bill had never seen the angel smile, now his piercing gaze looked severe. "*Go on with them,*" the angel said sternly. "*Since you've started with them, now you'll have to do it. But remember, if you do go south with them, you're going to suffer for it. Wake up Billy Paul and tell him, thus saith the Lord, Tomorrow morning is going to break warm and pretty. They will take Billy Paul early to Sunday school. Because the meetings have been so delayed, Ern Baxter is going to send Billy Paul back to get you so you can pray for the sick; be ready to go. Your son will come with a young man in a black car. On the way he will stop and pick up a second young man. After that...*" Here Bill saw two natives standing near a eucalyptus tree by a bridge. One of the natives, who was dressed in a white safari suit, had his arm raised and was about to strike the other native with a stick. The angel said, "*Billy Paul will call your attention to this. By these sign you will know that I have given you permission to go south. But remember, you'll suffer for it.*"

When he came out of the vision, the angel was gone. Bill woke up his son and said, "Billy, the angel of the Lord has just visited me." He told Billy Paul what the angel said; then he rushed to the room where Baxter, Bosworth, and Stadsklev were sleeping. "Brothers, wake up. I have 'thus saith the Lord.' He has given me permission to go south with you, but I'm going to suffer for it because it's not the perfect will of God. In fact, our meetings will not be as successful as they could be because we really shouldn't go. Tomorrow morning this storm will be over..." And from there, he told them the other details of the vision.

Sunday morning dawned as clear, calm, and warm as the angel said it would. Billy Paul went to Sunday school with Ern Baxter and the members of the National Committee. Soon two young men in a black car brought Billy Paul back to the house to get his father. Bill was ready. On their way down to the meeting grounds, they crossed a narrow bridge. There next to a eucalyptus tree stood two natives, one of them dressed in a white safari suit.

Billy Paul pointed. "Look, Daddy—that man's got a stick and he's going to hit that other man."

Bill nodded. "Remember what I told you last night, Paul? I can go south, but I will suffer for it."

Chapter 59
Durban at Last
1951

APPROXIMATELY 200 miles southwest of Klerksdorp lies Kimberley, a sprawling mining city of 60,000 people. William Branham arrived in Kimberley on Wednesday, October 17, 1951. His reputation preceded him. On his first night in Kimberly he prayed for the sick in a church that could seat 500. Unfortunately ten times that many people wanted inside.

The next morning, Fred Bosworth talked to the National Committee about getting a bigger place to conduct this faith-healing campaign. To his surprise, the committee said no. They had promised a particular pastor in Kimberley that the meetings would be held in his church, and now they felt they could not go back on their word.

So Fred Bosworth tried to reason with the pastor himself. "Look, brother, the streets and the fields are crowded with thousands of sick people wanting prayer. Do you mean to tell me that you still want to have the meetings in your little church building?"

"They promised me I could have the meetings in my church," the pastor said stubbornly, "so we'll have them in my church."

"Ridiculous," fumed Bosworth. Returning to the house where Bill was staying, Bosworth complained, "Brother Branham, did you ever hear of a preacher acting so selfishly?"

Bill quipped dryly, "This is that, 'exceedingly abundantly' you talked about earlier. Brother Bosworth, don't you see, we're out of the will of the Lord?"

Undaunted, Fred Bosworth decided to see what he could do on his own. Asking around Kimberly, he finally secured a local sporting arena that could hold thousands of people, and there they held the services for the next four days.

When Bill made plans to visit South Africa, he imagined himself preaching to black-skinned natives. Instead he found himself preaching to light-skinned Afrikaans of European descent. This frustrated him as much as the National Committee's "sacred" itinerary. He longed to see how the native population would receive a supernatural Gospel, but this was denied him until he had been in South Africa over 21 days. Finally, at the end of his week in Bloemfontein (100 miles South of Kimberly) the National Committee scheduled him for one Sunday morning service with non-Europeans.

The natives began to gather in Bloemfontein at the football field well before daybreak, October 28, 1951. By the time Bill arrived at 10:00 a.m., over 12,000 people were sitting on the playing field—a sea of black faces, many of the women wearing white or red bandanas. Ern Baxter explained God's plan of salvation through faith in Jesus Christ. When Bill came to the microphone, he explained the relationship between faith and healing. Then it was time to put faith to the test. One by one they came before the American evangelist—and one by one he told them who they were and what their troubles were. Before a dozen people had passed through the prayer-line, these natives were convinced that Jesus Christ was indeed present. After a single general prayer, hundreds of Africans were healed. In the weeks that followed, local pastors and missionaries assessed the results of this meeting by gathering testimonies of healings and miracles. The results were astounding: blind eyes opened, cancers healed, all manner of diseases cured, and cripples healed. One bus driver said, "I carried a lame man into my bus and drove him to the meeting, but when he returned, he could walk by himself." In all, local ministers and missionaries estimated that a thousand people were healed at this one Branham prayer service.

That was exactly what Bill had hoped to see in Africa— uncomplicated minds accepting Jesus when they saw Christ supernaturally displayed before them. Bill begged the National Committee to schedule more meetings for these natives; but the committee said no, rehashing their same argument about commitments to those dates already set. Bill could not believe the stubbornness and shortsightedness of these denominational men. They were acting like their itinerary was Jehovah's eleventh commandment.

Leaving Bloemfontein, the Branham party drove 900 miles southwest to Capetown. Here the meetings followed a similar pattern to those in Bloemfontein—five days of stirring healing services, with one Sunday morning set aside for the native Africans.

Bill was distressed at the treatment these black natives received. The meetings for white Afrikaans were held in a huge airplane hangar at Wingfield Airport. With the hangar doors open, over 10,000 people were able to participate in the service. The black Africans, on the other hand, had to use Drill Hall, a much smaller building inside the city limits. So eager was the native population to hear William Branham speak, people started lining up outside Drill Hall at 1:30 in the morning. By 6:00 a.m. the crowd had swollen to 8,000 souls. Unfortunately when the doors finally opened at 9:00 a.m., only 3,000 natives could squeeze inside. The myopic National

Committee had not even arranged to have loudspeakers set up outside the hall, so the people left in the street were unable to listen.

Bill felt his frustration rising like mercury in a thermometer on a summer morning. Certainly the National Committee must shoulder much of the blame for this muddle of poor planning. But Bill felt he too shared some of the guilt. He had agreed, however reluctantly, to follow the will of the National Committee, even though he knew it was not the will of the Lord. The angel had warned him that he would suffer for it. He wondered if this is what the angel had meant. It was not.

The campaign in Capetown ended on Monday night. On Tuesday they drove over 400 miles east along the coast, reaching Port Elizabeth before dark. The first meeting in Port Elizabeth was held the following night, November 7, 1951, in a large

William Branham ministering to the natives in Africa

auditorium called Feather Market Hall. Here again the organizers had drastically underestimated the need, and thousands of people could not get inside the building. Consequently, for the rest of the week in Port Elizabeth, the faith-healing campaign was held at Davis Stadium, a sports arena with ample room.

One morning Bill woke up with a twinge of pain in his abdomen. At first he dismissed it as nothing. When the pain persisted through the day, he began to worry. What if his mysterious stomach ailment was coming back to plague him? For many days now he had been feeling the cumulative effects of his strenuous schedule. Exhaustion had triggered his stomach trouble back in 1947. At that time he had been pushing himself for over a year, night after night, praying for long lines of sick and afflicted people into the early morning hours, until finally he had collapsed on the platform. Then illness had forced him to suspend his campaigns. His stomach had turned as sour as a lemon and he almost died from the complications. Was that going to happen again? The National Committee was pushing him hard, giving him no time to rest. They didn't understand how drastically these supernatural visions sapped his natural energy.

But worse than his exhaustion was the growing pain inside his abdomen. By the time he reached East London, 150 miles up the coast from Port Elizabeth, Bill was sure this pain was not his old enemy, stomach trouble. These cramps felt lower than his stomach, and the pain stabbed more sharply than nausea. When some of the other ministers traveling with him began to get sick too, Bill knew it came from something local, perhaps from something they ate or drank.

After five nights in East London, they headed for Durban, 300 miles farther up the east coast of Africa. While on the road, Bill saw a vision of a native woman lying on a cot. Soon the highway passed near a typical native village. Bill asked his driver to stop the car. Getting out, Bill and those traveling with him walked into the village, where Bill pointed out one hut that looked exactly like all the other huts around it. "In there we're going to find a woman lying on a cot. She's very sick with tuberculosis. She's a Christian woman and she can speak English."

When they entered the hut, there she lay, exactly as Bill had described her. The woman told them in English, "I have been praying a long time for healing. Jesus promised me that He would send a prophet from another land to pray for me, and that I would be healed."

The Lord Jesus kept His promise.

THEY REACHED Durban on Tuesday, November 20, 1951. Bill was impressed by the strong Asian flavor of this great metropolis. Rickshaws plied the avenues. Indian women, dressed in their traditional *saris*, shared the market place with black-robed Moslem women, and with dark-skinned native women, some of whom had multiple brass rings around their necks and wrists. Black-bearded Sikhs with white turbans on their heads and long knives tucked into their sashes, mingled with tall, almost naked African tribesmen painted with mud, their kinky hair decorated with little bones, and their earlobes stretched into long, fleshy loops. When Bill asked about this diversity, Reverend Schoeman explained that Durban had a population of 440,000, of which 130,000 were native Africans, 110,000 were European-Afrikaans and 200,000 came from India. Originally these Indians were imported as slaves to work in the mines. They still clung to their Asian heritage, including their religions of Hinduism, Buddhism, and Islam.

The first meeting in Durban was held Wednesday night at City Hall, and was restricted to white South Africans only. Those who could not get inside the building listened through loudspeakers positioned in the surrounding gardens. Expectations ran high and many who came in wheelchairs and on stretchers left without them.

On Thursday afternoon the service was moved to a giant horse-racing stadium called the Greyville Race Course. Over 20,000 people sat in the shaded grandstands, and still there was room for more. When Bill mounted the platform to speak, he was surprised to see the crowd made up of black natives, brown Indians, and white Europeans. He said to Sidney Smith, mayor of Durban, "I thought South Africa had segregation laws that prevented us from having whites and blacks at the same meeting."

"There are segregation laws," the mayor explained, "and if you'll look closely, the races are segregated. See all those fences?"

Now Bill noticed the lines of white picket fences crisscrossing the crowd. "But why do some of those fences run between black people?"

"Those fences separate different tribes—Bantu, Swazi, Xhosa, Zulu—there are over a dozen different tribes here, and some of them are enemies."

"Why couldn't we have done this in other cities?" asked Bill. "Then we could have reached more people with the Gospel."

"Durban is the only place where the government has given us permission to do this."

Now Bill understood why the angel of the Lord had told him to go directly to Durban and stay there until he was called away. Oh, if only he had not disobeyed the angel's directions. How he was suffering for that mistake. By now his abdomen ached continually. It felt like a rat was loose in his bowels, gnawing on his intestines. He had to grip the pulpit to keep himself from doubling over in pain—even as the prayer-line came forward, even as the visions broke before him and he discerned the secrets in the hearts of strangers, even as those same sick people were healed.

"Heavenly Father, forgive me," Bill prayed quietly, while he waited for the numerous interpreters to translate his last statement into 15 different languages. "I'm sorry for my mistake. Jesus, while You are healing these others, heal me too."

But no vision appeared for his relief. It seemed like God had turned His back on His prophet's need, while not overlooking the smallest need among the rest of His people. Remorsefully, Bill felt like he deserved this rejection.

The audience stirred with excitement as one by one the problems of those in the prayer-line were discerned without error, and the patients were healed. When a deaf-mute Indian boy heard and spoke for the first time in his life, the faith of the crowd swelled to overflowing. Bill raised his voice in prayer, exhorting the crippled, the sick, dumb, and blind to accept their healing now from the hands of the risen Savior, Jesus Christ. But long before the last interpreter finished translating this prayer, men and women, old and young, were climbing out of wheelchairs or pitching crutches aside; children were undoing the fasteners to their metal leg-braces and throwing these awkward contraptions away.

Tragically, even as the noise of victory grew louder, Bill was led away from the platform sobbing in pain, needing the support of two strong men.

Visitors continued to pour into Durban, slowing city traffic to the pace of a hippopotamus wading through chest-deep mud. By Friday afternoon, the crowd at Greyville Race Course doubled to over 40,000. Riding with Sidney Smith to the service, Bill saw many natives on the street carrying small, handmade statues. He had read about such idolatry in the Bible, but this was the first time he had ever seen it firsthand. "Look at those fellows with their idols," he commented.

The mayor said, "Some of them are Christians."

"Christians?" Bill gasped in astonishment. "Christians with idols?"

"Yes. Here a lot of natives who are Christians still cling to their ancestral idols."

"That's strange. I'd like to talk to one of them. Could you speak the language of that fellow standing there?"

"Probably. I can speak several native languages."

Pulling over to the roadside, the mayor and his guest got out of the car and approached a massive black man who was nearly 7 feet tall and must have weighed 300 pounds. As Bill got closer he could see the idol was speckled with dried blood. Through the mayor, Bill asked the native, "Are you a Christian?"

"Oh, yes," the native replied. "I have been a Christian for many years."

"Why are you packing that idol?"

"My father before me carried this god wherever he went. One day he was hunting alone in the veldt when a lion got on his trail. My father built a fire and prayed to this god using our witch doctor's enchantments, and the lion went away. Now I too carry this god wherever I go. If the god of the missionaries fails me, then this god won't fail."

"I think you're putting your faith in the wrong thing," Bill chided. "Being a hunter myself, I'm familiar with the ways of the wild. That idol didn't run the lion away; it was the fire." The native looked skeptical. Bill asked, "Are you coming to the meeting this afternoon at the racetrack?"

"Tomorrow," he grunted.

"Good. Then tomorrow you'll see that Jesus never fails."

The three services held on Sunday, November 25, 1951, broke the attendance record for Greyville Race Course. Not only were the grandstands full, so was the central field, where the different native tribes sat on the ground, divided by white picket fences like herds of cattle. Reverend Bosworth conducted the morning service and Reverend Baxter preached in the afternoon. The evening service was reserved for Bill to preach and pray for the sick.

By now Bill was used to speaking through 15 interpreters. It was a slow process, taking him an hour and a half to preach what would normally be a 15-minute sermon. Bill would say, "Jesus Christ is the Son of God." The first interpreter made noises like a chicken clucking; the second interpreter sounded like a jackal chattering; the third interpreter sounded completely different from the first two; and so it went down the line. (In years past Bill had often wondered about 1 Corinthians 14:10, where Paul said there was no sound without significance. Now, after hearing all these peculiar languages, he realized what Paul the missionary had meant.) Finally the fifteenth interpreter finished his sentence and Bill continued, "Jesus came to the earth to save sinners." The process began again.

While the interpreters took turns repeating this line, Bill walked to the rear of the platform and asked Sidney Smith, "What's going on down on the lawn? Is there a fight?"

The mayor had been watching the commotion also. "I can't tell. I'll send a policemen over to check it out." Soon the policeman returned to report, "Brother Branham, a native woman just gave birth down there in the crowd. She seems to be all right."

"Aren't you going to take her out of here?"

"We offered to do that, but she just wiped her baby off and began feeding it on her breast, saying she wanted to stay for the prayer service."

Such determination overwhelmed Bill. If the expectations of that new mother represented the desire of the rest of this crowd, today was going to be a tremendous healing service indeed.

No prayer-cards had been given out; instead several missionaries had simply picked a dozen sick people and lined them up for prayer. The first person to come forward in the prayer-line was a woman of East Indian descent. Her body was wrapped in a colorful *sari*, and her forehead was decorated by a red dot centered between her eyes—the *kumkum* symbol, considered a mark of beauty in the Hindu culture.

Just like Jesus did with a Samaritan woman, Bill talked with this woman briefly to contact her spirit. "Lady, why would you, being a Hindu, come to me, a Christian, for help? Why don't you go to your own priests?"

"They can't help me," the woman replied.

Above her a vision unfolded, showing her in a doctor's office listening to the doctor's diagnosis. Bill said, "Lady, you have tuberculosis. I believe if you will accept Jesus Christ as your personal Savior, He will also heal you."

Immediately the woman knelt on one knee, bowed her head, took her long skirt and wiped away the red dot from between her eyes. Bill saw a light flash around her. "Sister," he said, "Jesus Christ has just healed you. Go your way and serve Him the rest of your life."

A collective murmur rippled through the audience and Bill could see other Hindu women spitting on their fingers, then rubbing off their own red dots. Someone in crowd yelled, "Krishna!" Other Hindus picked up the chant. "Krishna! Krishna!" they shouted, thinking that the American evangelist had said the name of one of their gods. (Krishna is an earthly form of the Hindu god, Vishnu.)

Raising his hands to quiet them, Bill explained, "No, I never said Krishna. I said *Christ*," and he spoke the name distinctly, emphasizing the "t", "Jesus *Christ*. I am not Krishna; I am a servant of Jesus Christ."

The next person in line was a young woman of European descent. She appeared to be in good health, and as she drew near, Bill could feel a welcome spirit about her. He said, "I see you are a Christian." She replied that she was. "Sister, I see you going into a church. You belong to the Dutch Reformed Church." Then he paused, perplexed. Something was different about this woman. Often in a vision he would see a bright light burst around the patient, indicating the person was healed. But in this vision everything was getting darker, like the gathering shadows of approaching night. "Sister, a few days ago you saw a doctor. Your husband waited in the hall while the doctor examined you. Your husband has black hair and a mustache, and he was wearing a gray suit. The doctor is a gray-headed man who wears glasses. The doctor said you have a cyst on your ovary. It's not life-threatening, but the doctor still wants to remove it." The woman nodded yes. As Bill talked, the vision grew darker around her. He was about to say, "The Lord bless you and heal you, my sister," and let her pass off the platform with some hope; but before he could say this, the vision moved into a funeral procession and he saw the pallbearers carrying her coffin to her grave. Then Bill knew her life was about over, and he decided he might as well tell her plainly. "Lady, you're a strong looking woman. There is very little wrong with you, just that cyst on your ovary. But prepare for death, because thus saith the Lord, 'You're only going to live a short time'."

The woman's eyes grew wide and she gasped, "Sir?"

"That is right, sister. Just be sure your heart is right with God."

As this woman left the platform, a well-dressed white man led a native boy up the steps and across the platform. The man stopped a dozen feet from the American evangelist, while the boy came forward on his own. Bill took one look at the boy and said, "Anyone can see this boy's eyes are crossed. I can't heal him, but Jesus Christ can. Perhaps God will show me something that will encourage the boy's faith." He paused, watching the boy's past unfold. "I see a tall, thin Zulu woman holding a baby boy in her arms, showing him to her husband who notices that the baby is cross-eyed. I know the family is Christian because in the vision I see them praying before a cross." When this was repeated by the Zulu interpreter, the mother and father stood up in the audience, waving and shouting that it was correct.

Meanwhile, the boy had bowed his head.

Bill said, "I don't have to pray for the boy because he's already healed. You can pass by now."

The young Zulu raised his head and grinned. It was true; his eyes were now uncrossed and normal. The boy left the platform, but the man who had brought him up there did not. He came closer, saying, "Mr. Branham, I want to talk to you a minute."

Ern Baxter stepped in his way. "We can't let anyone talk to Brother Branham when he's under the anointing."

"I just want to ask him a question."

Turning toward the two men, Bill said, "It's all right, Brother Baxter. Let the doctor speak."

"How did you know I was a doctor?"

Bill ignored the question. "What can I do for you, doctor?"

"It's true, I'm a British doctor. I examined that boy before he came up here and I examined him again just a moment ago. His eyes used to be crossed and now they aren't crossed. How did you do that? Did you hypnotize him?"

"If hypnotism will straighten crossed eyes, you doctors ought to do it. But it wasn't hypnotism; it was the power of God."

"Mr. Branham, I'm just a church member. But now that I've seen a God so tangible He can straighten crossed eyes, I want to accept Jesus Christ as my Savior, and I'm willing to say that to your entire audience."

About ten minutes had passed since the woman with the cyst on her ovary had left the platform. While the British doctor spoke to the crowd, a messenger came up on the platform and jabbered excitedly to one of the interpreters, who then told Bill, "You know that woman you said must prepare for death? She just died. This man knows the husband and was sitting beside them. When the woman got back to her seat, she said to her husband, 'Well, what do you know about that;' and before he could answer her, she dropped dead right there." (Later they learned she died from a heart attack.)

Last through the prayer-line came a black man so hunched over that he walked on his feet *and* his hands. Obviously he was mentally retarded. A caretaker kept this hunchback from wandering by means of a chain secured to a dog collar around his neck.

"Look at this poor creature," Bill said sympathetically. "If I could help him, I would. The truth is I can't help him. But Jesus Christ can. This man's life cannot be hid because the angel of the Lord is here." When the vision came it revealed something unexpected. Bill said, "I know this boy grew up in a Christian home because I see a picture of Jesus hanging on the wall of his hut. He was born in this deformed condition. But right now he's not concerned about himself; he's worried about a brother. Four years ago his younger brother was hurt when he fell off a big yellow dog or goat. Now his brother is crippled and has to use crutches when he walks. Thus saith the Lord, 'His brother is healed.'"

At that moment a scream pierced the air. From way back in the audience, a tall black man stood and waved two stick-crutches over his head, shouting in his native tongue that he was the brother, and now he was healed.

The crowd boiled with noisy excitement because of this miracle, and it was many minutes before they quieted enough so they could listen. Bill watched the commotion patiently, then he turned his attention back to the pathetic man hunched over in front of him. A blue shadow appeared in the air, revealing a vision of this man standing up straight and walking normally. Bill said to the audience, "You can see that Jesus Christ healed this man's brother. If God will now heal this deformed, retarded man, how many of you here will serve the Lord Jesus?"

Black, brown, and white hands went up all over the stadium. Bill told the caretaker to remove the chain from around the man's neck. The caretaker shook his head, worried and perhaps a bit fearful. Bill insisted. "Stand the man on his feet and loose his chain. God has delivered him." Reluctantly, the caretaker obliged, unhooking the chain and lifting the man's shoulders. The man didn't need much help. His spine popped a dozen times as it uncurled, leaving him standing with perfect posture in front of 50,000 people. Bill slipped his arm around the man's naked waist and walked with him to the edge of the platform, then back to the pulpit. The man smiled and waved to the audience, confirming that his mind had been supernaturally restored to health.

The crowd seemed to rumble and move like an earthquake. Seizing his opportunity, Bill asked, "How many of you will now receive Jesus Christ as your Savior?"

Thousands upon thousands of hands went up. Ern Baxter said, "Brother Branham, I think they misunderstood you. They must have thought you were asking them if they wanted physical healing. You had better run that question through the interpreters again."

So Bill said into the microphone, "I was not asking you if you wanted physical healing. I was asking if you will accept Jesus Christ as your personal Savior. If you do, stand to your feet."

Thousands of people stood. Bill said, "Before Jesus will come into your heart, you must first renounce your false gods. You people who are packing idols, I want you to break them right now."

A cloud of dust rose over the field as men and women dashed their clay idols to the ground. First Bill prayed aloud for their salvation, then he prayed en masse for the healing of all those who were sick or afflicted. Thousands of these new Christians screamed out they were healed.

The next day at their hotel, Fred Bosworth could not stop talking about the Sunday night meeting. "Brother Branham, as the people left they made great stacks of their crutches, cots, wheelchairs, and braces. I stood there and wept my heart out. In all my 40 years of preaching the gospel and praying for the sick, I have never seen a meeting to match that one."

Mayor Sidney Smith said, "Brother Branham, come here and look out the window. Those trucks are filled with the crutches and things those people last night left behind."

When Bill looked, he saw seven large cattle trucks pass the hotel, followed by hundreds of people who were healed—natives from every tribe intermingled, no longer enemies, joined arm and arm, singing the Branham Campaigns theme song, "Only believe; only believe; all things are possible; only believe."

Smith said, "We estimated there were 50,000 people at that meeting last night—over 100,000 people if you count all three Sunday services. Yesterday there must have been 30,000 people who gave their hearts to Jesus Christ. There is no way to know how many thousands of people were healed."

"And me so sick I could hardly stand," Bill added. "We should have come straight to Durban from Johannesburg like the angel told us to do. By now it should be obvious to everyone that Durban is where the Lord wants us to be."

Unfortunately it was not obvious to everyone. Reverend Schoeman revealed that Ern Baxter, Bill, and Billy Paul would be flying to Salisbury, Rhodesia on Wednesday morning.

"And—and leave Durban?" sputtered Bill in dismay. "Why? Here is where the Lord is moving."

Schoeman dished up the same leftover reason: "We're just following the itinerary we set up over a month ago. We have you scheduled for two days in Salisbury, then down to Pretoria for a single meeting, then over to Johannesburg for one last meeting before you fly home. I don't understand why you're upset. You've had your meetings in Durban like you wanted."

"How far away is Salisbury, Rhodesia?"

"Eight hundred miles north of here."

Bill could scarcely comprehend the absurdity of these men. He pointed out the obvious, "There are over 50,000 people here in Durban who want to hear me preach. Many of them have walked for miles and miles to get here. Thousands of them are new Christians. Now all of a sudden, you're going to fly me 800 miles away; and you wonder why I'm upset?"

"I'm sorry, Brother Branham, but we promised this brother in Rhodesia we'd take you there, and we've got to keep our word."

Feeling too weak and sick to argue, Bill gave in, finishing the tour according to the National Committee's plan. In Salisbury he preached to a mere 1,500 people. The two days he spent in Rhodesia blurred in his memory like a bad dream. Then he flew back to South Africa where he had one meeting in Pretoria and two more in Johannesburg. During that last meeting in Johannesburg, he felt like he was going to die. Yet his own affliction didn't hinder his gift of discernment or the power of God. Among his many visions that night, he saw a woman in the audience who was blind. Pointing her out, he encouraged her to stand and accept her healing. She didn't respond, however another woman in the same row stood. Bill turned to this other woman and said, "I know you are blind also, but why did you stand up? You are a Jew and you don't believe that Jesus is the Christ. Do you think Jesus can restore your eyesight?" She nodded yes. Bill continued, "I can't ask Him to be your Healer unless first He is your Lord and Savior. If you will accept Him as the Messiah, raise your hand." She raised her hand and instantly her eyesight returned.

At last the time came for him to leave South Africa. The British doctor who had examined that cross-eyed boy in Durban, met Bill at the airport in Johannesburg and said, "I feel like God is calling me to be a medical missionary. Brother Branham, I owe it all to you. Thank you for coming." His thanks could be multiplied by a hundred times a thousand. There were reports coming in from the bush of 1,000 people a week being baptized. Churches all over South Africa were filling up with people who were newly excited about a real and living God—a tangible God. During their ten weeks in South Africa, William Branham's team had conducted 120 services in 11 cities with a combined attendance of around 500,000 people. God alone could tally the final victory, but Bill knew something of the cost.

Fred Bosworth accompanied the rest of the Branham party to the airport, although he was not flying out that day. Bosworth was going to stay in South Africa for another month to work with pastors and missionaries, helping them ground the thousands of new converts in Christ.

As Bill sat waiting for his plane to arrive, he squirmed in misery from the pain in his midsection. He seriously wondered if he would ever see Fred Bosworth again. Eventually his plane landed. The incoming passengers got off and soon the plane was ready for its new group of passengers to board. The moment had come to say good-bye. Putting his arms around his friend, Bill said, "Brother Bosworth, I'm 42 years old, and I guess my days are about over. Like Paul I can say I have fought a good fight; I have finished my course; I have kept the faith."[29]

"Nonsense," Bosworth snorted. "You're just a boy. I didn't even *start* preaching until I was 40 years old! Now I'm over 70 and still going strong. Brother Branham, you've just finished your education and received your diploma."

Bill agreed that he just finished his education, but he wasn't so sure about the diploma. He felt more like he had just failed his final exam.

---

[29] 2 Timothy 4:7

Chapter 60
The Angel's Prognosis
1952

"BILLY BRANHAM, mercy boy!" cried Dr. Adair, looking up from the lab report he was holding. "You picked up amebas in Africa." When Sam Adair finished reading the lab report, he shook his head sadly. "There is nothing I can do for you, Billy. I've got to send you to a specialist."

After more tests, Dr. Lukas explained the grim facts. "Mr. Branham, these amebas are parasites. They are transmitted as small cysts not much bigger than white blood cells. You probably picked one up in something you ate or drank. Typically symptoms appear about four to six weeks after these parasites enter the body. Yours is the worst case I've ever seen."

Bill remembered that he first felt abdominal cramps in Port Elizabeth, four weeks after he left Johannesburg. That meant He probably swallowed an amebic cyst in Klerksdorp. The timing was right. Oh, if only he had stayed in Johannesburg like the angel had told him to do, this never would have happened.

Dr. Lukas continued, "Invasive amebiasis is the third worst parasitic ailment there is, infecting hundreds of thousands of people worldwide. In most cases the amebas lie dormant. Although these infected people are now carriers and can spread the disease, they themselves are not affected. In other cases, like yours, the parasites become active. We don't know why. Right now these amebas are living off the mucus in your intestinal tract. We're going to try to control them there, because if they get out of the intestines, they head for the liver or the brain, and then the problems get worse. Unfortunately these parasites aren't much affected by drugs. I'm going to start you on a 60-day treatment plan."

While he was at the clinic, one of the tests required that he drink some barium meal. The doctor who was giving him this test said, "Mr. Branham, I hear you are a missionary."

"An evangelistic missionary, yes. I just returned from Africa."

"I studied to be a preacher too. It took me four years of school to find out there was nothing to Christianity. So I started studying the teachings of Muhammad, Buddha, Confucius, and many others. I was surprised to learn Christianity is not the only

Fred Bosworth

religion that talks about a virgin birth and a savior. I decided there's probably nothing to any of it, so I threw the whole mess away and now I'm an agnostic."

With his bowels aching and his mind filled with the dread of his condition, Bill did not feel up to sparring with such a shrewd man. Silently he prayed, "Lord Jesus, give me another chance when I'm feeling better."

After he got home and told his wife the dreadful news, Meda said, "Bill, remember Mrs. Shane from New Albany?"

"Isn't she that neurotic Sunday school teacher in Brother Johnson's church, the one I prayed for just before I left for South Africa?"

"That's her. While you were in Africa, she called me every few days. Now that you're home, she is calling me every day."

"How's she doing?"

"Terrible. She's getting so bad she can hardly leave her house. She wants you to pray for her under the anointing, but she doesn't think she can travel to a meeting."

"That doesn't matter. The way it looks now, I may never have another meeting."

"Bill, don't say that. Anyway, Mrs. Shane wanted me to ask you if the next time the angel of the Lord comes near, she could be the first one on the list to see you."

"Sure," said Bill absentmindedly. He was thinking how he had not seen the angel of the Lord since that fateful day in Klerksdorp when he had resigned to go along with the National Committee's itinerary, contrary to the will of the Lord. He thought, "Oh, how I've messed up my life."

Bill lived his next weeks in misery. The medicine did not help. Pain tormented him so much that he had difficulty sleeping. Night after night he paced the floor of his home, crying, begging, "God, please have mercy on me. If there is still some kindness in Your heart toward me, please forgive me. I'll never again knowingly step across Your line."

The Lord would not speak to him—neither by voice, nor by vision, nor through the written Word, even though Bill read his Bible constantly. Feeling helpless and isolated, Bill's mind slipped ever closer to the pit of despair. Oh, why had he been so foolish as to disobey a direct command from the Lord? Day after day he reexamined his dilemma in Africa, sifting the various elements, probing different solutions, trying to learn from his errors. Now he could see that his biggest mistake was getting tangled up with the South African National Committee, a group of leaders so inflexible that they could not bend even if God Himself asked them to change their plans.

Then Bill realized he had seen this same inflexible attitude among denominational preachers in America. Maybe it was not the men, but the system that was at fault. Every Christian organization lived by a preset list of creeds and bylaws, which often became dogmas so revered that members could not see the Word any other way. That was fine if they were always right. But what if they were wrong? What if God wanted to show them something more, and they wouldn't receive it because it didn't fit with their dogmas? In that case, their own inflexibility could condemn them to the judgments of God. What if denominational Christianity was actually hindering, instead of helping the Spirit of God?

After much soul searching, Bill decided his second mistake was being too sensitive to criticism. This sensitivity stemmed from his childhood rejection, when society ostracized him because of his family's bad reputation. Becoming a Christian had brought him the love and acceptance he had missed as a boy. But some of his childhood complexes remained, including his tendency to nervousness and his sensitivity to criticism. Now that so many thousands of people were clamoring for his attention, he wanted to please everyone, which was an impossible task. He decided that from now on he must do whatever God wanted him to do, no matter who he might offend in the process. He would be far better off to disappoint men than to disappoint the Lord Jesus Christ.

Unfortunately it was not always easy to know what the Lord wanted. Bill mulled over one criticism that had dogged him for years. Many Christians complained that he didn't pray for enough people during his healing campaigns. Hundreds of sick men and women came to each service wanting a personal prayer from him. Because the supernatural discernment taxed his body so heavily, Bill rarely had the strength to pray for more than a few dozen people on any given night of the campaigns. Many critics said that he should be more like Oral Roberts and other faith-healing evangelists, making a long line of people and moving them by as fast as he could touch them and pray a few words. Maybe his critics were right. Maybe his method was too slow. Sometimes Bill fretted over this puzzle for hours, wondering how God really wanted him to structure the healing campaigns. At other times Bill felt the question no longer mattered, because he might never preach again.

Early one morning, Meda found her husband kneeling on the floor, his head bowed over the seat of the couch, weeping.

"Bill, what is the matter?"

"Honey, if you only knew how bad I feel. Here I am, only 42 years old; my health is broken; my ministry is over; I'm in debt. What can I do? What does my future hold? It looks like the end of the road."

"Maybe you'll feel better after you've had something to eat," Meda suggested.

Bill had cried so hard that his eyes had almost swelled shut. Meda led him to the breakfast table where he nibbled on some eggs and toast. Lately his appetite had declined dramatically. Consequently his weight had dropped steadily over the past few weeks until he weighed a scant 110 pounds. His condition was getting worse instead of better.

About the middle of February 1952, Bill went back for more tests. Dr. Lukas shook his head as he studied the results. "Reverend Branham, I'm afraid the medicine I've been giving you isn't working. Next I'm going to use arsenic."

"Arsenic? Isn't that dangerous?"

"Yes, I have to be very careful with the dosage. But make no mistake about it, Reverend Branham, your condition is serious. Invasive amebiasis kills around 40,000 people a year. These active amebas can eat their way through the intestinal wall and get into the bloodstream, which carries them to the liver where they can form life-threatening abscesses. Sometimes the blood also spreads them to other parts of the body, including the brain. When that happens, you start a fever, and in ten hours you're dead."

Bill went home more disturbed than ever. He took his new medicine as prescribed, but the only thing it did was turn his skin yellowish orange.

About this time, his friend Dr. Sam Adair called to tell him about the misfortune of a mutual friend. "Billy, you know Delbert's mother died a few years ago. Delbert is 17 now, and he got out among the wrong crowd. Now he's in the hospital, dying with syphilis. I've given him all the penicillin his body can hold, and it's not doing any good. Just thought you'd want to know."

As sick as Bill felt, he mustered the strength to go over to the hospital and visit this long time family friend. When he entered the hospital room, Delbert said, "Brother Branham, I'm ashamed for you to come here."

"How bad is it, Delbert?"

"The doctor told me to make my peace with God."

"I know your mother was a Christian. How about you?"

"When I got out on my own, some of the boys told me it would be smart to start smoking; so I did. Then I started drinking a sociable beer with the gang, and first thing you know it had me."

"It's not too late to give your heart to Jesus Christ."

"I—I want to," the boy stammered, "but I'm afraid God won't receive me because I'm so sinful."

"Oh, yes He will," Bill assured him. "That's the reason He gave his life on the cross, to save sinful people."

"Do you think He'd take me now that I have this disease?"

"It's not your body you're presenting to Him. It's your soul."

"Then I come."

Opening his Bible, Bill read aloud John chapter 14, which begins: "*Let not your heart be troubled: ye believe in God, believe also in me. In my Father's house are many mansions: if it were not so, I would have told you. I go to prepare a place for you. And if I go and prepare a place for you, I will come again, and receive you unto myself; that where I am, there ye may be also. And whither I go ye know, and the way ye know.*

Thomas saith unto him, Lord, we know not whither thou goest; and how can we know the way?

Jesus saith unto him, I am the way, the truth, and the life: no man cometh unto the Father, but by me."

Finishing this chapter, Bill knelt by the bedside and prayed. Delbert raised his hands and sobbed, "Dear God, have mercy on my soul. Please don't let me die a sinner. With all my heart I believe Your Word is right, and I'm coming now to accept You as my Savior."

Bill stood up and patted Delbert on the shoulder. "Now let's talk about divine healing."

"It doesn't matter anymore whether I die or not." Delbert put his hand over his heart. "Something's happened in here and I'm not afraid to die now."

"Yes, Delbert, salvation is the main thing. But the same Lord Jesus that saved your soul, can also deliver you from your diseased body." Laying his hands on the young man's chest, Bill prayed again.

When Bill got home, he called Sam Adair and said, "Doc, why don't you give Delbert one more shot of penicillin."

"Bill, I've already given him more than enough antibiotics. If it was going to do some good, it would have done it by now."

"Would another shot hurt him?"

"No."

"Then would you give him one more anyway, as a favor to me?"

"Okay, but it won't do any good."

A few days later, Dr. Adair called back and said, "That last shot took. Delbert is going to lick this thing."

"That's wonderful," Bill said. When he hung up the phone, he was happy for his young friend, but sad for himself. "Lord," he prayed, "You healed Delbert. Why won't You heal me?"

DURING the last week of February 1952, William Branham returned to Dr. Lukas' clinic. "How does it look this time?" he asked.

Dr. Lukas didn't smile. "Every time I examine you, I find more amebas in your system. Reverend Branham, I don't want to alarm you, but you're a married man and have several children. You need to make sure your affairs are in order. There is nothing else medical science can do for you. If those parasites get into your bloodstream, you'll start running a high fever. It will be bad enough if they lodge in your liver, but if they get to your heart or brain, you'll live about ten more hours and that's it."

Bill went home distressed. That night he again paced the floor, praying, crying, begging God for mercy; but now he felt more desperate than before. Every half-hour or so he would check his temperature to see if he was starting a fever. What was his family going to do without him? Billy Paul would probably get along all right, but what about his babies? In March Rebekah would be six and Sarah would be one year old. How was Meda going to raise these two little girls by herself?

Around 11:00 Bill lay down and fell asleep. At three o'clock in the morning something woke him. He lay in the dark, listening to the ticking of the clock beside his bed. Suddenly he felt a light pressure which made his skin tingle. The angel of the Lord was near. Bill waited in tense anticipation. Then he heard that familiar voice say, "*Go to your baby and give her a drink of water.*" The pressure eased.

Getting out of bed, he wrapped his robe over his pajamas and walked down the hall to his girl's bedroom where he found Sarah standing in her crib, crying hoarsely, her face red and blotchy from the strain. She had been sick the last few days and had cried so much she had lost her voice. Bill picked her up, carried her to the kitchen, and poured her a glass of water. She drank it all. Bill thought, "Isn't that lovely of my Lord to do this for Sarah. Jesus is so sweet and caring."

Instead of putting Sarah back in her crib, he laid her in his own bed next to Meda. She fell asleep instantly. Bill went back to Sarah's room and laid down in the empty twin bed, but he could not fall asleep. For the umpteenth time he wondered, "What does my future hold? I guess it won't be long now until I'm gone. A fever will strike me... then, ten hours and it's all over... my wife will have these two little girls to raise alone." He sobbed aloud, "Oh, God, is there anything I can do?"

A faint noise disturbed the silence—faint but growing louder. It sounded like a whirlwind approaching. Bill flipped off his covers and sat on the side of the bed. "Dear God, are You coming with pardon for Your servant, or are You coming to take me away?"

A swirl of rainbow-colored light appeared, rising toward the ceiling. Out from beneath that light walked the angel of the Lord. He had his arms folded across his chest, and in one fist he held numerous sheets of white paper. The angel said, *"Insomuch as you were wondering about your future..."*

"Yes," said Bill, "I was wondering what my future holds."

The angel dropped several sheets of paper on the floor. Bill could see they had words written on each page, but before he could read them, the angel said, *"Look at this,"* and he showed Bill the remaining papers in his hand. They were all pure white, free from any marks. The angel flung these papers up in the air. Suddenly the room had no ceiling. The papers sailed into the night sky, going higher and higher until they looked like tiny specks the size of stars before they disappeared beyond the Milky Way. Then a voice boomed from heaven *"Your future is clear!"*

When Bill came to himself, he was still sitting on the side of the bed. The room was dark and quiet. Feeling numb and confused, he pleaded, "God, if I have found favor with You, please tell me: What about these amebas? Am I going to get over them? Please, Lord, if You have forgiven me my sin, will You speak to me one more time?"

Again that supernatural presence swept through the room and the angel stepped out from that light. When he spoke, his voice was compassionate, yet firm. *"Insomuch as you were wondering about those amebas, they will not bother you anymore."*

The angel departed, leaving Bill abounding in joy. He was healed. Healed! God had touched his body with a miracle. He was going to live to raise his family after all. He could even return to his ministry. Remembering his ministry, Bill thought, "While the angel was here I should have asked him how I should pray for the sick."

Suddenly the angel again stood before him. The angel's white robe reflected the supernatural light that circled above his head.

Bill said, "Different ones have been criticizing my meetings, saying that Oral Roberts and these other ministers pray for 500 people in the same time it takes me to pray for 15. You told me to get the people to believe me. Should I keep on doing it the way I'm doing, waiting for visions? Or should I pray for the people in a fast line the way Brother Bosworth says I should?"

"*Do just as you feel led to do,*" he replied. Then the angel disappeared.

"Do just as I feel led to do," Bill repeated. How encouraging. That was the very lesson he had learned from his mistake in South Africa.

Before long Bill felt that electrifying presence of the angel once more, and heard that familiar sound like fire being whipped by the wind in a steady rhythm: *Whoossssh, whoossssh, whoossssh...* Tonight was different from other visitations. Usually the angel brought only one message. Tonight he was appearing repeatedly.

The angel picked Bill up in the Spirit and set him down at the Durban meetings. He was standing at the north end of the Greyville Race Course looking south, exactly where he had stood when he had preached there a few months before. People filled the grandstands and grounds just as he remembered. As soon as he was convinced this was the same meeting, the angel lifted him up and carried him east. Bill watched the Durban meeting turn blue and fade into the west. Then the angel set him down in the midst of another crowd. These people were dark-skinned and skinny; many of them wore loin clothes and turbans. Bill assumed they were East Indians.

He heard a noise above him like the hum of a giant dynamo producing electricity. Looking up, he saw another angel descending from the heavens, clothed in a red robe, a great oscillating light gripped in his outstretched hand. The crowd below raised their arms and shouted praises to Jesus Christ. The angel above turned the power of his searchlight on high, illuminating the fringe of the crowd, showing how they stretched way back into the surrounding hills. It looked like an ocean of people for as far as Bill could see. The angel of the Lord, still standing beside him, cried out, "*There are 300,000 of them at that Branham meeting!*"

Stunned by the vision's power, Bill pitched forward onto the floor between the twin beds. When he revived, he could see daylight filtering in through the window blinds. He realized it must be early because the house was still quiet. Then he heard something curious. It sounded like the pages of a book fluttering in a breeze; only it couldn't be a breeze because the window was closed. Sitting up, Bill was startled to see his Bible rise off the night stand by the bed and float across the room, stopping in front of him, still hanging in the air. It was open to Acts chapter 27, where Paul was speaking to the crew of his prison ship during a terrible storm. A hand appeared above the text and pointed to the verses while Bill read: "*Sirs, ye should have hearkened unto me, and not have loosed from Crete, and to have gained this harm and loss. And now I exhort you to be of good cheer: for there shall be no loss of any man's life among you, but of the ship. For there stood by me this night the angel of God, whose I am, and whom I serve, Saying, Fear not, Paul; thou must be brought before Caesar: and, lo, God hath given thee all them that sail with thee. Wherefore, sirs, be of good cheer: for I believe God, that it shall be even as it was told me.*"

As soon as he finished reading this portion of Scripture, that floating hand flipped the pages back to Joshua chapter 1. It pointed at verse two and followed down the lines of print as Bill read: *"Moses my servant is dead; now therefore arise, go over this Jordan, thou, and all this people, unto the land which I do give to them, even to the children of Israel. Every place that the sole of your foot shall tread upon, that have I given unto you, as I said unto Moses...* That hand seemed to stress verses five and six: *There shall not any man be able to stand before thee all the days of thy life: as I was with Moses, so I will be with thee: I will not fail thee, nor forsake thee. Be strong and of a good courage: for unto this people shalt thou divide for an inheritance the land, which I sware unto their fathers to give them... Have not I commanded thee? Be strong and of a good courage; be not afraid, neither be thou dismayed: for the* LORD *thy God is with thee whithersoever thou goest."*

When Bill finished reading all of Joshua chapter 1, he reached for his Bible. Instantly it was back on the nightstand where he had left it.

A knock sounded on the bedroom door. Meda asked, "Can I come in?"

"That's strange," Bill thought. "Why would she ask if she could enter?"

Chapter 61
Three Witnesses
1952

M EDA BRANHAM knocked again. "Bill, are you all right?"

"Yes," he answered, "come in."

Meda stepped into the bedroom holding her sleeping baby. "Bill, has something happened? A few hours ago I had to get up with Sarah, so while I was up, I thought I would check on you; but when I came to this door, I had the strongest feeling that I shouldn't open it. I wondered if maybe there was a vision going on, so I sat in the living room and rocked Sarah until just now."

Bill looked at the time. It was six o'clock. The vision had held him for over three hours! "Yes, honey, it was a vision. The angel of the Lord has been here ever since three o'clock this morning. God has forgiven me and I'm going to get over these parasites."

"Oh, Bill," she gasped, "that is wonderful news!" A few minutes later her excitement softened into a question. "Bill, could you see that neurotic woman from New Albany today. She has begged me to call her the next time the anointing comes on you."

"Sure, honey. Tell her to come over around ten o'clock. First thing this morning I need to go to the bank and see about those check stubs for our income tax records. I'm also going to call Dr. Lukas and see if he can give me another examination."

While Meda went to phone Mrs. Shane, Bill sat down to think about what the vision meant. The first Scripture was easy, because it paralleled his misadventure in South Africa. Paul told those sailors if they would have only listened to him and stayed in Crete for the winter, they would not have lost their ship. Evidently Paul also had trouble with people who didn't believe he was led by God.

Paul suffered along with the crew for that mistake, but by God's grace, no lives were lost. For Bill, the lesson was obvious: never again would he follow men's ideas when the Lord was leading down another path.

Understanding how Joshua chapter 1 applied to him was more challenging. *"As I was with Moses, so I will be with thee: I will not fail thee, nor forsake thee."* Surely this was a declaration of God's commitment to this ministry. But what was the specific connection between his ministry and Joshua's? Was God commissioning him to lead the church into a spiritual Promised Land, the same way Joshua lead Israel into a natural Promised Land? That's how it sounded. *"...for unto this people shalt thou divide for an inheritance the land, which I sware unto their fathers to give them..."* Not only did Joshua lead the children of Israel in their fight to possess Canaan; after the battles were over, Joshua divided the land among the 12 tribes, directing them to their earthly inheritance. According to the apostle Paul, God promised the Christian church a spiritual inheritance. *"Now this I say, brethren, that flesh and blood cannot inherit the kingdom of God, neither doth corruption inherit incorruption. Behold, I shew you a mystery; We shall not all sleep, but we shall all be changed, In a moment, in the twinkling of an eye, at the last trump: for the trumpet shall sound, and the dead shall be raised incorruptible, and we shall be changed. For this corruptible must put on incorruption, and this mortal must put on immortality."[30]* Bill wondered if he was being called to lead the Gentile church into her spiritual inheritance.

Whatever else the vision meant, it was apparent that many battles lay ahead, and God was encouraging him to go forward boldly. *"Have not I commanded thee? Be strong and of a good courage; be not afraid, neither be thou dismayed; for the LORD thy God is with thee withersoever thou goest."* Picking up his pen, Bill wrote a brief account of this vision on the back flyleaf of his Scofield Reference Bible, so that he would always remember it and always have it with him.

During breakfast, Bill's mother-in-law stopped by to ask, "Is everything here all right? This morning I went to the sink to wash last night's dishes, and I felt the Lord was saying to me, 'Go over to Bill's house. Something has happened.'"

After Bill told Mrs. Broy about the angel's repeated visits earlier that morning, Bill remembered something the Bible said: *"...at the mouth of two witnesses, or at the mouth of three witnesses, shall the matter be established."[31]* Here was his second witness, confirming that what the angel told him was true. When breakfast was over, Bill called Dr. Lukas. "I'd like to get an examination this morning."

"What for?"

"I haven't got those amebas anymore."

"Yes, you've got them. Once a person gets those little devils, he has them for the rest of his life."

"This morning the Lord Jesus did something for me. I'd like you to check me over one more time."

---

[30] 1 Corinthians 15:50-53
[31] Deuteronomy 19:15; Matthew 18:16

Dr. Lukas hesitated. "Uh—well—I just examined you the other day. Your intestines are loaded with those parasites. But if you want to be examined again, come on over this afternoon and I'll take another look."

Bill got to the bank just as it was opening. His business did not take long. On his way out the door he suddenly felt like he shouldn't leave. Stepping over to the side of the lobby, he prayed quietly, "Lord God, what would You have me do?" He stood there for a minute, holding his briefcase under his arm. Then a voice sounded in his head, "Look at Bob Denison."

Bob Denison, one of the bank tellers, was a long time acquaintance of his. Bob was standing behind one of the teller windows with his head down. Bill walked over and said brightly, "Good morning, Bobby. How is everything today?"

When Bob lifted his head, tears glazed his eyes. "Billy, I don't know how you're going to take this, but this morning at three o'clock I woke up, and I had dreamed that I should tell you about my problem. Now here you are, so I hope you don't mind."

"No, Bobby. Go right ahead."

"Almost all of my people died of cancer. And now I have every symptom of it. I have been worried to death the last few days."

Taking Bob's right hand in his own left, Bill felt the pounding vibrations of a cancerous demon. Bill's left hand swelled as it turned red. "Bobby, let's pray that Jesus Christ will touch your body."

After just a short prayer, the vibrations stopped. The cancer was gone. Bill thought, "Here is my third witness."

By the time he got back home, Mrs. Shane had already arrived. Since she was too nervous to drive herself, two of her friends had brought her. Bill asked them to wait in the living room while he talked with Mrs. Shane in the den. A Baptist man had also come to the house wanting prayer. Bill had never met him before, but he knew him by reputation, because this man used to play professional baseball for Louisville, Kentucky. Now he was dying with cancer of the spleen, a condition for which medical science had no cure. Bill asked him to wait in a bedroom.

Bill entered his study, leaving the door open. Meda was in the next room. Mrs. Shane was pacing the floor, wringing her hands. Bill sat on a stool. "Howdy, Mrs. Shane. Please be seated."

Flinging herself down in a chair, she stuttered, "Br-brother Branham, is—is the angel of the Lord here?"

"Yes, sister, we're sitting in his presence."

"Good. Now you can cast this evil spirit out of me. I feel like any minute the ground might split open and swallow me."

"Just a minute, sister. We have to watch what we're casting out. Let's talk awhile first." He wanted to get her mind away from the issue so she would calm down. "Let's you and I take a little trip—"

"No!" she screeched. "I can't take a trip!" Her voice climbed hysterically.

"Relax," Bill soothed. "I was speaking about a mental trip. Let's go back to when God made man and woman, and put them in the Garden of Eden." He talked softly, soothing her nerves. Soon Bill saw a little black car speeding through the air between them. He asked, "Were you ever in a car accident?"

"No, Brother Branham. Why do you ask?"

"Oh, I saw something." He kept talking. Soon the vision returned, unfolding the ugly truth. "You got married during the last war, and your husband was shipped over to France. You got lonely and started running around with other men. One night you were out in a black car with a blond boy and you broke your marriage vow. On the way back, that black car was almost struck by a train as it crossed the railroad tracks."

Mrs. Shane screamed and collapsed on the floor. Meda dashed into the room to see what was wrong. Together Bill and Meda helped the woman get back up onto a chair. She shook uncontrollably and sobbed, "Brother Branham, don't you dare tell that to anyone!"

"Sister, right there lays your trouble. And you're never going to get better until you make it right. I don't care how many times they pray for you; they could stomp and scream and anoint you with 50 gallons of oil, and it wouldn't do any good. As long as you have unconfessed sin in your life, that devil has a right to stay there. If you want to get well, you're going to have to confess that sin to your husband and make it right."

"I have confessed it, Brother Branham. I confessed it to God a long time ago."

"It wasn't God you sinned against. You were a married woman. You sinned against your marriage vows."

"Brother Branham, I can't tell my husband. He'd leave me for sure."

"Sister, you know I've told you the truth. Nobody knows that sin except you, that blond boy, and God. You told me you've been seeing a psychiatrist for ten years. He couldn't drag that out of you. But that is your trouble. It's laying way down deep in your subconscious mind. You're never going to get well until you tell your husband about it and clean up your conscience."

"I can't do it," she sobbed. "I've got three children. It would break up our home."

"Your home might break up anyhow, because mentally you're not going to hold together much longer. You'd better go get your husband and talk it over."

"I—I can't," she bawled. "I just can't do it."

Bill stood up. "That's up to you, sister. I've done all I can do. I've told you what God showed me and you know it's the truth. The rest is up to you. I have to go now and see a man in the other room who has cancer."

She pleaded, "Oh, Brother Branham, don't leave me!"

Suddenly Bill saw a man standing beside Mrs. Shane. He was tall, with neatly combed black hair, and he was wearing a white jacket, which he turned so that Bill could read the word "CHEVROLET" printed across the back. Bill said, "Doesn't your husband work for the Chevrolet company?"

"Yes," she whimpered.

"He's a tall man with dark, wavy hair that he combs to the side."

"Yes. That's right."

"He's got the same sin to confess to you."

Her hands flew up to her cheeks. "No, not my husband! He's a church deacon."

"I don't care what he shows on the outside, God sees his heart. During the war, when your husband landed in England, he took a girl and lived with her. But that's not all. Just three days ago he snuck off with a black-headed woman who works in his office. She was wearing a pink dress. They parked under a beech tree in a green Chevrolet bearing an Indiana license plate. And right there he lived as untrue to you as you once did to him."

"I know the woman," she gasped. "And I know the car too."

"You'd better go call your husband and talk this thing over."

While Bill went to pray for the man with cancer, Mrs. Shane called her husband at work and asked him to meet her on the road. Her two friends drove her to the spot and waited until her husband drove up. When she got in the front seat with her husband, she said slowly, "I know I've kept you broke these last ten years, going every week to that psychiatrist. But now I think I've gotten to the bottom of my problem. I did something once, something bad, something that has haunted me ever since. I have to tell you what it is, and I hope you'll forgive me."

When she finished confessing her sin, her husband started to act indignant. She added, "And three days ago weren't you with a secretary from your office? Didn't the two of you park a green Chevrolet under a beech tree and do the same thing I did?"

He eyed her warily. "Who have you been talking to?"

"I was just up to see Brother Branham. He told me."

At this revelation, his hypocrisy deflated like a punctured tire. "Honey, that is the truth. If you'll forgive me, I'll forgive you. I'll go down to the church and resign as a deacon, and you resign as a Sunday school teacher. Let's get right with God and raise our children right."

Driving back to the Branham house, they walked up to the door with their arms around each other. Bill had just finished praying with the cancer patient. (The man had received his miracle.) Bill said to the Shanes, "I'm glad to see you got this thing worked out between you. Now we can call on the name of Jesus and make that devil move out."

A few minutes later, Mrs. Shane was a new woman.

LATER that afternoon, Bill showed up at the clinic. As busy as Dr. Lukas was, he still squeezed Bill into his schedule. "Now, what were you saying on the phone this morning?"

"I don't have those amebas anymore."

"Reverend Branham, you're probably just experiencing a temporary relief from the symptoms. That sometimes happens. Medically we call it a remission."

"No, doc, this is not temporary. This is permanent. I'm absolutely healed."

"Did you bring me a stool sample?" Dr. Lukas took this sample over to the clinic's laboratory. Soon he came back and said, "I'd like to check you further." When he finished this examination, he said, "Reverend Branham, the amebas are still there but they are no longer active. I've never heard of this happening before and I don't have any idea what would cause them to go dormant."

"I do," said Bill confidently. "The Lord Jesus healed me this morning about three o'clock."

The doctor said, "I'll have to examine you regularly for three months before I can say you're not infectious anymore."

"You can examine me every day if you want to."

As Bill was leaving through the waiting room, he saw Dr. Lukas' partner standing in the doorway of his office talking with a nurse. "Mr. Branham," said the doctor, walking over to shake his hand, "it's good to see you again."

In his mind, Bill prayed, "Lord, if You want me to talk to him about religion, let him bring the subject up. I don't want to push it on him."

The doctor said, "What do you think about those tribes in Africa? Aren't they getting more progressive all the time?"

"Yes, I suppose they are."

"There's a lot of East Indians transplanted to South Africa, aren't there?"

"That's right. The population of Durban is almost half Indians."

"I've read a lot about that. Hindus, aren't they?"

"Many of them are Hindus, but some are Moslems."

"A smart bunch of people, those Indians. In fact I think Mahatma Gandhi was the smartest man who ever lived."

"Every man has the right to his own opinion. But I differ with you there; I think it was Jesus Christ."

"I'll bet you didn't have much success getting those Hindus and Moslems to switch over to your religion, did you?"

"Oh, yes. We had about 30,000 converts in just one day."

"What?" the doctor blurted, dropping his cigarette on the floor. "Thirty thousand converts in one day?"

"If you question it, you can call Sidney Smith, mayor of Durban, and ask him. You'll find out that we probably made a low estimate."

"Are you sure they were Hindus?"

"Many of them were Hindus. When they saw the power of Almighty God moving in their midst, they believed it was the Lord Jesus, just like I told them it was. I watched hundreds of Hindu women wiping off the red dot from their foreheads when they accepted Christ."

Everyone in the waiting room seemed to be listening to this conversation. The doctor twisted his shoe over the burning cigarette he had dropped; then he patted Bill on the back and said, "Boy, you must be a genius."

"No, sir. I'm a seventh grade dropout. My Lord Jesus is the genius."

"Oh, I don't know," said the doctor. "That's going a little too far out on a limb for me."

"Excuse me for talking so straight with you, doctor, but you're missing something. You're a smart man, full of knowledge. But knowledge can only take you so far. There were two trees in the

Garden of Eden. One of them was the tree of knowledge and the other was the Tree of Life. When Adam left the Tree of Life to eat fruit off the tree of knowledge, he separated himself from his Maker. Ever since then, man has been eating off that tree of knowledge, and it's destroying him. He learned how to make metal and what did he create? Swords and arrows. Then he discovered gunpowder. After awhile, he invented the automobile. That has killed more people than gunpowder. Now he's got himself an atom bomb."

"But if man hadn't invented any of that, he'd still die."

"No, not if he had stayed with the Tree of Life. He would have lived forever. Death came because he left the Tree of Life for the tree of knowledge. But man can still live forever if he comes back to the Tree of Life, which is Jesus Christ."

"I don't know about that," the doctor muttered.

"I'm not against education," Bill finished. "But the problem you smart fellows have with your education is you try to reason everything out. You climb up the tree of knowledge as high as you can go, but when you get so high and can't get any higher, you reject everything you can't understand. The tree of knowledge is all right, but when you get as high as you can on that tree, you should jump over to the Tree of Life and keep right on climbing. That's what faith in God's Word is all about."

Chapter 62
Left Turn at Lake Michigan
1952

ALTHOUGH HIS SYMPTOMS vanished the day he was healed, William Branham could not go back to work immediately. His life-threatening struggle with amebas had left him weak and emaciated. It would take four more months before he would feel strong enough to resume his strenuous schedule of holding one faith-healing campaign after another.

In April 1952 Fred Bosworth called with a tempting proposal. "Brother Branham, in Baltimore they're offering us this air-conditioned auditorium free for the entire month of July. The building seats 10,000 people. Five hundred ministers have signed up to sponsor the meetings: Methodists, Baptists, Full Gospel, you name it. Five hundred of them are willing to cooperate. You can't beat that."

"If God tells me to go there, then that's where I want to go. But so far, I don't feel led to go to Baltimore."

A few days later Ern Baxter called. "There are people all over the country wanting you to come. So many cities are asking for you: Hammond, Zion, Chicago, Battle Creek, Minneapolis, and San Francisco. I could easily fill your schedule for the rest of 1952. So what are you planning to do?"

"At this moment I have no leading at all."

Baxter suggested, "Then let's go into Chicago. They've got a large arena waiting for you there."

"That sounds all right."

"Shall I secure it?"

Bill hesitated. "No, better wait awhile."

That afternoon Bill took his wife to a planetarium. As he watched the artificial night sky scroll across a domed ceiling, the Holy Spirit nudged him and said, *"Stay out of Chicago for now. Turn aside to Hammond and Zion."* When Bill got home he phoned Ern Baxter, asking him to set up meetings in Hammond, Indiana, and Zion, Illinois.

Baxter said, "That takes care of July. Where do you want to go next?"

Bill said he had no leading beyond Zion. Ern Baxter sighed. "Brother Branham, we have to have specific dates in order to secure these large auditoriums. What about Battle Creek?"

"I think it will be all right. I have two places I'm considering after Zion: Battle Creek, Michigan, and Minneapolis, Minnesota. I'm leaning a little toward Battle Creek because I've been to Minneapolis before. But don't make any long term commitments."

Unknown to Bill, Ern Baxter promptly called his contact in Battle Creek and committed Bill to a campaign that would begin August 16 and last 14 consecutive nights.

Early next morning Bill dreamed he saw a muddy wave heading for a beach house where his wife lay sleeping. Desperately he rushed to Meda's rescue, getting her out just moments before the giant wave smashed the beach house into fragments. Bill woke up sweating. He relaxed when he saw his wife sleeping peacefully beside him. He thought, "My, what an awful dream. I wonder if it means something."

Then, abruptly, he was sitting in a boat floating on deep blue water. Like day and night are similar yet different, so is a vision similar yet different from a dream. Dreams are shadows of reality, coming to closed eyes in the dark of sleep, leaving fuzzy impressions that are difficult to remember. A vision comes to wide-open eyes, striking the senses like sunlight and leaving distinct images in the brain. As far as Bill could tell, he really was sitting in a boat on a lake so large that the shore looked like a thin line in the hazy distance. He heard a sound like a small motor coming closer—*putt-putt-putt-putt*. Looking back, he saw a shadowy shape moving beneath the surface. It came slowly toward the stern of the boat, but just before it rammed him, it turned left and darted away. Then it circled and came at the stern of his boat again, turning at the last moment and darting to its left. Bill leaned over the edge of the boat, hoping he could see what this strange object was. Instead, he saw a road under the water that came to "T" beneath his boat—one road going left and the other going right. Now he heard the angel of the Lord say, "*This is telling you to turn left.*"

Suddenly Bill was back in his bedroom, sitting up in bed, wide-awake. He felt bewildered. What had happened? He had dreamed about his wife, and then—did he fall back to sleep and have a second dream? It seemed more vivid than a dream; the images sparkled with clarity, as though he was actually there sailing on a lake. But if it was a vision, what did it mean? It didn't seem to make sense. He pondered the experience for a long time, trying to understand it; but finally he gave up.

AFTER a seven-month hiatus, William Branham resumed his evangelistic ministry on July 13, 1952, starting with an ambitious eight-day faith-healing campaign in Hammond, Indiana. Praying for the sick in America was different than it had been in Africa, where seeing one miracle could inspire hundreds of people to believe Christ for their own healing. In Africa his job had been easier, because the angel told him if he could get the people to believe him, then nothing would stand before his prayer, not even cancer. Using his gift was still as exhausting as running a marathon, but at least in Africa he felt like he was running on dry ground. Praying for the sick in Hammond was like trying to run through knee-deep water. The crowd in general seemed cool and reserved towards the supernatural discernment. Although many people had enough faith to be healed, Bill kept feeling skepticism oozing from the audience like slime from a stagnant bog. At the beginning of the prayer-line, a woman came forward who looked healthy and strong. Bill said, "Because you are my first patient tonight, I want to talk to you just a moment. I believe we are strangers, aren't we?"

"Yes."

"You and I each have a human spirit. When this anointing comes on me, that is a Spirit too. That's the angel of the Lord, which is a Messenger sent from God. It is a part of God, an attribute of God, a gift of God sent to bless you. If you have a spirit of unbelief, then It can't bless you. If your spirit is willing, then It might tell you something and bless you."

"Now, you're conscious that something is going on. It's his presence, the angel of the Lord who is standing just a few feet away from me right now. Yes, my sister, I see you're suffering with headaches. Recently you were sitting in a chair reading, when one of these headaches came. In the vision I see you rubbing your head. Oh, you were reading my book.[32] You thought, 'If I go to those meetings and have him pray for me, maybe these headaches will cease.' Your headaches are caused by a female trouble. I know you've been told other things, but that's wrong. The doctor made

---

[32] He is referring here to the book *William Branham, A Man Sent From God* written in 1950 by Gordon Lindsay.

an error. In order that you might know I'm God's prophet, I'll tell you something else: you belong to the church called Christian Science. I seen you in a Christian Science reading room. Is that right? If it is, raise your hand."

As she raised her hand, Bill saw a flash of light surround her. He bowed his head and prayed, then opened his eyes and raised his head in time to see the light of the angel glide away from him, heading out over the audience.

"Excuse me, something's going on. I'm watching a vision of someone holding their head the same way, but it's a colored lady." Bill pointed and spoke, even as the vision rolled before his open eyes. "It's that woman with the yellow blouse on sitting right there. Don't you have sinus headaches? If that's right, stand up on your feet. Do you believe on God's Son, Jesus Christ? In the name of the Lord Jesus Christ, I ask for God's blessing upon you that those headaches leave you and never come again."

Turning to the audience, Bill said, "Every skeptic in here ought to feel ashamed of himself."

Skeptics continued disbelieving anyway. Later Bill learned that another evangelist had recently preached in Hammond, and this man's version of divine healing had soured these people to the idea. Many in the crowd suspected that the discernment was nothing more than a trick connected with the prayer-cards. On Tuesday night Billy Paul passed out 100 prayer-cards. But when the Spirit descended, It urged Bill to ignore these cards and ask instead for those sick people without prayer-cards to raise their hands. Identifying several rows of people without prayer-cards, he asked these men and women to form a prayer-line to his right.

First in line, an elderly woman shuffled up the steps to the platform. Bill said, "You don't have a prayer-card. You just came in here tonight and sat down and are kind of surprised I called you. I'm just your brother. I said 'brother' because you are a Christian.

I know that because I feel the welcome of your spirit. I'm talking to you like our Master did with the woman at the well, when He said 'bring Me a drink.' He wanted to start a conversation with her so he could catch her spirit. When I catch your spirit, the vision moves in. Then I can only say what I see. But if I am able to know what is wrong with you, will you believe me to be His prophet?

"I see you've been shook up lately. Something has happened that has given you a real hard shaking. You've got several things wrong with you. You're anemic, you have female trouble, and you've been nervous for a long time. But what you really fear is that cancer. You're afraid it's going to take your life... which it *is* going to take your life if God doesn't give you mercy. If that is right, raise your hand to the people."

She raised her hand. Again Bill confronted the skeptics. "To you who thought I was an impostor, thinking it was mental telepathy, me reading these things off of a prayer-card, aren't you ashamed of yourself? God will deal with you for that. God be merciful to your sinful soul." He turned back to the woman, bowed his head, and prayed for her healing in the name of Jesus Christ. "Now, my sister, go on home and forget all about that cancer condition; you're going to be well."

From that point on, skepticism in the audience evaporated into the hot July night. For the rest of the week God's Spirit moved freely in Hammond. Bill was so impressed with the improvement of faith in the audience that during one service he tried an experiment to see how many people he could pray for in one night. He was hoping that he could pray for a hundred or more, and that their faith would be so high that they wouldn't pull him into visions. But enough visions came to him anyway so that after 78 people had passed through the prayer-line, Bill collapsed in exhaustion.

The next morning he felt strong enough to continue the campaign, but he knew better than to try that very often, because his body could not stand the strain. Visions appeared unbidden. He could neither coax them on, nor shut them off. When enough faith pulled on his gift, the discernment flowed. His body could endure this for about a half-hour each night, no more. Too much time spent in that other dimension could kill him, just like it almost did in 1948. Still, he was glad he had tried his experiment last night. Now he knew he must continue to use prayer-cards to limit the number of people he prayed for during each service. If the audience could not believe after watching the supernatural discernment in the prayer-line, then there was nothing more Bill (or for that matter, God) could do for them.

IN AUGUST William Branham began his campaign in Battle Creek, Michigan, a small city of 40,000 people on the eastern shore of Lake Michigan. After a few meetings, he felt perplexed. The gift of God was operating perfectly, but just like in Hammond, the Christians in Battle Creek did not seem to be grasping its significance, so their faith remained flat. But unlike Hammond, Indiana—here in Battle Creek Bill could not put his finger on the problem. Perhaps he was just spoiled by the enthusiasm he had seen in South Africa. He told Ern Baxter, "There's something wrong. I don't know what it is, but I want to find out. Tomorrow afternoon I'm going out in the woods to pray about it until I know."

The next morning he drove out to a secluded spot by a lake where he could pray undisturbed. Kneeling among wild grape vines beneath a majestic oak tree, he soon lost himself in prayer. Suddenly he was out on the lake in a little motorboat. Its engine went *putt-putt-putt* as it headed north parallel to the eastern bank. Then the boat turned left toward the western shore of the lake.

The angel of the Lord appeared beside him and said, "*Close your meetings in Battle Creek and turn aside to Minneapolis at once.*" The angel vanished, and a moment later Bill was back on shore, kneeling beneath that shady oak.

Now Bill understood the vision he had seen at home in April. Then he had been praying about whether he should visit Battle Creek, Michigan, or Minneapolis, Minnesota. The clear blue waters of his earlier vision represented Lake Michigan. If he had held up a map of the area, Battle Creek lay to the right of Lake Michigan; Minneapolis lay to the left. All along God had wanted him to turn left, but for some reason he had not understood. Now he was in Battle Creek, contrary to the will of the Lord. Worst of all, his manager had arranged a two-week campaign, and there were still eight days left to go. Extracting himself from this commitment was going to be painful.

As soon as Bill got back to the hotel, he told his manager what he had to do. At first Ern Baxter thought he was joking. When he finally realized Bill was serious, Baxter called for a conference with Reverend Floyd, the local minister who was coordinating the Battle Creek campaign. Bill explained his vision and what he must do.

Understandably Reverend Floyd was troubled. "Brother Branham, I believe God wanted us to set up these meetings in Battle Creek."

"I'm not disputing you there. I don't know why I didn't recognize that for a vision back in April when I was still home, but now I do; and now I must obey what God wants me to do."

"Brother Branham," said Ern Baxter, "we have fourteen churches combined in this campaign. We have to consider all of the cooperating ministers here."

"That's right, we have to consider—" Bill stopped. He felt the presence of the angel of the Lord nearby. Suddenly he realized this was a test. God had allowed him to be confused about his April vision so he would end up in this predicament, which was similar to the one he had faced in South Africa—that is, the ministers wanted consideration, and his manager sympathized with the ministerial group. But God had told him to do something else. "Brethren," he said, "I love you. But the Holy Spirit tells me to go yonder to the other side of the lake, and I'm going. I won't make the same mistake I made in South Africa by waiting until something happens. I must be obedient to God."

"Brother Branham," snapped one frustrated minister at the table, "you claim to be a fundamentalist. Where would you ever find something like that in the Scriptures?"

"It's there," Bill answered calmly. "Philip was having a revival in Samaria, and the Holy Ghost called him away from it and sent him out in the desert to one man. That one man took the Gospel back to Ethiopia."[33]

Reverend Floyd frowned. "I don't understand why God would make it possible for us to arrange these meetings, and then send you away after you got here."

"Brother Floyd, what Battle Creek needs is a good old-fashioned Holy Ghost revival, not a healing campaign. A revival would get the people back on a spiritual line. Since the meetings are all set, why don't you have a revivalist step into my place."

Floyd shrugged. "Well, the Christians might understand, but I don't know about everybody else."

The room was quiet for a moment. Just then Bill saw that supernatural light blazing above Reverend Floyd's head. He said, "Brother Floyd, right now you're thinking about the time when the prophet Isaiah went up to King Hezekiah and told him God had heard his prayer."[34]

---

[33] Acts 8:26-39
[34] 2 Kings 20:4-6

Floyd raised his eyebrows. "Brother Branham, that's right."

"Confirmation," said Bill. "The Holy Spirit is here to prove this is the right thing to do."

"But how could you know what I was thinking?"

"Remember the Bible said that Jesus perceived their thoughts.[35] It's the same Holy Spirit."

Reluctantly, these ministers agreed to bring in a revivalist to preach the remainder of the Battle Creek campaign. As difficult as it was to disappoint his sponsors, Bill felt good that he was obeying his Lord. His predicament in South Africa was a lesson he would never forget.

That night, after Bill explained to his audience in Battle Creek why he was leaving the campaign early, he said, "You might not understand this, but I love you with undying Christian love; and God knows that is the truth. If I knew it was His divine will, I would stay here in this city for the next six weeks until a revival would sweep the whole city. I am willing, but I must be flexible in His hands and do exactly what He tells me to do."

---

[35] Luke 5:22

Chapter 63
When Love Projects
1953

IN FEBRUARY 1953 William Branham held a week-long faith-healing campaign in Tallahassee, Florida. One day while he, his wife, and his manager were having lunch in a downtown cafe, a smiling six-year-old girl waved at him through the front window. He waved back. Soon she came into the restaurant pulling her father along by his hand. They stopped at Bill's table and the girl said, "Brother Branham, do you remember me?"

"No, I don't believe I do."

"When you prayed for me, God healed my blind eye."

Her father explained that last year his daughter had severely damaged one of her eyes in an accident. Her doctor said she had no hope of ever seeing out of that eye again. But her father believed there was one last hope." He took his daughter out of the hospital, made a bed for her in the backseat of his car, and headed for Indiana, stopping only to eat and buy gas. They arrived in Jeffersonville on Sunday night and found Bill just leaving church. Bill prayed for this sweet little girl and now she was healed.

"Which eye was blind?" Bill asked.

"This one," said the girl. "I mean this one." She pointed first to one eye, and then the other. "You know, I don't remember."

Her father laughed and said, "It was this one."

Before she left, the little girl handed Bill an envelope that he slipped into his pocket and forgot about until he got home. When he opened it, he found it was a Valentine card with her signature beneath a lovely poem.

In May 1953, Bill conducted a strenuous faith-healing campaign in Jonesboro, Arkansas, holding seven meetings in six days. During this week, a minister in Jonesboro ridiculed divine healing on his local radio broadcast. Not only did he accuse William Branham of perpetrating a scam, he also challenged the public, saying, "I'll give $1,000 to anyone who can prove that a miracle of healing happened."

Within an hour after the end of this broadcast, dozens of people called Bill's manager offering to be that proof if Bill would accept the man's challenge. Bill gathered together a mixture of cases and said, "Let's go collect that $1000." One man brought along his doctor to verify he had once been dying with cancer. Another woman brought along her neighbor and her doctor, as well as her medical records, to prove she had spent twenty years in a wheelchair suffering from arthritis.

When they confronted this minister, in spite of all the weight of their evidence, the man sidestepped. "Well—uh—I can't—er—the money isn't here. It's at our denominational headquarters in Texas."

"Then tomorrow we'll fly to Texas and get it," said Bill decisively. "I want to put that money into a fund for missionaries."

Unfortunately none of the people who were his proof could go with him to Texas on such short notice. So the denominational minister suggested an alternative. "When we get to my headquarters, I'll take a girl and cut her arm with a razor blade. If you can heal that cut before my brethren, then they'll give you $1,000."

"You're suffering from a bad case of mental deficiency," Bill said in disgust. "How could a Christian make a sick remark like that? Sounds like the same thing they said to Jesus, 'If thou be the Son of God, come down from the cross and we'll believe you.'[36] That's the familiar old cry of the unbeliever: 'Jesus, show us a sign,'[37] when miracles were happening every day that those Pharisees weren't around to see. Or else if they did see a miracle, they said it came by Beelzebub, prince of the devils. It's always been that way. 'Master, we'll believe you if you go where *we* want and do what *we* want you to do.' But the Pharisees didn't have any strings attached to Jesus. He was free to do His Father's will. And so is He free today."

In June of 1953 Bill traveled to Connersville, Indiana, squeezing nine meetings into one week. After that, weary from months of campaigns around the country, he reserved the remainder of his summer to rest at home with his family.

Of course, he never could completely rest at home. People would constantly intrude upon his privacy. Bill had lived in his house on Ewing Lane for five years, and he had never eaten a meal with the window blinds open. Frequently strangers stood in his yard, waiting to see him, wanting to tell him their problems, hoping to ask his advice and to have him pray for them. They came at all hours of the day and night. Bill had seen as many as 30 cars parked in front of his house at the same time, some of them ambulances. Whenever he walked into a room, the first thing he did was pull the window blinds shut; otherwise somebody outside would see him there and either knock on the window or else just walk into the house uninvited, to reach him.

Bill couldn't turn anyone down who wanted prayer. He loved people and knew that most of these people were sincere in their hearts, seeking to get well, or trying to find peace of mind. He

---

[36] Matthew 27:39-43
[37] Matthew 12:38, 16:1; Mark 8:11; Luke 11:16

couldn't fall asleep at night knowing that some mother with a sick baby was camping on his lawn, or some man dying with cancer was sleeping in a car in his driveway, waiting for his prayer. He had to do what he could to help them. So whenever these strangers showed up at his house, he would pray for them in Jesus' name. Some nights, by the time he finished praying for the last person to come by, he didn't have enough energy left to change his clothes before collapsing into bed.

Even a simple chore like mowing the lawn became difficult because of his frequent visitors. Every time he got started, someone would drop by wanting prayer. Bill would change his clothes, counsel and pray with the newcomer, then change back into his work clothes and mow a little farther before the next person showed up. Day after day so many people came by wanting prayer that Bill couldn't finish his lawn. Sometimes it seemed like a losing battle. By the time he finished his front yard, the backyard had grown up into a ragged pasture again.

One afternoon there was a lull in the parade of visitors. Slipping into his work clothes, Bill hurried to the back yard and started his power mower. Soon he was cutting a swath through thick grass just as fast as he could push his machine. In the summer heat, it didn't take long for his shirt to be drenched with sweat, so he yanked it off and tossed it aside.

A martin box stood on top of a pole nailed to his back fence. Bill forgot that a swarm of hornets had built a nest inside this birdhouse. In his haste to finish his lawn, he hit the lawn mower into the fence hard enough to shake that martin box. Out swarmed a mass of hornets, angry and wanting vengeance. In a few seconds they surrounded him, circling in the air, some of them landing on his skin, ready to thrust their barbed stingers deep. Bill knew he was in serious trouble because this many hornets could sting a man to death. Then, suddenly, his fear changed to love. Continuing to push his mower, he said, "Little hornets, I'm sorry I disturbed you. I know that stinging is your God-given weapon to protect yourselves; but I don't mean you any harm. I'm a servant of God and I've got to get this lawn mowed so I can go back inside and pray for more of God's children. So in the name of Jesus Christ, go back to your nest. I won't bother you anymore."

Immediately the cloud of hornets lifted and flew straight back to their nest. Bill paused to watch in amazement. This was same thing he had experienced years ago when he had faced that killer bull. Love filled him, changing the course of nature. It was not a human love; this was something deeper, broader, fuller; this was what the Bible called *agape*, or divine love, the perfect love of God expressed through man. He wondered if this was what the prophet experienced when he was thrown into that den of hungry lions. Was it love that stopped the lions from eating Daniel?[38] Love had certainly changed the intent of these hornets. He realized that when love projects, grace takes over.

Bill resumed his work. Just as he finished mowing the backyard, several cars drove up and parked in front of his house. It was time to go inside and pray for more of God's children.

Later, he went to see why his daughters were crying. Entering the kitchen, he found Sarah sprawled on the floor, Rebekah sitting at the table and Meda standing next to the kitchen counter looking down at a sink full of dirty dishes. All three were crying.

Looking at her husband, Meda sobbed, "Bill, I'm going crazy. The children haven't had a bite to eat since breakfast. There have been so many people in our house today I haven't been able to get around the kitchen."

Now Bill knew why his little girls were crying. Not only were they hungry, their mother was creating an atmosphere of nervous

---

[38] Daniel 6:16-23

tension. He knew he could calm them down if he could just create the right kind of atmosphere...

Putting his arms around his wife, Bill said soothingly, "Yes, it's very bad sometimes. But remember, we're serving the Lord Jesus Christ. Think about this morning. Wasn't it wonderful to see that little boy take off those leg braces and walk normal?" In his heart he prayed, "Oh, Lord, help me here. Send Your presence and Your love to my dear wife." He said, "Meda, there probably won't be anybody else come for awhile. Let's get something ready to eat. I'll help you." He rolled up his sleeves and grabbed a dirty frying pan out of the sink.

"Oh, no you don't. You might be able to help me wash dishes, but you can't cook."

He smiled. "Who can't cook? You mean to tell me you've never seen me fry potatoes? I grew up on them."

One side of her mouth cracked into a tiny smile and soon she was herself again, sweet and cheerful. A moment later Rebekah and Sarah stopped crying. The atmosphere had changed.

AMONG his many visitors that summer was Dr. Morris Reedhead, who at that time was the head of the Sudan Missions, one of the largest Baptist missionary organizations in the world. Bill seated Dr. Reedhead in the living room and Meda brought in a pot of tea, which she left on the glass-topped coffee table.

Dr. Reedhead got right to the point of his visit. "Brother Branham, recently I talked to a Moslem boy who had just graduated from college here in America and was going back to his home in India. Not wanting to miss a chance to witness for the Lord, I said to him, 'Why don't you renounce your dead prophet Muhammad and receive the resurrected Jesus?' The young man answered, 'Kind sir, what can your Jesus do for me that my

Muhammad can't?' I said, 'Jesus can give you eternal life.' He answered, 'Muhammad promised me eternal life if I follow the Koran.' I said, 'Jesus can give you joy and peace.' He answered, 'Muhammad has already given me joy and peace. I don't need any more from Jesus.' I said, 'Jesus Christ is alive today. Muhammad has been dead for centuries.' He answered, 'If Jesus is alive, then prove it. Where is He?' I said, 'He's living in my heart.' He answered, 'Muhammad is living in my heart.'

"By this time I was so flustered I didn't know what to say. The young man could see my frustration and said, 'You see, we Muslims can command just as much psychology as you Christians. That is one reason why Islam is the greatest religion in the world today. But I will admit one thing: your Jesus promised you Christians more than our Muhammad promised us. I've read in your Bible where Jesus said he would be with you until the end of the world; and that the works He did, you would do also— casting out devils, raising the dead, healing the sick and the like.[39] Let me see Christians producing those same works and then I'll believe Jesus is alive.'

"I said, 'You are referring to Mark, chapter 16. But some of those verses were added at a later date. They may not be inspired.' He said, 'What kind of book are you following if some of it is inspired, and some of it isn't? All of the Koran is inspired.'

"Mr. Branham, I was dumbfounded. I'm a Christian scholar. I have so many doctorial and honorary degrees, I could plaster your wall with them. But that young Moslem had me, with all my theology, tied up in a knot. I changed the subject. Later, reflecting back on that conversation, I thought about you and I decided to come see you. I want to know—have all my Bible teachers been wrong?'"

---

[39] Matthew 28:20; Mark 16:17-18; John 14:12

"In one sense, yes. Education has its place. But, Dr. Reedhead, eternal life doesn't come by education; it comes by the new birth. Jesus said, *Ye must be born again.*"[40]

"Do you mean that accepting Jesus as Savior is not the same thing as receiving the Holy Ghost?"

"That is what Paul said. He told those Ephesians, *Have ye received the Holy Ghost since ye believed?*[41] See? That is *after* they already accepted Jesus."

"Brother Branham, I'm a Baptist, but I've been in Pentecostal meetings. Is there anything to that Holy Ghost experience they talk about?"

"Dr. Reedhead, there is a lot of falsehood and fanaticism out there. But that doesn't change the fact that there is a genuine Holy Ghost experience for the believer. The Holy Ghost that fell on Pentecost is the same Jesus today, and he gives the same kind of power."[42]

Dr. Reedhead said, "As one Baptist to another Baptist, I want to ask you something: Abraham believed God and it was imputed unto him for righteousness.[43] What more could Abraham do than believe God?"

"That is true," Bill agreed, "but God gave him circumcision as a witness and a confirmation that He had accepted Abraham's faith.[44] No matter how much you profess faith, until God gives you the Holy Spirit—the confirmation, the Seal of God—He has not yet recognized your faith. Ephesians 4:30 says, *Grieve not the Holy Spirit of God, whereby you are sealed until the day of your redemption.*"

---

40   John 3:7
41   Acts 19:2
42   Acts 2
43   Romans 4:3
44   Romans 4:11

Taking a deep breath, Dr. Reedhead asked, "How can I receive the Holy Ghost?"

"The only thing I know, brother, is to lay hands on those seeking the Holy Ghost."

"Would you lay your hands on me and ask God to give me the Holy Ghost?"

"I will."

Dr. Reedhead fell on his knees so fast that his elbows cracked the glass top of the coffee table. Bill didn't mind, because there in his living room he saw that seasoned Bible scholar receive the Holy Spirit of God.

IN AUGUST 1953, William Branham received a phone call from Leroy Kopp, pastor of Calvary Temple in Los Angeles. Reverend Kopp had sponsored several of Bill's campaigns in Los Angeles, including the one in which former Congressman Upshaw had walked without crutches for the first time in 66 years. Now Reverend Kopp wanted permission to make a documentary film about Bill and his ministry, which Kopp would call *Twentieth Century Prophet*. Bill agreed.

So one August morning, two trucks parked in front of Bill's house. A sign on the side of each truck read: Westminster Film Company, Hollywood, California. Bill was surprised at the amount of equipment these men set up inside his home: lights, microphones, a big box-like camera on a tripod stand, and electrical cords snaking over the floor. The producer wanted to paint Meda's face for the film, but Meda had never worn makeup in her life, so she refused.

The film began by showing Leroy and Paul Kopp walking past the impressive stone pillars that bordered the driveway entrance. These pillars had curved stone extensions sweeping back like the wings of an eagle. Next the camera focused on the front of Bill's home, showing the unusual entryway, where one side of the roof extended diagonally twice as far as the other side, making it look like a giant number seven leaning forward.

Bill greeted both men at the door and led them into his parlor. Green flower-print curtains covered the windows, accenting soft green walls. Above a stone fireplace hung an oil painting of the log cabin where Bill was born in 1909. On an end table sat a copy of the Houston, Texas, photograph that showed the angel of the Lord burning like a halo above Bill's head. The Kopp brothers sat on a red leather couch. Across from them, Bill sat in a green cushioned chair. Between them was the same coffee table that Dr. Reedhead had cracked while seeking the baptism of the Holy Ghost. The broken top had been replaced.

Leroy Kopp began the interview by asking Bill about his life and ministry. Although Bill had been a public speaker for 20 years, and was comfortable preaching in front of tens of thousands of people at one time, he was not used to being interviewed in front of a camera. He followed the script stiffly as he described his unusual childhood. He mentioned how, when he was seven years old, an angel spoke to him out of a whirlwind, saying, *"Don't ever drink, or smoke, or defile your body in any way, because there is a work for you to do when you get older."* He described how, in 1946, that same angel met him in human form and gave him a commission to take a gift of divine healing to the world, promising him two signs from God to prove his calling: first, the miracles and healings and, second, revealing the secrets of men's hearts. Bill told how the angel used Bible stories to explain to him his ministry, like the one where Nathanael met Jesus and was surprised that Jesus already knew about him;[45] and the story where Jesus talked to a Samaritan woman by Jacob's well, and knew her

---

[45] John 1:43-50

trouble without her telling him. She said, "'*Sir, I perceive that thou art a prophet... I know that Messias cometh, which is called Christ: when He is come, He will tell us all things'. Jesus saith unto her, 'I that speak unto thee am He.'*" It was only after Jesus revealed this secret hidden in her heart that the Samaritan woman recognized Jesus to be the Christ, the Messiah, the promised Savior of Israel.[46]

At this point the documentary took a curious turn. After an awkward pause, Bill said, "Concerning the campaigns planned for Israel, Brother Kopp, I will be happy to serve our Lord in Israel."

Reverend Kopp added, "Brother Branham, we think many Jews will come to believe that Jesus Christ is the Messiah when they see a Christian fulfilling the Old Testament prophecy in Joel 2:28: how that in the last days the Lord will pour out his Spirit upon all flesh. His sons and daughters would prophesy... and young men will see visions."

"Yes, Brother Kopp, I believe my ministry will be very effective to the Jews, because as the New Testament says, 'The Jews seek signs; the Greeks seek wisdom.'"[47]

These brief comments might seem out of place in this documentary without knowing their background. In 1950 Bill had conducted several meetings in Stockholm, Sweden. Lewi Pethrus, pastor of the largest Pentecostal church in Sweden, was so impressed by the gift of discernment in Bill's ministry, he suggested that Bill should go to Israel and display the power of Jesus Christ to the Jews. Bill considered the idea, but did not pursue it.

Meanwhile, Lewi Pethrus started a missionary outreach to Israel. Over the next two years his church distributed 1,000,000 New Testaments among the Jews in Palestine, concentrating on the new arrivals. For most of these people it was the first time

---

[46] John 4:3-26
[47] 1 Corinthians 1:22

they had read about Jesus. Many Jews told Pethrus, "If Jesus is the Messiah and He is still alive, then let us see Him do the sign of the Messiah and we will believe in Him." Again Lewi Pethrus thought about William Branham.

In the spring of 1953, Pethrus contacted Miner Arganbright, who was vice-president of the men Fellowship International, suggesting that FGBFI sponsor a William Branham faith-healing campaign in Israel, so that modern Jews could see the sign of their Messiah. Together these two men approached Bill with their plan. Miner Arganbright had just returned from Israel, where he had interviewed many incoming Jews as they got off the airplanes. Arganbright had asked one old man, "Are you coming here so you can die in Israel?" The Jew replied, "No, I'm coming here to see the Messiah."

Hearing this story set Bill's heart on fire. He thought, "This will be perfect for my ministry!" Now in August, while Leroy Kopp was filming *Twentieth-Century Prophet*, Pethrus and Arganbright were arranging a Branham campaign in Israel.

After Bill's comments on Israel, the documentary switched to his campaign at the Philadelphia Church in Chicago, August 29 through September 7, 1953. Although the film showed a segment from just one prayer-line, the five people Bill prayed for were representative of the tens of thousands he had prayed for in the past seven years. Two people were accurately diagnosed from the general audience. Then Bill prayed for a woman in the prayer-line without revealing her trouble. The next woman he discerned as anemic. Any skeptic might think he had guessed her problem correctly because she looked so pale. But the last woman's trouble would have been impossible to guess.

A middle-aged woman stood before the evangelist, wringing her hands nervously. Bill looked directly into her eyes and said, "I see you are strictly a stranger to me. You come from another city.

You've got a lot of trouble on your heart. And you've got heart trouble to begin with. Is that right?"

"That's right," she answered.

"There is a lot of blackness around you. I see a black sheet following you. Oh, it's a lie. (She nodded and began to quiver with emotion.) Somebody told a lie on you; and he was a man who professes divine healing. He said you were a witch. Is that true?"

"Yes," she sobbed, nodding as she covered her face with her hands.

"And you've got a stir in your church about it. Isn't that right? Your pastor is sick right now. He's got polio. Is that right?"

"Yes, sir."

"Sister, don't pay any attention to what those people tell you. They're lying. And the only thing wrong with your heart is that nervous condition which has got your heart worked up. Go on home in peace, and God bless you. You're all right. You're not a witch."

While the audience enthusiastically praised the Lord, Bill said, "I trust that God is blessing you to where you can't disbelieve any longer. It would be a sin for you to disbelieve now. After God has sent His Son and has done all these signs... sent His Bible, sent His preachers, sent His gifts... and you still disbelieve Him? ...then there is nothing left for you but to be condemned at the end.

"The only thing this discernment is to do is to glorify God by revealing Jesus Christ, that when He was here on earth He did this very same thing. And He said, 'When I go away, I will come again. A little while and the world will see Me no more (that's the unbelievers), but ye shall see Me (who? the believers), for I will be with you, even in you, to the end of the world.'[48] Then it's a

---
[48] John 14:3, 15-20

sin to disbelieve. 'Go ye and sin no more (or disbelieve no more) or a worse thing will come upon you,' said Jesus.[49] It's believe, or perish.

"But God is patient and merciful. When people don't take His Word, then signs and wonders are added into the Church, as Jesus

William Branham at the time of the filming of
Twentieth Century Prophet

---

[49]   John 5:14; 8:11

Christ promised He would do.[50] And to my honest belief, I believe God is finishing up right now with the Gentiles and will turn to the Jews right away. The Gentiles will be left with their creeds and dogmas and their cold, formal denominations. The real Church will be taken up in the Rapture, and the Gospel will go to the Jews. Amen. Amen means 'so be it.'"

---

[50] John 14:12; Mark 16:15-18

Chapter 64
Anointing for Life
1953

STRANGERS intruding upon his privacy were not the only stresses William Branham had to deal with at home during that summer of 1953. Recently his son had started rebelling against his strict Christian upbringing. Like many teenagers, Billy Paul wanted to live his life without responsibilities or restrictions. Unfortunately this attitude was tempting him down a dangerous path. Bill looked for the right moment to bring the matter up with his son.

One night while Bill was praying, he saw a vision of his son at a booze party, jumping out of a window and tumbling head-over-heels toward the ground, out of control. In terror Bill cried out, "Oh, God, don't let him die! He's the only boy I've got!" The vision ended with an inconclusive snap, jerking Bill alert, his temples dripping sweat. He prayed, "Lord, please don't let my son be killed like that."

Sometime after midnight, Billy Paul tiptoed into the house with the smell of beer on his breath. The next morning Bill let his son sleep as long as he wanted. When Billy Paul got up around ten o'clock, his first thought was to go visit a friend. Bill was washing his car in the driveway when Billy Paul sauntered out the front door. Bill shut off the hose and said, "You got in late last night, didn't you, son. Do you want me to tell you where you were?"

"No, sir," Paul replied. He knew his father could do it.

"You're starting down the wrong road, Paul."

"Dad, I want to see what it's like out there."

"Son, do you believe your daddy loves you?"

"I know you do."

"Good, because what I'm going to tell you, I'm saying in love. I can't have you working in the meetings anymore because it reflects badly on my ministry. Not only that, you can't live like that and still stay here."

"Daddy, I wanted to leave home anyway. I want to see what the world is all about."

"Don't do that, Paul. Sin will take you farther than you want to go, and keep you longer than you want to stay. If you let it, sin will take control of your life; and it could end up costing you far more than you want to pay."

"Daddy, I want to go."

"Before you go, do me a favor. Hold up your arms like this." Bill spread his arms straight away from his sides. Billy Paul did as his father asked. Bill said, "Now turn around and look on the wall behind you. Your shadow is forming a cross. Two roads intersect at the center of that cross: one road leads to heaven; the other leads to hell. You can't walk both roads at the same time. Today you are standing at that crossroad. I can tell you what is right, but you've got to make the choice yourself. But if you start down the wrong road, somewhere along the road God is going to turn you around, because I claim you under the token.[51] It might be a rough road back; but it's your decision."

---

[51] Exodus 12:13

Billy Paul chose the wrong road.

Several days later Dr. Pilai, the archbishop of the Presbyterian church in India, stopped by Bill's house to try to persuade him to hold a Christian faith-healing campaign in India. Bill and Meda were getting ready to take their girls to a dentist in New Albany, so Bill asked the archbishop to come along. While Meda took Rebekah and Sarah into the dentist office, Bill and Dr. Pilai sat in the car, discussing the archbishop's proposal. Suddenly Bill felt impressed to get out of the car. He ignored the feeling. Presently he heard a voice whisper, "*Get out of the car immediately.*" Now he knew the Lord wanted to speak to him alone. Excusing himself, Bill got out and walked down the street. Soon the angel of the Lord said, "*Return home as fast as you can. Billy Paul is in trouble.*"

Arriving home, Bill found his mother-in-law standing on the front porch, sobbing hysterically, "Billy Paul is in the hospital, dying." Bill calmed her down enough to get the story. Billy Paul had been staying with her. Yesterday he went fishing and fell in the lake. This morning he complained about a sore throat, so Mrs. Broy urged him to go see Dr. Adair. The doctor gave him a shot of penicillin, not knowing until it was too late that Billy Paul was violently allergic to penicillin. Shortly after the antibiotic entered his bloodstream, his heart stopped. Dr. Adair revived him with a shot of adrenalin, but his allergic reaction continued. An ambulance rushed Paul to the hospital where doctors were now struggling to keep him alive.

When Bill reached the hospital, he ran toward the emergency room and met Dr. Adair in the hallway. Dr. Adair said, "I didn't know he'd be allergic to penicillin. I've given it to him before and he didn't have a reaction. But this time he did. We've given him three shots of adrenalin, but his pulse keeps dropping. I'm sorry, Bill; I may have killed your boy."

"Doc, you're my friend. I know you've done your best to save him. Can I see him?"

"We've got a tube in him, and he's unconscious, but go ahead."

Bill walked into the emergency room and shut the door. Billy Paul lay on his back with a plastic tube threaded into his nose. His body was swollen and his skin looked a deathly blue, except the skin around his eyes, which was black; his jaw hung slack, leaving his mouth wide open. Life-support machines gurgled and whirred softly in the background.

Dropping to his knees, Bill prayed desperately, "Dear God, as far as medical science is concerned, my son is gone; but I am asking You to be merciful and don't let him go."

Minutes passed, and then he saw the same vision he had seen a few days earlier, only this time with a twist. He saw Billy Paul jumping out that window, saw him tumbling head-over-heels through the air; but this time he saw two strong arms reach out, catch him, and lift him back up to the window. Then he heard Billy Paul say, "Daddy, where am I?" That was not part of the vision.

Bill rose from his knees and stood beside the bed. "You're in the hospital, Paul. Don't worry. Everything is all right now."

A few minutes later Bill called for the nurse. Billy Paul wanted the tube taken out of his nose. When the nurse checked the boy's pulse, she found it was normal.

Unfortunately this brush with death did not cause Billy Paul to repent. After his release from the hospital, he slipped right back into his wrong-headed ways—frequenting pool halls, drinking, smoking, playing poker, and gambling. It would take a much stronger lesson to show him the right road. That lesson was not long in coming.

On September 13, 1953, Billy Paul turned 18. In October Bill took his family to Colorado for a vacation. Since Billy Paul was living on his own and not keeping in touch with his parents, neither Bill nor Meda knew their son was having health problems when they left on their trip. Paul was bleeding inside. He ignored his symptoms for as long as he dared, going to see a doctor only after the pain in his stomach doubled him over. Immediately Dr. Brenner admitted him to a hospital.

Billy Paul's condition was critical. He had developed intestinal ulcers, possibly caused by the alcohol he had been drinking so heavily. The bleeding alone posed a serious threat to his health. Even worse, scar tissue had formed over one ulcer, blocking his intestines, cutting off circulation and killing cell tissue. Gangrene had set in. Dr. Brenner warned him of the danger, advising him that a colostomy needed to be done soon or he would die.

Billy Paul stalled. He wanted desperately to get a message to his father, thinking that if only his father could pray for him, then everything would be all right. He had seen it happen in his father's faith-healing campaigns and at home—miracle after miracle, hundreds upon hundreds of times. Why couldn't it happen to him? Surely it *would* happen if only his father was there to pray. But no one knew exactly where his father was or when he would return. After a delay of several days, Dr. Brenner insisted that the operation could not safely be postponed any longer. Paul's life was at stake. Reluctantly, Mrs. Broy signed permission for Dr. Brenner to operate on her grandson.

The next morning as Billy Paul waited nervously for his operation, he lamented his fate. Within an hour Dr. Brenner was going to remove part of his lower intestine and feed the loose end out through a hole in his abdomen into a plastic bag. For the rest of his life he would be doomed to wear that plastic bag. He thought about what his father had told him: "Sin will end up costing you far more than you want to pay." Oh, why had he turned his back on the Lord Jesus Christ?

He felt a hand on his shoulder and heard his father's voice. "Hi, Paul."

Relief swept over him. "Daddy, I've been trying so hard to reach you. Where have you been?"

"I was vacationing with the family in Colorado. Paul, remember that night in Vandalia, Illinois, when God let you see His angel?"

Billy Paul recalled the swirling wisp of fire that he had seen form into a man. The angel had stood in the corner of their hotel room with his arms folded across his chest. How well he remembered that face, so stern and powerful. "I could never forget that night, Daddy."

"That same angel met me in the Colorado Rockies and said, '*Go to Billy right away. He's in trouble.*' Son, the way of a transgressor is hard."

"Pray for me, Daddy."

Bill shook his head. "Not yet, son. I didn't do the sinning; you did. First you need to ask God to forgive you. If you're ready to make Jesus Christ your Lord, I believe He will heal you."

There in his hospital bed, Billy Paul turned around, went back to the center of that crossroad, and this time he chose the right road, the one that leads to eternal life. Then his father prayed for his healing.

When Dr. Brenner came in to see his patient before the operation, Bill asked him to examine Paul one more time. After numerous tests, Dr. Brenner said, "Reverend Branham, I don't understand it. Your son has quit bleeding and I can't find any trace of gangrenous infection. It's like a miracle happened."

"And you don't know the best part," Bill said. "Paul had left the Lord Jesus Christ, but today he came back. That is the greatest miracle of all."

IN NOVEMBER OF 1953, William Branham held a nine-day faith-healing campaign in Owensboro, Kentucky; then on November 29 he started a long campaign in Palm Beach, Florida. While he was in Palm Beach, Gordon Lindsay called to ask him if he would speak at the Voice of Healing convention in Chicago on Friday night, December 11. Bill had planned on being in Palm Beach until December 15, but because last summer he had promised Lindsay (and also Joseph Mattsson-Boze) that he would speak in Chicago at the Voice of Healing convention, he agreed to cut his Florida meetings short. As soon as he finished talking with Lindsay, he called Mattsson-Boze to let his friend know the day he would be in Chicago. Since he would only be speaking one night at the convention, Mattsson-Boze asked if he would preach Saturday night and Sunday morning at the Philadelphia Church in Chicago. Bill said he would be glad to do it.

He finished in West Palm Beach on the evening of December 6. That same night he and Billy Paul (who was again helping him in his campaigns) left for home. Taking turns, they drove straight through the night and the next day, arriving home around three o'clock the following morning. As Bill was getting ready for bed, the angel of the Lord entered his bedroom and said, "*Something is wrong in Chicago.*"

Bill asked, "Is it in the Philadelphia Church?"

"*No,*" said the angel as he opened a vision. Bill saw Gordon Lindsay, editor of *The Voice of Healing* magazine, turn to another man and say, "Go tell Brother Branham that. But don't let him know I had anything to do with it." When the vision faded, the angel said, "*That man is going to confront you at the convention and take you out of the meeting.*"

The angel vanished before Bill could ask another question, leaving him wondering what it meant.

On December 11, 1953, Bill arrived at the Voice of Healing convention 45 minutes before his time to speak. A man named Velmer Gardner met him at the door, took him by the arm, and hurried him through the lobby into a side room. Gardner seemed eager to shut the door. Soon another man came in and introduced himself as Reverend Hall from *The Voice of Healing* magazine. Bill recognized Mr. Hall as the man who Gordon Lindsay had talked to in the vision.

Gravely Reverend Hall said, "Brother Branham, we hear you are planning to speak at the Philadelphia Church tomorrow night and Sunday. The Voice of Healing has decided that if you preach for Joseph Mattsson-Boze, then we won't permit you to speak tonight at this convention."

"What is wrong with preaching for Brother Boze?"

"Well, some of the churches in Chicago don't like him. And to keep unity at our convention here, we just made this decision."

"Who do you mean by 'we'?"

"The board of directors at The Voice of Healing. Gordon Lindsay didn't have anything to do with it."

Bill knew better. Now he could see what this was all about. The whole thing stank of politics—The Voice of Healing organization and some Chicago churches were trying to pressure him into conforming to their ideas. If he had not weathered that storm in South Africa, he might have buckled under this pressure now. He remembered what the angel told him the night he was healed of amebas: "*Do just as you feel led.*"

"Way last summer I promised Brother Boze I would hold at least one meeting for him during the time of this convention and I'm going to keep my promise."

"Then you can't speak tonight."

"Fine with me. I'll just go in and listen to the service."

Getting up, Bill opened the door. Before he got two steps away from that room, Gardner and Hall caught his arms and hustled him through the lobby toward an exit. The doors to the convention hall were open and Bill heard someone announce, "We're sorry to say Brother Branham will not be speaking tonight. He has a brother who is sick, and so he couldn't come."

How cleverly stated, because it was partly true. Bill's brother Howard *was* sick. Not long ago the Lord had shown Bill a vision of their father, Charles, descending from heaven and marking out the grave where Howard would be buried. But Bill didn't know *when* his brother would die, nor had Howard's illness influenced this trip to Chicago in any way.

It was another lesson in how strongly church politics could affect his ministry, regardless of how hard he tried to stay above it. And he had tried. Not only were all of his meetings interdenominational, he purposely kept his preaching simple to avoid offending the many different denominational ministers who supported his campaigns. He always preached on salvation and healing through the death, burial, and resurrection of Jesus Christ—themes which most Christians could at least come close to agreeing on. Whenever he had a burden to preach something beyond this, he did it at his home church in Jeffersonville, Indiana. But in an international ministry like his, because it was impossible to please everyone, it was also hard to avoid the pitfalls of church politics. His experience at this Voice of Healing convention made that painfully clear.

AS SOON AS William Branham got home from Chicago, he learned that George Wright was dying. Without even taking time to unpack, Bill got in his car and headed for Milltown. George Wright had been his friend since the early days of his ministry. Over the years Bill had spent many pleasant hours on the Wright's farm, tramping over the wooded hills hunting squirrels and rabbits. They had enjoyed many good meals together and discussed many Bible questions around the Wright's kitchen table. Together they had shared many adventures. George had even accompanied Bill on the night Georgie Carter was healed from tuberculosis after spending nine years in bed. By the time Bill turned down the familiar country road leading to the Wright's farm, he was misty inside with nostalgia.

George Wright was so glad to see Bill that he tried to talk too fast and went into a fit of coughing, spitting up blood. When his voice returned, he said slowly, "Oh, Brother Branham, we tried to reach you in Chicago. Did you get our telegram?"

"No, Brother George. It never got to me. What is your condition?"

"Blood clots started in my legs, then lodged in my knees. A specialist came out from Louisville to examine me. He said I've only got three or four more days to live. He said that when those clots dislodge, they'll either go to my brain and paralyze me, or else they'll go to my heart and kill me outright."

Falling across the bed, Bill begged God to let George live. He stayed at the Wright's farm several more days, continuing to pray for his old friend. Early each morning he shouldered his shotgun and trudged up the snowy, wooded hill behind the house, hunting for rabbits. On the third morning, coming back down the hill, Bill counted ten cars parked in the yard. He knew what it meant. The public had discovered he was here and people were coming for prayer. In all good conscience he couldn't stay at the Wright's farm any longer. Mrs. Wright did not need a gaggle of strangers around her door at a stressful time like this.

While he was packing his clothes, Meda called him on the telephone. "Bill, you need to come home right away. Remember Mrs. Baker—that Jewish widow who does Christian missionary work here in town? She wants you to pray for her daughter."

Bill didn't know Mrs. Baker personally, although he knew her by reputation because she was often mentioned in their local newspaper. She was a Jew who had converted to Christianity, attended Moody Bible Institute of Chicago, graduated with honors, and then moved to Louisville, Kentucky. For many years she had been an active missionary among the Jewish population in her area. Although Bill didn't know Mrs. Baker, he did know her daughter, Ruth. A few years earlier Ruth gave birth to a boy with clubbed feet. Bill had prayed for this deformed baby and Jesus Christ had healed the little boy completely.

"I was just planning on leaving here anyway," Bill said. "What is the matter with Ruth?"

"She just had another baby and some complications developed. Mrs. Baker called it septicemia. I guess that means blood poisoning. The baby is all right, but Ruth is in critical condition. She's over in the Baptist hospital."

"I'll stop by there before I come home," Bill said.

Shelby Wright, George's 40-year-old son, carried Bill's suitcase out to his car, which was parked by a giant willow tree in the front yard. Shelby said, "Brother Branham, I know you've been trying to give Mom hope; but what do you really think about Dad? Is he going to die?"

"Yes, Shelby, I believe your daddy is going to die. He's 72 years old. God only promised him 70 years.[52] I've asked God to spare

---

[52] Psalms 90:10

him, but God hasn't answered me a word about it. George is a Christian, so he's ready to go. I suppose God is going to take him home now."

"Oh, I know Dad is ready to go. But you know what bothers me the most? For years Dad has testified to everyone around Milltown that God is a healer. Now some of those people are mocking him, saying if God is such a healer, why doesn't He just dissolve those blood clots? And the man who is laughing the loudest is the Church of Christ minister."

That afternoon Bill stopped at the Baptist hospital. Mrs. Baker was standing in the hall outside her daughter's room, fussing with another woman and a Catholic priest. As Bill walked up, the other woman said to Mrs. Baker, "But she's my daughter-in-law and I don't want her to go to hell. I want my priest to anoint her for death."

"Just a moment," Bill interposed. "You should let me go in first. I'm Brother Branham and I've come here to anoint Ruth for life." This statement really sent Ruth's mother-in-law into a tizzy. Bill suggested, "Why don't you let her husband decide?"

Ruth's husband, a man in his twenties, definitely preferred Bill to go in first and anoint his wife for life. Grumbling, the mother-in-law stepped aside to let Bill pass.

Ruth was lying in a coma, her soul fluttering between life and death. Bill knelt by her bed and spent ten minutes asking Jesus Christ to be merciful and let her live. Finally he stood up, wiped a tear from his eye, and picked up his hat and coat. Before he could leave, he saw the Pillar of Fire appeared over Ruth's bed. Instantly the light drew him into a vision. Bill saw Ruth standing in a kitchen, stirring a pot of soup. She looked down at a rambunctious little boy running around the room. Putting one finger up to her lips, she said, "Shhhh. The baby is sleeping." Then the vision left him.

Smiling with confidence, Bill strode out into the hallway. There stood Ruth's husband, the doctor, the priest, and the two grandmothers, all in a group. Bill said to Ruth's husband, "I have some good news for you, son. Thus saith the Lord, 'Ruth is going to be all right.' Tonight she is going to get worse; but in the morning she'll start getting better. Within 36 hours she'll be well enough to go home. If she isn't, then I'm a false prophet."

While Mrs. Baker and her son-in-law rejoiced, the priest looked quizzically at the doctor, who shook his head and walked away. Scowling, Ruth's mother-in-law snapped, "Son, haven't we had about enough of this nonsense? It's time for the priest to anoint her for death."

The young man stood in the doorway and wouldn't let that priest go into Ruth's room. Finally the priest left. When Ruth's mother-in-law started scolding her son, he cut her off, saying, "Mother, do you remember when your first grandson was born with clubbed feet? I took him over to Brother Branham's house for prayer. Brother Branham saw a vision and said that within 24 hours our boy's feet would straighten out. The next morning we ran to his crib and it was just the way Brother Branham said it would be. So, if Brother Branham says, 'thus saith the Lord, in 36 hours Ruth is going home... well then, good-bye; I'm going home to get the house ready for her."

As Bill was leaving the hospital, Charlie McDowell met him on the front steps and begged him to ride with him over to Frankfurt, Kentucky, and pray for his mother. Doctors had just operated on the 61-year-old woman for cancer. They found her body so full of malignancy they didn't even bother sewing her back up; they just taped the incision closed, because she would be dead in a few hours anyway.

It was late at night when Charlie McDowell and Bill got to Frankfort. At the hospital Bill simply laid his hands on Mrs.

McDowell and asked for her healing in the name of Jesus Christ. Then he left, getting home around five o'clock in the morning. Several strangers were sleeping on his doorstep, waiting for him. Obligingly he prayed for each one, then dropped into bed exhausted.

A few hours later sunlight woke him up. It was nine o'clock, Monday morning, December 28, 1953. Slipping his bathrobe over his pajamas, he walked down the hall toward the bathroom. When he passed by the doorway to the living room, he was surprised to see an attractive young woman standing there. He said, "Good morning, ma'am. What are you doing in here?"

She didn't speak to him. Instead she turned her head and spoke to someone in the kitchen. Bill looked to see who it was. That is when he realized this was a vision, because the kitchen he saw was not *his* kitchen. Mrs. McDowell stood there, leaning against some kitchen cabinets, talking on the telephone. Bill thought to himself, "That's the woman I prayed for last night."

Just then he heard an unusual noise behind him. Puzzled, he turned to see what it could be. There stood a weeping willow tree. Yellow clods of clay were falling from the sky, making a *plop-plop* sound as they filled a large, rectangular hole at the base of the tree. There was something about those willow branches that looked familiar. Yes, it was the willow tree that stood by George Wright's house. He heard the angel of the Lord say something about 'graves,' but he didn't catch what it was, so he asked God to repeat the vision. Suddenly he was standing behind the pulpit of his church in Jeffersonville. George Wright came in the main door, walked down the aisle, and shook Bill's hand. The angel said, "*Thus saith the Lord, George Wright will dig the graves of those who are laughing at him.*" Now Bill understood that George was going to be all right.

After breakfast, he called Charlie McDowell to tell him his mother would be coming home from the hospital. Then he called the Wrights.

Shelby answered the phone. "Brother Branham, Dad is almost paralyzed this morning."

"It doesn't matter. He is going to be all right. Go tell your daddy I have 'thus saith the Lord' for him. He is going to dig the graves of those people who are laughing at him."

"Brother Branham, did you know that my dad sometimes works at the cemetery as a grave digger?"

"No, Shelby, I didn't know that." But now that he did know, the vision made more sense.

Detail by detail, the visions became reality. Mrs. McDowell felt better immediately. Her doctor examined her again and was shocked when he could not find any cancer. In fact her case baffled the entire hospital staff. A week after she was prayed for, she went home and resumed her normal chores. Every day she enjoyed a long telephone conversation with her daughter, just like Bill had seen her doing in that vision.

Two days after Bill told George Wright 'thus said the Lord,' the blood clots in his knees dissolved harmlessly. After that, he quickly recovered his health. One Sunday morning he opened the door of Branham Tabernacle, walked down the aisle to the front and shook Bill's hand, just like Bill had seen him do in the vision. Concerning those who had mocked him during his illness because he had testified that Jesus Christ is a healer, within a year he saw five of them buried, including the Church-of-Christ minister. George Wright lived well into his nineties.

As for the young mother dying from septicemia, the next morning her blood tested free from toxins. The following morning she took her newborn baby home from the hospital. Mrs. Baker sang for joy. In her missionary work, she zealously testified how Jesus Christ had healed her daughter. Soon the Christian organization that sponsored her withdrew its financial support. An officer of the organization explained, "We don't have anything against William Branham, but neither do we want our program entangled in the controversy surrounding divine healing."

When Bill heard this, he said, "Then they are out of God's program. Signs and wonders will always vindicate God's program. As long as there is a world, there will be a supernatural God here to control things, and He will always have somebody He can put His hands on. Tonight He's got a church all around the world. His church has a lot of things about it that's got to be ironed out. I can't iron them out; no man can. That is God's business. He will take care of it. No matter how many manmade programs raise up, every one of them will fall. God Himself will set up His program. As far as I know, His program is for people to be baptized into Jesus Christ and be led by the Holy Spirit, free from condemnation."

Chapter 65
Called Out of Egypt
1954

WILLIAM BRANHAM was planning to go overseas again on February 23, 1954. However, by the first of January, his managers had still not secured his itinerary. Campaigns in Israel and India looked certain, but South Africa remained questionable. Some members of the National Committee seemed to be dragging their feet. Then in January something startling happened that made Bill change his plans.

One day a carload of people showed up at his house wanting prayer. He settled them in the living room, then went to get something and saw another man standing in the doorway. At first he assumed it was someone from this same group, someone who had just been slower in getting out of the car. What puzzled him was the peculiar way this man was dressed. He looked like the East Indian Sikhs Bill had seen in Durban, South Africa. His black hair and dark complexion contrasted sharply with the white turban wrapped around his head.

The man was standing in the doorway with his head bowed. Bill walked over and greeted him cordially, "How do you do, sir"

Raising his head, the East Indian said, "Brother Branham, don't go overseas until September."

That was an unexpected response. Bill didn't know what to say. He turned and motioned with his hand, saying, "Won't you come in?" When he looked back, the man was gone. He had simply vanished! Bill stood in the doorway, stunned.

More cars followed the first, and it was midnight before he finished praying for people that day. He went to bed around one o'clock, but a few hours later he awoke, having dreamed that he should not go to India until September. He roused Meda and told her his dream; then he went back to sleep and dreamed the same thing again. The next morning he called one of his managers and told him to reschedule his foreign campaigns for September in accordance with the vision and the dreams.

Since his trips to Africa, the Middle East, and Asia were now postponed, his managers proceeded to fill his schedule with campaigns across North America. In the first three months of 1954, Bill held meetings in Wood River, Illinois; Hot Springs, Arkansas; and Shreveport, Louisiana. After these, he held an eight-day campaign in Phoenix, Arizona. Then he moved on to Carlsbad, New Mexico, before returning east to Columbus, Ohio, where he held a huge meeting at the coliseum (a meeting that included the cooperation of 400 ministers and their congregations.) At the end of March he returned home to hold meetings in Louisville, Kentucky, and Jeffersonville, Indiana.

In April Bill took some time off from his work, but as usual that didn't guarantee him any rest. Sick and needy people sought him out at all hours of the day. One busy Saturday afternoon, when the number of visitors thinned to just a few, Bill said to Meda, "If anybody else calls, tell them to just go to church in the morning and I'll pray for them there. I'm getting so tired, honey, I can't hold myself together."

After the remaining visitors left, Bill took Meda for a drive in the car. He had no destination in mind; he just wanted to get away from the house so he could relax for awhile. He drove south of New Albany along a scenic highway that wound around and over the top of some hills. The modest elevation provided a pleasant view of the surrounding countryside, showing a mix between cornfields and woodlands. Eventually they came to a place where the road curved along the top edge of a cliff.

As he maneuvered his car into the first turn, he saw the angel of the Lord like a white fog before his eyes. The windshield turned completely white. For three or four miles he blindly guided his car around every turn while his eyes watched something happen 8,000 miles away, literally. Meda kept talking to him as she watched the beautiful scenery beyond the cliffs. After a few minutes she glanced at her husband to see why he wasn't answering her. The instant she saw his glassy stare, she knew he was lost in a vision. "Bill!" she gasped.

Snapping back to consciousness, Bill brought his car to a stop on the side of the road. "Sweetheart, I have to pray for Brother Bosworth right now. I saw him get off a train in South Africa and collapse. I saw them pick him up and put him on a stretcher. He's in a hospital now, seriously ill. I must pray for him at once." Walking a short distance up the wooded hillside, he knelt and prayed.

The next night after church, one of the four phones in his house rang. Bill answered. A Louisville operator for Western Union said, "Mr. Branham, I have a telegram for you from Durban, South Africa. It's from Dr. Yeager. He says, 'Pray for Reverend Bosworth at once. Stricken after stepping off train. Hospitalized. Expected to die.'"

By the time Bill got a telephone call through to Durban on Monday, Fred Bosworth was not only healed, he had already left the hospital to continue his work.

For over a month now Bosworth had been traveling through South Africa, trying to arrange more Branham campaigns in the country. So far it was like trying to put a scratch in a diamond. Most Christians in South Africa wanted William Branham to return and hold more healing campaigns, but many of the church leaders did not. The National Committee of South African Churches had the final say on the matter. Certain powerful members of the National Committee argued that Branham's high-profile ministry undermined the influence of poor local pastors. To an old veteran evangelist like Bosworth, this smelled like a rotten excuse used to hide their jealousy.

After weeks of debate, the National Committee finally denied William Branham's request for a visa. Once again his ministry was hampered by church politics. Nor would it be the last time.

IN SEPTEMBER 1954 William Branham began his third trip overseas by flying from New York City to Lisbon, Portugal, where Baron Von Blomberg was waiting for him. Baron Von Blomberg was a German aristocrat, well educated, and well traveled (he spoke seven languages). In 1950 Von Blomberg met Bill in Finland and was impressed by the supernatural power of Christ so visibly displayed in Bill's ministry. Since the Baron had connections all over the world, including monarchs and other political leaders, Von Blomberg offered to set up Bill's itinerary on this trip. After Portugal Bill was scheduled to visit Italy, Egypt, and Israel; then he would fly to Arabia, and finally, India.

In Lisbon, Von Blomberg had arranged for Bill to dine with the President and members of his cabinet. Beyond this, the Baron had not been able to arrange a campaign in Portugal, because the Roman Catholic Church used its political clout to prevent him from securing any large auditoriums. Bill had to settle for two meetings at a Pentecostal church in the foothills on the edge of the city. But those two meetings glowed with miracles, setting the tone for the rest of this foreign tour.

Leaving Portugal, Bill, Billy Paul, and Baron Von Blomberg flew on to Italy. While in Rome, Bill visited the underground dungeon where the apostle Paul had been imprisoned for his faith. Gazing into a cold, dismal prison cell, Bill's heart swelled with love for Paul, that gallant messenger who took the Gospel to the Gentiles. Rejected by the world, even misunderstood by many Christians of his day, yet through all his years of struggle he never faltered or turned away from his commission. Paul knew he was carrying the greatest treasure on earth: the good news that Jesus Christ rose from the dead to give eternal life to all those who would believe in Him, both Jews *and* Gentiles. Because Paul stood firm in his calling, every Christian down through the centuries had benefited. That struck Bill as a powerful lesson he could apply in his own ministry.

On his second day in Rome, he was scheduled to meet the Pope at three o'clock in the afternoon. Baron Von Blomberg told him how he must act—how he must kneel on one knee; then the Pope would extend his hand and Bill must kiss the Pope's ring and address him as "His Holiness" or "Holy Father."

Bill shook his head. "That's out. Cancel the audience. I'll call any man Reverend, or Doctor or any other title he wants, but not Holy Father. Jesus said, 'Call no man Father but God.'[53] When it comes to worship, there is only one man I will worship and that is Jesus Christ."

So instead of seeing the Pope, Bill toured the Pope's home. Vatican City is a unique independent state situated in the heart of Rome. Although it occupies only 0.15 square miles, it is the center of government for the Roman Catholic Church, and its influence touches every country on earth. Bill was amazed at the

---

[53] Matthew 23:9

rich splendor of St. Peter's Basilica, the Vatican Gardens, and the Palace of His Holy Office. The wealth contained in these buildings was astonishing. Visiting the Vatican museum, he saw a magnificent triple-decked crown, representing the Pope's jurisdiction over heaven, purgatory, and hell. A Latin inscription read VICARIUS FILII DEI, meaning *Vicar of Christ,* or *in place of the Son of God.* What a contrast between the riches of Vatican City and the dingy prison cell not far away where Paul the apostle spent the last years of his life. It was a striking lesson that wealth did not mean truth. Bill thought, "The Gospel doesn't glitter, it glows."

In a park not far from the Vatican City, a Christian evangelist was holding revival meetings in a large tent. Bill wandered over to see what was going on. After Bill introduced himself, the local evangelist graciously stepped aside, turning his service over to the world-famous American. There in the City, Bill preached the Word of God and prayed for the sick. God supplied the miracles.

FROM ROME Bill flew to Cairo, Egypt, where he spent one day sightseeing, visiting the Sphinx and the pyramids, and seeing for himself that the Great Pyramid was missing its capstone. To him this seemed symbolic because the Bible spoke of Jesus Christ being *the* Capstone—or as the King James Version put it, 'the head of the corner.'[54] There is only one structure where the cornerstone and the headstone are both the same shape, and that is a pyramid. Bill believed that sometime in the mist of ancient history God had allowed this massive structure to be built as a testimony to His great plan, and that soon the real Headstone would set Himself at long last in His proper place.

That evening he dined with Egypt's King Farouk. The next morning, as Bill waited in Cairo's international airport for the

---
[54]   Psalms 118:22, Matthew 21:42, Luke 20:17, Acts 4:11, 1 Peter 2:7

plane that would take him to Jerusalem, his excitement grew stronger. Soon he would be standing in Israel, land of the Bible prophets, birthplace of Jesus, home of the blinded Jews, many of whom were still looking for their Messiah. A meeting was scheduled in Jerusalem for that very afternoon. Although most Jews discounted Christianity as false, because of the unusual nature of Bill's ministry, Lewi Pethrus still expected around 5,000 Israelis to attend. Advertisements posted around Jerusalem suggested a connection between his "gift of discernment" and the "sign of their Messiah."

Bill believed it was the perfect environment for his ministry. Devout Jews reverenced their prophets. Imbedded in the Mosaic laws were the two qualifications of a true prophet: first, he would see visions; and second, his accuracy would be 100%.[55] Bill imagined what it would be like when he called a prayer-line in Jerusalem and the discernment began. Surely those Jews would recognize the sign of their own Messiah? He imagined the whole audience receiving the baptism of the Holy Ghost, just like those 120 disciples did on the day of Pentecost.[56] If that did happen, the Gentile age would be over. Jesus said, *"Jerusalem shall be trodden down of the Gentiles, until the times of the Gentiles be fulfilled."*[57] As soon as Israel as a nation accepts the Gospel of Jesus Christ, the Gentile Bride of Christ will be caught away with her Bridegroom, while the rest of the world plunges into the agony of a great tribulation. The Jews will then have 3½ years to preach the Gospel of Christ before the last great battle. According to the book of Revelation, when the dust settles on the battlefield of Armageddon, the sun will rise on a millennium of peace and perfection.[58] Bill could scarcely contain his excitement. This

---

[55] Numbers 12:6 and Deuteronomy 18:15-22
[56] Acts 2
[57] Luke 21:24
[58] Revelation 16:16; 20:1-3

afternoon he might be preaching the most important sermon of his life.

The plane had landed, but he still had thirty minutes until it was time to board, so he walked over to a gift shop. Picking up a small elephant carved out of ebony, he considered buying it as a present for Doctor Adair. The elephant's miniature tusks appeared to be carved out of real ivory. Suddenly he heard someone say, *"Don't go."*

Bill looked around, but no one was paying any attention to him. "Maybe I imagined it," he thought, and he started for the purchase counter. Then he heard it again, distinctly, saying, *"Don't go. This is not the hour."*

There could be no mistaking the angel's voice, but Bill could hardly believe what he was hearing. The meetings were set. The plane was waiting. What did it mean? He put the carved elephant back on its shelf. Leaving the crowded passenger terminal, he walked behind an airplane hangar so he could be alone. There he prayed, "Heavenly Father, in just a few more hours I'll be in Palestine standing in front of your blinded children. I'll challenge those Jews to believe the sign of their Messiah. When they recognize that it is You doing the discerning, they will receive the baptism of the Holy Spirit just as sure as anything. Isn't that what you want?"

The angel of the Lord appeared, suspended in the desert air like a spot of bright, white fog. Bill shrank back against the hangar. The Holy Spirit said, *"Stay out of Palestine. This is not your place. This is not the hour. The cup of iniquity of the Gentiles is not yet full. There is still more gleaning to do."*

That spot of bright fog evaporated into the stifling desert heat, leaving Bill gasping. What should he do now? It would not be easy to cancel his campaign in Israel on such short notice. He might even kindle some bitter feelings among those who had worked so hard to get him into Palestine. But his painful lesson in South Africa could not be forgotten. He was determined to do whatever the Holy Spirit told him to do, regardless of the consequences.

Returning to the terminal, he changed his ticket from Jerusalem, Israel, to Athens, Greece. That left Baron Von Blomberg saddled with the unpleasant task of flying on to Jerusalem and canceling today's meeting. The Baron would link back up with him in Saudi Arabia, where Bill was scheduled to dine with the king of Arabia.

In Greece Bill visited the ruined temple of Ares, Greek god of thunder and war (known to the Romans as Mars), where Paul the apostle had preached the Gospel to those ancient Athenians.[59] That night in his hotel room, Bill studied his Bible, trying to make sense out of what the Lord had told him in Egypt. He thought he had understood his ministry before this. Apparently he had missed something. But what had he missed?

The Holy Spirit said, *"Stay out of Palestine. This is not your place."* So he had been wrong to think he could show modern Israel the sign of their Messiah. It was an honest mistake. In 1933 the Lord told him, *"As John the Baptist was sent to forerun the first coming of Jesus Christ, so are you sent with a message to forerun His second coming."* John the Baptist introduced Jesus to the Jews. Then Jesus vindicated Himself by producing the sign of the Messiah: knowing the past (and future) of people he had never met before, and revealing their secret thoughts.[60]

For the past five years Bill had been demonstrating the sign of the Messiah in his meetings. When the anointing came down and the visions occurred, he could discern the past, the future, and the secret thoughts in the minds of people. This discernment was always perfect because he wasn't doing it; Jesus Christ gave

[59] Acts 17:22
[60] Matthew 12:25, 21:1-7; Mark 14:12-16; Luke 2:34-35, 6:8; John 1:5, 2:24-25, 5:19, 10:37; Hebrews 13:8.

each vision and did every miracle. Bill was like a microphone plugged into an electric amplifier. A microphone is silent until somebody speaks into it. God was speaking, and His Holy Spirit was amplifying this gift of discernment until Christians could hear it all around the world. Because the Lord had told Bill that his ministry would parallel John the Baptist's ministry, it had seemed only logical that he should go to Israel and demonstrate this sign of the Messiah to the Jews.

Now Bill could see he had overlooked one simple fact. The Bible doesn't talk about two comings of Jesus Christ; it talks about three. The first coming happened nearly 2,000 years ago. Around the year AD 30, John the Baptist introduced Jesus to the Jews as their Messiah, their Savior. When Israel rejected Jesus and crucified Him, that gave the rest of the world (the Gentiles) an opportunity to be saved.[61] Jesus promised He would come again, this time to the Gentile church, revealing Himself and catching up His Gentile Bride in what is known among Christians as the Rapture.[62] The Bible says Jesus will come this second time like a thief in the night.[63] When it happens, no one will know about it except His Bride. After this, Jesus will return once more to the Jews. His third coming will startle the world, *"and every eye shall see him, and they also which pierced him."*[64] This time the Jews will receive Jesus as their Messiah.

So, if it wasn't Bill's place to introduce the Messiah to modern Israel, where was his place? He searched the Scriptures for an answer. The key seemed to be in Luke 1:17, in the fact that Elijah's spirit motivated John the Baptist. The "spirit of Elijah" was really the Holy Spirit acting through a personality like Elijah's. God needed John to have the spirit of Elijah in order for John to accomplish the difficult tasks his ministry required of him. Bill

---

61   Romans 11:11,15,25,30
62   1 Corinthians 15:51-54; 1 Thessalonians 4:15-17
63   Matthew 24:42-44; 1 Thessalonians 5:2; 2 Peter 3:9-10
64   Revelation 1:7

turned back to 1 Kings 17 and read again about Elijah, so he could compare Elijah's life and ministry with that of John's.

In 2 Kings chapter 2 he read the story about Elijah's last day on earth. God appeared as a burning fire and caught Elijah away in a whirlwind while Elisha, who was Elijah's apprentice, watched. At that moment a double portion of Elijah's spirit fell on Elisha, who promptly picked up Elijah's cloak, struck it on the Jordan River, and cried out, "Where is the God of Elijah?" The river separated and Elisha walked to the other side on dry ground. Right there God showed mankind that the spirit which inspired Elijah could be transferred to another prophet. In Elisha's lifetime he performed exactly twice the number of miracles that Elijah did, proving that he did indeed have a double portion of Elijah's spirit. Elisha could even discern by vision, which he demonstrated when he told the king of Israel what the king of Syria said in his bedroom.[65]

Turning to Malachi 4, the last chapter in the Old Testament, Bill read, "*For, behold, the day cometh that shall burn as an oven; and all the proud, yea, and all that do wickedly, shall be stubble: and the day that cometh shall burn them up, saith the* LORD *of hosts, that it shall leave them neither root nor branch... Behold, I will send you Elijah the prophet before the coming of the great and dreadful day of the* LORD." Many Bible scholars taught that Malachi 4:5 referred to John the Baptist, because the angel Gabriel said that John would have the spirit of Elijah, and Jesus indicated that John was Elijah.[66] But these teachers stopped short of the full truth. It was wrong to assume that Malachi 4:5 referred only to John the Baptist. When the Jews asked John if he was Elijah, John said flatly that he was not.[67] Instead he identified himself with Isaiah 40:3—"*The voice of him that crieth in the wilderness, Prepare ye*

---

[65] 2 Kings 6:12
[66] Matthew 17:12-13; Luke 1:17
[67] John 1:21

the way of the LORD..."[68] Jesus identified John with Malachi 3:1, *"Behold, I will send my messenger, and he shall prepare the way before me."*[69]

Who then was Malachi referring to when he prophesied, *"Behold, I will send you Elijah the prophet before the coming of the great and dreadful day of the LORD"*? This had to be one of those Scriptural passages that had more than one meaning—like Hosea 11:1, which said, *"When Israel was a child, then I loved him, and called my son out of Egypt."* Hosea was referring to the time when God sent Moses to Egypt to rescue the children of Israel from slavery. But Matthew said Hosea 11:1 was also a prophecy which was fulfilled when Joseph and Mary, who had fled to Egypt to escape King Herod, brought the child Jesus out of Egypt and back to Israel after Herod died.[70]

Malachi 4:5 had to have a compound meaning also, speaking of more than one coming of Elijah. In Matthew 17 the disciples asked Jesus, *"'Why then say the scribes that Elias*[71] *must first come?' And Jesus answered and said unto them, '**Elias truly shall first come**, and restore all things. But I say unto you, That Elias is come already, and they knew him not, but have done unto him whatsoever they listed. Likewise shall also the Son of man suffer of them.' Then the disciples understood that he spake unto them of John the Baptist."* When Jesus said this, John the Baptist was already dead. So when Jesus said, *"Elias truly shall first come, and restore all things,"* Jesus was speaking about a future event.

Since there would be three comings of Christ, and since the first coming of Christ was preceded by a prophet-messenger with the spirit of Elijah, it followed logically that the second and third comings of Christ would each be preceded by a prophet with the spirit of Elijah. In all, there would be five comings of Elijah's

68   Matthew 3:3; Mark 1:3; John 1:23
69   Matthew 11:7-14; Mark 1:1-2; Luke 7:24-28
70   Matthew 2:12-15
71   Elias is the Greek form of Elijah

spirit: the first time in Elijah, the second time in Elisha, the third time in John the Baptist, the fourth time in a prophet-messenger to the Gentiles at the end of the Gentile age, and the fifth time in a prophet to modern Israel.

Why was the spirit of Elijah so special that God chose to use it repeatedly in His great plan? When Bill compared the lives of Elijah and John the Baptist, he found many remarkable similarities. Both men were rugged individuals who loved the wilderness and knew how to endure hardships. Both men had the courage to speak against the spiritual corruption around them. Elijah looked into King Ahab's face and said, "Thou and thy father's house has troubled Israel in that ye have forsaken the commandments of the LORD, and have followed Balaam. Now therefore gather all Israel, and the 450 prophets of Baal, and the 400 prophets of Jezebel's groves, gather them unto Mount Carmel for a showdown."[72] John looked at the Pharisees and Sadducees and said, *"Brood of vipers! Who warned you to flee from the wrath to come? Therefore bear fruits worthy of repentance..."*[73] Neither Elijah nor John was tempted by money, power, fame, or women. Both men denounced immorality: Elijah condemned Queen Jezebel's idolatry,[74] and John rebuked King Herod for living in adultery with his brother's wife.[75]

Both Elijah and John the Baptist had their shortcomings too. After Elijah's victory on Mount Carmel, he fled from Jezebel's wrath and hid in the wilderness. During his journey he got so depressed that he asked God to kill him.[76] John also went through moody periods. When John was in prison he got so despondent that he sent a message to Jesus and asked, "Are You the one who should come, or do we look for another?"[77] Noticing these faults

---

[72] 1 Kings 18:18-19
[73] Matthew 3:7-10 (NKJV)
[74] 1 Kings 21:17-23; 2 Kings 9:36
[75] Matthew 14:3-4
[76] 1 Kings 19:1-4
[77] Matthew 11:3; Luke 7:19

encouraged Bill. It showed him that everything Elijah, Elisha, and John the Baptist accomplished was the result of God working through them. They couldn't rely on their own strength. It reminded him of how the Lord told Paul, *"My grace is sufficient for thee: for my strength is made perfect in weakness."*[78]

Although Elijah and John were both prophets, they were rejected by most religious leaders of their time. No doubt these leaders were jealous of Elijah and John because neither man came through established religious channels. Elijah, Elisha, and John were not connected with any organization. That gave them the freedom to preach their messages without having to worry about what anyone else thought. And all three men preached the Word of God fearlessly, without compromise. That was the kind of spirit God wanted in his prophets, especially those three men ordained to forerun the comings of Christ. Only the spirit of Elijah was rugged enough to withstand the intense pressures of opposition which would inevitably come against that sacred commission *"to make ready a people prepared for the LORD."*[79]

Behind that Egyptian airplane hangar, the Holy Spirit said to him, *"This is not your place. This is not the hour. The cup of iniquity of the Gentiles is not yet full. There is still more gleaning to do."* But Israel's hour must come, just as surely as the sun rises in the morning to scatter darkness. After warning Israel about the great end-time destruction, Malachi 4:2 said, *"But unto you that fear my name shall the Sun of righteousness arise with healing in his wings."* Revelation 1:7 said about Jesus Christ, *"Behold, he cometh with clouds; and every eye shall see him, and they also which pierced him..."* ("They" meaning the Jews.) Zechariah 12:9-11 prophesied of it. The apostle Paul spoke of it in Romans 11:25-27. The Jews will finally receive Jesus Christ as their Savior, and it will be a prophet with the spirit of Elijah who will introduce the Messiah

---

[78] 2 Corinthians 12:9-10
[79] Luke 1:17

again to Israel. Bill felt that this fifth and final Elijah would be one of the two witnesses in Revelation 11:311, because one of these witnesses had the power to prevent it from raining, and the only other prophet in the Bible who had the power to cause a drought was Elijah.[80]

When the Jews finally do receive their Messiah, the Gentile age will end. Then the wrath of God will be poured out on the Gentiles who rejected Christ.[81] As dreadful as that might sound, it must happen before Jesus Christ can rule in a peaceful and perfect kingdom.

Bill didn't know when this would happen, but he did know God was waiting for two things. First, He was waiting for the sins of the Gentiles to accumulate to a certain level. The Holy Spirit said, *"The cup of iniquity of the Gentiles is not yet full."* Jesus said that, *"Jerusalem shall be trodden down of the Gentiles, until the times of the Gentiles be fulfilled."*[82] God had once said something similar to Abraham about his enemies, the Amorites. He said He would not judge the Amorites until their iniquity was full.[83] Back then the Amorites ruled much of Canaan (Palestine). Even in Abraham's day the Amorites were a sinful, amoral culture. By the time God destroyed them, the Amorites' polytheistic religion had degenerated beyond simple idolatry and had embraced divination, religious prostitution, and child sacrifice. Bill could see the modern Gentile world heading that direction also, even to the point of child sacrifice. Wasn't abortion a form of child sacrifice? Could modern governments become so amoral as to legalize the slaughter of unborn children?

The second thing God was waiting for was the salvation of all His children. When His last son or daughter receives the baptism of the Holy Spirit, at that moment the Gentile church

---

80 1 Kings 17:1
81 Malachi 4:1; Matthew 24:21; Revelation 2:22, 7:14
82 Luke 21:24
83 Genesis 15:13-16

will be raptured, that is, they will be caught up into a higher dimension. Then the door of salvation will close to the Gentiles; then Revelation 22:11 will be fulfilled: *"He that is unjust, let him be unjust still: and he which is filthy, let him be filthy still: and he that is righteous, let him be righteous still: and he that is holy, let him be holy still."*

Bill closed his Bible, satisfied that now he better understood the Scriptural position of his own ministry in relation to Israel. Previously he had assumed there would be four comings of Elijah's spirit; now he could see there must be five. His own ministry had nothing to do with Israel. He was called to preach the Gospel to the Gentiles, and that is what he would continue to do: praying for the sick, preaching salvation in Jesus' name, finding one here and one there who would listen—gleaning, always gleaning; gathering up souls like grain for the Master of the Harvest; doing his best to prepare people for the coming of the Lord.

Chapter 66
A Showdown in India
1954

L EAVING GREECE, William Branham flew to Riyadh, capital of Saudi Arabia, where he joined Baron Von Blomberg for dinner with King Saud. Saudi Arabia is a strict Moslem country with laws against Christianity, so there could be no meetings there. Flying on to India, he landed in Bombay during the fourth week of September 1954, and was greeted by dozens of Christian missionaries and church leaders.

The archbishop of India's Methodist church said to him, "Mr. Branham, I hope you're not coming here as a missionary. We know more about the Bible than you Americans do. After all, it's an Eastern book. Saint Thomas preached the Gospel here 1,900 years ago. But we heard God has given you a gift that makes the Bible live again. That is what we want to see."

"Certainly," Bill replied. "I want to show your people that Jesus Christ is the same yesterday, today and forever."

Even though he had been told that Bombay was overcrowded with poor people, he was not prepared for the constant motion he saw everywhere: people jostling along the sidewalks, spilling out into the streets so that his taxi, with horn blaring, had to weave constantly to get by them. Black hair and dark skin predominated; some of these people looked even blacker than the Negroes of

Africa. All of them were skinny and very few of them wore shoes. Many women were fully dressed in traditional *saris*, while many of the men wore only loincloths. Variations abounded. Bill's interpreter pointed out certain ethnic groups: a black-bearded Sikh wearing a turban and a long knife tucked into his sash; a Bengali mystic monk dressed in a saffron-colored robe; a Muslim Sufis covered all in white and sporting a goatee; a Tamil from the south, leading a dwarf pig on a leash tied through a hole in the pig's ear; a fakir sitting with his arms and legs twisted into a Yoga pose; a Parsee fire worshiper bowing in front of a little altar set up on the sidewalk; a Jain with a mask over his mouth to prevent him from accidentally swallowing an insect, which he believed would be murder. Besides these, Bill saw countless beggars, peddlers, fakirs, monks, and merchants. Chickens, goats, and Brahman cows wandered about freely.

The squalor in the streets was disgusting. Garbage was piled everywhere, rotting and stinking in the heat and humidity, breeding cockroaches, flies, mosquitoes, rats, disease, and despair. The buildings, built up to ten floors high, looked as though they might collapse at any minute. A missionary told Bill that these flimsy structures housed one of the highest concentrations of humanity on earth: in some parts of Bombay the population density soared as high as 200,000 people per square mile.

Bill had been raised in poverty himself, and he had seen much poverty among the Black people in the American South and in Africa... Yet, never before had he seen people as destitute as these beggars with their tin cups outstretched, hoping to get a single rupee to buy half of a pound of rice, enough food for three days. Entire families, who had nowhere to go, were camped on the side of the streets. They had a spot on the sidewalk that they considered *their* spot, and that is where they slept while the pedestrians walked around or stepped over them.

The Christian missionary explained to Bill that India had gained her freedom from Great Britain only a few years earlier. The sudden loss of British support had left this giant country bankrupt. Growing enough food to feed her population of 400,000,000 people posed a significant challenge for the Indian government. Hunger gnawed in the bellies of millions of Indians daily. Bill could see it in their eyes, especially the beggars—like the leper holding a tin cup between two white stubs that once were hands; and the boy with elephantiasis, who was dragging one gigantic foot that looked like a tree stump.

After checking into the Taj Mahal Hotel, Bill was taken out to have dinner with the mayor of Bombay and other government officials, including India's Prime Minister, Jawaharlal Nehru—a highly educated man who spoke perfect English. During their meal, Nehru looked over at his guest and said, "Mr. Branham, I do believe you are ill."

Bill looked down at his bowl of sheep's feet cooked with rice and seasoned with olive oil. It tasted so flat, he felt like vomiting. Politely he replied, "I think it's just the food. It's a little different from what I'm used to."

Nehru wasn't convinced. When Bill got back to his hotel, he found Nehru's personal physician waiting to examine him. Everything seemed fine until the doctor checked his blood pressure. "Mr. Branham, are you feeling overly tired?"

"Yes, sir, I am. Why? What's wrong with me?"

"Your blood pressure is dangerously low. In fact, it is so low, I don't see how you are still alive. I advise you to return to America as soon as possible and get your doctor to look at you."

"I have two meetings here in Bombay," he answered wearily, "then I can go straight home."

The next evening his sponsors took him to a huge Episcopal church for his first meeting. The government wouldn't let him hold an open-air campaign because they could not guarantee his safety. Back in January a female evangelist from America, Mrs. Dowd, had come to India and conducted some open-air meetings on the outskirts of Bombay. She advertised herself as a Christian who was preaching divine healing, but she put too much emphasis on money. When she tried to collect an offering from the poor people in her audience, a riot broke out. Mrs. Dowd was knocked unconscious with a brick, and two people were stabbed to death. The memory of that fiasco still lingered in the minds of city officials. (Now Bill understood why the Lord had told him to postpone his trip until September.)

The Episcopal church where he would be holding his meetings was huge. It could hold several thousand people in the sanctuary, with room enough on the church grounds outside for twenty times that many. In addition, loudspeakers were strung up for many blocks along each street near the church so the overflow crowd could hear the service. Hundreds of Christian pastors and missionaries in Bombay and the surrounding areas were cooperating to promote these meetings. This fact, coupled with William Branham's worldwide fame, had drawn a crowd that the mayor estimated to be around 500,000 men, women, and children. There was no way to know for certain, but Bill thought the crowd was probably closer to 300,000 people, because that is what the angel told him in a vision back in February of 1952.

That night Bill explained to his audience how Jesus Christ, the Son of God, is the same now as He was 1,900 ago; therefore if He rose from the dead and is alive today, then we can expect Him to act the same now as He did back then. When it came time for the prayer service, there was no way to pass out prayer-cards in such a vast crowd, so Bill asked several missionaries to choose some bad cases and put them in a line. One by one they came forward and Bill told them who they were, told them what their troubles were, and prayed for them. He couldn't pronounce their names, so he spelled them out letter-by-letter, and every detail was correct. But this supernatural knowledge did not convert the audience, which was used to seeing Indian magicians perform unexplainable tricks. Then a mother led her young son up the steps to the evangelist. Through an interpreter she explained that her son was born deaf and dumb. The huge crowd hushed, waiting, listening. They had heard this American boasting about the power of his God; now they would see if Jesus could really do what the American said He could do.

Bill prayed, "Lord, You promised the Christian believer that if he would ask anything in the name of Your Son it would be given to him, if it was according to Your will. So that these people may know You are the only true and living God, I'm asking for the deaf-and-dumb spirit to leave this child now, in the name of Jesus Christ."

Stepping behind the boy, Bill clapped his hands. Startled, the boy jumped. Turning to look at Bill, the child uttered the first sound that had ever passed through his lips, which the microphone picked up and amplified to hundreds of thousands of people. The audience rumbled with a noisy excitement that would not subside, forcing the meeting to end sooner than anyone had planned. But the stage was set for a spectacular finale.

What is more, the huge crowd at this Branham campaign aroused the curiosity of leaders from India's other religions, who asked if they could meet with the American evangelist. The next day Bill was taken to a Jain temple where he would be interviewed by a group of spiritual leaders representing over a dozen different religious sects of India: Hinduism, Taoism, Jainism, Buddhism, Confucianism, Islam, Brahmans, Sikhs, Zoroastrians, and others. All of these men opposed Christianity, and each leader gave Bill a question or a criticism. A Jain monk said, "If America is a Christian nation, why did they drop an atomic bomb on Japan, killing over 100,000 civilians?" A Moslem caliph added, "And why do they allow their women to strip down in public until they are practically naked?" Bill answered that not everyone in America lived by the principles of Jesus Christ. A Brahman priest asked, "If Jesus was such a holy Man, why did He have to die?"

Bill answered, "Jesus was not an ordinary man. God himself came down to earth in the form of Jesus Christ in order to die for the sins of man, so that man could live forever. The only requirement God made was that man believe in what Jesus did."

A Buddhist monk asked, "How can the death of Jesus take away our sin and give us life?"

Because India swarmed with insects, Bill used an illustration these men could relate to. "Sin is like a deadly bee. Eventually it will sting every man, causing that man to die. But death is in the flesh, not the soul. After a bee stings, it leaves its stinger behind, so it can't sting anymore. God had to become flesh in order to take away the sting of death. That is what Jesus did. Jesus let death sting Him, and so He robbed death of its power. Now, if any man will believe in what Jesus did, he can live forever. And Jesus proved it by rising from the dead."

A Sikh challenged, "If Jesus rose from the dead, why can't we see him?"

Bill answered, "I know Jesus Christ has been represented to you by Christian missionaries in the form of Bible doctrines, pamphlets, schools, hospitals, and orphanages. I support every one of those things; but still, Christ has not been fully presented to you. If you will come to my meeting tonight, you will see Jesus Christ presented in His supernatural power."

Surprisingly, they agreed to attend.

That evening it took two hours for Bill's motorcade, surrounded by a company of policemen, to force its way through the crowd and deliver him to the Episcopalian church. Once inside, Bill was surprised to see policemen standing four rows deep in front of the pulpit. Beyond these policemen, the first row was occupied by those religious leaders who Bill had talked to at the Jain temple earlier in the day.

The church was packed with thousands of people. Outside, several hundred thousand more people crowded as close as they could get to the loudspeakers so they could hear the American evangelist. During his sermon, Bill explained why Jesus Christ died and rose from the dead, using again the analogy of a bee losing its stinger after it stings. Finally it was time for Jesus Christ to reveal Himself in power. After a number of people with internal problems came through the prayer-line, there came forward a man with something outwardly wrong, something that could be seen by everyone. Billy Paul led a blind man past the barrier of policemen and up the steps to his father. Bill gazed with pity at this scrawny man, clothed only with a loincloth, whose eyes were as white as Bill's shirt. Soon he saw this man rising in the air, shrinking into a vision, growing ever younger until he reached the day when he could still see. Family members appeared. Then he saw this man worshiping the sun with so much sincerity that he watched it all day until his retinas were completely destroyed by the sun's ultraviolet rays. Now he was a beggar. The vision ended with no sign of a miracle.

Bill spoke to the beggar through his interpreter, while the public address system amplified his words to a million ears. "You are a married man and you have two children, both of them boys. Your name is—uh—" He couldn't pronounce his name, so he spelled it. "You are a religious man, very sincere. You worship the sun. Twenty years ago you stared at the sun all day long and it caused you to go completely blind. Is that true?"

The beggar confessed it was true. Since the vision had not specified that the man would be healed, Bill was just going to pray for him and move on to the next case. Suddenly the vision returned. There it was! Bill saw himself laying a hand across the blind man's eyes, and he saw what would happen next. Confidence surged through him. There weren't enough devils in hell to stop it now. The visions never failed; they couldn't fail, because they were "thus saith the Lord!"

Pointing at Bombay's religious leaders sitting in the front row, Bill said, "Gentlemen of the religions of India, this afternoon you were telling me how great your gods are and how insignificant is the God of the Christians. Now I want to ask you, what can your gods do for this man? I know you would say the man is worshiping the wrong thing, and you would try to bring him around to your way of thinking. You Buddhists would make him a Buddhist; you Mohammedans would make him a Moslem. We have the same thing going on in America: the Methodists want the Catholics to become Methodists; the Baptists want the Methodists to become Baptists; and the Pentecostals want them all to become Pentecostals. That's just psychology—changing their thinking from one philosophy to another. But surely the God who made this man can also restore his sight? So which god is real? If one of the gods represented here tonight can heal this man, will you people agree to worship that God and that God alone? If you will, raise your hands."

An ocean of hands went up, both inside and outside the building.

"Gentlemen of the religions of the world, here is your opportunity. Can any of your gods give this man back his sight? If any of your religions are real, I challenge you to come forward right now and prove it."

The auditorium became as quiet as a library. Outside, parents hushed their children so they wouldn't miss whatever might happen next. Bill felt like the prophet Elijah standing on Mount Carmel challenging the 400 priests of Baal to a showdown.[84] The

---

[84] 1 Kings 18

religious leaders of Bombay did not stir. "Your priests and monks are awful quiet," Bill taunted. "Why don't they come up here and heal this man?" Nobody answered. "Because they can't do it, that's why. Neither can I, but Jesus Christ can. Not only can Jesus give this man eternal life, He can prove it right now by giving him back his sight. He showed me a vision of it happening, so if it doesn't happen, I'm a false prophet and you have a right to kick me out of India. But if it does happen, you are obligated to accept and believe in the resurrected Jesus Christ. Will you do that?"

Again arms went up everywhere.

Laying one hand across the beggar's eyes, Bill prayed, "Heavenly Father, I know you will give this man his sight, because you showed me a vision of it. I have made each one here promise that they will receive You as their personal Savior if You will do this. God who made heavens and earth, and who raised Jesus from the dead, now let it be known that You are God. I ask it in the name of Jesus Christ."

As soon as he pulled his hand away from the beggar's face, the man shouted something in his own language that turned the crowd into a hurricane of noise and motion. He could see! Joyously the beggar hugged Bill; then he ran across the stage and hugged a policeman; then he turned and hugged the mayor of Bombay, all the while screaming, "I can see! I can see!"

Policemen tightened their lines to keep the audience back, but it was no use. The crowd surged forward like an ocean wave cresting toward a beach—fathers with leprosy and mothers with sick babies, all of them striving to touch the American evangelist. The police could not stop an ocean wave. Hastily they pulled Bill and Billy Paul back toward an exit, while desperate people grabbed at Bill from the other direction. He barely made it to the safety of a waiting car, losing only his shoes and his coat pockets to those clutching hands.

The next morning Bill stood in front of his hotel room window and gazed down on the street below. It looked like an ant hill, black heads moving in every direction, rickshaws threading their way through the crowd, peddlers hawking their wares right next to beggars pleading for a pittance so they could eat one more day. The whole scene troubled Bill so much that he couldn't eat his breakfast. He thought, "They are human beings and they deserve to eat just as much as my Sarah and Becky do." Taking the oranges and crackers that were in his room, he went down to the street and gave them away to the most needy people he could see. A crowd formed around him, hands outstretched, begging. When the food was gone, he emptied his pockets, handing out every rupee he had left in his missionary fund. Then he was broke; and still the beggars pressed him, pleading in words he didn't understand. He did understand their faces, and the desperation on those faces twisted Bill's heart into spasms of agony—especially when he saw a young mother, her face pockmarked with the remnants of some disease, one arm clutching her shrunken baby, her other hand imploring Bill to give her something to feed her starving child. He had nothing more to give. He went back to his hotel room sick at heart and heavy in spirit. That afternoon he left for home.

Chapter 67
Something Haunting Him
1954

WHEN WILLIAM BRANHAM got home from India, he spent five days in bed. All his muscles ached. He felt so tired he could barely move, and yet he still had trouble sleeping. This was partly due to the eleven-hour difference in time between Jeffersonville and Bombay, which made his body think day was night. But low blood pressure and frayed nerves also contributed to his malaise. Worst of all, his spirit had sunk as low as his blood pressure.

He had plenty to brood about besides his poor health. Ern Baxter had resigned as his campaign manager, and the army had just drafted Billy Paul. Worse than both of these put together was the feeling that something was wrong with his ministry. It wasn't having the effect it should. In 1946 the angel had told him: *"As Moses was given two signs to prove he was sent from God, so you will be given two signs."* One sign Moses demonstrated was a miraculous healing, thrusting his leprous hand into his cloak and pulling it out visibly restored to normal. But Moses only had to show that sign once, and after that the Israelites followed him all the way to the Promised Land.

Today God was beckoning people to a spiritual Promised Land, trying to lead them away from man-made theology toward an understanding of Jesus Christ as the fulfillment of God's plan. Just as the Israelites reached their Promised Land by the supernatural experience of walking through the Red Sea on dry ground, so today people could only reach this spiritual Promised Land by a supernatural experience, being baptized by the Holy Spirit. Jesus referred to this land when he said, *"Elias truly shall first come, and restore all things."* Peter referred to it again in Acts 3, saying, *"when the times of refreshing shall come from the presence of the Lord; And he shall send Jesus Christ, which before was preached unto you: Whom the heaven must receive until the times of restitution of all things..."*

Bill believed that "the times of restitution" were here, and he felt his ministry should have led the Christian church to their spiritual Promised Land. For eight years he had crossed America, Europe, Africa, and Asia, verifying the presence of Jesus and demonstrating Christ's power. Out of the tens of thousands of visions he had seen, not one time had his discernment been wrong—not once! Perfection came only from God. Why couldn't the Christian denominations see that the sign of the Messiah was in their midst? This was a sign that had not been on earth for over 1,900 years! It should have caught their attention like an erupting volcano or an atomic explosion. This sign, coupled with Israel becoming a nation, should have told every believer that the end was near. It should have caused Christians to seek God desperately for the baptism of the Holy Spirit. It should have ignited them with a burning zeal for the Word of God. It should have made all the denominational leaders drop their differences and come together as one giant army for the cause of Christ. In short, this sign of the Messiah should have shaken the Christian community to its foundation and rebuilt it into the image of Jesus Christ, the Word.

Why were none of these things happening? After eight years of watching Jesus Christ show Himself in their midst, most Christians remained lukewarm. They sat stiff and starchy in their denominations, satisfied with their church socials and missionary programs, content to let their leaders tell them what to believe. Where was the *"glorious church, without spot or wrinkle"* spoken of by Paul?[85] Where was the church, *"prepared as a bride adorned for her husband,"* spoken of in Revelation?[86] Where was the love, the desperation, the zeal, and the faith of the true believers?

Discouragement settled around Bill like a suffocating cloud of dust. The angel had told him, *"You will take a gift of divine healing to the peoples of the world,"* but the angel had not told him how to go about it. Nor had the angel been specific about how he should use the two signs that had been given him to prove he was sent from God. Bill wondered if he had misused his prophetic gift by concentrating too much of it on divine healing. After all, Oral Roberts, Tommy Hicks, Tommy Osborn, and many other evangelists were getting acceptable results in their faith-healing campaigns without demonstrating supernatural discernment. Perhaps if Bill focused his gift strictly along prophetic lines, and used his influence to settle people firmly in the Word of God, perhaps then his ministry would have a lasting effect on the Christian community.

Over the past eight years Bill had preached mostly short sermons, telling Bible stories and personal experiences that could raise the faith of his audiences enough so they could believe God for their healings during the prayer services that followed. Because people attended his campaigns from all denominations, Bill confined his teaching to a few basic doctrines—like how to receive salvation and healing through faith in Jesus Christ. Although these subjects are essential, they are still just the

---

[85] Ephesians 5:27
[86] Revelation 21:2, 9-11

beginning lessons in living an abundant Christian life.[87] The book of Hebrews scolded some early Christians for not maturing, saying: *"For though by this time you ought to be teachers, you need someone to teach you again the first principles of the oracles of God; and you have come to need milk and not solid food."* The writer of Hebrews likened these early Christians to babies, and he urged them to grow up, saying, *"Therefore, leaving the discussion of the elementary principles of Christ, let us go on to perfection. . ."*[88] Bill felt that his ministry, with its supernatural vindication, could help the modern Christian church go on to the perfection in Christ that was mentioned in the book of Hebrews. To accomplish this, Bill knew he would have to feed his audiences more than just the milk of God's Word; he would have to feed them solid food. He needed to teach Christians the difference between truth and error, between Bible doctrines and man's traditions. In doing this he realized he would offend some people; maybe he would offend a lot of people. That could not be helped. If his ministry was going to have a lasting impact on the Christian church, then he would have to teach the meat of God's Word regardless of how many people that might offend. God had blessed him with worldwide influence. He wanted to use his influence to establish Christians firmly in the Word of God.

But first Bill had to pull himself back together. The constant burden of his ministry, especially the strain upon him from discernment, had worn him down again until his nerves felt tight enough to snap. A man could only take so much pressure before he broke. Bill needed to get away for awhile to renew his strength. Fortunately it was October, the month he always reserved for hunting. In a few weeks he would be camping high up in the Colorado Rockies, far away from the pull of the crowds. There he could drink in the beauty of rushing streams, and clear his

---

[87]   John 10:10
[88]   Hebrews 5:12-14; 6:1a (NKJV)

head among the lofty peaks. There he could freely commune with his Maker and feel at peace. Such experiences rejuvenated him. During the rest of the year, whenever the pressure of his ministry seemed too great, he would often close his eyes and picture some beautiful mountain valley he had visited, and try to recapture the peace he had felt there.

Now in his misery, while staying in bed through much of the day, Bill thought about a time he went hunting in Canada back in 1952. He camped way up north in British Columbia, at least 100 miles from the nearest paved road. Using a horse, he explored high valleys squeezed between rugged mountains. One day he trailed a big grizzly bear. He didn't want to shoot it; he just wanted to get close enough to take some good pictures. All afternoon he tracked that bear through heavy underbrush, giving up only when dusk made the trail impossible to follow. It was a long ride back to camp. A full moon bathed the forest, giving his horse enough light to see its steps. At one point the trail crossed over a ridge and down the side of a mountain through an old burn-over, which is a place where years ago a fire had raged, killing the trees, but not burning them down. Now the dead trees stood erect in the moonlight, like hundreds of white tombstones dotting the mountainside. When Bill was halfway across that burn-over, the wind picked up, moaning through dead, unyielding branches like the spirits of ancient Indian warriors. It was the spookiest place he had ever seen.

He stopped his horse on a knoll. As he gazed out over that eerie moonlit cemetery of dead trees, he thought about what the prophet Joel had written: "*That which the palmerworm hath left hath the locust eaten; and that which the locust hath left hath the cankerworm eaten; and that which the cankerworm hath left hath the caterpillar eaten.*"[89] This spooky mountainside reminded Bill

---
[89] Joel 1:4

of many cold, formal churches he had seen. Let the Holy Spirit sweep over them like a mighty rushing wind, and they stayed so stiff with rigor mortis that all they could do was moan, "The days of miracles are past. This doesn't fit into our program. There is no such thing anymore as divine healing—or prophets; or visions; or the baptism of the Holy Ghost; or the gifts of the Spirit."

Bill thought, "Lord, why did You stop me on this knoll? Is there a lesson here You want me to learn?" Looking down he noticed a new growth of pine trees poking up through the underbrush. Green and flexible, these young shoots swayed and danced in the wind. Suddenly Bill shouted, "Hallelujah! They act like they're having a Holy Ghost revival." There was his lesson. Out of the ashes of those old dead churches God promised to raise up a new crop of Christians who would believe His Word in all Its power.

The next day in camp he read the rest of Joel's prophecy: "*Fear not, O land; be glad and rejoice: for the LORD will do great things... I will restore to you the years that the locust hath eaten, the cankerworm, and the caterpillar, and the palmerworm, my great army which I sent among you. And ye shall eat in plenty, and be satisfied, and praise the name of the LORD your God, that hath dealt wondrously with you... And it shall come to pass afterward, that I will pour out my spirit upon all flesh; and your sons and your daughters shall prophesy, your old men shall dream dreams, your young men shall see visions... And I will shew wonders in the heavens and in the earth, blood, and fire, and pillars of smoke. The sun shall be turned into darkness, and the moon into blood, before the great and the terrible day of the LORD come. And it shall come to pass, that whosoever shall call on the name of the LORD shall be delivered...*"[90]

AT THE END of October 1954, after hunting for several weeks in the Colorado Rockies, William Branham returned home

---

[90] Joel 2:21-32

refreshed in body but still troubled in spirit. He felt like there was something more he should be doing, but he didn't know what it was. Perhaps he was merely anxious to begin teaching more doctrine during his campaigns.

On Sunday, October 24, 1954, preaching at his home church in Jeffersonville, Bill said, "Many of you here have watched me since I was a kid preaching the Gospel. And I haven't varied one speck from the Gospel I started with. I still teach the same thing, because it wasn't given to me by some seminary, neither was it taught me by a man. It came by revelation of the Bible. That's right. Therefore, I know it came from God and I've stayed with the Gospel."

"Many years ago I preached water baptism in Jesus Christ's name. I preached the cleansing of the human soul by the blood of Jesus Christ through sanctification. I preached the baptism of the Holy Ghost as a confirmation or sealing of God's people away in the Kingdom. You know that's right. I taught divine healing. I taught the second coming of Jesus Christ. I taught feet-washing and communion as sacraments of the church. I taught holiness before the Lord. I taught all these things from the beginning."

"I also taught that speaking in tongues is not the evidence of the baptism by the Holy Ghost. Singing, shouting, speaking in tongues, any of these signs might be present, and yet they aren't infallible evidences. There is only one person who can say the Holy Ghost is there, and that is God Himself. He is the judge. I've seen them sing, shout, and speak in tongues, but their fruits proved that they didn't have it."

These were some of the doctrines he wanted to teach during his faith-healing campaigns. By placing more emphasis on such fundamental truths, he hoped the effect of his ministry would be greater and more lasting.

Bill's final healing campaign for 1954 was scheduled to begin Friday night, December 3, in Binghamton, New York. He arrived in Binghamton a day early, and settled into his hotel room. On Friday morning he woke at seven o'clock. Billy Paul was still sleeping.[91] Quietly Bill slipped out of bed and looked out the window at the city. He saw the traffic blur, then disappear, as he was drawn into a vision.

In this vision he was conducting an open-air meeting, but he couldn't tell where. The people coming through his prayer-line had black hair and reddish skin like American Indians. It was night. The people were shouting and praising God for healing them. Bill saw one woman come through the prayer-line holding a pair of socks in one hand and a necktie in her other hand. Bill thought that was odd. Then the vision vanished and he was back in his Binghamton hotel room.

He got out his notebook and wrote this vision down. Several years before he had started keeping a record of his visions. Of course he didn't need to write down visions he saw during the prayer-lines. More and more of his meetings were being recorded on magnetic tape, which meant he could remember these visions by listening to what he said under the anointing. But visions he saw *between* meetings, these he wrote down so he wouldn't forget them. This particular one in Binghamton, New York, showed why it was a good idea. As the campaign progressed and the discernment multiplied, his Friday morning vision faded from his memory until it was almost gone... almost.

---

[91] Before Billy Paul reported for his army physical, his father told him, "Don't worry, son, you won't have to go in, because God has called you to work with me." After his physical, a doctor asked Paul, "How long have you had heart trouble?"

Paul said, "I didn't know I had heart trouble." The army doctors warned him that he had heart trouble. According to their tests his heart was bad enough to warrant giving him a permanent deferment. Billy Paul went home worried that he might die any day. When he told his father, Bill laughed and said, "I told you that you wouldn't have to go in, because God's called you to work with me. Now go downtown and have Dr. Adair check your heart."

Sam Adair ran an electrocardiogram on Billy Paul, then assured him that there was nothing at all wrong with his heart.

William Branham ministering in India

Two weeks later back in Jeffersonville, Bill told his own church, "My next campaign will begin on January 12 in Chicago, first at the Philadelphia Church, and then we move to a larger auditorium somewhere in the city. After that I will be going out west to Phoenix, as the Lord will provide."

"I am desperately in need of you people to pray for me—not for my health. By the grace of God I am this morning in perfect health, as far as I know. I'm very happy and thankful for that. But I am in need of spiritual guidance. I keep feeling like I'm a failure. Something just keeps haunting me, saying, 'Oh, you're such a poor excuse.' That might be so, but I want to do the best I can with what I've got. So I'm longing for more guidance from the Holy Spirit to let me know what is the right thing for me to do. Because after you get to be 45 years old, if I'm ever going to be at any age the best for the Lord, it seems to me it should be right now, because at 45 all the kid things are passed away, and you're settling down, turning gray—you know, mellowed out. It's the time in life when you really should be anchored and strong, at your very best. If I'm ever going to know what I have, seems like I should know it now. And I'm so thankful for what He has shown me in His Gospel."

"But somehow I just can't feel satisfied yet. I hunger for more of God. I feel like there is something I ought to be doing, and I just can't quite get to doing it right. It seems to me like there is something else out there for me to do. I'm almost touching somewhere, but not quite. If I could only get to that spot, then I would be fine."

On the last day of 1954, during a New Year's Eve service at his home church, Bill said, "Tonight I'm thankful to know that the great Jehovah God—who once roared on Mount Sinai, who once stood on another mount and taught the beatitudes, who raised from the dead—He is in our midst tonight. He is the same now as He was then. And to think that the God of heaven would humble Himself to come down and associate with poor people like us, not much of this world's goods... He loved me so much that He came down and saved me by His grace; nothing I deserved, but He saved me because, before the foundation of the world, He predestinated me to be saved—in His own foreknowledge before the world began. And every other man and woman that's saved, He did the same for them. Oh, what a wonderful, marvelous thing."

"My whole heart's desire is for this year (if God will hear my prayer) I want this coming year to be the greatest year I've ever had in my life. I have now, by God's grace, won over half a million souls to Christ. I hope by this time next year to make it a full million, because (if God is willing) I want to start through the foreign countries again, just as soon as we're financially able to do it."

"I know the day is passing; the hours are way spent. Twilight is falling, friends, and I want to do all that I can, because this is the only time that you and I will ever be mortal. This is the only time in all eternity that we'll ever have the privilege of winning someone to Christ. Let's do everything that we can do. Let's put every hour that we possibly can to His glory. That's my intention for this coming year. By God's help, and with your prayers, I'll make it."

His ministry would change—and change dramatically; but in a far different way than he expected.

Book Five:
The Teacher and His Rejection

(1955 — 1960)

Jesus said to them, "Have you never read in the Scriptures: 'The stone which the builders rejected has become the chief cornerstone. This was the LORD's doing, and it is marvelous in our eyes'?"

—Matthew 21:42 (NKJV)

Chapter 68
Shifting His Emphasis
1955

HAVING MADE his decision to teach on a wider range of
Biblical doctrines, William Branham eagerly looked forward
to another year of faith-healing campaigns. But first he needed
to regain his strength. He rested through Christmas and into
the first few weeks of January 1955. On Sunday January 9 he
spoke at his home church in Jeffersonville, Indiana, taking
both the morning and the evening services. Then on Thursday
evening, January 13, he began a faith-healing campaign at the
Philadelphia Church in Chicago, Illinois, where he preached 13
times in 11 days. Pastor Mattsson-Boze gave him liberty to speak
on any subject he wanted. Bill used this freedom to deliver several
doctrinal sermons—among them: "Fundamental Foundation for
Faith," "Position in Christ," "The Seven Compound Names of
Jehovah," and "Earnestly Contending for the Faith."

On Monday night, January 17, he told the spiritual side of his
life story. He explained how, as a young man, he was confused
when Christian ministers told him that his visions came from
the devil. Bill described the afternoon in 1946 when he fled to a
cabin in the woods and sought God for answers. Sometime in the
dark beyond midnight, a supernatural light appeared in the air.
From the midst of that light stepped a man. He stood over six feet

tall and weighed at least 200 pounds. His white robe contrasted sharply with the dark hair that surrounded his beardless face.

Speaking to this audience sitting comfortably in a warm Chicago church, Bill tried to convey the terror he felt at that moment. "Honest, friends, I thought my heart would fail me. Just imagine! Put yourself there. It would make you feel the same way. After hundreds and hundreds of visitations, it still paralyzes me when He comes near. Sometimes I almost completely pass out. If I stay too long praying for the sick, I *will* go completely out.

"So I was sitting there looking at him. He had a deep voice, and he said, '*Do not fear. I am sent from the presence of Almighty God.*' When he spoke, I recognized that voice as the same one that had spoken to me since I was three years old. I knew that was him. He said, '*Do not fear. I am sent from the presence of Almighty God, to tell you that your peculiar birth*—(as you know what happened at my birth up there in that Kentucky cabin in 1909. That same Light hung over me when I was born)—*and your misunderstood life has been to indicate that you are to go all over the world and pray for sick people. Regardless of what they have, if you get the people to believe you, and be sincere when you pray, nothing shall stand before your prayers, not even cancer.*'"

"I said, 'Sir, I'm a poor man and I live with my people who are poor. I'm uneducated. They wouldn't listen to me.'"

"He said, '*As the prophet Moses was given two signs to vindicate his ministry, so you will be given two gifts to vindicate your ministry.*[92] *One gift will be a sign in your hand—when you pray for a sick person, hold the person's right hand with your left hand. Then just stand quietly. Demon-caused diseases will have a physical effect on your body, which will allow you to identify them. Then you pray. If the swelling leaves your left hand, then the disease is gone from the*

---
[92] Exodus 4:1-8

person. Pronounce them well. If it doesn't leave, just ask a blessing and walk away.'"

"I said, 'Sir, I'm afraid they won't receive me.'"

"He said, *'If they won't hear the first sign, then it will come to pass that you will know the very secrets of their hearts. This they will hear.'"*

"I said, 'Sir, that's why I'm here tonight. I have been told by clergymen that those visions that come to me are wrong.'"

"He said, *'You were born into this world for that purpose.'"*

When Bill finished his testimony, an unseen presence settled beside him, overwhelming his emotions with a sacred awe so tangible that it made his skin tingle. He knew the angel of the Lord was standing beside him. Then he felt the angel leave him and glide over the audience. He could see it plainly now, an amber ball of fire, shining like a camera flash that would not fade. Bill watched its movement closely, knowing that his visions were somehow connected with that light. The angel stopped over a black woman. Bill felt her faith pulling on his gift.

"There's a colored lady sitting here with her hands up. Stand up so I can single you out. I'm just a man, but Jesus Christ is the Son of God, and He sent His Spirit to vindicate these things. If God will tell me what's wrong with you (and you know there's no way for me to have contact with you at all) will you believe with all your heart?"

The woman answered, "Yes!"

"God bless you. Your high blood pressure has left you. That's what you had. Isn't that right? Then sit down. You feel different, don't you, lady? Yeah. That's right."

"The little lady sitting next to you, she is suffering with arthritis and a female trouble. Isn't that right, lady? Stand up just a minute—the little lady with the red dress on. You were so close to the angel that now the vision has come to you. You have arthritis, female trouble, and something else... You are worried about your husband. He's a drunkard. He won't go to church. If that's right, raise your hand."

She confirmed with her upraised arm.

"God bless you, lady. Go home now and receive your blessing. You're healed. I saw it turn light around you."

The angel floated to the back of the sanctuary. Bill kept talking to the crowd while he waited to see where the light would stop. "Have faith in God. What do you all think about it way back there? Do you believe? Be reverent."

"There is a lady wearing a scarf sitting back there in the corner. I see that light hanging over her. She is suffering with heart trouble. Her husband is sitting next to her. He has an upset stomach. Isn't that right, sir? Raise your hands up if that is true."

In the back row of the building a man raised his hand.

"Sir, you with your hand up, I see in the vision you have the habit of smoking. Quit doing that. You smoke cigars. You shouldn't do that. It makes you sick. Isn't that right? If it is, wave your hand like this. That is what's upsetting you. It's bad on your nerves. Throw those nasty things away and don't do it anymore, and you'll be all right—and your wife's heart trouble will leave her too. You believe that? Isn't that right? I can't see you from here, and you know that; but you're carrying cigars in your front pocket. That's right. Lay the things out and put your hand over on your wife; tell God that you are through with that kind of stuff, and you'll both go home well. Blessed be the name of the Lord Jesus!"

The audience rumbled with excitement. Bill could actually feel their faith rising, pulling on his gift from every angle. He kept his eyes fixed on the Pillar of Fire as it moved over the heads of the people. "Have faith in God," he said. "I can't do this within myself; it's only His sovereign grace. Do you believe? I can only say these things as He shows me. Do you realize that this is not your brother doing this? It's your faith operating a divine gift. You are standing in His presence. Just a minute..."

He watched the light glide back toward him. It stopped over an old man. "In this corner I see a colored man sitting there, kind of elderly, with glasses on. Stand up a minute, sir. Do you believe me to be God's servant? You're thinking about somebody else, aren't you? If that's right, wave your hand."

As the man waved, Bill said to the audience, "I see that light hanging above him. It hasn't broken into a vision yet. If Almighty God will tell this man what his trouble is, will the rest of you receive your healing? There is a man standing 15 yards away from me. I have never seen him before in my life. If Almighty God will reveal what's wrong with that man, every one of you ought to walk out of here a well person. What more can God do?"

"Sir, there is nothing much wrong with you. You're weak and have a little problem with your prostate, but that's not your trouble. Your problem is your son, who is in a state mental institution because he has a dual personality. Isn't that right? Wave your hand if that's true. See, that's exactly right."

"Now, how many believe that Jesus Christ the Son of God is here? Let's stand and offer praise and receive our healing."

The microphone amplified Bill's prayer over the noise of the crowd. "Almighty God, Author of Life, Giver of every good gift, You're here, the same Lord Jesus Christ, the same yesterday, today, and forever. Satan, you've bluffed these people long enough. I adjure thee by the living God—whose presence is here in the form of the Pillar of Fire—I adjure thee in the name of Jesus Christ to leave these people and come out of them."

"Now, every one of you raise your hands, praise God, and receive your healing!"

Many did, but not all.

AFTER his January campaign in Chicago, William Branham traveled southwest to Phoenix, Arizona. Billy Paul Branham, Jack Moore, and Young Brown went with him. Bill had 12 services scheduled at the Shriner Temple in Phoenix, Arizona, beginning Sunday, February 20, 1955.

The Saturday before these meetings started Bill drove into the desert outside of Phoenix, looking for a place to pray. He still wasn't sure what he should do about his method of praying for the sick and needy. Why couldn't he be more like the other evangelists who had faith-healing ministries? In the time it took Bill to pray for five people, Oral Roberts could pray for fifty. Oral Roberts laid his hands on people and prayed for them as they walked by him. Bill, on the other hand, put people in a line, then called them forward one by one so he could discern each person's need through a supernatural vision. Not only did Bill's method take longer, the visions themselves taxed his body severely, limiting how many people he could personally touch each night. A single vision tired him more than if he had spent an hour digging a ditch with a pickax and shovel. After 15 visions in a row, he would feel so tired he could barely stand. If he tried to continue beyond this point, he risked collapsing from exhaustion, which had happened on several occasions. His son, Billy Paul, and his current manager, Jack Moore, watched him closely to make sure he didn't overdo it.

Although Bill often explained this phenomenon to his audiences, many people still didn't understand. Even his associates had trouble understanding. Gordon Lindsay once asked, "Why couldn't you just discern one or two people, then step back and pray for the rest of the prayer-line like we do?" For some reason his gift of discernment didn't work that way. When the angel stood beside him during a prayer-line, the visions just came. He couldn't control them. Many times it felt like people were actually pulling the discernment out of him by their faith.

On this particular Saturday in the desert outside of Phoenix, Bill knelt in the shade of a boulder and asked God to help him pray personally for more people in each meeting. The sun rose higher, baking the red sand and causing heat waves to blur the distant mountains. Everything that could move sought shelter in whatever shade was available. The plants had to endure this heat, but God gave them the special ability to do so. Here the desert was covered with tall, straight saguaros cactus, the bushy cholla cactus, and the whip-like ocotillo cactus, as well as many other cactus varieties.

After a while Bill felt the angel of the Lord draw near. Suddenly the desert vanished. Bill found himself standing on a platform in an auditorium, facing a line of people waiting for prayer. Behind him he noticed a short, bald-headed man and a tall, thin man, neither of whom he knew. A short woman wearing a brown suit coat with a matching skirt walked toward him. In her arms she carried a baby wrapped in a blanket. She stopped a few feet in front of him, close enough for Bill to see her light complexion, her dark eyes and black hair. Looking down into her arms, he saw a tiny, pasty-skinned infant who looked like it was near death. After Bill prayed, God healed the baby. Then the angel stepped into view and said, *"When you see this come to pass, your ministry will change."*

Every night in Phoenix, he expected this vision to be fulfilled. It didn't happen during that campaign, but something else astonishing did. On Wednesday night, February 23, 1955, Bill was halfway through his sermon when suddenly he saw a vision. (He rarely saw visions while he was preaching; usually they came under the anointing during the prayer service.) He continued to preach as he watched this vision unfold, incorporating it directly into his sermon.

He described the vision like this, "Yonder I see Adam and Eve in the Garden of Eden. I see Adam put his arm around his sweetheart to walk out with her, for God had condemned them. Adam was not deceived; he didn't have to walk out. But he walked out because he loved his wife. He walked out with both eyes wide open. I hear something that sounds like clapping. What is it? It's that bloody sheepskin smacking against their thighs, the blood running down their legs, which speaks of redemption, pointing towards a time when they will get back into Eden.

"Now let's change our scene. Four thousand years later in Jerusalem... there - coming through the streets I see someone... bumpity, bumpity, bump... out of the gate towards Golgotha... I see a little Fellow with a crown of thorns on His head and a cross over His shoulder. Look! All over His back there are little red spots of blood. As He walks they get bigger until they become one big spot. There He is, moving up the hill, going to Calvary, His poor shoulder rubbing on the cross, the old bee of death buzzing around Him...and then it stung Him. But, friend, you know that if a bee ever stings anybody deeply, it can't sting anymore because it pulls it's stinger out. After that it can fly, but it can't sting. Like Paul said, 'O death, where is thy sting? O grave, where is thy victory?'[93]

"Christ, the kinsman Redeemer has made a way of escape for every believer on this earth today. The bee of death might buzz, trying to make us afraid, but it can't hurt us because we can point back to Calvary, where God Himself was made flesh and held the stinger of death, taking our place as sinners and paying the price. And He laid out the welcome mat for us, saying, 'Whosoever will,

[93] 1 Corinthians 15:55

let him drink the water of life freely' and 'whoever comes to Me I will in no wise cast out.'[94]

"John 3:16 says, 'God so loved the world that He gave His only begotten Son...' Adam so loved Eve that he went out of the Garden with her, knowing she was wrong. He was innocent, but she was guilty. But Adam said, 'I'll go with her.' Likewise Christ looked at His church, and knowing she was wrong, still He went with us to take our place as a sinner, to die for us, to take the sting out of death for us. Sinner, how can you reject such matchless love?"

After the meeting ended, Bill and his associates stayed up until one o'clock talking about this vision. On Thursday night he mentioned it to his audience. He felt this vision confirmed his decision to teach more doctrine.

During the Friday night meeting he said, "Tonight, how many people in the building have prayer-cards? Let me see your hands. Well, that's a good, nice number. Now, I intend to pray for everyone who has a prayer-card. I can't bring them all through the line. As you can see, my strength becomes depleted quickly after a few visions, so I can't get to all of them that way. But my meetings are not based upon me personally contacting each person. They are based upon the exaltation of the Lord Jesus Christ and His resurrection through preaching and demonstrating the Word of God. By hearing the Word preached, people should believe that the Lord Jesus in His resurrecting power is in our midst and is doing the same things He did when He was here on earth, as a vindication of His everlasting omnipotence. He is here with us and will be forever. Christian believers, we will never be without the Lord. We are associated with Him for eternity. Isn't that wonderful? Jesus said, 'I will be with you always...'[95] My meetings

---

[94] Revelation 22:17; John 6:37, respectively
[95] Matthew 28:20

are based on the principle that the believer should just look and live."[96]

Although this campaign was going to run through Wednesday, March 2, 1955, there was no meeting scheduled in Phoenix for Saturday night, February 26. That Saturday Bill drove 100 miles east so he could hold one prayer service for the Apaches at the San Carlos Indian Reservation. The last time he had preached at San Carlos was in 1947, two years before his second sign appeared. Back then he could only discern diseases by the sign in his hand. When that 1947 meeting began, the Indians were reluctant to come forward for prayer, thinking he was probably a fraud. In a community as tightly-knit as the Apaches, where everyone knew everyone else, after they saw an outsider accurately diagnose the first few patients, their suspicion vanished and they eagerly formed a line which kept Bill praying half of the night. Miracles flowed as freely as water down the White Mountains in spring.

Now, in 1955, the Apache Indians were eager to have another faith-healing service on their reservation. As soon as Bill arrived, one woman came out of a tar-papered shack, knelt in the yard, bowed her head, and prayed continually through the entire service.

Young Brown and Jack Moore accompanied Bill on this excursion, but Billy Paul stayed behind in Phoenix. Since Billy Paul usually distributed the prayer-cards before each meeting, Bill had not given any thought to this detail until he was already at San Carlos. Then he realized he didn't have any prayer-cards to keep order in the prayer-line. Fortunately, these Apaches stayed orderly without such a device. Bill planned to pray for as many

---

[96] He is referring here to the principle of faith. "Look and live" alludes to a story in Numbers 21:4-9. When a plague of poisonous snakes attacked the Israelites, Moses raised a brass serpent on a pole. God said whoever looked at that brass serpent would live. The brass serpent symbolized sin that was judged. That Old Testament story was a type of Jesus on the cross (John 3:14-15). Jesus bore the sins of mankind on the cross. Whoever looks on Him, in faith, will live forever.

people as he could, then after his strength failed, his associates would continue praying until they had touched everyone in line.

To begin the prayer-line, a mother walked forward with a baby in her arms. The mother wore a traditional Apache dress, with its ankle-length wool skirt having pastel patterns woven into its fibers. Bill talked with her a minute to discern her spirit. She was concerned about her baby. His first vision of the night showed how glaucoma had blinded this baby's eyes. A simple prayer to an Almighty God reversed the course of nature. As Bill moved a finger in front of the baby's face, those little eyes focused and followed the movement.

That first miracle triggered a chain reaction of faith, which rapidly spread through the tribe. Soon deaf people heard, crippled people walked, and numerous diseases succumbed to the power of Jesus Christ. As Bill came to the end of his strength, a missionary named Mitchell brought up a little Apache girl. Bill knelt and asked her a question, but she didn't answer.

Reverend Mitchell said, "Brother Branham, she doesn't speak English. She is blind."

Bill waved his hand in front of her face. She didn't flinch. He prayed for her, and then waved his hand in front of her face again. Her young eyes stared at a black future, unresponsive. Looking at this beautiful little Indian princess, a great sadness swept over him. Suddenly he saw a strange vision. He saw himself take this girl's hand, fly up through the heavens with her, and together they entered the throne room of God. There lay the blood of Jesus on the throne. That blood could heal this girl if only she could believe it, but she didn't have enough faith. Then came the strangest part. God accepted Bill's strong faith in the blood of Jesus in place of the girl's minimal faith. Instantly he was back at the Indian reservation, kneeling beside that little Indian princess. He said, "Brother Mitchell, something happened. It looked like

I was going up through the sky with this child in my hand…" He swung his arm toward heaven as he talked. At this sudden movement, the girl jerked her hands up to her mouth in surprise. She could see!

Reverend Mitchell immediately took the girl to the reservation's doctor, who examined her and confirmed the miracle. Meanwhile Bill faced the next person in line, a man who was also blind. When the vision broke, he saw this man was the father of the girl who had just been healed. That night God's grace restored his sight as well.

By now Bill was so tired that his lips felt numb and his legs felt like rubber. Jack Moore wanted him to quit, but Bill said he thought he could tolerate one more vision. A young Apache woman hurried forward, carrying a pair of socks in one hand and a man's necktie in the other. She handed these articles to Bill, who took them thinking she merely wanted him to hold them while he prayed for her. She had something else in mind, which the vision promptly revealed. Bill said, "These socks belong to a loved one of yours who has a disease in his feet, and you want him to be healed when he puts them on. This necktie is for your husband, who is an unbeliever. You want him to receive the Holy Ghost when he ties it around his neck." The woman said this was exactly what she wanted. Bill said, "If you can believe it, in Jesus' name you can have what you are asking for."

Later that night, while they were driving back to Phoenix, Young Brown and Jack Moore talked excitedly about the Apache meeting. Young Brown was amazed at how many Indians Bill had prayed for before he ran out of strength—around 30 people, twice as many as usual. Brown wondered how Bill could have endured the strain of those visions so long.

Bill was wondering the same thing. He knew it was the people themselves who operated his gift. Although his discernment was a supernatural gift, it could not heal anyone. The most it could do was to raise faith by showing people that Jesus Christ was present, willing, and able to heal them. At the beginning of his international ministry the angel of the Lord told Bill, "*If you can get the people to believe you, nothing will stand before your prayer, not even cancer.*" What each person received from his ministry depended on that person's faith. Perhaps these Apaches simply had more faith than most other Americans, which in turn reduced the strain on him. He saw the same thing among the natives of South Africa and India. It seemed like Western culture's emphasis on education and intellectual reasoning often hindered, instead of helped people believe the Word of God.

While Jack Moore and Young Brown discussed the meeting, Bill thought about the woman who wanted him to pray over a necktie and a pair of socks. Something about that necktie and those socks stirred his memory. When he awoke the next morning, those socks still tumbled around inside his thoughts. Eventually the Holy Spirit said, "*Pick up your vision book.*" Opening his notebook to the last entry, he skimmed back through the notes of his visions until he found it. On December 3, 1954, in Binghamton, New York, at seven o'clock in the morning, God had shown him a vision of last night's Apache meeting from one end to the other, including the woman holding the necktie and socks.

That Sunday in church (February 27, 1955) Bill said, "The most hallowed meeting I ever had on American soil happened last night at the Indian reservation. I'm used to preaching to 15,000 to 18,000 people. Last night there were only 500 or so, but never before in America have I seen the Spirit of God flow so freely."

Before he began his sermon, he wanted to clear up a misunderstanding. Earlier in the week he said that Adam was innocent and Eve was guilty. Evidently some people (including ministers) had called Jack Moore to ask if Brother Branham believed that Adam had not sinned in the Garden of Eden. Now Bill tried to explain what he had meant. "Some of you thought I said Adam did not sin. Adam *did* sin, and was condemned just like Eve. The lambskin as a redemptive robe over him showed that. But Eve did wrong, thinking she was doing right. She was deceived. Adam was not deceived.[97] He sinned with his eyes wide open, knowing exactly what he was doing. He deliberately took his position with his wife because he loved her. And Jesus, not ignorant of what He was doing, took His place with the sinner, the Church, so that He might redeem the Church back to Himself. See? Adam was a type. Through the first Adam, all died; through the Second Adam, all live.[98] Because Adam loved Eve, he willingly took on her sin and was condemned. Because Christ loved His Church, He willingly took on our sins and was condemned, died, and was sent to hell. That's right. God wouldn't have sent Him to hell pure. He was condemned. He died as a sinner. Christ never sinned Himself, but He took our sins upon Himself; and on the third day God raised Him up, conquering death and offering eternal life to everyone who will believe on Him."

Bill hoped this explanation clarified his earlier statements. It was not the first time someone had not understood him correctly. He realized the more he taught "meatier" doctrines, the more such misunderstandings would happen. That didn't discourage or dissuade him from his new purpose. His vision of the first Adam and the Second Adam verified his conviction that he was called to teach as well as evangelize. He wanted to use his God-given influence to ground people firmly in Biblical truth. He felt that if Christians could ever grasp a revelation of the resurrected Jesus Christ in their midst, everything would change.

---

[97]   1 Timothy 2:14
[98]   1 Corinthians 15:20-22

Chapter 69
A Solemn Warning
1955

WILLIAM BRANHAM'S campaign in Phoenix ended on Wednesday, March 2, 1955. The next day he drove to Los Angeles, California, to begin a five-night campaign at Angelus Temple, the church founded by Aimee Semple McPherson, a famous woman evangelist of the 1920's. Then he moved to a larger building in Los Angeles for two meetings sponsored by the Full Gospel Business Men's Fellowship International (FGBMFI). The Fellowship's vice-president, Miner Arganbright, had rented the Stock Arena for Friday and Saturday night, March 11 and 12.

Bill hoped these two campaigns would turn out better than the one he had held in California the previous summer. Back in August 1954, when he preached at Calvary Temple in Los Angeles, the nightly crowds were much smaller than his sponsors expected. Afterward, Bill learned that many people refused to attend because they didn't like the church where his meetings were being held. Even though he was not connected with any denomination, conflicts between denominations still affected his ministry.

He had been visiting the West Coast regularly since 1947. At first his California meetings had exploded with faith and miracles, and every year he returned, his crowds grew larger than the previous year. Lately that trend had reversed. Christians in Orange County seemed to be losing interest in his supernatural gift. Certainly, movies and television shows were causing many people to lose interest in activities that would feed their souls. Perhaps the television and movie industry was even sucking some Christians into its illusions, dulling their spiritual senses to the sign of the Messiah in their midst; or perhaps jealousies and rivalries among denominations were making church leaders unwilling to cooperate with one another. Whatever the reason, attendance at Bill's campaigns in California had been dropping over the past three years.

Bill remembered a conversation he had with a Baptist preacher the first time he came to Los Angeles in 1947. The minister warned: "Brother Branham, now that you're on the West Coast you'd better be careful what you preach about."

That puzzled him. "I'm preaching divine healing. What's wrong with that?"

"Oh, I believe in divine healing too," the minister replied, "but out here in California it's different. Pick up a Saturday paper and look for yourself. Out here the worst fanaticism you have ever seen is tied in with divine healing—strange people with all kinds of theories and funny feelings that they call signs from God. If you're not careful, you'll cause that kind of stuff to multiply and scatter even more."

At that time Bill answered, "Look, sir, my gift comes from God. I believe it will bless Christians. My desire is to see this broken up bunch of Pentecostal people come together in one accord. They've got the greatest thing in the world—the baptism of the Holy Ghost. Surely those people with spiritual minds will see my gift and understand what I'm trying to do."

The Baptist minister answered, "I'm not doubting your gift or your motives, but Brother Branham, God be with you." He spoke this phrase solemnly—not as a blessing, but more like a warning. Back then, Bill did not know what this preacher had meant. He was about to learn.

On Monday, March 7, 1955, Bill woke at three in the morning. Unable to fall back asleep, he got up to pray. Soon he felt the angel of the Lord come into his motel room. Moments later, a vision took him for a ride.

Now he was standing on the top of a bluff, which gave him a panoramic view of Los Angeles. Directly below him was a street lined with palm trees. Squawking vultures fluttered everywhere, some flying between trees, others flocking around a dead animal on the road. Every species of vulture was represented. From the top of a palm tree, one vulture called to the group feeding on the road kill, shouting, "I've got it." One of the vultures on the road looked up from his meal and shouted back, "I've got it too." This started a racket, with every vulture squawking to his neighbor, "I've got it! I've got it!"

Bill wondered what this strange, noisy scene meant. Suddenly on the bluff beside him stood the same Baptist preacher who had given him that solemn warning on his first trip to Los Angeles. The preacher looked straight into Bill's eyes and said sternly, "What did I tell you eight years ago, Brother Branham?"

"Sir, I apologize. I thought surely they would understand."

The angel of the Lord stepped up to the edge of the bluff on Bill's right side. The angel said, *"So did Moses think that theIsraelites would surely understand."*[99]

Then the vision faded back to his room.

---

[99] Acts 7:22-29 Moses' first attempt to deliver the Israelites was sincere, but inappropriate, and therefore it did not succeed.

ON FRIDAY NIGHT in the Stock Arena, Bill told this vision to his audience and publicly apologized to that Baptist preacher for not heeding his warning. Then he tried again to make the people understand. For two nights he explained the difference between the seal of God on the believer and seal of the antichrist on the unbeliever. He taught that the seal of God was the baptism of the Holy Ghost, which caused a Christian to accept *all* of the Word of God as inspired. The antichrist spirit also claimed to love God, but this spirit could not accept everything in the Bible as true.

Bill said, "People with the antichrist spirit are lukewarm, borderline believers who will come right up to the Holy Spirit, and then say, 'I don't believe in such stuff.' They can come as far as their leader Judas—very fundamental in doctrine, but when it comes to receiving the baptism of the Holy Ghost, then they say, 'Oh, that's fanaticism; there's nothing to it.' They might believe the Word intellectually, but they can't believe it from their hearts.

"The antichrist spirit will be a religious spirit. Jesus said it would be so close to the real thing until it would deceive the very elect, if possible.[100] That throws a different light on it, doesn't it? It's a religious spirit; one that can dance, shout, cast out demons, and do miracles—and still it is antichrist. Jesus taught that not everyone who calls Him 'Lord' will enter into the kingdom of heaven. On Judgment Day many people will say to Him, 'Lord, have we not prophesied in Your name, cast out demons in Your name, and done many wonders in Your name?' Then Jesus will tell them, 'Depart from Me you workers of iniquity. I never knew you.'[101]

"You can't base your salvation on emotions. In India I saw people work themselves into a frenzy, screaming at the top of their lungs, and then walk barefoot through a pit of fiery coals

---
100   Matthew 24:24
101   Matthew 7:21-23

without getting burned—and they deny there ever was such a man as Jesus Christ! So emotions don't mean anything.[102] What matters is the fruit of the Holy Spirit: love, joy, peace, patience, goodness, and gentleness.[103] That's right. I don't want to hurt your feelings, but it must be told. You've seen the Holy Spirit go forth in my ministry with this gift of discernment. Now it's come to the place where I want to tell you the truth about these other things as well."

A few minutes later he related his vision of the vultures that were feeding on carrion, yet claiming to have the truth. Bill said, "Brethren, you don't understand what my ministry is all about. The God of heaven is trying to bring you together. But every time I come here, the crowds get smaller and smaller. No matter what I try to do, some people still label my ministry as a cult. Brothers and sisters, this great Pentecostal movement will never prosper until you break down your prejudices and put your hearts together in unity of spirit. If you keep on rejecting it—remember that Laodicea, the last church age, turns lukewarm and God spews it from his mouth.[104] Hear the Word of the Lord!

"The Pentecostal church is cooling off and getting too starchy. That's the reason you can't cooperate with one another—you're paying more attention to your organizations than to Jesus Christ. Each church is trying to outshine the others by putting up the fanciest building in town. What does God care about church buildings? If you believe Jesus is coming soon, why are you putting millions of dollars into your buildings? That money should be spent on the mission fields, spreading the Gospel to those who have never heard.

"You Pentecostal people have let down your standards, permitting sin to come into your churches. It used to be that

---

[102] Matthew 7:13-20
[103] Galatians 5:22
[104] Revelation 3:14-22

Pentecostal women wore long hair and dressed nice. Now most of them cut their hair, put on makeup and wear short, skintight dresses—and still say they are baptized with the Holy Ghost? I believe that the Holy Ghost will make you dress decently and live right. If the Holy Ghost condemned those things in the beginning, He is still the same Holy Ghost tonight. He doesn't change.

"I am afraid there is something that didn't start out right in the beginning. Amen. Oh, my, I hate to say that. But how can I keep from saying it, when it's pushing out of me just as hard as it can?

"Tonight the Christian Business Men brought me out here to this big arena so we could be free from denominational tags. This place ought to be jam-packed with ministers shaking one another's hands and praising God for sending a revival. But too many ministers have told their people, 'Don't go out there because he doesn't belong to our group.' My brethren, that is the devil getting between you, separating you, breaking you apart. Can't you see what I mean?

"So if that Baptist minister is here tonight, I apologize again. Instead of my ministry bringing Christians in California together, it has encouraged fanaticism. Everybody has to smell a demon or stomp on a devil. Oh, brother, if you believe me to be God's servant, hear my voice tonight. Come back to the Gospel. Pray that the Holy Spirit will give you enough love to break free from all these prejudices. Humble yourselves and pray that God will mold you into His image. Then you won't be tricked by any of these false vines that try to impersonate the genuine gifts of God."

WILLIAM BRANHAM knew his gift struck many people as unorthodox. He often tried to explain to his audiences how his visions worked, hoping that such an explanation would help

Christians avoid misconceptions. Some people misunderstood him anyway.

One time a young Pentecostal man came to Bill asking for help in his marriage. The man said, "My wife is a staunch Lutheran and I can't get her to see the baptism of the Holy Ghost. Brother Branham, I've seen you handle devils in your meetings, so when my wife makes fun of me, I command that devil to leave her in Jesus' name. No matter how forceful I am, I can't get that devil to leave her. Now it looks like we're going to get divorced."

"Brother, you're going at it the wrong way," Bill replied. "When she starts in on you like that, say, 'Bless your heart, dear. I love you,' and be really kind to her. Do something nice for her, and all the time keep praying for her silently in your heart. God will take care of the rest."

Three weeks later this man called Bill to report, "My home is revolutionized. My wife is a different person."

"Which is more powerful," Bill asked, "screaming and kicking, or putting your arms around her in love? Always remember that God is love. That's how I cast out those devils in my meetings, through the power of love."

Most misconceptions were not as easy to correct. Worst of all were the preachers who had seen or heard about Bill's gift and were trying to impersonate it for their own gain, causing much confusion among Christians. Some of these preachers were outright frauds, playing on the gullibility of honest, but spiritually ignorant people. Other preachers embraced the gifts of the Holy Spirit sincerely, but were not careful to handle these gifts in a Scriptural manner, and so they became almost as harmful as the frauds.

Bill knew one mixed-up preacher who, claiming to have a gift of discernment, said, "This woman has three devils in her. One of them is named Jeff, and another one is named Seth. They're each a different color. One devil is green, another one is blue, and the last one is pink." When Bill heard this, he prayed, "Oh God, have I ever said anything to give people such ideas? Don't let that happen, God. Many of those people are struggling so hard, trying to see the Kingdom of God. How could they flock by the hundreds to listen to such tommyrot as that? Let them hear the voice of the Great Shepherd, so they won't follow the voices of these strangers."

The truth about Bill's gift of discernment was far more powerful and startling than any of these imitators could imagine. When the anointing came on him during a prayer service, it was like a curtain had been pulled aside from a window, giving him a glimpse of the spiritual world beyond. He could feel the angel of the Lord a few feet away from his right side, and often he could see the angel, looking like a Pillar of Fire hanging in midair. When people in the prayer-line walked forward into the presence of that angel, Bill could tell whether they were believers or unbelievers because a faint halo surrounded Christians and they brought with them a spirit of welcome. If doubt troubled a Christian, Bill saw it as a dark streak following behind. If a believer was being tormented by a devil, Bill saw it as a black, wavy shadow overhead.

In general devils appeared like dark clouds, cold and indifferent. A person contemplating suicide was surrounded by a black fog of demons prodding that person to commit the act. If someone was dying, Bill often saw this as a dark shadow surrounding the head. Then he would say that the person was shadowed by death. Often when a devil that caused a specific disease was exposed on the platform, it would scream for help from nearby devils who also caused the same disease in others. Bill saw this as a dark streak running from the person on the platform to someone in the audience. Then he could expose both devils at once. His diagnosis was never wrong.

Under the anointing of the Spirit to discern, Bill could actually feel the faith of people pulling on his gift. The main reason he had a prayer-line at all was to isolate the faith of the person for whom he was praying. He knew that his gift operated by the faith of each individual. When people came forward for prayer, it took just a few words of conversation with them to bring on a vision. If Bill kept talking, the vision continued until he was physically exhausted. To delay the inevitable, he tried to say just enough to raise each person's faith to the point where he or she could accept supernatural healing from Jesus Christ. Even without a vision Bill could often tell when a Christian was healed, because the halo around that person suddenly flashed extra bright. Often the angel of the Lord would leave the platform and move out over the audience. Then all Bill needed to do was watch where the Pillar of Fire stopped; the vision always broke under that light. Sometimes in a meeting, the faith of Christians grew so great that Bill could actually see their faith like a milky mist hanging over his audience. When this happened, so many people pulled on his gift at once that he had difficulty discerning individual problems. Usually at this point he would dispense with the prayer-line and offer a general prayer for the healing of every sick person in the building.

Despite the many times he tried to explain the spiritual aspect of his gift, most people could not comprehend it. There was no harm in that. The harm came when people used his explanation of this supernatural gift to try to duplicate his ministry. This became painfully clear one morning when a middle-aged woman came to Bill's house seeking his help. He invited her into his living room. Meda was cooking breakfast. The woman sat in the cushioned chair, took off her shoes and stockings, tucked her legs under herself, and then rubbed her hands together nervously. Her face looked haggard. When Bill asked her what was wrong, all she said was that she felt funny. He pressed her for more details, but she remained vague and mysterious.

Then a vision came, piercing to the heart of this mystery. "Lady, you come from St. Louis," Bill said. "Your husband is on the police force there."

"Yes, that's right. How did you know?"

Bill didn't answer her question. He was still watching this vision unfold. He said, "You used to be a lovely housekeeper, but recently your house looks like a pigpen. Your grown daughter is there now taking care of your husband."

"You're right. Who told you that?"

"When you started feeling funny, you went to see a doctor. He gave you a hormone shot. Then you went down to a certain church where a minister said you were possessed by devils. He sent you to see a preacher out in California, who told you that you had seven devils. You believed him because you thought that explained your funny feelings. Then you listened to a woman preacher who said you had five devils. She told you to come to Jeffersonville and see me about it."

"Yes, that's all true. How did you know? Did my daughter call you?"

The vision ended, snapping Bill back to his living room. Now he could answer her. "The Holy Spirit told me those things by vision."

The woman pulled her legs out from underneath her and sat up straight. "Now I can get to the bottom of this," she said eagerly, smacking her hands together. "I haven't eaten in several days, and I'm not going to eat until I find out what happened to those two devils. If I can learn why those two devils left me, I can make the rest of them go the same way."

"Lady, you haven't got any devils to begin with."

"I haven't?"

"No, ma'am. Didn't you watch your mother go through the change of life? The same thing is happening to you. What do you think those hormone shots were for?"

"I don't know."

"They were for menopause, that's what."

"Are you going to pray for me and cast it away?"

"There's nothing to cast away. Your funny feelings aren't caused by devils. It's just a natural condition of life. Your body is changing so you can't have any more children. That happens to every woman eventually."

Her face relaxed noticeably. The smell of frying bacon turned her head towards the kitchen. "Kind of hungry?" Bill asked with a wry smile. Soon she was sitting at the kitchen table eating bacon, eggs, and toast. When she finished her second cup of coffee, Bill said, "Go home now, straighten up your house, and then bake your husband a nice apple pie. When he comes home tonight, sit on his lap, throw both your arms around him, kiss him, and tell him you love him. From now on, live like a Christian woman ought to live."

Watching her drive away, Bill thought about the two preachers in California who told this gullible woman she had devils. He wondered if those preachers had ever been in his meetings. He hoped they were not trying to pattern their ministries after his. Bill thought again about that Baptist preacher and his solemn warning, "God be with you."

Around this time a young man drove to Bill's house in an old Chevrolet pickup truck. Bill sat on his porch and listened to this young man's problem.

"Brother Branham, I own a used car lot in Minneapolis. A couple of years ago my wife went to a Pentecostal church and got the Spirit. She wanted me to go with her to church, but I told her, 'No, I'm not the religious type.' Then a few months ago something happened that shook me up. I had just sold a car to an elderly woman and was hanging up my coat, when I got to wondering if I had given her both sets of keys. When I checked in my coat pocket, I found a piece of paper that said, 'Where will you spend eternity?' That question touched me so deeply, I turned my business over to an associate and went home to seek God. I went to one of Billy Graham's meetings. He told me if I raised my hand and accepted Christ as my personal Savior, then the issue would be settled; I would spend eternity with Jesus. I raised my hand, but I still didn't feel it was settled. So I visited a Nazarene church. The Nazarene people told me unless I got happy enough to shout, I wasn't saved. So I prayed until I shouted, but I still didn't feel it was settled. Next I went to the Pentecostal church. Those people told me if I spoke in tongues, then my eternal destination would be settled. They prayed with me half the night until I spoke in tongues, but I still didn't feel it was settled. Then I met some people from *The Voice of Healing* magazine. They told me you are a prophet. They said if I came here, you could tell me what I need to know. Brother Branham, how can I know where I am going to spend eternity?"

"Well, brother, first I want to tell you I'm not a prophet; I'm just His servant. But you don't need a prophet to straighten you out; you just need the Word of God. Mr. Graham, the Nazarenes, and the Pentecostal people told you the truth; and yet it's not the truth, not completely. To raise your hand, to shout or to speak in tongues is not receiving Christ. Receiving Christ is receiving the person of the Lord Jesus Christ."

The young man nodded like he understood, but the expression on his face still looked confused. "Where can I find Jesus Christ?"

"You said the moment you read that note, something struck you and you wanted God. Before that time you were going away from Him. Then suddenly you did a U-turn and headed the other direction. What changed your mind?"

"I don't know."

"God came into your heart right there when you looked at that piece of paper."

"You mean I've had it all along?"

"Certainly, brother. That's what conversion means—to turn around."

"Brother Branham, will you pray for me?"

Bill smiled and shook his head. "You don't need prayer. The truth has made you free. That is the work of the Holy Spirit—the person, not a thought. The Holy Spirit is the personage of the Lord Jesus Christ who we accept into our hearts, who gives us a new and different attitude to everything in life."[105]

---

[105] John 8:30-36; 14:15-19; Acts 3:19-21

Chapter 70
True and False Vines
1955

INDIANA WEATHER IN THE SPRING can be a temperamental companion. Sometimes the sun warms the cornfields for a week or two of balmy, windless days. Then the weather snaps and storm clouds boil over the horizon—giant cumulus clouds with puffy white mounds on top, gray middles, and bluish-black at their bottoms, sailing across the sky like an armada of war ships, cannons flashing and explosions thundering, drenching the earth with life-giving rain.

William Branham's life also had some blustery days in May of 1955. As Meda came to the end of her third pregnancy, the winds of adversity blew against Bill until it seemed like a tornado threatening to destroy his family. A well-known woman preacher prophesied that Meda Branham was going to die during this childbirth. This woman claimed that God had sent her to lead William Branham, and because he refused to follow her leadership, God was going to slay his wife. She printed this dire prophecy on postcards and sent them across the country to many different churches.

Unfortunately, Meda heard about this prophecy and quite naturally it upset her. She was already nervous about this pregnancy. In 1946 her first daughter, Rebekah, had to be taken by cesarean section. Five years later, her second daughter, Sarah, was also born cesarean. After both of these pregnancies, her doctor warned her not to have any more children—that to do so would be dangerous, and could even be fatal. Now she was about to have another baby and here was this horrible prophecy. For a while she tried to ignore it, but as her operation drew near, her courage faltered.

On May 18, 1955, the day before Meda's third cesarean operation, Bill found his wife in tears. He tried to reassure her.

"I want Margie to come with me, Bill. I don't feel like going to the hospital." Meda Branham and Margie Born, 1955 were bosom friends. Margie had been with Meda during both of her previous cesarean operations, but this time she was away from Jeffersonville due to a family emergency.

Bill answered, "Look, honey, we love Margie, but Margie is not our God. Margie is our sister. We're not depending on Margie; we're depending on the Lord Jesus."

"Bill, do you think I'm going to die?"

"I don't know, but the baby's going to be born. You're going to have a Joseph."

"Is this him?"

"I don't know, honey. I can't say, but God said you were going to have Joseph, and we're going to have Joseph. I don't care what anyone says differently, we're going to have Joseph. The same God who has told me all these revelations, He told me that. He has never failed on those other things, and He won't fail on this one either."

He did his best to encourage her, but she was so torn up over the dire prophecy that she was inconsolable. That tore Bill up inside. He needed to talk to God about this whole situation, so he got into his car and drove towards Green's Mill. All the way there he kept thinking about how God had specifically told him he would have another son. That was almost five years ago…

BACK IN JULY OF 1950, Bill held a tent meeting in Minneapolis, Minnesota. One day while he was in his motel room, he rejoiced as he read in Genesis about the life of Joseph the patriarch. Bill went into the closet where his clothes were hanging, pulled the door shut, and continued rejoicing, crying tears of joy.

He could see clearly that Abraham represented election; Isaac represented justification and love; Jacob represented grace; and Joseph represented perfection—that is, he was a perfect type of Christ. Joseph was loved by his father and hated by his brothers because he dreamed spiritual dreams. For 20 pieces of silver his brothers sold him into slavery, just like Judas betrayed Jesus for 30 pieces of silver. After many hardships and even imprisonment, Joseph was elevated to the place of a ruler in Egypt, second only to Pharaoh himself. From that position he was able to save his family from starving to death in a famine. Likewise, Jesus was tried, condemned, and sent to the prison of hell; but He rose from the dead and was elevated to the right hand of the Father, with all the power in heaven and earth at His command. Now Jesus could save His family on earth from eternal death.[106]

"Oh," Bill rejoiced, "I'll be so happy someday when I cross over to meet Joseph and shake his hand. To see Daniel and ask him how he felt when that Pillar of Fire stood there and held off those lions all night long. To see the Hebrew children, how they came out of the fiery furnace with that Pentecostal wind around them whirling. What a wonderful time!"

---

[106] Genesis chapters 30-50 (especially 37:28); Matthew 26:15; Acts 2:36; 1 Corinthians 15:4; Hebrews 12:2, etc.

"God," Bill prayed, "I want to thank You for a man like Joseph; a man who once lived on the earth; a man in flesh like I am; a man who could believe You and take Your Word. Thank You, Lord. Thank You for such a man." Bill sympathized with Joseph the patriarch. Joseph couldn't help being spiritual. He saw visions. He interpreted dreams. Most of his brothers hated him for it. He couldn't help it because that was just who he was. As Bill continued to pray he said, "Oh God, if You ever give me another boy, I'll name him Joseph."

As Bill was rejoicing, he heard a clear voice say within him, *"You will have a boy and you will call his name Joseph."* It wasn't an audible voice, nor a vision; but he heard it inside his head just as clearly as he heard a car door slam outside his motel room.

Bill thought, "Well now, that's fine. I thank You, Lord." And he went out from there a very happy man, telling his family, his church, and many other people about it.

Bill knew there are three levels of faith. The first level is basic hope, like when you say, "I hope you'll get well;" or, "I'm believing with you, trying to use all the faith I can." That is basic human faith—the kind everyone has to some degree. The second level is divine revelation, which is the kind of faith you have when God reveals something to you. You know in your heart it is going to happen; yet there is nothing outward that you can point to for proof it will happen; you just have a revelation that it will. The third level is a vision, which is prophetic, that is "thus saith the Lord." That level is always perfect. Bill felt he now had a divine revelation that someday he would have a son through Meda.

In the summer of 1950 Meda became pregnant. Bill wondered if this baby would be their Joseph. When the baby was born in March of 1951, it was a girl. They named her Sarah. After the cesarean operation, the doctor explained, "Mr. Branham, your wife's pelvic bones don't unhinge like they should in childbirth;

they are solid like a man. Really, she should never bear another child; her womb is too thin. You had better let me tie those fallopian tubes."

"No, I can't let you do that, doc."

"She shouldn't have another child. If she ever carries another baby, it might kill her. We had an awful time in there. She just barely came through it."

"I still can't let you tie those tubes, doctor. God told me I was going to have a son."

"Well, you might get married again and have that boy yet."

"No," said Bill, shaking his head. "God said I was going to have a son by Meda." Even though he had not seen it in a vision, it was written on his heart by divine revelation. By faith he knew it would happen.

Not everyone shared his faith. After Sarah was born, one man called Bill on the telephone and laughed at him. "Say, you know what? You meant Josephine."

"Sir, God told me I was going to have a son and I'd call his name Joseph."

Three people in his church (who had left a certain denominational church) decided he was a false prophet. "Wait a minute," Bill answered, "I never said *when*; neither did God say *when*. God told Abraham he was going to have Isaac, but Ishmael was born in between that time. That didn't take away from the promise. Someday I'm going to have a boy by Meda and we'll call his name Joseph, just like God said."

Four years had passed since then, and now Meda was going to have another baby...

BILL TURNED off the highway and drove to the Green's Mill area. He parked his car and headed towards his cave, which was at least a 30 minute hike from the highway. As he was walking through the woods, he saw that supernatural light hovering over a bush, floating in the air between two trees. A voice said, "*Turn and go back to your car. Your Bible will be laying open.*"

When Bill got back to his car, he saw that the wind coming through four open windows had blown the pages of his Bible open to 1 Chronicles chapter 17. Curiously Bill read versus 1 through 15, which tells how King David told Nathan the prophet that he wanted to build a solid temple to shelter the Ark of the Covenant (which at that time was still sitting in a tent). Impulsively Nathan said to David, "Do all that is in your heart, for God is with you." But that night the Lord appeared to Nathan and said, "Go to my servant David and remind him how I took him from being a shepherd and made him the King of Israel. I have been with him and I have cut off his enemies wherever he went." Nathan continued as a mouthpiece for God, saying to David, "*And it shall come to pass, when thy days be expired that thou must go to be with thy fathers, that I will raise up thy seed after thee, which shall be of thy sons; and I will establish his kingdom. He shall build me a house...*" Just as soon as Bill read the words *his sons*, he thought, "Oh my! There it is—Joseph!" He felt that the Lord was telling him not to worry—Joseph would be born and all would be well. He wept for joy.

Bill got into his car and drove home. As he pulled in to his driveway, he saw Meda taking out the garbage. She could hardly walk, she was so big with their child. Her face looked pale, almost gray. Bill ran over to her, put his arms around her, and said, "I want you to be of good courage."

Meda sniffed back her tears. "Why do you say that?"

"You know where I've been?"

"I have an idea."

"I have 'thus saith the Lord.' Honey, Joseph is coming. Joseph is on his road. Don't worry; everything will be all right now."

Meda had lived with her husband long enough to know that when he said 'thus saith the Lord,' the matter was truly settled. She had seen it happen too many times to doubt it. Finally, she relaxed.

At seven o'clock the next morning (May 19, 1955), Bill drove his wife to the hospital. The doctor, seeing that her baby had already dropped into the birth canal, exclaimed, "Oh mercy, goodness! Nurse, hurry! Let's get her into the operating room." Bill kissed his wife and said, "Honey, it won't be long now. In a few more minutes Joseph will be here."

They rushed Meda into the operating room. Bill waited and walked the floor with all the other anxious fathers who were wearing out the carpet. A few minutes passed and then the nurse came back to the waiting room, "Reverend Branham?"

"Yes, ma'am?"

"You have a fine seven-pound, three-ounce boy."

"Joseph, you've been a long time getting here. Daddy's kind of glad to see you."

The nurse said, "You called him Joseph?"

"That is his name."

A FEW DAYS after Joseph was born, Miner Arganbright stopped by Bill's house for a visit. Miner was a short man. Bill once joked that it took both Miner and his wife together to make one full-sized person. Despite his friend's small physical stature, Bill considered Miner Arganbright a giant in faith. He was vice-president of the Full Gospel Business Men's Fellowship

International. He also edited that organization's monthly magazine, *Full Gospel Business Men's Voice*, which regularly printed articles about the Branham Campaigns. Bill had known Miner for several years and respected his Christian character. He was humble, kind, generous, and always sensitive to the leading of the Holy Spirit.

Sitting on the edge of his chair, Arganbright said, "Brother Branham, I have a great revelation from the Lord."

Bill leaned forward. "Yes, sir?"

"The Lord wants me to go to Zurich, Switzerland. Do you want to go with me?"

Relaxing back into the cushions of his chair, Bill said, "I've got one night in Denver, Colorado. Then I've got a week in Macon, Georgia. After that I'm free. Let me think about it."

Praying about Switzerland left Bill with mixed feelings. God didn't tell him directly that he should go. Still, the more he thought about it, the more he felt that if Miner Arganbright had a revelation about this trip, it must be God's will.

BILLY PAUL BRANHAM knocked persistently on his father's hotel room door. No answer came, not even a stirring from inside. Billy Paul knew his father was deep in prayer for the evening service. On any other night Billy Paul would have left and tried again 15 minutes later—but not tonight. He kept knocking lightly and called, "Daddy, better come on; you're going to have to preach again tonight. Brother Jack isn't there."

Jack Moore had arranged for the meetings in Macon, Georgia, to start on Friday, June 3, and run consecutively for ten nights. A scheduling conflict prevented Moore from being there during the first three meetings. However, he promised Bill he would show up by Monday. Now it was Tuesday night and Jack Moore still had not arrived. That meant Bill would have to preach again before he prayed for the sick. He would have preferred to have his manager preach a preliminary, faith-building sermon. That way Bill could concentrate on the prayer service, which would conserve his strength. The anointing to preach and the anointing to see visions were completely different—the latter more strenuous than the former. Switching from one to the other put an extra strain on him; but he could do it if necessary.

This campaign in Macon was held outside in a football stadium. Folding chairs lined the football field. After four nights of miracles, not even the threat of rain could dampen the interest of these people—every folding chair on the field was occupied, as well as most of the bleacher seats. An elevated platform was built near one goal line. When Bill climbed the stairs to the podium, he still didn't know what he was going to preach. It wasn't until he greeted the people that his subject came to him.

He opened his Bible to the book of Joel, where the prophet spoke about a plague of insects that damaged every fruit tree and vine in the land of Israel. First he read Joel 1:4, "*That which the palmerworm hath left hath the locust eaten; and that which the locust hath left hath the cankerworm eaten; and that which the cankerworm hath left hath the caterpillar eaten.*" Then he read Joel 2:25, "*And I will restore to you the years that the locust hath eaten, the cankerworm, and the caterpillar, and the palmerworm, my great army which I sent among you.*"

His voice echoed slightly from the time lag between a dozen speakers strung up on light poles around the playing field. "God likens His church unto a vine. Jesus said, 'I am the Vine; you are the branches.'[107] Therefore, the life that was in Christ has to be in every branch. So if Christ preached the kingdom of God by healing the sick, every branch as it comes up will have to do the

---
[107] John 15:1-6

same thing, because they will have the same life in them that is in the vine."

So far he was covering familiar ground, but from this point he trod a new path and planted new seeds. He said there are two spiritual vines on the earth: one true and the other false. These two vines grow side by side so that their branches intertwine, which sometimes makes it difficult to tell which branch goes to which tree. But Jesus said, "By their fruit ye shall know them."[108]

"Remember," Bill stressed, "the antichrist spirit is religious. Jesus said in the last days it would be so close it would deceive the very elect if possible."

Referring to the book of Genesis, Bill showed how both Cain and Abel were religious; both were believers; both built altars; and both offered sacrifices to God. Cain worshipped God just as sincerely as Abel did. In fact, Cain's offering was more beautiful than his brother's. Cain offered fruit and flowers, whereas Abel offered a slain lamb. Cain's anger boiled when God rejected his offering, but accepted his brother's. Abel had a spiritual revelation that it wasn't fruit that caused sin to enter the world; sin came through blood. Abel realized that the only way sin could be atoned was through the shedding of blood, speaking of a day when the Lamb of God would give His own blood for the sins of fallen mankind.[109]

Bill followed these two vines from Genesis to Numbers chapter 23, where the children of Moab struggled against the tribes of Israel. These Moabites, who were descendants of Abraham's nephew Lot, worshipped the same God as Israel did. Just as Israel had a prophet in Moses, so Moab found a prophet in Balaam. Moab offered Balaam a lot of money if he would ask God to curse Israel. Balaam accepted Moab's offer. To approach God,

---

[108]   Matthew 7:15-23
[109]   Genesis 4:2-8

Balaam sacrificed seven bullocks and seven rams on seven altars. According to the Levitical laws, that was fundamentally correct.[110]

Here Bill shocked some people in his audience by pointing out, "You can be ever so fundamental and orthodox, and still be on your road to hell." He explained, "Although these two vines were growing side by side—both religious, both fundamental—it is only by their fruit they shall be known. Compare Judas with the other disciples. For years Judas was just as fundamental as the rest of them; but right before Pentecost, Judas showed his fruit—he couldn't go on to Pentecost and be born again. Many people don't believe there is an experience of being born again. They think it's all in your mind. No, brother, it happens in your soul.

"Compare Jesus with the Pharisees. Both believed in Jehovah God and both believed in the fundamentals of the Law, but supernatural signs and wonders vindicated Jesus. The apostles also had that vindication. So did the early church. And so will the true vine be vindicated in every age. Jesus said, 'In My name they shall cast out devils, lay hands on the sick and they shall recover.'[111] That is the difference between those two vines. They can both believe the fundamentals, but only the true vine has the Spirit and can see the light for their day. Remember, Paul said *the letter killeth, but the spirit giveth life.[112]*"

Bill knew this was a striking departure from his usual faith-building sermons; but that was his new commitment, to spend more time in each campaign teaching Bible fundamentals. Tonight he emphasized the most important fundamental of all: *Ye must be born again.[113]* No doubt he was making some people feel uncomfortable. That could not be helped. He could only hope that when these people saw the supernatural discernment in the

---

110 Numbers 23:1, 29; 1 Chronicles 15:26; 2 Chronicles 29:21; Job 42:7-8; Ezekiel 45:23
111 Mark 16:15-18
112 2 Corinthians 3:6
113 John 3:1-8

prayer-line, they would realize that what he taught them was the truth.

Later that evening, after he changed the mode of the service over to praying for the sick, visions cascaded one after another, each discernment cutting to the heart of somebody's problem. The second woman in line stood in front of him. Before she could say anything, Bill said, "Just a moment." He turned toward the audience, watching, listening. "It's an evil spirit screaming for help. I see a dark streak between this lady beside me and that woman sitting down there with her foot propped up on a chair. They both have cancer. This lady up here has cancer in her throat." He spoke to the woman standing beside him. "Have faith, lady. You're very nervous. They tried operating on you and now your voice comes out a hole in your throat. You're not from Georgia. You're from Melrose, Florida. Your name is Mrs. E. M. Robinson." A collective murmur rippled through the stadium. Bill laid his hand on Mrs. Robinson and rebuked the demon of cancer in Jesus' name. Then he spoke to the other woman sitting in the audience. "Sister, your cancer is on your breast. In the vision I can see the doctor's examination." Bill rebuked that demon of cancer also in the name of Jesus.

A young Methodist preacher watched this from high in the bleachers. Willard Collins thought, "This is not like the Methodist church. I've never seen anything like it before. I'm too far away to see much. Tomorrow I have to get closer."

The next night Willard looked for an empty chair near the platform. He couldn't find one. Even the space between the platform and the first row of chairs was filled with people sitting in wheelchairs and lying on cots. Willard stopped and asked an elderly black man how long he had been sick. "I've been bedridden for 17 years," the man replied. Noticing how withered the old man looked, Willard believed him. Unable to find a chair up close, Willard again took a seat in the bleachers.

During the service that night, William Branham said to one woman in the prayer-line, "You are suffering with a hideous thing called cancer. There is a death spirit hanging near you. But there is one thing you need more than healing, and that is salvation for your soul. You are a sinner. If you will repent now and give your life to Jesus Christ, He will heal you."

After she repented, she was healed. Bill watched her go briskly down the steps to the grassy field below. The angel followed her. While the woman walked along the aisle between the rows of folding chairs, the angel left her and moved over the section of cots and wheelchairs. Suddenly Bill pointed at the old colored man Willard Collins had talked to earlier. "You, sir, on that cot—do you believe me as God's prophet? You have no prayer-card, do you? You don't need one. Will you accept me as your prophet and obey me? Then get up from that cot, go home, and eat your supper. Jesus Christ will make you well. Amen."

The old man threw his spindly legs over the edge of his cot and stood. Someone steadied him for a minute. Then he walked on his own down the full length of the football field, and walked right out of the stadium.

Willard Collins felt his blood pounding in his neck. "This is real!" he thought. "I want in that prayer-line." For years Willard had suffered from an ulcerated stomach, which forced him to live on a strict diet of bland foods. For the first time in years he believed he could get well—if he could have William Branham pray for him.

Getting in the prayer-line proved to be difficult. Only 100 prayer-cards were passed out each night, and from that group only 15 to 30 people were selected to be in the line. Every night hundreds of people came to the stadium early to request a prayer-card. On Thursday night, Willard did not receive one. Disappointed, he wandered around for a while looking for a seat as close to the platform as he could get. Not only was there a place up front that was set aside for wheelchairs and cots, there was also a place reserved for people who were tape-recording the service. Willard noticed a small vacant space between two tape recorders. Running back to his pickup truck, he got a folding chair, brought it back into the stadium, and squeezed in among the tape recorders.

After William Branham had prayed for a dozen people in the prayer-line, he walked down the steps to the field, and walked among the cots and wheelchairs, praying for one here and one there. Then he stopped in front of Willard, put his hand on Willard's shoulder, and prayed, "Father, he's sick too. Heal him." Walking back up the steps to the stage, he stood before the microphone and said, "You probably couldn't see it, but the angel of the Lord led me to every person that I went to when I left here."

Willard Collins didn't see the angel, but he felt his presence. After the evangelist touched him and prayed, a strange sensation flowed through Willard's body. It felt almost like cool water passed over him and through him. From that day forward he could eat whatever he wanted. His stomach never bothered him again.

On the last night of this campaign, a certain woman came through the prayer-line. Bill told her exactly what her trouble was and how many operations she had undergone. Then he told her she didn't live in Macon, she lived in Augusta, Georgia, adding her name and address, even though he said he had never seen her before in his life. Although Willard had watched Branham discern the secrets of hundreds of people during this campaign, that fact did not lessen his amazement at this one. Then something happened that troubled him deeply. A woman sitting behind him said to her neighbor, "Brother Branham sure missed it that time. I know that woman and she doesn't live there."

Doubt pushed a sharp, wicked needle into Willard's faith. He had heard William Branham say, "If I ever tell you something wrong in discernment, don't believe anything else I tell you because that means I'm no longer being led by the Holy Spirit." Willard Collins saw the logic in that statement. If Branham could make a mistake in discernment, he could also make a mistake in doctrine. The question was, did he really make a mistake? Collins had to know. Over the next few days he played detective, asking this person and that person until finally he discovered the truth. It turned out that two days before she entered the Thursday night prayer-line, the woman in question had moved to a new house in Augusta, and her acquaintance sitting in the audience had not known she had moved. She did indeed live at the address William Branham had given.

Chapter 71
Controversy in Switzerland
June 1955

FLYING OVER FRANCE, William Branham looked down on a patchwork quilt of fields in various shades of green. Rivers meandered between the hills. Roads crisscrossed the landscape, sometimes intersecting at small villages, and other times getting lost in a maze of city streets. Cotton ball clouds cast a polka dot pattern of shadows across the ground. The hills got bigger until they became mountains. Eventually he saw Lake Zurich, looking like a greenish-blue serpent resting in a long, curving valley between Alpine peaks. A city crowded around the northwestern end of the lake. Soon the airport came into view. His plane started down into what looked like a serene valley. Actually, he was descending into a storm of religious controversy.

Bill landed in Zurich, Switzerland, on Saturday, June 18, 1955. Traveling with him were Billy Paul Branham; Fred Bosworth of Florida; Miner Arganbright of Los Angeles, California; and George Gardner of Birmingham, New York. Arganbright and Gardner had arranged these meetings with the support of the Full Gospel Business Men's Fellowship International (FGBMFI). Bill was scheduled to speak for nine days at the largest stadium in Zurich. Dr. Adolph Guggenbuhl—a Swiss lawyer, hotel owner, and FGBMFI leader—handled the arrangements in Switzerland

and also served as an interpreter for the American evangelistic team.

The controversy actually started earlier that week with the arrival of another famous American evangelist, Billy Graham, who was preaching his last service in Zurich the same day Bill arrived. Bill wanted to go and hear Billy Graham speak that night; but, tired from his long flight, he took a nap in his hotel room in the afternoon and woke too late to make it to the Graham meeting. Fortunately he was able to listen to it on the radio in his room. When Billy Graham preached that Jesus Christ was God Himself manifested in human flesh, Bill shouted, "Amen!" as loud as he could shout, because that was his message too.

That night he saw a powerful vision. He seemed to be standing in the air overlooking a huge model globe. The continents of Europe and Africa lay below him, with all of their hills and mountains rising to their proper heights according to the model's scale. On the highest peak in the Alps mountain range, near the border between Germany and Switzerland, sat a German eagle. The bird was watching a man riding a horse. The man looked like an English aristocrat dressed in traditional English riding clothes—red coat, red cap, white pants, and black leather boots. With keen eyes, the eagle watched this man ride across Europe and down through Africa, heading for the Cape of Good Hope. Bill heard the angel of the Lord say: *"All have sinned, and come short of the glory of God."*[114] When this vision left him, he felt so weak and numb that he was shaking.

On Sunday morning he woke to the clang and bong of church bells echoing across the valley. Zurich had so many bells ringing at once, Bill joked that the millennium must be starting. During breakfast, Dr. Guggenbuhl showed him a biting newspaper article about the Billy Graham crusade that was just ending in

---

[114]   Romans 3:23

Switzerland. This article didn't have anything good thing to say about Reverend Graham. His suit was too expensive; his cologne smelled too strong; and his hair was too wavy, as though he had spent hours in a beauty salon getting it fixed. The reporter didn't like his preaching style either. He said that Mr. Graham swung his arms wildly and shouted like a salesman trying to sell soap.

Bill was no stranger to attacks from the news media, but never before had he seen someone being criticized so furiously over such frivolous details. Dr. Guggenbuhl explained that this was not really about Mr. Graham's appearance and mannerisms. Billy Graham was preaching the supreme deity of Jesus Christ, which contradicted the doctrine of the Swiss Reformed Church—the oldest and largest Christian denomination in Switzerland. The Reformed Churches followed the teachings of Huldreich Zwingli, who was the most influential reformer in the Swiss branch of the Protestant reformation. Zwingli discounted the virgin birth of Christ, teaching instead that Jesus was the naturally born son of Joseph, and was only *called* the Son of God.

Bill thought, "If they criticize a man as polished as Billy Graham, what are they going to say about me?"

On Monday night, the first night of his campaign, Bill spoke to his audience for half an hour, trying to rouse their faith and prepare them for the prayer service. "I do not claim to be a healer. Jesus Christ is the only healer. I don't condemn doctors, hospitals, or medicine—these are God's gifts to us. Neither do I claim to take a doctor's place. But there are many things that doctors cannot do. Since that is true, we have a right to ask Jesus to help us. I believe He will do it. For nearly ten years now I have seen Him heal tens of thousands of people in my ministry: blind, crippled, twisted, lame, and halt. I have seen Him raise three people from the dead—two of them in the United States and one of them in Finland. He's the same Lord Jesus today as He was when He walked the earth.

"During His earthly ministry, Jesus also raised three people from the dead: Jairus' daughter, the widow of Nain's son, and Lazarus.[115] He could have raised more if the Father had showed Him more.

"Remember when Jesus was at the pool of Bethesda, He stopped by a man lying on a pallet. The man had been sick for 38 years, so the disease wasn't going to kill him. The place was crowded with people who were in worse condition than this fellow. Jesus healed only that one man. Why? He healed him because He had seen that man in a vision. When the Pharisees questioned Jesus about it, He said, 'Verily, Verily, I say unto you, the Son can do nothing by Himself; but what He sees the Father do, that doeth He.'[116]

"Now let us be reverent and take the right attitude towards the Lord Jesus. Your attitude towards any divine gift will determine what result you get from it. The sick woman who touched the hem of Jesus' garment felt His virtue, but the soldier who blindfolded Him and struck Him, saying 'If you're a prophet, tell us who hit you,' that soldier didn't feel anything.[117] It all depends on what attitude you approach Him with."

Bill continued along this line, trying to explain his unusual ministry using New Testament examples. When he called the prayer-line, the first person who came forward was a young woman. Bill said, "Everyone realizes these miracles cannot be done by man. I'm sure you Christians appreciate my position here. I'm representing your Lord and Savior, Jesus Christ.

"Now here stands a young woman. I've never seen her before in my life. We live thousands of miles apart. But God knows all about her. This is just like the time when Jesus stopped by a well

---

[115] Luke 8:40-56; 7:11-18; John 11:1-44, respectively
[116] John 5:1-19
[117] Luke 22:63-65

in Samaria and talked to a woman long enough to catch her spirit. He saw a vision of her trouble and said, 'You have five husbands, and the man you're living with is not one of them.' She said, 'Sir, I perceive you are a prophet. When the Messiah comes, He too will tell us things like that.' Jesus said, 'I am He.'[118] You see, revealing those secret things was the very sign of the Messiah. He is the same today."

Bill talked briefly with the young woman. Then he saw her shrink into a vision, and her secret was revealed. He said, "This woman is a Christian. She has throat trouble—tonsillitis. I hear a doctor telling her that her tonsils must be removed. She also has blood coming from her bowels. You speak English. You're not from Switzerland; you're from Germany. You came here by train and you must go back tonight. At home you have a grandmother who is dying with cancer and you also want her to be healed. If this is true, raise your hand so the audience can see." After she raised her hand, Bill said, "Go, lay your hands on your grandmother, for thus saith the Holy Spirit, 'You're going home to be well, in the name of the Lord Jesus Christ'."

Many visions and miracles followed.

The next morning, articles in Zurich's newspapers criticized Billy Branham worse than they criticized Billy Graham. The Reformed Churches called him a fraud and a quack, questioning his motives. This harsh criticism didn't reduce the size of that night's crowd (which approached the stadium's maximum capacity of 20,000), but it did put doubts in the minds of many (if not most) of the people who were sitting in the stadium.

When Bill was ready to pray for the sick and needy, he struggled under the weight of their doubts. On the platform where he could focus on one person at a time, his gift worked easily; but it wasn't moving out among the audience like it should. That hindered his

---

[118] John 4:1-26

entire campaign because the purpose of his discernment was to raise the faith of people so that anyone who needed healing could receive it from Jesus Christ.

That night, when the first person in the prayer-line stood before him, Bill said, "The man is beginning to move from me," which meant he was watching the man shrink into a vision. "He has cancer, which started in his side and has now gone into his liver. Unless God heals him, he will soon die." Snapping out of the vision, Bill said to his audience, "Now there is nothing you can hide. That voice speaking a moment ago wasn't me, your brother. It was Jesus Christ using my voice. What will happen next depends on this man's approach; what he thinks about it, that will determine what he receives." Apparently the man believed that Jesus Christ was there and able to heal, because after Bill prayed for him, he said he felt different.

The third person in line was a woman. Bill said, "I know nothing about this lady. The more I talk to her, the more the Lord Jesus will reveal to me through a vision. If God will tell me what you are here for, will you accept Him as your Healer? I see you being examined by a doctor who says you need to have your gallbladder removed. You don't want this operation, and that's why you're here tonight. I see you in a room praying for this opportunity. That is true. Your faith has saved you. In the name of Jesus Christ, be well."

Bill could feel waves of doubt coming from all over the stadium. Many people seemed to have the same attitude they would have at a soccer game. "Please, people, don't get up and move around," Bill said. "It's very irreverent. You're disturbing the Spirit." He discerned the problems of several more people in the prayer-line, and then he turned back to the audience. Pointing to a section of seats, he said, "What about you along there? Do you believe with all your heart? This is mysterious to you because you've never been taught the supernatural. You don't understand it. That same light that is anointing me has swayed over that part of the audience three times since I've been standing here—and you people won't move to it. Right now every one of you should be on your feet, healed. He is here! You just have to accept it."

Gradually skepticism dwindled and faith rose. Hundreds of people in the audience claimed their healing in Jesus' name. When Bill gave an altar call, thousands of people stood and surrendered their lives to Jesus Christ.

Not all of the people attending this Branham campaign were from Switzerland. Throughout the week, thousands of people poured into Zurich, coming from all over central Europe to hear William Branham preach. Miner Arganbright counted 180 buses from Germany lined up in the stadium's parking lot. During the day, so many strangers came into town that every public place bustled with activity. To avoid any problems his presence might cause, Bill spent most of his spare time in his hotel room; except for one morning late in the week, when the angel of the Lord told him directly, "*Get out and go down by the lake.*"

Bill asked his son to go with him. Billy Paul thought it was a bad idea. "Dad, somebody will recognize you. Then you'll get tangled up in a crowd and we'll have to get the police down there to fish you out."

"Well, the Lord is telling me to go down to the shore, so I'd better go."

Reluctantly, Billy Paul followed his father. Because Switzerland had not been bombed in World War II, Zurich retained its historic charm in good condition, having many cobblestone streets and ornately decorated brick buildings that were hundreds of years old. The lakefront area was developed into a tourist park with well-kept lawns and many trees, flowers, fountains, and promenades in front of the hotels, and well-groomed paths along the beach.

Bill strolled along the shore, enjoying the sunshine as much as the picturesque scenery around him. It felt good to be outside exercising his legs. Billy Paul was nervous about the hundreds of other people on the beach, some sitting on benches or lying on blankets, others strolling up and down the shore. After a while, when no one recognized them, Billy Paul relaxed.

Father and son walked a long ways together. Eventually they approached an old man sitting on a bench, hunched over a book that looked like a Bible. Tears dribbled down the old man's cheeks like dew glistening in the morning sunlight. Bill felt the presence of the angel. One more step transported him to a different country where he saw this same old man taking a handkerchief from a young woman with a withered arm. Five little children clung to the woman's skirt. The vision continued, giving more details before it dropped him back on that footpath by Lake Zurich.

"There he is," Bill said to Billy Paul, "the man God sent me down here to see."

"You aren't going to just walk up and talk to that man, are you Dad?"

"No, he's going to walk up and talk to me. He is from far away. You watch and see if he doesn't have something for me, something that pertains to a woman's arm."

"How do you know?"

"A vision struck me. Here we go. Just look out at the lake and walk by him."

Bill looked out over the blue-green water, watching little sailboats that swam as gracefully as swans. The lake curved, hiding its far end behind a huge mountain that thrust up from the water's edge. Many trees and shrubs dotted the mountainside, and several waterfalls poured over steep cliffs. The wake of a passing motorboat sent waves lapping against the beach.

Billy Paul said, "Daddy, that man is following us."

"I know it. When we go around this next bend, we're going to cross a footbridge, and he's going to overtake us right at that bridge."

Ahead of them the path curved around a building surrounded by a grove of trees. Rounding the bend, they came upon a footbridge over a creek that fed into the lake. When they were halfway over the bridge, the stranger caught up with them. "Brother Branham," he said in heavily accented English. Bill turned to face him. The man gave his name and said he was from Russia. Miraculously, several hundred Russians had managed to get visas to come to Bill's meetings in Zurich. Taking a white handkerchief out of his satchel, the old Russian handed it to Bill. He said that back home there was a mother who had hurt her arm so badly it wouldn't heal. Now her arm was withered and useless, making it hard for her to care for her five young children. The old man wanted Bill to pray over this handkerchief and tear it into six strips. He believed that when he returned to Russia, God would use those six anointed strips to heal that crippled mother and bless her five children.

Bill prayed over that handkerchief, and then cut it into strips with his pocketknife. As he handed it back to the elderly man, Bill asked, "How did you know I was in Switzerland?"

"I heard it through a Swiss radio station broadcasting into Russia."

"Did you ever hear of my meetings before?"

"Yes, Brother Branham. You once prayed for a dead boy in Finland and God brought him back to life. That story went deep into Russia. For years I have wanted to meet you; but how could I get past the iron curtain? The Communists would never allow me to visit America. Then I heard you were going to be in Switzerland. Today is a miracle."

Bill thought of the man by the pool of Bethesda, and of the woman who touched Jesus' robe.[119] Like those two people long ago, this elderly Russian had approached the promises of God with the right attitude.

---

[119] John 5:1-19; Matthew 9:20-22

Chapter 72
Opossum Fever
1955

WHEN HE RETURNED from Switzerland, William Branham found a white mountain of mail waiting for him at his office in Jeffersonville. That was not surprising. Whenever he was gone, his mail piled up like a never-ending snowfall. His two secretaries, Mr. and Mrs. Cox, handled most of it without needing Bill's direct attention. The majority of these letters came from people asking for prayer cloths. Bill would go out to his cave near Tunnel Mill and spend all afternoon praying over a roll of white ribbon. Then Mr. and Mrs. Cox would cut the ribbon into six-inch long strips and mail these strips free of charge to every person who requested one. Lots of letters contained testimonies about healings and miracles that happened during the campaigns, or from receiving a prayer cloth. Letters like these did not require an answer.

There were other letters that did need Bill's personal attention. Right now he had telegrams and letters from 400 major cities worldwide, asking him to hold faith-healing campaigns in their areas. Of course he could only accommodate a small fraction of these requests. He included each one in his prayers and asked God to lead him to the places he should go to next. His methods made it difficult for his managers to plan. They would prefer to schedule his meetings at least six months in advance. He wanted to be more flexible so he could follow the leading of the Holy Spirit on short notice. He had the first weekend in August scheduled for Campbellsville, Kentucky. Then he had a week to get ready for his trip to Germany. His campaign in Karlsruhe, Germany, would begin on the 12th of August.

Each week Bill also received dozens of telephone calls, telegrams, and letters from people asking him to come and pray for them personally. If they sent a letter, they often included a roundtrip airplane ticket with their requests. There was no way he could travel and pray for all these people in person. If he tried, that is all he would do with his time. He did pray for each of these people when he read their letters and telegrams, and he was always open to the possibility that sometime God might direct him to make a special trip.

One day he was studying in his den when the walls dissolved. He found himself standing on the sidewalk of a city street. None of the houses around him looked familiar. The door of a white house opened and out came a man holding a black bag. This man walked down the path, opened a gate in a picket fence, crossed the sidewalk in front of Bill, got into a gray car and drove away.

From somewhere behind Bill's right shoulder, the angel of the Lord said, "*Look on the other side of the gate.*" Opening the gate, Bill saw a hoe lying on the ground next to a cultivated bed of flowers. The angel said, "*Go to the door. You will meet a woman wearing a brown coat who is weeping because she is so worried about her sick boy. Ask to see the boy. She will take you to a bedroom. When you lay your hat on the bed, she will move it to the top of a television set. Wait until a woman wearing a red sweater comes into the bedroom and sits by the bed. When both women are in the room, then lay your hands on the boy and say, 'Thus saith the Lord, you are healed.'*"

Abruptly the scene changed. Now he seemed to be standing on a city street looking through the window of a variety store. A large, electric clock hung on the wall of the store. Bill heard a rhythmic squeak, squeak, squeaking noise. Turning to look for its source, he saw a nurse pushing a man in a wheelchair with squeaky wheels. A Bible lay on the man's lap. The angel said, *"Notice the time."* Bill looked again at the clock, noting that it was ten minutes until three o'clock. Then the angel said, *"Tell the man to rise and walk."* At that moment the vision ended and Bill returned to his den.

Like most of his visions, this one had stamped vivid impressions into his brain. As with all memories, Bill knew these could fade with time, so the first thing he did was write each scene down in his vision book.

Three days later, while reading his mail, one letter touched him differently than the others. A man in Denver, Colorado, who was dying from tuberculosis, wanted Bill to fly to Denver and pray for him at once. Although this letter was similar to dozens of other letters Bill had read in the last three days, this time the Holy Spirit inside him said, *"Go!"*

He flew to Denver, took a cab to the man's house, and prayed for him. Since Bill had several hours before the next plane left for Louisville, Kentucky, he decided to walk downtown. After strolling a dozen blocks through a residential neighborhood, he heard a door open and saw a man with a briefcase come out of a white house. A woman inside the house said, "Good-bye, doctor."

"Isn't that strange?" Bill thought. "It's like I've seen him somewhere before." The doctor walked through a gate in a white picket fence, got into a gray Ford sedan, and drove away. That fired a synapse in Bill's brain. He walked over and opened the gate. On the ground lay a hoe next to a flowerbed, just like he had seen in that vision a few days ago. Walking up to the door, he knocked. A young woman opened the door just enough to see out. She was wearing a brown coat, just like the angel had said. Her eyes looked red and moist.

"Hello," Bill said, taking off his hat. "Do you have a sick little boy?"

One of her eyebrows lifted in a quirky frown. "Yes, I do. Are you a doctor?"

"No, ma'am, I'm a minister. My name is Branham."

"I don't believe I know you, Mr. Branham."

"I'm a stranger in this city. My ministry is to pray for the sick, and the Lord has directed me to your house. Can I see your son?"

She thought for a moment and then, as if to say, "Why not?" she shrugged and opened the door wide. He followed her to a bedroom where a small boy lay shivering under a layer of blankets. Bill tossed his hat on the bedcover below the boy's feet. Instead of the mother moving it to the top of the television set, she sat in a chair next to the bed. Bill thought, "I can't say a word about the vision. I'll just have to wait until everything falls into place." So he asked the mother, "What is wrong with your son?"

"He has pneumonia. The doctor says it is very serious."

They discussed the boy's condition for several minutes, and then the mother picked up Bill's hat and put it on top of the television. Bill thought, "Well, that part is done, but I still can't pray for the boy." After a while an older woman wearing a red sweater entered the bedroom and sat down. At the same time, the mother got up and left the room! Bill waited patiently, chatting with the grandmother until finally the mother returned and everything was just the way he had seen it in the vision.

Bill said, "Stand up, both of you." He stood also. Walking to the head of the bed, he laid his hands on the child and said, "Thus saith the Lord, 'You're healed.'"

The boy called for his mother, reaching out his arms. She sat down on the edge of the bed and held him, laying her cheek on his forehead. She looked up in surprise. "His fever is gone."

Returning to the street, Bill looked in vain for a taxi. He was a little concerned about missing his plane, so he walked briskly toward the center of town, looking for a busier intersection so he could find a cab. Eventually he came to a row of stores. This seemed like as good of a spot as any to wait for a taxi. He went into a variety store to buy something sweet. While he was paying the cashier, he noticed an electric clock on the wall. The time was ten minutes to three o'clock. He knew he was in the right place at the right time. As soon as he walked out of the store, he heard the squeak, squeak, squeaking sound he was expecting. A nurse was pushing a man in a wheelchair along the sidewalk. Just like he had seen him in his vision, the man in the wheelchair had a Bible sitting on his lap.

Walking over to the invalid, Bill asked, "Do you believe that book?"

With a firm voice the man replied, "Yes, sir, I do."

"Good, because that book holds the words of eternal life. Did you ever read in it where Jesus healed the sick?"

"Many times."

"Do you believe that He can do the same thing today?"

"Yes, sir, I do."

"Then in the name of the Lord Jesus Christ, stand, because thus saith the Lord, 'You are healed.'"

Shifting his weight forward and grasping the armrests of his wheelchair, the man tried to get up. Startled, his nurse put one hand on his shoulder and pushed him back down, protesting, "You can't get up. You'll hurt yourself."

"Get up," Bill insisted. "Take my word for it—you're healed."

"Who are you?" the man asked.

"That doesn't matter. Rise, sir, in the name of the Lord."

The man pushed his nurse's hand away from his shoulder and stood. Then he didn't just walk, he ran. At that moment a taxi came around the corner and headed their way. Bill waved it over, and soon he was speeding towards the airport.

The next day he stopped by the Jeffersonville public library to read a Denver newspaper. It didn't take him long to find the article he was looking for. The headline read: "Mystic Healing of Man on the Street." Nobody in Denver knew what had really happened. Bill didn't see any point in telling them.

AFTER his June 1955 campaign in Switzerland, William Branham spent almost six weeks at home with his family. The only preaching he did was a weekend campaign in Campbellsville, Kentucky, and a few Sunday sermons at his home church. Orman Neville, who was the assistant pastor at Branham Tabernacle, eagerly stepped aside to let Bill address the congregation. Although Bill had tried to resign as pastor when he stepped into full time evangelism in 1946, his congregation wouldn't let him. They still considered him their pastor, even though he only preached in Jeffersonville occasionally. Over the years Bill had come to accept this arrangement as an outgrowth of their love and respect for him. Currently, with his emphasis shifting towards more teaching, it meant he had a pulpit where he could teach in depth. During his faith-healing campaigns, even though he was now teaching more doctrine, he still felt restricted in what he could say, and how deeply he could go on certain subjects. At home in Branham Tabernacle he could teach doctrine as thoroughly as time would allow.

On Sunday, July 24, 1955, he taught on demonology. He used many Scriptures to explain how demonic spirits can affect the lives of people, and he illustrated these points with examples drawn from his own experiences battling demons in his prayer services. He called this sermon, "Enticing Spirits."

Before he approached his text, he held a short dedication service, praying over several babies, dedicating them to the Lord. He didn't believe in baptizing infants. Instead he taught that the souls of children are safe in Christ until they become old enough to be held accountable for their own choices. The apostle Peter said, *"Repent, and be baptized every one of you in the name of Jesus Christ for the remission of sins, and ye shall receive the gift of the Holy Ghost."*[120] Baptism is a conscious public act by new converts, testifying that they have turned away from their sins to follow Jesus Christ. Since infants could not repent, they should not be baptized. However, Bill encouraged Christian families to bring their children to church and let a minister pray for God's blessing on these young lives. He quoted from Mark 10:13-16, where Jesus said: *"Suffer the little children to come unto me, and forbid them not: for of such is the kingdom of God... And he took them up in his arms, put his hands upon them, and blessed them."* One of the babies Bill dedicated to the Lord that morning was his own son, Joseph.

ALTHOUGH William Branham was taking a summer break from his busy evangelistic schedule, his time at home was not always restful. Out-of-town people stopped by his house at all hours, wanting prayer. Because he saw visions, many people thought of him as a prophet and believed if they could sit in his living room and talk to him about their problems, God would give His prophet a "Thus saith the Lord" specifically for them. They were right; but in their eagerness to hear a message from God, they didn't realize the strain these interviews put on the messenger.

---

[120] Acts 2:38

Most people in his own congregation did understand, and to lighten his burden, some of them tried to help their pastor whenever they could. One day in July, Banks Wood, who lived next door, mowed Bill's lawn. Early the next morning Banks and his wife crossed their property line to rake up the grass clippings in Bill's yard before the sun got too hot. About ten o'clock Bill went outside to thank his neighbors. While they talked, Leo Mercer and Gene Goad drove up. Bill jokingly referred to Leo and Gene as his "students." Like Banks Wood and Willard Collins, Leo and Gene had moved to Jeffersonville to be near William Branham and his ministry. When Bill traveled, Leo, Gene, and Banks often went along to tape-record his services. Then they duplicated these recordings and supplied them at minimal cost to the growing number of people who wanted copies.

Leo, Gene, and Mrs. Wood stood in the yard and talked to Bill. Soon Banks laid down his rake and joined them. The conversation turned to a local murder that happened a few days earlier. A young woman had smothered her newborn baby in a blanket, tied the bundle with wire, and dropped the dead baby off a bridge into the Ohio River. Bill used this tragedy to illustrate the decline in moral values he was seeing as he traveled across North America. Year by year it seemed to be growing worse. Unfortunately this moral decay was also creeping into churches.

This backward slide was especially noticeable among women. It amazed Bill how many Christian women were discarding their feminine heritage and adopting masculine traits, like cutting their hair, wearing pants, and even preaching the Gospel from the pulpit—all in contradiction to God's Word.[121] Every year more Christian women were leaning in the wrong direction. They were copying the sleazy styles of the world, trying to look alluring by painting their faces with makeup and wearing indecent clothes,

---

[121]   1 Corinthians 11:1-15; Deuteronomy 22:5; 1 Timothy 2:9-15, respectively

like tight, skimpy dresses or short pants, and even bathing suits that were so skimpy on material that they were really about the same thing as colored underwear. This shift in values affected children also. Instead of mothers teaching their children godliness and decency, they were teaching them ungodliness and indecency by their examples. Worst of all, many Christians didn't know these things offended the Holy Spirit.

Until recently Bill hadn't said much about things like these in his sermons, feeling it was the duty of pastors to correct their congregations. But too many pastors were not preaching against worldliness and carnality. Bill felt someone had to do it. If pastors wouldn't preach against it, then he would. People needed to know the difference between right and wrong. The standards of the church must be upheld if Christians wanted to be the Bride of Jesus Christ.

While he was talking, Bill noticed an opossum turn in his gate and waddle down the gravel driveway toward his house. That was odd. Although opossums are common in southern Indiana, they prowl at night and never travel during the day unless something disturbs them. In daylight they are practically blind. So why was this one here? Opossums usually shy away from people. Could this one have rabies? He studied it carefully. From a distance it looked normal. A little larger than a cat, it had coarse, grayish-white hair covering its body, fine white hair on its face, an elongated snout, small hairless ears, and a hairless, rat-like tail.

As it came closer, Bill noticed it was limping, dragging a front foot. Bill walked over to get a closer look. The animal didn't stop at his approach, but it was hobbling so slowly that Bill could study it easily. A wicked wound disfigured the side that he had not seen from a distance. Perhaps a car had hit it, or perhaps a dog had chewed it up. Whatever happened, its shoulder was mangled and bloody from a wound that stretched all the way up to its ear.

The leg was probably broken. Green flies buzzed around the open wound and maggots crawled in the pink flesh.

Using the handle of a lawn rake, Bill pushed the opossum over on its side so he could see the extent of its injuries. Normally in such a situation, an opossum would fall limp and play dead; but this one growled and bit at the rake handle. That is when Bill saw she was a mother trying to protect her babies. An opossum, like a kangaroo, carries its young in a pouch across its stomach. This mother was so weak that her stomach muscles couldn't keep her pouch closed. Bill counted eight tiny babies squirming inside her pouch.

"Gene, Leo, come here and I'll show you a lesson. See this mother opossum. She may be a dumb animal, but in my mind she is a real lady. She has more motherhood in her than a lot of today's women, especially that one who dropped her baby in the river the other day. That woman considered her baby a burden, and she killed it so she could run around to taverns and have a good time. Now consider this mother opossum. She probably has only a few hours left to live, and yet she will spend the last of her strength fighting to protect her babies."

As soon as Bill let up on the rake handle, the mother opossum struggled to her feet and limped the rest of the way to Bill's house, where she collapsed next to the porch steps.

Mrs. Wood said, "Brother Branham, you should kill her and put her out of her misery. You'll have to kill those babies too. They're so tiny, you won't be able to feed them yourself."

Bill shook his head. "Sister Wood, I can't do it."

"Why?" she asked. "You're a hunter. You've killed lots of game."

"Yes, I'm a hunter, but I only kill things I can eat or otherwise make use of. Or sometimes I've killed animals that were destroying other animals. I never kill just to be killing."

"This wouldn't be pointless killing. That opossum is going to die anyway, and then all those babies will starve. Killing them is the humane thing to do."

"I know you're right, Sister Wood, but for some reason I can't bring myself to do it."

"Then let Banks take them out and kill them."

"No," Bill said, "let's just leave them right where they are for now."

All day that mother opossum lay next to the porch, baking in the July sun. Everyone who came for interviews and for prayer noticed her and asked about her. Several times during the day Bill prodded her with a stick to see if she was still alive. Each time she grunted, but otherwise made no effort to move, not even when Bill set some food and water beside her. Once he poured water over her wound to chase away the flies, but they swarmed right back.

That evening Banks Wood knocked on his door and said "Brother Branham, you've ministered enough for today. Why don't you let me take you for a drive so you can relax a little?" Bill gladly accepted.

They spent the next few hours driving around the countryside, admiring woodlands and cornfields, farmhouses and barns, all the while talking about the goodness of God. When Bill returned home at 11 o'clock, he prodded the opossum to see if she was dead yet. She groaned pitifully and shivered.

That groan haunted him all night. For an hour he paced the floor thinking about how strange it was that a mother opossum had come to his house—in broad daylight, no less. After he went to bed, her groan seeped into his dreams. Early the next morning he stepped out on his front porch to nudge the opossum again with his foot. This time her back leg twitched, but otherwise she didn't move. She didn't even open her eyes. Bill knew it wouldn't be long now until she was dead. He went back in the house and sat in his den. Rubbing his face, he thought, "One way or another I'm going to have to do something with that opossum today. What should I do?"

Out of nowhere a voice said to him, *"Yesterday you called her a lady and used her for a sermon. You praised her for being a real mother."*

"Yes, that's right," Bill answered. "What about it?"

"She has laid at your doorstep like a lady, patiently waiting her turn for prayer."

"Well, I didn't know. I—" Bill sat up stiffly. His eyes looked around his den as he wondered, "What's happening? Who am I talking to? I was answering somebody."

Clearly he heard a voice say, *"I sent her to your house for prayer. Now she has laid by your door almost 24 hours and you still haven't prayed for her."*

Bowing his head, Bill said, "Dear God, was that You sending her to me? Forgive Your stupid servant for not understanding." Now he could see it plainly. The opossum could only have come from that patch of woods about 150 yards up the street. In order to reach his house, she first had to drag herself past four other houses, all closer to the road than his, all without fences. His was the only yard along this block that had a fence, yet she had limped down his driveway, refusing to stop until she reached his door. God must have been leading her.

Striding outside, he stood next to the mother opossum, raised his hands in the air, and prayed, "Heavenly Father, I know You lead Your children to be prayed for when they are sick. I also know You even care about sparrows.[122] If Your Holy Spirit has led

---
[122] Matthew 10:29-31; Luke 12:6-7

this dumb animal here to be prayed for, forgive me for being too stupid to know it. I pray thee, Heavenly Father, in Jesus' name, heal this gallant mother."

As soon as he mentioned *Jesus*, that mother opossum raised her head and looked in Bill's eyes. A minute later she rolled over, gathered up her babies and stuffed them back in her pouch. Then she got to her feet and took a few wobbly steps down the path. With each step she seemed to get stronger. By the time she scurried across the driveway, she didn't show the slightest sign of a limp. When she reached the gate, she stopped by one of the pyramid-shaped pillars and looked back at Bill, as if to say, "Thank you, kind sir." Then she turned, went through the gate and scurried up the street, heading for the safety of the woods.

Telling this story later, Bill said, "If God is concerned enough to take pity on an ignorant opossum, think of how much more He cares about His sons and daughters who are in need. The power of Satan is limited. The power of God is unlimited."

Chapter 73
Preaching in Germany and Switzerland
1955

DR. ADOLPH GUGGENBUHL considered William Branham's faith-healing campaigns in Zurich, Switzerland, a phenomenal success. The size of the crowds impressed him; so did the excitement and reverence he saw in the faces of all those people who heard the supernatural discernment and saw Jesus Christ heal the sick and perform other miracles. As soon as the Zurich campaign ended, Dr. Guggenbuhl asked William Branham to let him arrange an immediate follow-up campaign in Europe for that summer. When Bill agreed to return, Dr. Guggenbuhl scheduled two weeks of meetings for the middle of August 1955—the first week in Karlsruhe, Germany, and the second week in Lausanne, Switzerland. However, when the leaders of the Swiss Reformed Church learned about these plans, they did everything they could to prevent these meetings from happening. When their efforts in Switzerland failed, they flooded the German parliament with complaints and pressured that government into barring William Branham from entering Germany. Dr. Guggenbuhl drove to Bonn to lodge his own complaint. It didn't do any good. The influence of the Swiss Reformed Church had shut and locked the door. Dr. Guggenbuhl prayed about what to do next, and God showed him how to pick the lock.

After Germany's defeat in World War II, the country was divided into four sections. Each sector was supervised by one of the conquering Allied armies: American, English, French, and Russian. The city of Karlsruhe stood in the American occupied zone. Dr. Guggenbuhl decided to take his case directly to the American colonel in charge of that district.

A secretary ushered Dr. Guggenbuhl into the commander's office. The colonel greeted him politely, and then sat behind his desk to listen. Dr. Guggenbuhl explained, "I represent an American evangelist who believes God wants him to preach in Germany this month. But the Reformed Churches oppose his doctrine, so they convinced the government to deny him entrance. My argument is this: If they let Billy Graham come in and preach, why can't this other man?"

The colonel leaned back in his chair and asked, "What do they have against this fellow?"

"He prays for the sick and gets results—big results—miraculous results. I think the Reformed Church is uncomfortable with the idea of a supernatural God who people can see in action."

"'Prays for the sick,' you say. Hmmm. Who is this evangelist?"

"His name is William Branham."

"Brother Branham!" The colonel rocked forward in his chair. "My mother was healed in a Branham meeting back in Virginia. She rose out of a wheelchair. Tell Brother Branham to come on. I'll personally see to it that he gets in."

Although the Reformed Church didn't keep Bill out of Germany, they did keep him from using the Black-Forest Auditorium in Karlsruhe, even though the city council had previously given its verbal consent for the use of that building.

Thankfully, the Reformed Church's opposition didn't stop Dr. Guggenbuhl, who immediately explored other options. Soon he came up with a workable plan. He rented a soccer field from a sports club. Then the town of Duerkheim supplied a huge rectangular tent which they pitched in the center of that field. The city council of Karlsruhe, perhaps feeling a little guilty, helped to fill this tent with chairs. It was a giant undertaking, but when it was completed this makeshift cathedral could shelter up to 8,000 people from either sunshine or rain. Whether or not it could withstand a windstorm was questionable.

On Thursday, August 11, 1955, Bill and Billy Paul Branham, Fred Bosworth, and Miner Arganbright boarded a plane in New York City and flew to Karlsruhe, Germany. They began their faith-healing campaign on Friday night. Many thousands of people filled the canvas cathedral, with several thousand more standing outside, looking in through the open door-flaps. Seventy-seven buses and hundreds of cars waited in the parking field. The next two days opened Germany's eyes to the supernatural. On Sunday afternoon Bill offered eternity to every man, woman and child who accepted the blood sacrifice of Jesus Christ as atonement for his or her sins. Thousands of people accepted this invitation. That night Jesus again proved He was alive: first, through His perfect discernment; and second, through His powerful miracles.

After the service that night, a squad of German military police escorted Bill and Billy Paul to their car. Communist terrorists had threatened to assassinate the American evangelist, so the government had assigned this squad of policemen to protect him. As Bill got near the black sedan that was shuttling him back and forth to the meetings, another car veered from the street and careened through the parking lot, heading straight for the evangelist and his son. Bill jumped into the backseat, but Billy

Paul was still in the fanatic's path. Just in time, Bill jerked his son out of harm's way.

The next morning the leader of a spiritualist cult asked to meet with the American evangelist. Dr. Guggenbuhl refused to let the man have an interview. The offended cult leader said to Guggenbuhl, "Today I and my followers will cast a spell on Branham's meeting. We'll conjure up a storm so big it will blow the whole place down. We'll show him our power." When Dr. Guggenbuhl told Bill about this threat, Bill wasn't concerned, knowing that the power of Jesus Christ could prevail over any spell of the enemy.

That night Fred Bosworth preached about faith and healing in Jesus' name, laying a foundation for the prayer-line to follow. All day a gentle breeze pushed cumulus clouds across the sky, sometimes hiding and sometimes revealing the sun. Shortly after Bill climbed the stairs to the platform and greeted his audience, the breeze stiffened, sucking the canvas inward on its wooden framework, then snapping it out like a billowing sail—sucking it in, snapping it out, over and over like monstrous lungs gasping. Distant thunder warned the crowd of worse weather approaching. Bill continued talking on the subject of faith and healing, telling the story of blind Bartimaeus sitting by the Jericho road, crying for Jesus to stop and heal him.[123] Soon the howling wind made it difficult for the crowd to hear him, even with the help of the loudspeakers. The thunderheads blew nearer, rumbling like the battlefront of an approaching army, with cannons firing and shells exploding. The wind tugged relentlessly on a canvas structure that was not built to withstand such stress. It swirled around the edges of the door-flaps, threatening to lift the building like a kite.

Bill knew this was not an ordinary storm. Since the first crack of thunder sounded, he had been praying for the Lord to show

---

[123]   Referring to Mark 10:46-52

him what to do. Now he saw a small dark shadow drifting over the crowd. He watched that shadow until he saw it settle over a group of 15 men sitting in a row. They pointed feathers at him and mouthed words that he couldn't understand. (Later he learned they were chanting, "In the name of the Father, the Son, and the Holy Ghost, we call forth a storm to destroy you.") Then he noticed another row of men across the aisle doing the same thing—perhaps 30 men in all, waving feathers and chanting. While Bill studied these men and their peculiar actions, a vision parted the curtain between dimensions, revealing the leader of this cult bowing to the unbound devils around him.

Turning to his interpreter, Bill said, "Brother Lauster, don't interpret this." Then he bowed his head and prayed, "Lord God, Creator of heaven and earth, I stand on German soil in the name of Jesus Christ. You sent me here for the salvation of these people. Satan, I command you in Jesus' name to depart from here." Raising his head, he looked at that cult leader and said softly, "You child of the devil, like Jannes and Jambres stood against Moses, so do you have the power to perform miracles.[124] But you can't touch the supernatural God. Because you've tried to destroy this service, you'll have to pay a price."

Suddenly Bill saw the Pillar of Fire in front him, just beyond the edge of the platform, hovering over a woman who was strapped securely to an ambulance stretcher. By vision, he foresaw something miraculous. "There," he said, pointing. "The woman lying there strapped to that bed—she has tuberculosis, and her backbone is eaten in two. Somebody untie those straps."

A distinguished-looking man sitting in the front row stood and objected. "You can't do that! I'm her doctor. She must remain completely immobilized or she could die."

---

[124] Exodus 7:11-12 and 22; 2 Timothy 3:8

"Untie her," Bill insisted, "for thus saith the Lord, 'She is healed.'"

Someone undid the straps and the woman on the stretcher, lifted by faith, stood. The audience uttered a collective gasp as she walked barefoot down the sawdust aisle. This first miracle of the Karlsruhe campaign lit a fire of anticipation in thousands of hearts and shook many doubters awake, but not all…

Ten minutes had passed since Bill had rebuked the cult leader whose spell had conjured this storm. During that time, the wind had dropped to a whisper and the clouds had evaporated, letting the setting sun kiss the canvas cathedral goodnight. Bill finished his sermon, and then called 15 prayer-card numbers. As these 15 people formed into a line on his right, Bill noticed that the man who had challenged him was now slumped forward in his seat. "Brother Lauster, look at that man over there. See how his head is forward and his arms are hanging limp. Something has happened to him. Send someone over there to see what is wrong."

When they investigated, they discovered that the cult leader couldn't move. A group of ushers had to carry him out of the building. Bill never did learn what became of him.

While everyone on the platform was watching this little drama end, an usher led a blind girl up the steps to the platform and left her standing alone. That was a mistake. Restless, the blind girl wandered ahead looking for the American evangelist. Bill saw her just as she was about to step off the edge of the platform. Hastily he grabbed her and pulled her back.

In German she said, "I want to meet the man who is going to pray for me."

Mr. Lauster said, "He is holding your hand."

The girl hugged Bill so warmly that his heart melted with pity. She looked so innocent in her flower-print dress, her hair parted down the middle and braided into two long plaits. She was about eight years old, the same age as his daughter Becky.

Suddenly a vision shrank this girl to the size of a newborn baby. Bill saw her cradled in her mother's arms. Her mother was a tall, thin, blond woman. Her father was a heavyset man who had dark hair. Next Bill saw a doctor lean over the baby, examine her eyes, and pronounce her blind. When the vision left him, Bill told his audience what he had seen, even as he searched their faces, looking for the parents. He saw the girl's mother sitting a few rows back. Bill said, "Of course I have no power to heal her. Jesus Christ is the only healer."

He looked down at the blind girl who was still clutching him desperately. As he watched, she seemed to separate into two girls, her twin peeling away like a shadow, stepping out over the edge of the platform, skipping through the air, pointing at different objects. Now Bill knew what was going to happen. He prayed, "Heavenly Father, I left my daughter Becky crying for me at home in order to come here and pray for this child. Please heal her in Jesus' name." Gently he lifted her face from his shoulder. She looked past him, gazing toward the ceiling. Then she said something in German. Lauster interpreted, "Brother Branham, she is asking what those round things are above us." She could see the electric lights overhead. Bill held two fingers in front of her face. "How many fingers am I holding up?" he asked through his interpreter.

"Two," she replied, raising two of her small fingers to match.

Her mother screamed and ran for the platform so fast that she lost a shoe on the stairs. Soon she was smothering her daughter with kisses. The little girl asked, "Are you my mother?"

"Yes, dear," she replied.

Cradling her mother's face with her little hands, the girl said over and over, "Oh, mother, you're so beautiful...so beautiful."

Seeing this miracle, the crowd spontaneously sang the hymn, "Crown Him, Crown Him, Lord of all the Earth."

Later, an usher led a middle-aged man up to the podium. When Bill asked this man a question through his German interpreter, the man replied by making signs with his hands. It took a few minutes to find someone who could interpret sign language, but eventually Bill learned this man was born deaf and dumb. After praying for his healing, Bill knew the once deaf-mute could now hear and talk. Since the man had never before heard or spoken a word, one language was as good as another to test his healing. Bill whispered to his German interpreter, asking him to tell the sign-language interpreter to tell this man to repeat what he heard Bill say. Then Bill said, "Mama."

The man mumbled out a semblance of "mama."

Bill said, "I love Jesus."

The man slurred together something, which sounded close to, "I-wuv-Jesus."

Bill said, "Praise the Lord!"

A little more clearly the man said, "Praise-the-Lord."

Although the thunderclouds outside vanished, the air inside the canvas building thundered with praise to Jesus Christ. That night God did more than silence a storm; He also silenced scores of critics.

After ten days in Germany, the Branham team traveled 200 miles south of Karlsruhe to Lausanne, Switzerland, a city situated on the northern shore of Lake Geneva, not far from the eastern border of France. Thousands of French-speaking people filled a giant arena to listen to the man who said an angel of God stood beside him when he prayed for the sick. By the end of that week, even some ministers in the state church were almost convinced it was true. On Saturday morning, August 27, 1955, around 40 ministers from various denominations gathered in the banquet hall of a luxury hotel in Lausanne to eat breakfast with the visiting evangelist. Bill sat at the head table with Guggenbuhl, Bosworth, Arganbright, and another man who acted as spokesman and interpreter for the Swiss ministers.

After breakfast, the spokesman said, "We know that something supernatural is happening in your meetings, but we're not sure what it is. We can't understand how you can see visions. Could you give us a scientific explanation of how it works?"

"I can't explain it because it's God—and you can't explain God; you've got to believe Him. I could give you a lot of Scriptures on visions, but you already know most of those. As far as a scientific explanation, I have none. The closest thing is the pictures that have been taken of the angel of the Lord, which prove scientifically that He is real."

"Reverend Branham, we have a professional photographer with us today. If that angel comes here this morning, can we try to photograph it?"

"You can if you don't use a flash. Under the anointing, I see the angel of the Lord as a bright light. If I'm watching the angel when someone snaps a flash, I get mixed up, and it can even break up the vision. That's why I don't let people take flash pictures during my meetings."

The photographer assured Bill that a flash would not be needed because the tall windows of the banquet hall let plenty of sunlight into the room. While he was setting his camera up on a tripod, the spokesman said, "Reverend Branham, be sure to signal the cameraman if you see the angel."

"I'll let you know if he comes."

"Thank you. Some of us are thinking about taking your message into our churches, if we can just prove that it's not witchcraft."

"Witchcraft?" Bill was shocked. "Brethren, really! Witchcraft? That's ridiculous. It's absolutely impossible for a demon to have anything to do with divine healing. Every Scripture is against it. Jesus Himself said, 'If Satan can cast out Satan, his kingdom is divided and can't stand.'[125] See? He can't do it. Healing comes only from Jesus Christ."

"Well, your discernment is the part that is giving us trouble. Some of our leaders say it's a trick. They think you go around town in the daytime talking to people; then you give them a prayer-card and call on them that night, so you already know about them."

"Ask the people later. They'll tell you. I've never seen them before in my life."

"Maybe you're reading their minds."

"How could I read their minds? I can't even speak their language. When I'm telling the visions, sometimes I have to spell out their names letter-by-letter because I can't pronounce them."

"Maybe you're using mental telepathy to read what they wrote down on their prayer-cards."

"Can mental telepathy open the eyes of the blind? Brethren, be reasonable. Who is it that can heal the sick and foretell the future? Do you even believe in an all-knowing, all-powerful God?"

"Oh, we believe in God—but this is so different from what we've been taught."

Bill grew tired of their wishy-washy opinions. He said, "Brethren, your trouble is that you're spiritually blind, and that's a whole lot worse than being physically blind. The eyes in your head are seeing things that prophets and great men have longed to see, and still you won't believe it. Well did Isaiah speak of you, saying, 'You have eyes, but you can't see; and ears, but you can't

---

[125] Mark 3:22-30

hear.'"[126] He spoke these pointed words in a gentle tone, which made them sound like a good-natured warning, and they seemed to be received good-naturedly by his listeners. The questioning continued for a while. Finally Bill asked everyone to stand and join him in prayer. Suddenly he felt the presence of the angel of the Lord. "Just a moment, gentlemen. The one who I am speaking of is here now."

Upon that cue, the professional photographer snapped a series of pictures in quick succession. At the same time a vision was opening a window of revelation for the evangelist. Bill said, "The gray-headed man standing across the table from me is an Italian. Sir, you used to be the leader of 32,000 communists. You were raised a Catholic, but later you picked up a Bible and read where Jesus Christ, the Son of God, died to save you from your sins— and you accepted it. Now you run an orphanage and a school way up in the mountains. The reason you haven't touched your breakfast is because you've got a stomach ulcer that many times won't let you eat a thing."

The Italian confirmed that every word of it was true.

Bill said, "Thus saith the Lord, 'Go ahead and eat your breakfast. Your stomach is healed.'"

Gingerly, the Italian tasted a bite of eggs. When that bite settled nicely, he attacked his food like a starving man. Bill asked the ministers in the banquet hall, "What kind of prayer-card telepathy did that fellow use?"

Later that day when the professional photographer developed his film, he was surprised to find that some of his pictures had a light in them that wasn't visible when he clicked the shutter. He immediately showed these pictures to Guggenbuhl, who in turn showed them to Bosworth and Branham. Dr. Guggenbuhl could scarcely contain his excitement. These four sequential pictures

---

[126] Matthew 13:11-17; Isaiah 6:9-10

clearly caught the angel of the Lord descending into the banquet hall.

The first photograph looked normal. It showed 40 ministers standing to pray in front of their tables. The hotel staff had connected these tables in a rectangular pattern with the longest two lines of tables running north and south. The ministers stood on both sides of their tables facing each other with heads bowed. The camera was fixed on top of a tall tripod centered at the south end of the room. Since Bill faced the camera from the middle of the table at the north end of the room, the picture captured a clear, though distant view of his head. Behind him stood an entire wall of glass windows and glass doors looking into the hotel lobby. The windows to the outside were located on the right side of the photograph, so the morning sun lighted the eastern side of everything in the room, while casting all the western sides in shadow.

In the second photograph the shadows were scattered and rearranged, not by the overhead electric lights (which the photograph showed were turned off), but by a strange ball of fire hanging midway between the floor and the tall ceiling, apparently coming down directly over the place where Bill was praying. This supernatural light was about three or four feet in diameter and seemed to be vibrating so fast that the camera couldn't freeze its form, leaving its edges fuzzy and indistinct.

The third picture showed this cotton ball of light surrounding Bill's head, completely hiding it from view.

In the fourth picture all the ministers were seated except for Bill and his interpreter. The light had shrunk to about two feet in diameter and now looked like a halo behind Bill's head—howbeit a lopsided halo that weighed more heavily on his right shoulder. Bill had his left hand raised to the level of his eyes, apparently stressing a point as he spoke.

Photo 3. Lausanne, Switzerland

Photo 4. Lausanne, Switzerland

Dr. Guggenbuhl said, "The photographer used a German-built camera that is one of the best in the world. He took a dozen pictures in the banquet hall before he took these, and he took a dozen pictures after he took these—and all of them turned out normal, so it couldn't be something wrong with the camera."

Bill examined the photographs carefully. "That is the angel of the Lord, all right. See in this first picture where everyone is standing—that's when I first felt the angel's presence. Then here in the second picture, you can see the angel like a ball of fire coming down toward me. In the third picture, you see it completely covering my head. That was when the vision happened. Here in this last picture, you see it leaving me. Notice how it moved away from my right side. The angel always stands on my right. That's why in my meetings I always have the prayer-line come up on my right, so the people stand near the angel."

"Do you think this will convince those ministers?"

"If they are true believers in God, it will. If they're not true believers, nothing is going to convince them."

During his last sermon in Lausanne, Bill again admonished the Swiss Reformed Church for their belief that Jesus was not virgin born. He preached, "Not long ago a woman in America said to me, 'Brother Branham, you brag too much on Jesus in his earthly journey. You make him divine.' I said, 'He was divine.' She said, 'He was a great prophet, but still he was just a man, and I can prove that by the Bible.' I said, 'I'd like to see you try.' She turned to John chapter 11 and read me the part about Jesus weeping at the grave of Lazarus. She said, 'Only a man could weep.' I said, 'Lady, He was a man when He wept at the grave of Lazarus. But when He commanded Lazarus to come forth, and a man who had been dead four days stood on his feet and lived again, that was more than a man; that was more than a prophet—that was God!'

"Jesus was a man when He fell asleep in the boat. He was so tired from preaching all day and praying for the sick, that the storm didn't wake Him. That little fishing boat was tossed around by those big waves like a cork stopper. Ten thousand devils of the sea swore they would drown Him that night. He was a man when His disciples shook Him awake; but when He looked up toward heaven and said, 'Peace, be still,' and the storm obeyed Him,[127] that was more than a man—that was God!

"He was a man when He hung on the cross and died for our sins, the supreme sacrifice. But on Easter morning when the stone rolled back from His tomb and He walked forth, He proved He was God!"[128]

Just like in Zurich two months earlier, this second European campaign of 1955 was a phenomenal success. After evaluating the results from these two weeks of meetings, the Branham team estimated that somewhere upward to 100,000 people either committed their lives to Jesus Christ or were healed by Him in Germany and Switzerland that summer.

---

[127] Mark 4:36-41; also, Matthew 8:23-27; Luke 8:22-25
[128] Matthew 28:1-15; Mark 16:1-14; Luke 24:1-49; John 20:1-23

Chapter 74
The Angel Teaches Him How to Fish
1955

AFTER HIS SUMMER CAMPAIGNS IN EUROPE, William Branham scheduled only two more long campaigns for the last quarter of 1955. He preached eight nights in Chicago during the first two weeks of October, right before he went on his usual fall hunting trip in the Colorado Rockies.

In November, Miner Arganbright arranged an 11-day campaign in San Fernando, California. These California meetings were held in a canvas circus tent, which the Full Gospel Business Men's Fellowship set up in a field, hoping that neutral territory would overcome the denominational divisions that had frustrated Bill's efforts in Orange County over the past two years. A neutral location didn't help. On the first night of this campaign the crowd filled less than half of the seats in the giant tent. True, it was a Thursday night, but midweek services had not hampered the turnout at his campaigns in other parts of America. Despite the small crowd, Bill preached with as much sincerity to the hundreds of people in the tent as he would have to thousands. Although his meetings had always been nondenominational, many of his sponsors were Pentecostals simply because Pentecostal people believed strongly in gifts of the Holy Spirit, such as tongues, prophecy, divine healing, and miracles.

On Friday night Bill preached a sermon he called, "Where I Think Pentecost Failed." He wanted to turn the church around. He said, "If we know where we made our mistake, the best thing to do is go right back there and start over again from that point."

He talked about two types of Christians—fundamentalists and Pentecostals. The fundamentalists know where they stand in the Bible, but they don't have much faith to accompany their knowledge. On the other hand, the Pentecostals have a lot of faith, but too often they don't know where they stand in the Scriptures. It's like two men, one of whom has money in the bank, but doesn't know how to write a check; the other man knows how to write a check, but doesn't have any money in the bank. If those two men could get together, they could buy something. Likewise, Bill felt that if fundamental doctrine and Pentecostal faith could be combined in the hearts of more people, a great revival would erupt.

He said, "If you Christians could only realize that *now*—present tense—*now* you are the sons and daughters of God, then you could fill out a blank check for anything God has promised.[129] Instead you're pushing the blessings way off somewhere in the future. You won't need divine healing in the millennium. *Now* you are the children of God, and joint-heirs with Jesus. Everything Jesus died for at Calvary is your possession. Satan doesn't want you to realize it, but if you will just take God at His word, your resources are unlimited."

He told a story to illustrate what was missing in the lives of so many Christians. When Reverend Billy Graham held an evangelistic campaign in Louisville, Kentucky, over 30,000 people filled out decision cards, saying they were going to live for Jesus

---

[129] 1 John 3:2

Christ. A few months later Billy Graham came back to check on these "converts" and was surprised when his team could only find a few hundred people who were still living for the Lord Jesus. Why would that be? Bill explained that there are two different ways to come to Christ. One way is through an intellectual decision; the other way is through a "born again" experience. One type is a choice in the mind; the other is a transformation in the heart. Jesus said, *Ye must be born again.*[130] That is a spiritual birth, not an intellectual conception.

Next Bill outlined what he thought had gone wrong with the Pentecostal movement. He stressed that he didn't have anything against the people in the various organizations, noting that he had friends in all denominations. It was the basic idea behind organized religion that bothered him.

He explained that the Roman Catholic Church organized Christianity first, forcing its ideas on millions of illiterate people for hundreds of years. Martin Luther pulled away from Catholicism, following the Pillar of Fire. Luther preached that people couldn't earn salvation; rather, it comes as a gift from God. Luther emphasized the Scripture: "*The just shall live by faith.*"[131] Unfortunately, Luther's followers organized into their own denomination. The Pillar of Fire moved on, shedding more light as it went, but the Lutherans couldn't move with it because they had already drawn up documents saying what they believed. Later John Wesley followed the Pillar of Fire into a message of sanctification and holiness, calling it the second work of grace. His preaching caused a revival in England that swept around the world. Unfortunately his followers organized the Methodist church and carved their doctrines in stone. The Pillar of Fire moved on, but the Methodists couldn't move with it because they were already organized around their doctrines. In 1906 the Pillar of Fire shed more light on the baptism of the Holy

---

[130] John 3:7
[131] Habakkuk 2:4; Romans 1:17; Galatians 3:11; Hebrews 10:38

Ghost, bringing forth gifts of the Spirit, such as speaking in tongues and prophecy. The people who received this light called themselves Pentecostals. It became the fastest growing Christian movement in the world. So, what did the devil do? He talked the Pentecostals into organizing, which made them draw boundary lines and build fences. They also carved their doctrines in stone, just like earlier movements did.

Bill warned his audience, "The Pillar of Fire is moving out again, and the Pentecostal people are so organized they can't move with it. God's fire will keep moving just like it did in every age. So don't ever draw boundary lines. It's all right to say, 'I believe this,' but don't end it with a period; end it with a comma, meaning: 'I believe this, *plus* as much more as God will reveal to my heart.'"

For the rest of this San Fernando campaign, Bill preached his usual faith-building sermons meant to inspire people to accept Jesus Christ as their savior and healer. Each night miracles happened in the prayer-lines. Normally this would have boosted attendance as fast as word-of-mouth could spread the news. It didn't work that way in San Fernando, California. The crowds remained small. Five days into the campaign, Miner Arganbright mentioned that offerings were lagging far behind expenses. He asked Bill to let him put pressure on people to put more money into the collection plate when it was passed through the audience each night. As always, Bill refused to allow anyone to ask for money in his meetings. He knew other evangelists who appealed long and hard for larger donations. Bill always thought such tactics weakened credibility. When his own ministry began, he promised the Lord he would never beg for money, and he was determined to keep his promise. After the last service on November 20, Miner Arganbright told Bill that the San Fernando campaign had ended $15,000 in debt.

Bill drove back to the motel cabin where he and his wife and son were staying. It was two o'clock in the morning. Even though they planned to leave for home at 4:30, Bill didn't feel like sleeping. Instead he walked away from his cabin, found a secluded spot, and knelt to pray. A bright moon dimmed the stars. Soon the chilly night air seeped through the thin fabric of his pants, causing him to shiver automatically. He scarcely noticed the discomfort.

He thought of the promise he made to God nine years before when he first started these faith-healing campaigns. When the angel of the Lord told him to take this gift of divine healing to the peoples of the world, Bill realized that such an enormous task would expose him to great temptations. In the Bible he noticed three dangers that could ruin a ministry: money, women, and popularity. Balaam fell because he was greedy; Samson fell when he lusted for Delilah; and King Saul fell when his pride caused him to disobey God so he could be popular with his people.[132] Bill felt that neither women nor popularity could tempt him much, but he was not so sure about money. He realized it would cost thousands of dollars to hold big campaigns around the world. Was it possible that Satan could use this need for money to make him stumble? To make sure this never happened, Bill promised God he would stay on the evangelistic field as long as God met his needs and he never had to ask people for money. For nine-and-a-half years God had supplied all of his finances.

Through his prayer, Bill struggled with indecision. He knew God had specifically called him to do a job, and he had promised God he would do that job as long as God provided the funds. God had done that until this week. So, what should Bill do now? Should he continue to do the job God assigned him, or should he keep his promise to God and end his evangelistic ministry? For two hours Bill prayed for direction, wrestling with every

---

[132]   Numbers 22-24; Judges 16; 1 Samuel 15, respectively

possibility he could imagine. Shortly after four o'clock, he stood up, brushed the dirt from his knees, and slowly walked back to the cabin. His choice seemed clear—he must keep his promise to God and quit evangelizing.

The moon was setting in the west. The sky in the east was lightening as dawn approached. Meda and Billy Paul were already packing the car. Seeing her husband's tear-streaked face, Meda asked, "Bill, what's the matter?"

"Oh, I was just out talking with the Lord." He couldn't bring himself to say he was quitting. He decided he would tell his family in Arizona. When they crossed the Arizona line, he still couldn't bring it up. Texas—he would tell them in Texas. The panhandle of Texas came and went, and still he kept quiet, thinking...

What was God trying to tell him? It was not just the small crowds in San Fernando that made him wonder. During the last few months he had seen a change happening all over the United States. Where once he got thousands of letters a week, now he was getting only hundreds. Of course this had not changed his finances. Rarely did any of these letters contain money. He mailed out prayer cloths for free. What puzzled him was the decreasing interest in his ministry. Could it have something to do with his decision to teach more doctrine? Or was it just a change in the mood of the whole country?

He wondered what he should do now. How would he provide for his wife and children? Here he was, 46 years old, with little education, minimal business experience, and very few marketable skills. Maybe he could get his old job back at Public Service Indiana. Maybe he and Banks Wood could go into business together building houses. Banks was a good carpenter. Bill figured that the quicker he went back to work, the quicker he could pay off that $15,000 he owed.

It seemed ironic that he should suddenly be so deeply in debt. If he had kept one-hundredth of the money people had offered him personally, he would be a multimillionaire by now. He had always turned down these gifts. He felt that if he had a large bank account, he might trust in money instead of trusting in the Lord. His church paid him a modest salary of $100 a week. Most of the money collected during his campaigns went to pay for campaign expenses. If there was any money left over, he gave it to Christian missionaries or charitable causes. This approach kept his "Branham Campaigns" checking account near a zero balance. It might not be the most business-like way to handle his ministry; but then, he had never tried to be a good businessman; he just tried to be a good evangelist.

Recently the Internal Revenue Service notified him that they wanted to audit his campaign finances. He wasn't worried about an audit, but it did seem strange that the IRS should choose to audit his ministry at this particular time. What was the Lord trying to tell him? Was there something still wrong with his ministry? Did something else need to change?

No one could deny the impact his ministry had made on the Christian church in the past ten years. Besides the hundreds of thousands of people saved and healed in his campaigns, he had inspired hundreds of similar ministries. Many of these upstarts were genuine Holy-Ghost-filled men—but not all of them, and perhaps therein lay the problem. Some of these copycats were trying to impersonate a ministry they did not understand, and by trying to copy him, they were sowing spiritual confusion among Christians.

Bill thought about the 16-year-old girl who recently came to his house for an interview. She was terrified because some preacher in California, who claimed to have the gift of discernment, told her she had cancer. When Bill took her right hand in his left hand, he could instantly tell she didn't have cancer. The girl left his house relieved. Bill wondered how many other people that particular preacher had deceived.

One time Bill visited a meeting where a man claimed to have the gift of healing in his right hand. Every time he touched someone to pray for them, he hollered, "Feel that? Do you feel it?" After the meeting, Bill met him behind the tent and said, "It's a lie, and you know it. Sure you can fool a lot of people, but someday you'll have to answer to God for it; and what then?"

Another time Bill visited a meeting where a woman claimed to have the gift of discernment. She said things like, "The Lord told me that someone in the audience is backslidden," and, "The Lord told me that someone here has kidney trouble. Will you raise your hand if you are that one." Bill thought, "Any large crowd is bound to have backslidden Christians and people with kidney trouble. That's not spiritual discernment—she's using psychology."

At a different church service, Bill watched a minister pray for a man with heart trouble by jerking him up and down, while the minister's wife beat on the floor with a stick and hollered, "Shoo! Get out of him, devil! Shoo, shoo!" Even worse than this was the evangelist who slugged his patients in the stomach with his fist, claiming he was forcing the devils out. Another time, Bill heard a man say he could smell sickness and demons. Why would anyone listen to such unscriptural tommyrot? No wonder the world scorned and laughed at the idea of divine healing. No wonder so many Christians were confused about spiritual gifts. With so much falsehood around, it masked the real thing.

Another day passed while the miles rolled under his wheels— Oklahoma, Missouri, Illinois, and finally Indiana. When they were almost home, Bill told his family about his decision to quit evangelism. Billy Paul said, "Daddy, you had better be careful. Didn't Paul say, 'Woe unto me if I don't preach the Gospel'?"[133]

"I never said I would stop preaching the Gospel. I said I was going to stop these evangelistic campaigns. I'll still preach at the tabernacle. Maybe Brother Neville can take the Sunday morning services, and I can take Sunday nights. I might even rent a hall sometime for an international meeting where I pray for the sick."

Night had fallen, but the dim lights of the dashboard revealed the concern in Meda's face. She said, "Bill, you know I would love to have you home with me and the kids. But look at what your ministry has done. It's started a worldwide revival. I can't see why God would have you quit like this. I hope you know what you're doing."

"Well, I know one thing: I need to keep my promise to God."

"God never told you to leave the field," said Billy Paul. "That's something you told God."

"You're right, son. We expect God to keep His promises to us, so we should try to keep our promises to Him."

"Daddy, I think you're making a mistake."

"If I am, let's pray that God will correct me."

They got home around four in the morning. Before Bill crawled into bed, he prayed again for God to show him what to do next. Then, in spite of his troubled mind, he fell asleep.

Meda got up at 6 a.m. so she could get Becky ready for school. Her movements in the room woke Bill. He sat up on the side of the bed and rubbed his sleepy eyes. "Honey, this morning I'm going to call the public service company and see if I can get my old job back. If I can't get that, I'll see if Brother Banks wants to go into business with me. I've got to earn some money so I can start paying off that debt."

---

[133] 1 Corinthians 9:16

"Bill, you told me that some of the brothers in California underwrote that campaign. So in that sense, the debt has been paid."

"True, but that wasn't my promise to God. The way I see it, now I owe those brothers $15,000."

"Bill, I hope you know what you're doing," Meda said.

"Well, I think..." He didn't finish his sentence. Something strange was happening. Instead of looking at his wife, he was watching two grubby boys walking toward him along a dirt road. Their bare feet stirred up a cloud of dust that settled on their ragged pants. They were not wearing shirts. Both boys had straggly black hair, dark eyes, and brown, sun-baked skin. One of them was pulling a wagon with wooden wheels. "Sweetheart," Bill said, "look who's coming."

"What are you talking about?" Meda asked. By now, Bill was too far into the vision to answer her. Then his wife left the room and the vision became everything.

Something powerful carried him past the children until he came to Miner Arganbright, who smiled and said, "Brother Branham, everything is ready. We've given out all the prayer-cards and we've got a way to get you in and out. The meeting has already started, so go on in."

"Thank you, Brother Arganbright." Bill walked past his friend toward an outdoor arena filled with thousands of brown-skinned people. The crowd was listening to a preacher who talked from a platform built in the center of the arena. Bill asked a group of ministers, "Who is that man?"

A minister with blond hair said, "They put him up there."

"Who are *they*?" Bill asked.

Without answering him, the ministers walked away, all except the man with blond hair. At that moment, the preacher on the platform said, "You are all dismissed." The crowd started to leave.

"He shouldn't have done that," Bill protested. "He didn't make an altar call."

"It's all right," said the blond man, holding up a sack of money and shaking it so Bill could hear the coins clinking. "We've already taken up the offering."

Disgusted, Bill snapped, "Since when is an offering more important than souls won to Christ?"

Ignoring that question, the man said, "You'll be preaching later this afternoon."

By now the arena was almost empty. A light rain began to fall. Bill quipped, "We'll be lucky to have 12 people come out this afternoon."

The man shrugged and said, "Wasn't Jesus left with just 12 men after he told the people the truth?"[134]

From somewhere behind Bill's right shoulder, the angel of the Lord said, "*By this you will know…*"

Then the angel took him farther into the vision. The next thing Bill knew, he was holding a soft baby shoe in one hand and a shoelace in the other. He was trying to thread this fat shoelace through the tiny eyelet on the shoe. He couldn't get the shoelace to start. Every time he tried to push it through the hole, more end-fibers bent sideways, stopping it from going through. Twisting the end of the shoelace into a tight point, he kept trying; but the more he tried, the farther back the shoelace unraveled. The task looked impossible. The diameter of the shoelace was just too big to fit through that little eyelet.

The angel of the Lord asked, "*What are you doing?*"

"I'm trying to lace up this shoe, but I can't do it. The string won't go through the hole."

"*You're doing it wrong. Use the other end.*"

---

[134] John 6:28-69

He had been concentrating so intently on lacing the baby's shoe that he hadn't noticed how long the shoestring was. It went all the way to the floor where it looped back and forth into a sizable pile. Spotting the other end, Bill could see that it was small enough to fit easily through the eyelet.

The angel said, *"Don't you understand? You can't teach Pentecostal babies supernatural things. If you try, you will only cause carnal impersonations."*

Then the angel took him farther into the vision until he came to a beautiful lake surrounded by green trees. The water looked as clear as glass. Bill could see schools of little fish swimming near the shore; and farther out, he could see a few large rainbow trout. Lots of fishermen were casting from the shoreline, but they were only catching little fish. Bill thought, "I'm a good fisherman. I think I can catch those big trout way out there."

The shoelace had turned into a fishing line, and the baby's shoe had now become a lure and hook. A fishing pole lay on the ground by his feet. Bill picked up the fishing pole and reeled in the line. From behind him, the angel said, *"I will teach you how to fish, but I don't want you to tell anyone else how to do it. Just keep it to yourself."*

"I understand."

"First, tie a lure on the end of your line and bait the hook. Then cast your line way out into deep water. Let the lure sink a ways, then pull on it gently. That will bring the small fish around. When you feel one of these nibble at the bait, pull the line again, just a little harder than the first time. That will scatter the small fish, which in turn will attract the attention of the big ones. When you feel one of those big fish nibble at the bait, pull hard to set the hook firmly in its jaw. Then you can reel it in."

Bill started to do what the angel said. While he was baiting his hook, the other fishermen came over to watch. These fishermen were all Christian ministers and they were excited to see him there, saying things like, "Praise the Lord, it's Brother Branham. He's a real fisherman. Let's watch how he does it. He can show us how to catch a lot of fish."

Basking in all this attention, Bill said, "Sure, I'll show you how it's done." He cast his line far out into the lake and let the lure sink. "Now, brethren, those little fish are fine, but we want to catch the big ones too. Here's how you do it. First give a gentle tug on your line. That will attract the little fish. When a little fish nibbles on the bait, jerk the line again, just a little harder, but not too hard. The little fish will scatter, and the big fish will come around to see what's going on. One of those big fellows is bound to strike at the lure."

Bill demonstrated this technique, giving his line its first gentle pull. Sure enough, a school of little fish swam toward his shimmering lure. This excited the ministers, who slapped each other on the back and gushed, "Hallelujah! Praise the Lord! This is wonderful!" Their enthusiasm infected Bill. By the time he felt a nibble on his lure, he was so eager to catch a fish that he yanked too hard on his pole, jerking his line out of the water and all the way back to shore. The line fell around him in a tangled mess. He had indeed caught a fish, but one so small he wondered how it ever got its mouth over the lure. The ministers lost interest and wandered off.

Now the angel of the Lord stepped into view. His black hair and olive-brown skin contrasted sharply with his white robe and turban. He folded his arms across his chest and frowned. "*You did exactly what I told you not to do.*"

Bill felt ashamed of himself. "I know I didn't do it right," he apologized feebly, as he struggled to untangle the mess around him. "I jerked it too hard the second time."

"Don't get your line all tangled up in these kinds of times," the angel admonished. *"This fishing lesson is symbolic of your ministry. The first pull is when you took people by the hand and could feel the vibrations of their diseases. The second pull is the discernment, which let you tell them the secrets of their hearts. I made you a seer before the people, but you were always trying to explain it. You shouldn't have done that. You took a supernatural gift and made it into a public show. By doing that, you caused a lot of carnal impersonators to rise and spread confusion."*

"I'm so sorry. I'll try to be more careful after this." To Bill's great relief, he finally got his line straightened out. Reeling up the slack, he drew back his arm for another cast. Before he could throw out his line again, the angel took him even farther into the vision.

Now he was standing high in the air—not outside; but rather, he seemed to be inside some kind of structure. Above him stretched a domed ceiling like that of a cathedral or a gigantic tent. Bill had never before seen such a huge canopy. Below him, thousands of people sat in rows facing a platform at one end of the tent. Hundreds of people were kneeling in front of this platform, weeping softly and worshiping Jesus Christ. Apparently this was an evangelistic meeting and the preacher had just made an altar call. Bill said, "Now that's more like it."

A kindly looking gentleman walked up to the pulpit and said in a soothing voice, "While Brother Branham is resting, let's form the prayer-line. Everyone with a prayer-card line up over here on my right."

Bill was facing the same direction as the crowd—that is, he was looking towards the pulpit on the platform. From his vantage point above this meeting, he watched the people with prayer-cards stand and move to their left, forming a line that continued all the way to the back of the tent and on outside. This was very different from his current meetings. Not only were there far more people in line than usual, the whole structure of the prayer-line was different. In front of the prayer-line hung a canvas curtain, blocking the view of the platform from those people standing on the floor. Things were different up on the platform too. Between the prayer-line and the pulpit stood a rectangular building about 12 feet wide by 20 feet long, with a door on each end. A woman holding a notebook stood by the door facing the prayer-line. Another woman stood by the door near the pulpit.

Puzzled by all this, Bill looked around for the angel of the Lord so he could ask him to explain. The angel was standing in the air beside him, off to his right. Above the angel swirled that supernatural light, throwing off licks of flame, roaring with the pulsating sound of a whirlwind. Then something happened that Bill had never seen before. The Pillar of Fire left the angel of the Lord and glided down through the auditorium until it came to that small building on the platform. For a moment the light hovered above that little building. Then it settled straight down through the roof into the room below.

As soon as the Pillar of Fire was hidden from sight, the angel of the Lord said, "*I'll meet you in there. This is the third pull.*"

Now the prayer-line moved. The first patient in line was a woman on an ambulance stretcher. Two men carried her through the curtain, up the steps, and across the platform to that little building. The woman, who was standing by the door nearest to the prayer-line, wrote down the sick woman's name and affliction in a notebook. Then the two men carried the stretcher into the little room. The crowd hushed as everyone focused their attention on the rectangular building standing on the platform. Suddenly the door nearest to the pulpit opened and out came that same woman pushing her stretcher in front of her and praising God as loud as she could shout.

The dark-haired woman, who was standing just outside the door that was nearest to the pulpit, asked the healed woman, "What happened in there?"

"I don't know what happened," the excited woman answered. "I was paralyzed for 20 years, and now look at me! I feel like I was never crippled!"

The second person in the prayer-line was a man on crutches. He hobbled into that little room, but soon he leaped through the door nearest to the pulpit, shouting, holding his crutches high in the air. Again the dark-haired woman asked, "What happened in there?"

The man answered, "I don't know; but look at me! I can walk!"

Bill said to the angel of the Lord, "I don't understand. What is going on in that little room?"

The angel answered, *"Did not our Lord say, 'When you pray, you shall not be like the hypocrites. For they love to pray standing in the synagogues and on the corners of the streets, that they may be seen of men... But you, when you pray, go into your room, and when you have shut your door, pray to your Father who is in the secret place; and your Father who sees in secret will reward you openly?'"*[135]

"Yes, that is what our Lord told us to do."

The angel said, *"I will meet you in that room. This is your third pull. It will not be a public show."*

Bill gave a single nod and said, "I understand."

Now the angel carried him down into that little room on the platform, and told him what to do for the third time. Then the angel told him a secret. Referring to that conversation, Bill said, "Christian friends, when I leave this world, that secret will still be in my bosom. But mark my words, you watch what is going to take place next."

---

[135] Matthew 6:5-6

Chapter 75
Mexico: Mystery and Miracles
1956

WHILE THE GRASS in his yard shivered under a blanket of snow, William Branham pondered the most powerful vision he had yet seen. A meeting of his that was mysteriously canceled? An unsuccessful attempt to lace a baby's shoe? The angel of the Lord teaching him how to fish? And finally, a mysterious little room set on a platform next to an empty pulpit, and the whole thing placed underneath a giant canopy? These images lingered, and their hidden meaning tantalized him. For a long time this vision preoccupied his thoughts. Although he dutifully kept the secret that the angel gave him in that little room, the impact of that secret colored much of what he read in the Bible and much of what he preached for months thereafter. One night in December 1955, he felt too excited to fall asleep. At 10:30 he woke his wife and asked, "Honey, can I preach to you for a while?"

Meda rolled over to face her husband. She rubbed her eyes, smiled and said, "Sure, Bill, go ahead."

Bill preached to his wife until midnight. He said, "The Christian faith is based entirely upon rest. A Christian is not tossed about. A Christian doesn't run from place to place. A Christian doesn't fuss, and fume, and worry about things. A Christian rests.

It's all finished for the believer at Calvary. Oh, disappointments may come, but the Christian is still resting, knowing that God is able to keep His promises. We Christians know that no matter what problems come—whether hunger, sickness, or even death—nothing can separate us from the love of God that is in Jesus Christ. We are at rest. Let this old ship toss any way she wants to toss in the storms of life, our anchor holds us securely in place. Our faith doesn't rest in our own abilities, or in our church, or in our friends. Our faith rests entirely upon the finished work of Jesus Christ. Sure, all kinds of storms and troubles will arise, but our ship can't sink because we are anchored in the Word of God."

On January 1, 1956, he expanded on this theme in a sermon he called "Why Are People So Tossed About?" He talked about those Christians who are constantly being tossed back and forth by the storms of life. This type of Christian is sometimes up and sometimes down. One day he feels victorious, and the next day he is discouraged. One day he is worshiping God, and the next day he might be back in the world. Why? Because he only has a mental conception of God's Word. He came to Jesus through intellectual knowledge, rather than through a supernatural experience in his soul.

To clarify his point, Bill used the story of the Israelites' journey from Egypt to the Promised Land. Since the Israelites didn't bring food with them, every day God gave them a natural bread that He supernaturally prepared. The Israelites called this bread *manna*.[136] They couldn't store up manna during the week. If they tried, it corrupted by the next day. Each morning they had to gather only as much manna as they could eat that day. Likewise, Christians must feed each day on Jesus Christ, the Bread of Life.

Although this manna would usually not keep more than one day, there were a few exceptions. Since God had commanded

---

[136] Exodus 16

the Israelites to work only six days a week, the manna they gathered on the sixth day always kept through the seventh. Also, God instructed Moses to put some manna inside the Ark of the Covenant. The Ark of the Covenant was a rectangular box that sat in the innermost room of the tabernacle, the room known as the Holiest of Holies. The manna inside that Ark never went stale; generation after generation it smelled as sweet as freshly baked bread. Spiritually speaking, this perpetual freshness is available to Christians also.

To explain what he meant, Bill compared a Christians life with the tabernacle that God commanded Moses to build in wilderness of Sinai. The tabernacle had three parts—the courtyard, the holy place, and the Holiest of Holies. (1) Anyone who came to the tabernacle had to enter the fenced courtyard first. This area was open to the sky. The courtyard is where the altar for animal sacrifices stood, and the laver filled with water where the priests washed before entering the tent. (2) The tent itself was divided into two rooms by a heavy curtain. The outer most room was called the holy place and it contained a lamp stand with seven branches for seven flames. The holy place also contained an altar for offering incense and a table for a special kind of bread called showbread, which signified God's presence. (3) The inner room was called the Most Holy Place or the Holiest of Holies. This sacred inner room contained only one piece of furniture—the Ark of the Covenant. The lid to this Ark was called the Mercy Seat. It was not a chair, but a location. No one ever sat on the Mercy Seat because above it were carved two angel-like creatures facing each other, with their wings spread so that all four wing-tips touched over the center of the Mercy Seat. The Ark of the Covenant contained some manna, the stone tablets upon which God wrote his Ten Commandments, and Aaron's rod that budded.[137] These three parts to the tabernacle have multiple layers of meanings,

---

[137] Hebrews 9:2

representing (among other things) God's triune nature of Father, Son and Holy Ghost; and man's triune makeup of body, spirit and soul. In this sermon Bill used the three parts of the tabernacle to symbolize the three stages of salvation: (1) justification, (2) sanctification, and (3) the baptism of the Holy Spirit.

The tabernacle in the wilderness had only one entrance, and only those who believed in Jehovah could go through it and see the altar. That scenario was a type or shadow of salvation through Christ. From the moment Jesus became the Great Sacrifice, from that moment forward a person can only receive eternal life if he or she believes in Jesus Christ. But that is just the first step. Believing in Jesus is like entering the outer court of the tabernacle. The man who enters the outer court believes that Jesus died to save him from his sins. That makes him justified by faith. That's good. But he is still in the open air, subject to every change in weather. Some days are sunny and he feels great. Other days are cold and stormy, and he feels miserable. Clouds cause the light from the sun and stars to vary constantly.

Sanctification is the second stage of grace. The man who is sanctified by the blood of Jesus Christ is in a better position than the man who stops at justification. The sanctified man has quit smoking, quit drinking, quit lying, quit stealing, and so forth. He treats people right and is living holy before the Lord. He is like the priest who entered the holy place of the tabernacle. The holy place was more comfortable than the outer court. It sheltered the priest from the wind and rain. In the holy place he didn't have to rely on the changing lights in the sky because he got his light from the golden lamp stand with its seven flames. But these seven lights did not illuminate perfectly. The lamps needed daily attention. Sometimes the wicks would carbonize, dimming the flames and smoking up the room. Sometimes a lamp would go out and have to be relit.

There is one more stage of salvation—the baptism of the Holy Spirit. That is when a Christian steps behind the veil into the Holiest of Holies and lives his life in the Shekinah Glory of God's presence. The Shekinah Glory is a mystic light, a soft glowing light, steady and utterly dependable. Its source is God Himself, so there can never be any variation.

Bill said, "Yet men and women can live good lives, and love God by a mental conception. But the real hiding place is in the heart, hid with Christ. When Christ the Holy Spirit comes into your heart, He is in you with your temperament, and He's living His own life through His own will—through you. So yielded you are, that Christ speaks the kind of words He would speak, He thinks the kind of thoughts He would think—through you. He does the kind of works He would do—through you. You are yielded and resting.

"What a beautiful picture of a consecrated Christian—yielded, Christ working through. Paul said, 'For me, to live is Christ and to die is gain. It's not me that lives anymore, but Christ that lives in me.'[138] Christ living in the surrendered soul of the individual—speaking through the lips, thinking through the mind, seeing through the eyes, and acting through the temperament. Then the things of the world pass away. How can it be anything but sweet and pleasant all the time? Christ has control. Amen.

"You see it? Christ is in you, so your whole makeup is Christ. Your attitude, your desires, your appetite, your everything is Christ; so you are yielded and resting, with everything perfect. No matter how dull it looks, or how black it looks, still it's the same—Christ is in you. He thinks through your mind the very way that He would if He was here on earth. You are no longer your own because you're surrendered.

---

[138] Philippians 1:21; Galatians 2:20, respectively

"Once a year Aaron, the high priest, went into the holy place of the tabernacle.[139] The congregation watched him. Aaron had to be anointed right, dress right, and walk right. He wore bells on his garment, and as he walked those bells played, 'Holy, holy, holy, unto the Lord.' He took with him the sacrificial blood of the atonement. He was anointed with the rose of Sharon, and the anointing rolled off his beard plumb to the hem of his robe. He walked into the inner court in the presence of God, the veil fell behind him, and he was hidden from the outer world.

"Praise God, there is a hiding place, an abiding place. You can walk in the presence of God and be hidden from the things of this world. You won't hear them anymore because it's soundproof. The world is on the outside, gasping and looking. You're on the inside, in the presence of the eternal God, eating from this manna that will never be contaminated and will never give out.

"When a man lives in the presence of the King, everyday is fine. He has found the secret place.[140] He has gone behind the veil and it has closed behind him. He doesn't see the world. The holy place was made soundproof by sheepskins and goatskins, but this secret place is made soundproof by the baptism of the Holy Spirit that hides a man in Christ. There he becomes a new creature and he walks daily before God in this manner.[141]

"What a beautiful picture of the believer in the presence of God. All things were given to Christ. All God was, He poured into Christ. All Christ was, He poured into the Church. Jesus said, 'At that day you will know that I am in My Father, and you in Me, and I in you.'[142] Oh, the privilege that believers have, if they only could accept it."

---

[139]   Exodus 30:10; Leviticus 16; Hebrews 9:7-14, 25-26
[140]   Psalms 27:4-5; Psalms 91:1; Matthew 6:6
[141]   2 Corinthians 5:17; Galatians 6:15-16
[142]   John 14:20

In conclusion Bill said, "The man who walks behind that veil shuts out the world. He sits beneath the interlocking wing tips of the Cherubim, surrounded by the Shekinah Glory of God. That light never gets dim, never goes out. The believer rests by the Ark of the Covenant and eats from the golden pot of manna that is always fresh. He doesn't have a worry in the world. Everything is taken care of. God is over him, listening to his prayers, and answering his prayers. Not only that, but this believer is living right in the presence of the King of kings, God in His Shekinah Glory! Problems can't get to him in there. He won't listen to them. The whining of the world is left outside.

"Friends, if you ever come into Christ like that; if you can get into a place where the world is dead, and you are living only in the Shekinah Glory, living in the presence of the King, then every day will be sweet to your soul. Oh, my! All is well! All is well! Nothing can harm you. Oh, what a place."

To prove his point, he quoted Hebrew 10:19-22:

> *Having therefore, brethren, boldness to enter into the holiest by the blood of Jesus,*
>
> *By a new and living way, which he hath consecrated for us, through the veil, that is to say, his flesh;*
>
> *And having an high priest over the house of God;*
>
> *Let us draw near with a true heart in full assurance of faith, having our hearts sprinkled from an evil conscience, and our bodies washed with pure water.*

He would repeat this theme many times in 1956, teaching that the tabernacle was an earthly representation of heavenly truth, as Paul the apostle taught, "Who serve the copy and the shadow of the heavenly things, as Moses was divinely instructed when he was about to make the tabernacle. For He [God] said, 'See that you make all things according to the pattern shown you on the mountain.'"[143]

The three parts of the tabernacle represented many things. In God's numerology, three is the number of perfection. God has three different ways of expressing Himself to mankind: as a Father, as a Son, and as a Holy Spirit. Man is made up of three parts: a body, a spirit, and a soul. Salvation has three phases: justification, sanctification, and the baptism of the Holy Spirit. The tabernacle in the wilderness had three parts: the outer court, the holy place, and the Holiest of Holies. Bill knew that his own ministry would have three parts too: the first, second, and third pull on that fishing line in the vision. The huge tent at the end of the vision also had three parts: the congregation at one end, an elevated platform at the other end, and that little building on the platform. Bill knew the first and second pulls represented the first two stages of his ministry: the sign in his hand and the discernment by vision. He didn't know yet what the third pull might be, but the angel made it clear it would somehow be connected with that little room on the platform into which the Shekinah Glory descended. The angel said, *I will meet you in that room. This is your third pull. It will not be a public show.*

The "third pull" was not the only part of the vision that puzzled him. He wondered how much of it was symbolic and how much of it would happen literally. Why did that kind-looking gentleman say, "William Branham is resting"? Why was there a curtain in front of the prayer-line? Why did the line continue all the way outside the tent? Why did the people in the prayer-line go into that little room? What happened in that mysterious room?

Since there was no way to know how much of the vision was symbolic, Bill called his two managers (currently Jack Moore and Miner Arganbright) and asked them to look into renting

---

[143]   Hebrews 8:5

or buying the biggest tent they could find. Miner Arganbright suggested setting it up for a month in Phoenix. Bill liked that idea. Because his campaigns often gained momentum with each day they continued in an area, he always wondered if staying longer in one place would produce a revival. However, this plan fell through when another evangelist, A. A. Allen, scheduled a faith-healing campaign in Phoenix for the same month. Bill canceled his own meetings, realizing it wouldn't work to have two evangelistic campaigns in Phoenix at the same time.

Miner Arganbright suggested another plan. Mexican army General Narciso Medina Estrada, who was a Christian, had asked Miner Arganbright to bring a Branham Campaign to Mexico City. Would Bill consider holding some meetings in old Mexico?

When Bill prayed about this, the angel of the Lord came to him and said, "*I never told you to go to Phoenix. I told you to go to Mexico.*" That explained a few more details about the vision he saw last November. Those two ragged boys he saw at the beginning of the vision were Mexican children, and so were all those people who were dismissed from that meeting before he had a chance to preach.

Bill asked Miner Arganbright to arrange a campaign in Mexico, telling him in detail about the vision he had seen. A few days later Arganbright called back and said, "We've secured the bullfighting arena in Mexico City. It will hold around 60,000 people. The first meeting will be the 16th of March. I will meet you and Jack Moore that morning at the Regas Hotel in Mexico City." Arganbright could not hide his excitement. "Brother Branham, we have at least a hundred ministers in two dozen denominations cooperating with us. What's more, this is the first time in Mexican history that their government has welcomed a Protestant evangelist into their country. I'm expecting some wonderful things to happen."

Bill spent the first two months of 1956 flying around the United States, preaching one night here and two nights there. These were not faith-healing campaigns. He didn't want to pray for the sick until he reached old Mexico, since that is where he expected his new ministry to begin.

On the 16th of March, Bill flew to Mexico City, accompanied by Billy Paul, Jack Moore, and Young Brown. Also traveling with him was Roberto Espinosa, a Mexican-American minister who would be his interpreter during the campaign. After checking into the Regas Hotel, he hired a taxi to drive them out to the bullfighting arena. Dark clouds had gathered and a light rain was falling.

The taxi driver said, "We don't have rain very often at this time of year."

Bill elbowed his manager in the ribs and said, "What did I tell you? Now, watch, there's going to be some kind of trouble when we get there. The place will be empty."

"Brother Branham, how could it be?"

"I don't know, but that's what I saw in a vision last year."

When they got to the bullfighting stadium, Jack Moore stared in amazement at the circle of 60,000 concentric seats, all of them empty. He said, "Brother Branham, if I wasn't a believer in your gift before this, I certainly would be now."

Later they learned that during that morning thousands of people had gathered in the bullfighting arena, waiting for the evening prayer service to begin. In the afternoon, when it began to rain, someone had used the public address system to dismiss the crowd. Reverend Abel Medina, one of the main organizers of the campaign, told Bill that he didn't know who was responsible for dismissing the crowd. Worst of all, their contract for the bullfighting arena had suddenly been annulled. At that moment, neither Reverend Medina nor General Estrada could put a personal name on their enemy, although they were sure they knew the name of the organization for which he worked. Jack Moore gritted his teeth and said, "I'm going to find out who is behind this fiasco."

Bill shrugged. "Go ahead and try, but you won't find out. Nobody you talk to will know anything about it."

While Bill and Billy Paul flew home to Jeffersonville, Arganbright and Moore stayed in Mexico City, hoping to straighten out the mess. Jack Moore tried for two days to find out who had dismissed the crowd and canceled the meetings. He walked from office to office, talking to government officials until his jaws hurt. Nobody he talked to seemed to know anything about the matter. Meanwhile Arganbright worked with General Estrada and Reverend Medina to salvage the campaign. Since they had lost their contract for the bullfighting arena, they had to find another suitable place to hold the meetings. They found a site in Tacubaya, a suburb of Mexico City.

On Saturday, Miner Arganbright called Bill and asked him to come back to Mexico. Bill went out to his cave to pray about it. Early Sunday morning he saw a vision of dead fish lying all over the ground. The angel of the Lord said, "*Go back to Mexico. This is not the perfect time, but I will be with you.*"

So, on Monday, March 19, 1956, just a few days after he left Mexico, Bill and his son returned. General Estrada had secured a soccer field in Tacubaya for two weeks. Bill would be praying for the sick each night through Friday night. After that, Reverend Abel Medina would continue the campaign using local evangelists.

At nine o'clock on Monday morning, people came to the soccer field. Since here there were no grandstands or bleachers, they sat on the playing field all day waiting for the evening meeting to begin. Hour by hour their numbers grew. At six o'clock in the evening, Billy Paul Branham shuffled the prayer-cards and gave them to a Mexican man who passed them out. Then Billy Paul followed this man through the crowd to make sure he didn't sell any of the cards. By the time Bill arrived at eight o'clock, there were approximately 10,000 people waiting to hear him speak. Bill wondered how he could ever get to the platform. His sponsors had already worked this problem out. The platform was built against a tall wall that separated the soccer field from a public road. Bill was driven to the street side of this wall. Then he climbed a ladder to the top of the wall, where two men looped ropes under his armpits and lowered him down the other side to the platform.

After greeting the people, Bill read Jude 3, emphasizing the phrase: "...*earnestly contend for the faith which was once delivered unto the saints.*" Then he told the story of the Samaritan woman, explaining that Jesus had never seen her before, yet he told her the essential history of her life.[144] He followed this with the story of Nathanael. Philip told Nathanael, "I have found the Christ." Nathanael asked, skeptically, "What proof do you have?" Philip said, "Come and see." When Nathanael came before the Nazarene, Jesus said, "Here is a true Israelite." Nathanael asked, "How do you know me?" Jesus said, "Before Philip called you, while you were sitting under that fig tree, I saw you."[145] How did Jesus see him? He saw him in a vision. The Spirit of God knows everything; and Jesus, who is the manifestation of God in flesh, knows everything about us.

Bill said, "Tonight the Lord is here to do miracles. I don't do the miracles. I am like this microphone in front of me. If I don't speak, the microphone cannot transmit anything on its own. Likewise, I am only an instrument in the hands of God. The Lord Jesus Christ is the one who heals; I am only the means by which God manifests

---

[144] John 4:5-39
[145] John 1:43-51

healing. I act in agreement with the promises of His Holy Word, because I believe what He promises in His Word."

A woman named Enriqueta Arellano was the first of 25 people in the prayer-line. She walked up the stairway to the platform and stood before the American evangelist. Bill said, "This woman is as much of a stranger to me as the Samaritan woman was to Jesus. But I can tell you what her trouble is. I can see her in a hospital having an operation. The wound has not healed properly and she is afraid it might be cancer. Is that true?" Tearfully, she announced to the audience it was so. After a short prayer, Bill said, "Rejoice! The Lord has healed you!" Enriqueta walked off the platform looking like a new woman.

Several more people came through the prayer-line with equally astounding results. Then a man named Mariano Santiago stood before the evangelist. Bill said to the audience, "If God will tell me why this man is here, will all of you believe in Jesus Christ?" Turning to Santiago, Bill said, "You came here to have me pray for your hernia. But there is another reason too. You are a minister of the Gospel from Veracruz, and your church is called Calvary. You want me to pray over some handkerchiefs so you can give them to sick people in your church."

While this was going on, an usher informed Reverend Medina that a demented young man was standing in the prayer-line, holding a prayer-card with a woman's name written on it. When Medina investigated, he found that the young man did seem to be mentally ill, but he did not seem to be dangerous. From the fringe of the crowd stepped the young man's mother. She said that the prayer-card belonged to her. She was sick, but more than anything else she desired her son to be healed, so she had given the card to him. Reverend Medina sympathized with her desire. However, there were so many sick people who had not been able to get a prayer-card that Medina feared any deviation from their announced procedure might cause a riot. He asked the mother to switch back with her son in the prayer-line, which she did.

When she finally stood on the platform, Bill said to her, "You are a Catholic and you pray with a rosary. You are here because you desire that a loved one be healed, and that person is your son. God has fixed everything. Go in peace."

That night the same thing happened in Mexico that happened in Africa, India, and also on the Apache Indian Reservation. The simple faith of these Mexicans accepted the discernment at face value; that is, they believed it was Jesus Christ revealing Himself among them. Miracles blossomed as abundantly as desert flowers after a spring rain.

A storm front was still affecting the weather in this region. All day scattered rain clouds billowed over the mountains. On the first night the wind blew, but it didn't rain on the crowd. The next day, however, a light rain fell all afternoon. That didn't discourage people from coming to the meeting. By the time Bill arrived at eight o'clock to pray for the sick, the crowd had swollen to around 25,000.

The fifth person who came through the prayer-line was an old blind man. Bill watched as he shuffled forward, led by one of the Mexican ushers. The old man kept asking the usher a question. Espinosa interpreted for Bill. "He's asking if he is near the American evangelist. He wants to touch you."

A few moments later, the usher placed the blind man's shaky hand on Bill's lapel. Dropping to his knees, the old man pulled a string of rosary beads from his pocket and started to chant "Hail Mary, full of grace..." Bill stopped the man and urged him to get up, saying, "You don't need to do that here, Papa."

The old man wore a frayed straw hat, torn and sewn back together with twine. Unkempt gray hair jutted out from beneath his hat. An untrimmed gray mustache hid his upper lip. His trousers and coat were ragged and dusty, and he wasn't wearing a shirt. This pitiful man touched a nerve of sympathy deep in Bill's heart. He thought, "If my daddy had lived, he would have been about this man's age. How cruel life has been to this old fellow. He may never have eaten a full meal in his life, or owned a decent suit of clothes, or a pair of shoes. Besides all that, now he's staggering in darkness, unable to help himself."

Bill looked at the man's bare feet. They were dusty and calloused, with long toenails that curled up. For a moment Bill thought about giving the man his shoes. Then he realized they wouldn't fit; this Mexican's feet were much larger than his own. Bill glanced at the man's shoulders, thinking that maybe he could give him his coat. The old man's shoulders were too broad; Bill knew his coat wouldn't fit either.

The blind man took off his hat, dropped his forehead on Bill's shoulder, and wept. Not only could Bill feel the man's pain, something inside him entered into the man's suffering—something that went beyond compassion, beyond reasoning, into a realm of love that could pray the prayer of faith with absolute sincerity.

Suddenly a vision bloomed like a cactus flower, showing the old man jumping with joy. Bill knew then it was finished. Gently he lifted the man's head. The man blinked twice, and then shouted, "Gloria a Dios! Veo! Veo!" which meant, "Glory to God! I can see! I can see!" Dropping to his knees, he tried to kiss Bill's shoe. Bill pulled him up. The old man gave Bill a hug, then dashed around the platform, hugging Arganbright, Brown, and other ministers on the platform, shouting, "Gloria a Dios!" People by the thousands picked up the refrain, "Gloria a Dios!"

A miracle like this was too spectacular for the Catholic-controlled media to suppress. Thousands of Mexicans heard about it the next morning. Among them was a young mother whose baby was stricken with pneumonia and was struggling for every breath. Sometime that morning while this mother waited to see a doctor, her baby gasped for one last breath and then stopped breathing. Frantically, she called for the doctor. His efforts to revive the infant failed. Gravely the doctor told her she should leave her dead baby in his office and he would call for an undertaker.

Something in that young mother refused to let go. She figured that if God could give sight back to an old man, why couldn't He give life back to her baby. She told the doctor she would take the body with her, and from the doctor's office she went straight to the field where the American evangelist would be praying for the sick that night. By the time she got there, it was early afternoon and the soccer field was already two-thirds full of people. A drizzling rain was falling. She took her place at the back of a long line of people waiting for the hour when prayer-cards would be passed out.

That night when Bill climbed over the wall and was lowered by rope to the platform, he was surprised to see a large pile of coats and shawls waiting for him. Miner Arganbright explained that many of those without prayer-cards had piled these articles on the platform for Bill to pray over. They believed just touching a coat that he had prayed over could heal them. Bill was happy to do this, remembering the time Paul had prayed over a pile of handkerchiefs and aprons in Ephesus.[146] Bill knew it would work today the same as it did back then. These Mexicans understood the concept of faith. As always, Bill stressed to them that their faith must be firmly fixed on Jesus Christ, who is the only healer.

Not long after the prayer service started, Bill noticed some kind of trouble in the prayer-line. It looked like a woman in the back of the line was trying to get past the ushers. Bill watched her scramble right over their heads and dash for the platform. A

---
[146] **Acts 19:11-12**

roar went up from the surrounding people. Some men who were acting as ushers caught this woman and dragged her back to the end of the line. A moment later she scooted under their legs and made another dash for the platform. Again they caught her and dragged her back, but she wouldn't give up.

Soon Billy Paul came up on the platform and reported, "Daddy, we can't hold that prayer-line together much longer. A woman back there has a dead baby in her arms and she's desperate to have you pray for it. The trouble is, she doesn't have a prayer-card. All of those people in the prayer-line have been waiting here since early morning. If I let that woman through without a prayer-card, it might start a riot. But she's frantic and the ushers can't keep her back. What should we do?"

Bill turned and looked at his manager. Jack Moore was a small man like Bill. They were both about the same age, and both of them had thin hair on top with bald foreheads. Bill said, "Brother Jack, she doesn't know who I am. Why don't you go back there and pray for her dead baby? That should satisfy her and calm her down."

Jack Moore nodded and walked down the stairs to the grass. Bill turned back to the microphone and was about to speak to the audience when he saw a toothless Mexican baby floating in front of him. The baby was sitting on a blanket, cooing, laughing, and flailing its arms the way infants do when they are excited. Bill said, "Wait a minute, Brother Jack. I better handle this myself. Tell those ushers to let the woman through."

Billy Paul shook his head. "I can't do that, Daddy. It might cause a riot."

"Billy, I saw a vision."

"A vision? That's different." Billy Paul knew better than to question a vision.

"I'll go down there and tell the ushers," said Espinosa. Soon the ushers stepped aside and let the woman pass.

She dashed to the platform like a soccer player sprinting for the goal. Falling in front of the American evangelist, she cried, "Padre! Padre!" Bill and Espinosa lifted her so she was again standing. She was a pretty woman in her early twenties. Her eyes were swollen from a day of tears. Perhaps this was her first child, which she now held lifeless in her pleading arms. Bill couldn't see the baby; all he could see was its stiff form under a wet blanket.

"When did the baby die?" Bill asked.

She said her baby died that morning in a doctor's office. Bill said, "Brother Espinosa, don't interpret this prayer." He laid his hands on the wet blanket and prayed, "Heavenly Father, I do not know what all this means, but just a few minutes ago I saw a little baby in front of me, cooing and playing. If that vision showed this dead child, let life return to it in Jesus' name." At that moment, the baby squalled and kicked beneath its blanket. The mother screamed and clutched her wiggling child to her chest.

Bill said sternly, "Brother Espinosa, don't publish this yet. Have this woman take you to her doctor. I want a written statement from her doctor proving this baby was dead."

At the end of the prayer service, Bill asked how many people, after what they had just seen, would raise their hand and give their lives to Jesus Christ. Thousands of hands went up. Astonished, Bill turned to Espinosa and said, "Tell them that I don't want Catholics or Protestants to raise their hands. I only want to see the hands of people who have never received Jesus Christ before." Espinosa stressed this to the crowd, but it did not seem to change the number of hands in the air.

The next day, Roberto Espinosa obtained a signed affidavit from the doctor who had examined that woman's baby and had pronounced it dead. Only then did Bill give permission for this story to be published, first in the local newspapers, and later in *The Voice of Healing* magazine.

While Bill was packing to leave Mexico, a Catholic reporter called on him for an interview. After questioning Bill about the many miracles that happened over the past five days, the reporter asked, "Do you believe our Catholic saints can perform miracles?"

"If they're living, they can," Bill answered shrewdly.

"In the Catholic church, you can't be a saint until you're dead," the reporter countered.

"That might be what the Catholic church says, but in the Bible, Paul wrote a letter to 'the saints who are in Ephesus.' They were certainly alive at the time."

"We read the Bible too. But if there is any question, we believe what our church says over what the Bible says, because the Pope hears directly from God." Bill frowned. The reporter said, "I take it that you are a non-Catholic."

"Yes, I am a Protestant, which means I protest the Catholic church—not the people in the church, those people are souls for whom Jesus died—but I protest the Catholic system that rules those people and turns them away from the Bible."

Such candor surprised this Mexican reporter. "Mr. Branham, what church are you affiliated with?"

"The church of the Lord Jesus."

"I don't think I've heard of that denomination."

"That's because it isn't a denomination. It's the body of Christ. The Bible says, 'By one Spirit we are all baptized into one body.'[147] Organizations don't count. What matters is a person's faith in Jesus Christ—and that faith comes by believing the Bible."

---

[147] 1 Corinthians 12:13

"You realize, Mr. Branham, that the Bible is merely the ancient history of the Catholic church."

"I would differ with you there. I have read a lot of history and as far as I can see, the Catholic church didn't come into existence until the time of Constantine, nearly 300 years after the death of the last apostle."

"Mr. Branham, what is your overall opinion of the Catholic church?"

"I wish you hadn't asked me that; but since you did, I'm going to tell you. The Catholic church is the highest form of spiritualism there is."

This shocked the reporter. "Where did you ever get such an idea?"

"Anyone who tries to talk with the dead is a spiritualist. And you Catholics are always trying to talk with dead saints, asking them to intercede for you."

"Mr. Branham, you talk to Jesus Christ, and He died."

"Jesus didn't stay dead. He rose from the grave and is living today. If my campaign in Mexico proves anything, it proves that Jesus Christ is alive!"

Chapter 76
America Stands Like Israel at Kadesh-Barnea
1956–1957

LIKE HIS CAMPAIGNS in Germany and Switzerland, William Branham's campaign in Mexico was a phenomenal success. During his five nights in Tacubaya, an estimated 20,000 people gave their lives to Jesus Christ. It was easy for Bill to see how Mexico fulfilled the first part of his December 1955 vision, but it did not fulfill everything. The baby's shoe and the fishing lesson were allegories he could easily grasp, but the tent portion of the vision was not as easy to understand. Did it merely symbolize the "third pull" of his ministry, or was he really going to preach in a gigantic tent or cathedral? He didn't know. Just in case it was going to be literal, Bill asked his managers to search for the biggest tent they could rent or buy. The vision had clarified one thing for him—he now knew that God expected him to continue his evangelistic work.

Miner Arganbright wanted him to return to either Europe or Africa in July. After praying about these suggestions, Bill said no to both continents. The Holy Spirit compelled him to stay on American soil. He felt an urgency that he had never sensed before, as if this was a pivotal year for the Gospel in America. Many times during 1956 Bill said, "I predict that the United States of

America will either receive Christ, or she'll start falling from grace this year. Now, the Lord hasn't told me that. Still, I believe that America is either going to receive Christ or turn Him down flatly this year—and I predict that she will turn Him down."

In January of 1956 he preached a sermon in Jeffersonville that he called "Junction of Time." In this sermon he identified seven major places in history where the omnipotent God changed course and began something new. During each of these junctions God visited the earth in a special way. The word "junction" means "two things coming together," and in his sermon the word referred to the natural and the supernatural. Bill identified these junctions as the time of Noah, the time of Moses, the time of Abraham, the time of Elijah, and the time of Jesus. Bill dwelt in detail on this fifth great junction. He said, "John the Baptist was a prophet. Gabriel was the angel. They appeared about 33 years before a junction of time. God forewarned people that the junction was at hand. Look at what took place. We see John standing by the Jordan River, preaching, telling people about the mighty one who was coming. After a while, there appeared none other than the omnipotent one Himself, wrapped in a little bundle of flesh. Great Jehovah God revealed Himself in His Son, Christ Jesus. One night Jesus slept in a little boat tossed about by a storm. He didn't pay any attention. He was tired. But time had come to a junction and something had to happen. He put his foot on the rail of the boat and said 'Peace, be still.' I tell you, the very Creator of the heavens and earth lay in that boat and nature had to obey. When omnipotence speaks, miraculous things take place. Amen."

Concerning our own day, Bill said, "I believe that we are living at the near appearing of the second coming of the Lord Jesus. The first time He came as a baby. This time He's coming as King of glory to take vengeance upon all who obey not the Word of God... Teaching of the Word is a very fine thing. We know faith comes by hearing the Word. But it always takes the miraculous to vindicate that the omnipotent God still lives and reigns. We must have the miraculous. And I believe that the Church is now standing on the threshold of the greatest vindication of omnipotence that the world has ever known... We're at a junction. What is the next thing? Jesus Christ shall come again the second time in glory to receive all those who are dead in Christ and alive in God. God will bring every one with Him, the meek shall inherit the earth, and the great millennium will begin. There will be no more war, and neither will there be any more sickness, trouble, or heartache. We will live here in His presence forever and ever. And all these signs and things show we are at the junction."

After his campaign in Mexico, he continued to pray for the sick in his meetings, but more and more he was teaching. The angel had explained how divine healing was the bait on the hook that would catch people's attention. The hook was the Word of God. That was the important thing. Christians needed to be grounded in the fundamental principles of their faith, lest their faith be in vain.

In Sturgis, Michigan, he again taught on the three courts of the tabernacle, stressing how important it is for Christians to step behind the veil into the Holiest of Holies, which symbolizes the baptism of the Holy Spirit. He said, "Many professing Christians are always having a hard time, always struggling to hold on. I believe it's because they lack correct Bible teaching. There is actually no such thing as a Christian 'holding on.' Christ does the holding. The whole Christian principle is based upon rest. Jesus said, *"Come unto me, all ye that labour and are heavy laden, and I will give you rest."*[148] Notice, it's not what you do; it's what Christ has done for you that brings rest. Someone told me they were seeking God. That is an error. No man ever sought God; God

---

[148] Matthew 11:28

seeks man. After Adam sinned in the Garden of Eden, he ought to have been running through the garden hollering, 'Father, Father, where are You?' Instead, God was the one who went through the garden, calling, 'Adam, Adam, where art thou?'[149] Adam was hiding. That is the nature of man."

Besides teaching more during his campaigns, Bill was teaching more at Branham Tabernacle too. Whenever he was in Jeffersonville on a regular church night, Reverend Orman Neville gladly stepped aside so that Bill could address the congregation. These Jeffersonville sermons did not merely rehash what he was preaching elsewhere. During his evangelistic campaigns, the large mix of people limited how far he could go on a subject. At Branham Tabernacle he felt free in his spirit to go as deeply as necessary to thoroughly explain sound doctrine. Most of his sermons in Jeffersonville were tape-recorded. He realized the far-reaching effects these tape-recorded sermons could have. Each week more and more people requested his recorded sermons. Many people were keeping these sermons indefinitely and listening to them repeatedly.

On May 27, 1956, he preached in Jeffersonville about Kadesh-Barnea, that oasis in the desert of Sinai where the Israelites camped while 12 men spied out the Promised Land. When the spies brought back a mixed report, the Israelites had to make a decision: should they go forward and try to conquer the land, or should they turn back into the desert and look for another place to settle? True, many formidable obstacles stood in the way of conquering Canaan, but God had promised them that land. The real question was spiritual: should they believe Moses, or shouldn't they? After all, it was Moses who told them God had promised them the land. Most of those Israelites decided not to believe Moses, and as a result they had to spend 40 years wandering

---

149   Genesis 3:9

around in the desert until they all dropped dead. It was their children who finally possessed the Promised Land of Canaan.

Bill said that the Christian church in America was in the same position. He felt that in 1956, America was camped at her own Kadesh-Barnea. Her decision was still pending.

On June 3, 1956, Bill preached on "The Lamb's Book of Life." Because he was in Jeffersonville, he could talk about predestination more freely than he could in his faith-healing campaigns. Using the Bible, he proved that the names of everyone who would ever be saved were written in the Lamb's Book of Life before the world was made.[150]

On June 17, he preached "Revelation, the Book of Symbols." He presented the scene in Revelation chapter 5, where God sat on a throne in heaven, holding a book that was closed and sealed with seven seals; and no man in heaven or on earth was found worthy enough to take the book and break open its seven mysteries. Then the Lamb of God stepped forward. He *was* worthy, so He broke open the seven seals. The prophet Daniel saw this same book and said it would be sealed until the last days. Then Bill touched on Revelation chapter 10—how an angel would come down from heaven with a rainbow over his head. This angel would put one foot on land and one foot on the sea, and would swear by Him who lives forever that in the days of the seventh angel, the mystery of God should be finished.

Bill read from Revelation chapter one: "*The Revelation of Jesus Christ, which God gave unto him, to shew unto his servants things which must shortly come to pass; and he sent and signified it by his angel unto his servant John...*" Bill paused and inserted, "An angel! How is He going to signify it? God gave the Revelation of Jesus Christ to His servant, a prophet, and signified it by an angel. Amen! I hope you see it."

---

[150] Revelation 13:8; 17:8

He continued to read: "*Who bare record of the Word of God, and of the testimony of Jesus Christ, and of all things that he saw. Blessed is he that readeth and they that hear the words of this prophecy, and keep those things which are written therein: for the time is at hand.*" Bill said, "Look, when is the time at hand? When the Revelation of Jesus Christ has been revealed to the body of Christ, and Christ has been revealed as not dead, but alive, living in His Church, doing the same things He did back then: the same ministry, the same Gospel, the same sign of the resurrected Christ. When He is revealed by His angel unto the Church, then the time is at hand. And from that day unto this, never has the mystery of Jesus Christ been revealed until these last few years. The time is at hand!"

WHEN WILLIAM BRANHAM preached in California back in 1954, he mentioned to his audiences that in two more years it would be 50 years since the Holy Spirit started a revival at the Azusa Street Mission in Los Angeles—a revival that restored the gifts of the Spirit to the church, most notably the gifts of tongues, interpretation of tongues, and prophecy. That revival actually began at an informal house meeting in Los Angeles on April 9, 1906, when a man named Edward Lee spoke in an unknown tongue. At this group's next meeting, an African-American preacher named William Seymour preached on Acts 2:4, prompting six other people to speak in tongues before that night ended. Other people soon received the gift of tongues as well. News of this revival spread quickly through the surrounding Los Angeles' neighborhoods. After just a few days the house on Bonnie Brae Street couldn't hold all the people wanting to attend these meetings. By April 14, 1906, this informal group of Christians moved their meetings to an old building at 312 Azusa Street, which later became known as the Azusa Street Mission.

The revival that sprang from this humble beginning in April of 1906 spread around the world and began the 20th century Pentecostal movement.

In 1954 Bill suggested to his California audiences that it would be nice to have a 50-year anniversary rally commemorating the 1906 Azusa Street revival. This idea caught on among Pentecostal ministers, who organized a jubilee rally for September 16-22, 1956—September being the month in 1906 when the Azusa Street Mission published its first newsletter called *Apostolic Faith*.

In September of 1956 Bill took a train from Jeffersonville to Los Angeles to attend this Azusa Street rally. He was scheduled to speak twice during the week. Around 5,000 people filled Angelus Temple on the first night he preached. Demos Shakarian, president of the Full Gospel Business Men's Fellowship, introduced him to the audience. During his introduction, Shakarian aptly stated the legacy of the Azusa Street revival when he said, "Pentecost is not a denomination; it is an experience."

Bill expanded on this theme in his sermon, "Azusa Jubilee." He explained that the word "Pentecost" means the 50th day, and the word "jubilee" means the 50th year. For the Jew, Pentecost refers to one of the feasts prescribed by the Mosaic Law. For the Christian, Pentecost refers to the 50th day after Jesus rose from the dead, the day when the Holy Spirit was first given to the Christian church. Like the word "Pentecost," the word "jubilee" also comes from the time of Moses, and is actually a statute of the Mosaic Law. God commanded the Israelites to observe a year of rest every 50th year. During a jubilee year, lands had to be left untilled, alienated property was restored to owners, and slaves were set free.[151] The Mosaic laws contained some interesting provisions for the freeing of slaves. When a year of liberty came, if any slave wanted to stay

---

[151] Leviticus 25:8-13

with his master, he could. Such a slave would then have a hole punched through his earlobe to signify he wanted to remain a slave forever.[152] Ultimately, every slave made his own choice during the year of jubilee.

Using "jubilee" as his context, Bill presented the same choice to every man, woman, and child enslaved by sin. He said, "This is a beautiful type which can be applied today because today every person must choose between taking the seal of God, or taking the mark of the beast. Paul said, "Faith comes by hearing, and hearing by the Word of God."[153] When a man hears that he can be free, and refuses to accept his freedom from sin, then he is sealed away from God and receives the mark of the beast. When men and women hear this marvelous Gospel of the Lord Jesus Christ, which tells them they must be baptized by the Holy Spirit, they have to make a choice. If you accept it, you receive your freedom in Christ. If you refuse it, you are marked and sealed away from Christ. So it makes a difference what your attitude is towards the Word."

He talked about the men and women who gathered at the Azusa Street Mission in 1906—ordinary people who humbled themselves before God and lay in prayer for hours until the world dimmed to insignificance and the Word of God brightened into a fire in their souls. Bill preached that if Christians in 1956 did the same thing, they would get the same results.

His sermon stirred hundreds of people to come forward and ask God to baptize them with the Holy Ghost. Still, not everyone liked what he preached. Some people were offended when he said that sin in the church was hindering revival. After the service, one woman said to another woman, "Branham is wrong about that. As Americans we have a right to smoke cigarettes and wear shorts if we want to. If I had been sitting near a door, I'd have run out

---

152 Exodus 21:2-6; Deuteronomy 15:12-17
153 Romans 10:17

of there." The second woman was a friend of Bill's and she relayed this comment to him.

The next night Bill preached on "The Lamb and the Dove." When John the Baptist saw Jesus walking toward him, John said, *"Behold the Lamb of God, which taketh away the sin of the world."* After Jesus was baptized, John said, *"I saw the Spirit descending from heaven like a dove, and it abode upon him."*[154] Bill pointed out that the lamb and the dove are two of the meekest creatures in the world. Why did God use them as symbols of Himself? The Son of God always obeyed His Father. Jesus Christ had a right to live, but as the Lamb of God He meekly gave up His human rights, allowing Himself to be sacrificed on Calvary so that all those who believe in Him could live forever. Jesus was our example. As He obeyed the Father's will, so ought we. Jesus also likened His people to sheep. He called Himself the Good Shepherd who is seeking His lost sheep.[155] A sheep willingly gives up its wool to the person who shears her. Likewise, Christians must willingly give up their rights to sin in order to follow the Good Shepherd into a better life.

During the last quarter of 1956, besides teaching on his usual subjects of love, grace, faith, and divine healing, Bill preached on some harsher topics, like sin and God's judgment. In Jeffersonville he preached "The Handwriting on the Wall," a sermon which equated the attitude of Belshazzar at his drunken party in Babylon to the attitude of many Americans toward the Word of God. (Daniel interpreted the supernatural writing on the wall as "Thou art weighed in the balances and found wanting.")[156]

Later that year Bill preached on "The Blushing Prophet," referring to Ezra's embarrassment when he saw all the sins and perversions in Israel. Bill drew a comparison between Ezra's day

---

[154] John 1:29-36
[155] John 10:11-14
[156] Daniel 5:25-27

and America in 1956. He said, "This is not an easy subject to speak on. I could think of many things that would be easier to speak on, but, brother, if somebody doesn't stand up in this sinful, adulterous day and call out a warning, then what is going to happen? Somebody has to speak about these things. Perhaps Ezra didn't want to do it in his day, but he did it anyway."

Bill didn't just preach on topics like this in Jeffersonville. More and more during his evangelistic sermons, he was preaching against sin and calling for a return to holiness, stressing the need for Christians to shun the immoral fashions of this world and live sanctified, holy lives before God. Frequently he quoted the words of an old church song:

> We let down the bars; we let down the bars,
> We compromised with sin.
> We let down the bars, and the sheep got out,
> But how did the goats get in?

Then he would answer the question, "The goats got in because you let down the bars. You compromised with sin."

On October 5, 1956, he preached a sermon in Chicago he called "Painted Face Jezebel." He used the story of Jezebel, the infamous wife of King Ahab, to show how a woman should not act.[157] He drew a parallel between Jezebel's immorality and the moral decline of women in modern America, a moral decline that was even seeping into Christian churches. He preached against women wearing shorts and pants, cutting their hair, wearing makeup, and smoking cigarettes. He taught that wives should be submissive to their husbands, and should not try to rule over them in the home. He said, "If the Holy Spirit is in me, you had better get right by that stuff before Judgment Day. And don't let

---

[157] 1 Kings 21:1-24; 2 Kings 9:30-37

your pastor tell you anything different, because this is 'Thus saith the Lord,' in God's Word.

"Remember, when sins like that go on among the people, God always has somebody who will stand up and tell them about it. In Jezebel's day, God had a prophet named Elijah the Tishbite who walked right up to the king and said, 'Ahab, you're wrong. God will make you answer for that kind of stuff.' What did Jezebel do? She hated Elijah for telling her what was right and wrong. Sure. If you tell the truth to people, many times they will hate you instead of repenting. They ought to repent and thank God for letting them know what the truth is. That's right."

Bill didn't confine his criticism to women. He said, "I am ashamed of you weak Christian brothers who will let your wives do such things. It shows what you are made of. If you aren't man enough to put your house in order, God be merciful to you." Lest people should get a wrong impression, Bill clarified what he meant. "Please understand me. Your wife is not a doormat; she is your sweetheart. You should set down and talk to her about these things; reason with her; read the Bible together and pray together. If more Christian men did that, these sins would not be in the church."

He knew he offended some people by speaking so bluntly. Although he hoped it would be seen as constructive criticism spoken in love, he knew not everyone would see it that way. As the reality of 1956 closed and the promise of 1957 opened, Bill told his secretary, "Brother Cox, I have determined in my heart to preach against sin. I'm going to just lay the truth before the people and wherever it belongs, God can put it in its rightful place."

ON SUNDAY, January 20, 1957, William Branham was sitting in his den putting the last touches on a sermon he called "The Impersonation of Christianity," when an old friend from

Canada stopped by his house to visit. Bill could not help noticing how much his friend had aged since he had seen him last, which reminded him of how much he himself had aged. In 1947 this Canadian minister had sported a mustache as black as Indiana topsoil. Now at the age of 50, his mustache was mostly gray. Bill was 48 years old, and his own hair—once thick, dark, and curly—was thinning and graying too.

His friend said, "Brother Branham, two years ago I thought the Lord called me to minister in the United States. For a while I worked as an evangelist. While traveling around your country, I noticed mostly two kinds of churches—either they are cold, formal and indifferent, or else they are loose and fanatical. A few months ago a church in the States asked me to be their pastor. I had my doubts when I saw them beating on the piano and kicking over chairs. They calmed down when I preached, so I hoped I could reach them. At the end of my sermon I said, 'Let us worship the Lord and consecrate our lives to Him.' At that moment an idiotic young man ran up to the pulpit and said, 'Amen, preacher, look at my hands—oil has been dripping out of my hands all morning. Hallelujah! If the people come up here now, I will give them this anointed oil for healing.' I said, 'Sonny, find yourself a seat and sit down.' Brother Branham, do you know what happened? The elders came forward and told *me* to find a seat and sit down!" The Canadian dropped his face into his hands and cried the tears of discouragement.

Bill laid a hand on his friend's shoulder. "I know what it's like. I see both groups everywhere I go: the intellectual churches on the one side and the emotional churches on the other. And sometimes each side is against the other so that it's hard to find a way to approach them both with the real Gospel."

"Brother Branham, as a traveling evangelist yourself, how are you able to balance your ministry between those two extremes?"

"It's just the grace of God."

"Well, I'm going back to Canada and try to escape from these evil spirits."

About that time Bill's secretary, Rhode Cox, knocked on his front door, ready to drive him to church. On their way to Branham Tabernacle, Bill thought, "Lord, my Canadian friend is right. Since the day I laid the cornerstone in my tabernacle, it has been a long, hard struggle, both of those extremes pulling on me, while I'm standing in the middle of the road trying to present the true Gospel. Last year I tried so hard to stabilize the people, to get them balanced in the Word so that Christians would forget their differences and come together in unity. Last year I felt such an urgency to teach, like it was America's year of decision. But today, very little has changed. What about these American churches, Lord? What will happen to them?"

As clearly as Bill heard the car engine, he heard a voice say, *"What is that to thee? Follow thou Me."*

Rhode Cox stopped at a stoplight and flipped on his turn signal. Bill let his thoughts drift back to the morning in 1933 when he laid the cornerstone in Branham Tabernacle. After showing him a vision of the finished building, the angel shocked him by saying, *"This is not your tabernacle."* Then the angel carried him to an orchard. Overhead the blue sky was clear of any clouds. The angel said, *"This is your tabernacle."* The orchard had just two rows of trees: one row of plum trees and one row of apple trees. At the end of each row sat an empty pot. The angel said, *"You are to plant in those two empty pots."* In the vision Bill broke off an apple tree branch and stuck it in one pot, then he broke off a plum tree branch and stuck it in the other pot. Instantly a tree grew out of each pot. Both trees developed fruit. A voice from heaven said, *"You have done well. Hold out your hands and reap the harvest."* A mighty wind blew hard enough to shake the fruit loose. Bill caught an apple in one hand and a plum in the other. The voice said, "*When you come out of this vision, read 2 Timothy 4.*" Since the day of that vision, Bill read this chapter often:

> *Preach the Word; be instant in season, out of season; reprove, rebuke, exhort with all longsuffering and doctrine.*
>
> *For the time will come when they will not endure sound doctrine; but after their own lusts shall they heap to themselves teachers, having itching ears;*
>
> *And they shall turn away their ears from the truth, and shall be turned unto fables.*
>
> *But watch thou in all things, endure afflictions, do the work of an evangelist, make full proof of thy ministry.*

In 1933 that vision puzzled him. Looking back from 1957, he could now see what it meant. That blue sky represented his worldwide ministry. When God called him to an international ministry in 1946, he went forth as an independent evangelist, not affiliating himself with any Christian denomination. That left him free to go anywhere he was invited. Still, because Pentecostal people embraced and emphasized spiritual gifts, it was not surprising that Pentecostal churches became some of his biggest supporters. The two rows of trees in that orchard represented the two largest factions within the Pentecostal movement: the Trinitarians and the Oneness. Although both groups had much in common, conflicting views on the Godhead separated them. Simply put, the Oneness group believes in one God, claiming there is no difference between the Father, the Son, and the Holy Spirit. The Trinitarian group believes that the Father, the Son, and the Holy Spirit are three distinct persons who together make one God.

For many years Bill walked carefully between these two factions, trying not to offend either so he could fellowship with both. But ever since his emphasis had shifted to teaching the fundamentals of the Christian faith, he could no longer avoid the subject of the Godhead. After all, the nature of God was the starting point of truth. How could Christians grow closer to their Maker unless they first know who God is?

Now Bill began to teach on the nature of God during his evangelistic sermons. In essence, he said that the Oneness view and the Trinitarian view were both wrong, and the truth lay between these two extremes. He taught that God is indeed only one. The Father, the Son, and the Holy Spirit are not three different persons in one God, but rather one Person manifesting Himself in three different offices. In the Old Testament, God showed Himself as the omnipotent Father. In the New Testament, God became a man in order to redeem His people. Finally, God indwelt His people in the form of the Holy Spirit. Bill said, "Oh, what Pentecost needs is a good Bible lesson; then you wouldn't have so much nonsense going on. Jesus Christ is the Son of God. He had the Spirit without measure. God didn't partially dwell in His Son, but all of God was in His Son, Christ Jesus.[158] All of God was poured out in Christ. All that Christ is, He poured out on the Church. But Pentecost, you keep refusing it. See? Jesus said, *'If I do not the works of my Father, believe me not. But if I do, though ye believe not me, believe the works: that ye may know, and believe, that the Father is in me, and I in him'*."[159]

On February 3, 1957 he attended a Full Gospel Business Men's convention in Evansville, Indiana. At this one-day convention Dr. Roy Weed, a presbyter for the Assemblies of God churches in Indiana, publicly criticized Bill's position on many issues, presumably the Godhead, water baptism, the evidence of the baptism of the Holy Spirit, and the conduct of Christians. Dr. Weed's criticism was: "Brother Branham says he tries to walk in

---

[158] Colossians 2:9
[159] John 10:37-38

the middle of the road on these issues. That isn't good ethics. A man who walks in the middle of the road will get run over."

When Bill was given a chance to answer him, he said, "Dr. Weed, this road we're traveling is a one-way road. You either go forward with God, or you fall off one side or the other. We don't need all this formal stuff; neither do we need all this fanaticism that we have today. The skies are loaded with the genuine Holy Spirit; there is no need to take a substitute. Why try to get to heaven on some sensation when God's Word says you can't do it? Why accept a substitute—either by joining a church, or by getting into some group that says you have to jump up and down, or have oil run from your hands, or blood from your face? That stuff comes from hell. It's not in God's Word. If you believe me to be a prophet of God, receive my word and stay away from such stuff."

Lately Bill was preaching against fanaticism a lot. For many years Christian fanaticism had festered on the West Coast, but now it seemed to be spreading and infecting other parts of the country. One preacher in Los Angeles gained national attention because blood appeared on his hands when he prayed for the sick. This man claimed it was the anointed blood of Jesus Christ. Amazingly, thousands of people flocked to see this deception. It disgusted Bill and he publicly condemned it, saying that it could not be the blood of Jesus. If it was, it meant the physical body of Jesus had returned, and that was nonsense. Since it was not the blood of Jesus, it was meaningless. No Scripture connected drops of human blood with divine healing. Repeatedly, Bill scolded Christians for accepting signs and wonders that didn't match God's Word. Everything a Christian thinks, says, and does must agree with the Bible.

On February 10 through 17, 1957, he preached in Minneapolis, Minnesota. His next campaign was scheduled to begin February 26 at the Madison Square Garden in Phoenix, Arizona. He had a week at home before he left for Phoenix. During that week he constantly received phone calls from ministers who were worried about the fanaticism that was creeping into their churches. Invariably they asked for his help. One day he received 30 of these calls in less than two hours. The ministers said variations of, "Brother Branham, that West Coast fanaticism has struck my part of the country. Leave Phoenix alone and come here. Surely my people will hear you. If they don't, I'm afraid of what might happen."

"Brother, I can't come now," Bill answered. "I promised the brethren in Phoenix I'd go there. You are a man of God. Stand behind your pulpit, take the Word of God, and preach it straight. Jesus said, *'My sheep hear my voice,* and *a stranger will they not follow'.*"[160]

His campaign in Phoenix lasted two weeks. One night he explained fanaticism in a sermon he called "God Keeps His Word." He took his text from the story of Moses leading the children of Israel out of Egypt. Exodus 12:38 said that *"a mixed multitude went up also with them."* That mixed multitude was in addition to the Israelites. The mixed multitude saw Moses show supernatural signs in Egypt, and they flocked around his supernatural vindication, but they were unconverted in their hearts; they were just trying to impersonate the real believers. The same thing is happening today.

Bill spoke about William Seymour, that one-eyed Negro preacher in Los Angeles, California who received the baptism of the Holy Ghost in 1906 at the Azusa Street Mission. He said, "From there God stuck His torchlight in the hands of people who wanted that same Pentecostal experience described in the book of Acts. God restored the gift of speaking in tongues. You Pentecostal people received it. But what happened? You made a

---

[160] John 10:27; John 10:5, respectively

doctrine that the initial evidence of receiving the Holy Ghost was speaking in tongues; and you said that no one could get the Holy Ghost without speaking in tongues, and everyone who spoke with tongues had the Holy Ghost. When you made a dogma out of it, God took the torchlight out of your hands.

"Then you Oneness people started baptizing in Jesus' name. That is all right, because it's in the Bible. But what happened? You organized and put a period after it, so God took His torchlight away from you. Then God started an interdenominational move of divine healing. What has happened? Too many men have built their ministries upon fantastic sensations. The Pentecostal movement has fallen face down into emotions that have no Scriptural foundation. God's Word is His foundation.

"Listen, brother, you are not saved by a sign or a sensation. You are saved when you meet the conditions of God's Word. I am not saved because I feel like I'm saved. I'm saved because God gave the promise and I met God's conditions; and upon God's Holy Word I can defeat Satan seven days in a week, and as many nights, because it's God's Word. Jesus said, 'He that hears My Word and believes on Him who sent Me has everlasting life and shall not come into judgment, but has passed from death to life.'[161] That's what the King of kings said. Do you believe it?"

When he was at his home church in Jeffersonville he spoke even more bluntly on this subject. He taught that Satan could impersonate every gift of the Holy Spirit. Of course he based this on Scriptures; but he also showed how many heathen cultures do Satanic things that parallel what Christians might call "Spirit-filled experiences."[162] If the presence of spiritual gifts could not be used as proof of a Spirit-filled life, then "speaking in tongues" could not be the evidence of the "baptism of the Holy Spirit." He preached, "If you say, 'Oh, hallelujah, I spoke with tongues,'

---

[161] John 5:24
[162] Matthew 7:21-23; 1 Corinthians 13:12; 2 Corinthians 11:13-15

that doesn't mean any more than if you played a tune on a guitar. Though you spoke with tongues, though you shouted and ran up and down the aisles, and cried tears like you've been peeling onions, it doesn't mean one thing unless your life backs it up. Now, if you do those things plus you have the life—amen, that's fine. But you can do those things without having that life. So then none of those things is the evidence of the Holy Spirit. Jesus said, 'By their fruit ye shall know them,' and the fruit of the Spirit is love, joy, peace, longsuffering, goodness, gentleness, faith, meekness, temperance."[163]

All through 1956 and 1957 he shocked and offended many Pentecostal people with statements like these. Many of his supporters wavered in their support.

---

[163] Matthew 7:16-23; Galatians 5:22-23

Chapter 77
Dividing an Inheritance
1957

BANKS WOOD had a good reason for buying a house next door to William Branham. In January of 1950, his wife Ruby persuaded him to attend a Branham meeting in Louisville, Kentucky. Banks had been raised in the Jehovah's Witnesses movement, so the idea that Jesus Christ could heal sick people today seemed ridiculous to him. That night in Louisville, Banks Wood watched in amazement as William Branham discerned the problems of strangers. He thought, "This seems right, but how can I be sure those people are really getting healed?" Then he saw William Branham pray for a boy who was crippled from polio. The boy rose from his wheelchair, ran up the stairs to the platform, and shouted his thanks to Jesus for healing him. That touched Banks deeply because his own little boy, David, was crippled from polio. Banks felt like he had stumbled across something real.

Banks Wood decided he had to know more about this unusual ministry, so he and his wife visited the next Branham campaign, which happened to be in Houston, Texas, at the end of January 1950. They were sitting in the audience on the night when the Pillar of Fire was photographed above William Branham's head. Banks drove home to Kentucky with a lot on his mind.

In August of 1950 William Branham held a two-week-long campaign in Cleveland, Ohio. One night Banks, Ruby, and little David Wood joined thousands of other people who flocked into a large tent. During the prayer service, William Branham turned away from the prayer-line, looked out over the audience, and said, "Way in the back sits a man with his family. Your name is Wood—Banks Wood. You're not from this city. You live near Crestwood, Kentucky. You are a Jehovah's Witness by faith. You've got a boy sitting there with a paralyzed leg drawn up underneath him, and your wife suffers with a tumor. Thus saith the Lord, 'They're both healed.'"

The evangelist turned back to the prayer-line. For a shocked moment, Banks and Ruby stared at each other, not knowing what to do. Then Ruby felt something cool pass through her body. She touched her side where the tumor had been. "Banks," she gasped, "Feel this. The knot is gone."

He felt his wife's side for the ominous lump. It wasn't there. He said to his son, "David, get up." Even while David squirmed to obey, his crippled leg straightened. He stood on two solid, working limbs. Not surprisingly, David Wood did not want to sit back down.

Nor was it surprising that Banks Wood surrendered his life to Jesus Christ. Selling his house and his construction business in Kentucky, he moved to Jeffersonville, Indiana, so he could attend church weekly at Branham Tabernacle. After he bought the house next door to Bill, the two neighbors became good friends.

When Banks Wood accepted Jesus Christ as his Lord and Savior, his father, mother, brothers, and sisters (all of whom were staunch Jehovah's Witnesses) disowned him. Banks did not see any of them for many years. Then one morning in April of 1957, his brother Lyle showed up at his door. The two brothers sat at the kitchen table and talked.

Eventually Lyle said, "Banks, I came here to see if I could talk some sense back into your thick head. What kind of fanaticism have you got tangled up with?"

"This isn't fanaticism, Lyle. Look at David's legs."

"Ah, nonsense. Our daddy raised us to know better than that. He always warned us against these hellfire preachers. I can't believe you really fell into such a mess. What kind of a quack are you listening to anyway? He must be a smooth talker to get you to quit building houses and follow him around the country like you do."

"No, he's not a smooth talker. Actually, he talks kind of plain. But the Spirit of God is with him."

"Well, if I ever meet this Branham fellow, I'll give him a piece of my mind."

"There he is, out mowing his lawn. I'll call him over."

Stepping outside, Banks waved for his neighbor to come over. When Bill entered the kitchen, Banks introduced his brother. Bill offered Lyle a vigorous handshake, but the hand he shook was cold and limp. They sat down to talk behind cups of coffee.

Lyle eyed Bill suspiciously. He didn't think this man looked like a preacher. He was wearing overalls and a floppy straw hat tipped far back on his head. His face bristled with beard stubble that might have been a day or two growing. Sweat glistened from his balding forehead and soaked his white T-shirt under his armpits. Right now he looked more like a hard-working farmer than a world-renowned evangelist. Lyle said, "So you're the preacher that has taken Banks on this wild goose chase."

"No, sir, I'm not. I'm just his brother in Christ. But I do preach the Gospel."

Banks told Lyle about some of the miracles he had seen in Bill's campaigns. Lyle listened stiffly, showing no interest. After listening to Bank's testimony for ten minutes, Bill said, "I suppose you don't believe any of this, Mr. Wood."

"I certainly don't. There is no such thing as divine healing. It's just a bunch of made-up nonsense that you've got my brother mixed up into. As for these so-called visions..."

While Lyle was giving his opinion, a vision flashed before Bill's eyes. He said, "Mr. Wood, I see you are married to a blond woman and you have two blond-headed boys, about six and eight years old."

Lyle gave his brother an accusing look.

"You think Banks told me that," Bill continued. "He didn't. He hasn't told me anything about his family. But if that didn't convince you, maybe this will. You've been cheating on your wife, and it's caused a separation. The night before last you were with a young woman with auburn hair. You heard a knock at the door and you were going to answer it, but she wouldn't let you. So you hid in her bedroom while she answered it. When you peeked out the window, you saw a man standing at the door wearing a dark suit and a red tie. That was another one of her lovers, and it's a good thing you didn't go to the door, because he had a gun in his hand and he would have blown your head off."

"Who—who told you that?" Lyle stuttered.

"Almighty God just showed me a vision of it happening."

Lyle felt light-headed. "Mr. Branham, every word you said is the truth. I think I'd better surrender my life to the same Almighty God who told you that secret."

Full of enthusiasm, Lyle went home to tell his family about his conversion. Within a week his sister attended one of Bill's meetings and she too was converted. That alarmed their father, who decided he had better meet this Branham character for himself, so he could straighten his family out.

On Monday afternoon, May 13, 1957, Bill turned his car into his driveway and saw an elderly gentleman standing in the yard. Bill walked over and introduced himself.

"So you're Mr. Branham," the man said gruffly. "I've heard a lot about you. My name is Wood—Jim Wood. Banks and Lyle are two of my sons. Do you know where Banks is?"

"Banks and Ruby usually go grocery shopping about this time of day. Won't you come inside and refresh yourself with a glass of water?"

It didn't take Bill long to learn that he and Mr. Wood had some common interests. First they talked about growing up in Kentucky; then they talked about how much fun it was to hunt squirrels and fish for bluegills and crappies. Rather than plunging right into the subject of Jehovah God, Bill asked Jim Wood to go fishing with him tomorrow, thinking that such a trip would give them plenty of time to discuss religion. He suggested that Banks and Lyle could come too. Jim Wood liked the idea.

That night it rained hard. The next morning Banks said, "Well, I guess there's no need of us going fishing today. The streams will all be muddy and the fish won't bite."

"We can still try," said Bill. He had a few days until his next campaign began in Saskatoon, Canada, and he needed to relax and unwind.

So, the four men packed their camping and fishing gear into the trunk of Banks' car. Banks and his father sat in the front seat; Bill and Lyle sat in the back. Banks drove. Their destination lay over 150 miles southeast near Dale Hollow Lake. Bill planned to fish on the lake behind Wolf Creek Dam. This area was not far from Burkesville, Kentucky, where he was born. Because some of his relatives owned land on the lake and had a boat he could borrow, Bill fished this spot often.

While they were crossing the Ohio River into Kentucky, Bill prayed silently, "Lord, somehow help me to get through to this honest old farmer's heart." Soon he felt himself slipping into a vision. The car vanished and he was somehow further ahead in time, watching the future reveal its secrets. When the vision ended, he said, "Mr. Wood, so you may know this Gospel that I preach is real, today every stream and lake we pass will be muddy, until we get to our destination. The lake behind Wolf Creek Dam will be blue and clear. We shall fish until about 3:30 this afternoon without catching anything. Then I'm going to start hooking catfish. I've never caught any catfish in these waters before, but today I'm going to catch a string of them, totaling about 25 pounds. Mr. Wood, you're going to fish right beside me using the same bait, but you're only going to catch one, and Lyle will catch one. The next morning I'll catch a scaly fish. I couldn't see exactly what kind, but it will be large for its species. That will be the last fish we'll catch on this trip. We will fish the rest of the day without even getting a bite. That is 'Thus saith the Lord'."

One side of Jim Wood's mouth curled up slightly in a smirk of disbelief. He looked over at Banks and winked. But the old man started to wonder when they topped the last hill and looked down on Wolf River Dam. The water in the reservoir behind the dam was just as blue and pretty as it could be. Obviously, it had not rained much on the region above the dam.

They fished for crappies, bluegills, trout, and bass without success. In the middle of the afternoon Bill changed his bait and immediately hooked a catfish. Over the next several hours he caught a string of catfish, while Jim and Lyle each caught one and Banks didn't catch any. They quit fishing around 11 o'clock that night. No one mentioned the prophecy from that morning, although it simmered in everyone's thoughts.

On Tuesday morning the sun came up smiling. After a breakfast of fried catfish, the fishermen took their fishing poles and tackle boxes and headed for the lake. As they were baiting their hooks, Bill reminded them, "There is another fish coming, and that will be the last one we'll catch on this trip." On his first cast, Bill hooked a scaly fish with a red belly. It weighed about a pound, which was large for that species of brim.

They continued to fish, but no one caught anything else. Every few hours Banks, who knew how precise Bill's visions were, suggested that they quit and go home. Jim Wood wanted to stay. He was determined to catch another fish and prove them all wrong. The old gentleman moved from spot to spot along the bank, frequently changing his bait and his technique, trying to find some combination that would work. He fished all afternoon, through the evening, even after dark, all the way up to midnight. He didn't even get a nibble.

Early Wednesday morning they dismantled their camp. Bill had to go home because Thursday he was leaving for Saskatoon. While they were packing the car, Banks asked his father, "What do you think about it now, Dad?"

"Well-l-l-l-l," he drawled, fidgeting with his tackle box, "if a fellow can see fish before he catches them, I guess that's all right."

Bill saw his opening. "But I can't always do that, Mr. Wood. God showed me that vision for your sake. The Bible says, if you wonder whether or not a man is a prophet, watch his prophecies. If his prophecies don't happen, then he's not a prophet and you can ignore him; but if they do happen, then you should listen to him because he has the Word of the Lord.[164] I know Mr. Russell is considered a prophet in the Jehovah's Witnesses movement. But Mr. Russell prophesied that Jesus Christ would return in 1914. When that didn't happen, he said it was a 'spiritual' coming. But

---

[164] Deuteronomy 18:15-22

that's not right, because Jesus came back to earth spiritually on the day of Pentecost in the form of the Holy Ghost. That is what the book of Acts is all about. So you see, Mr. Russell can't be a prophet." Bill continued along this line, showing three other places where Russell's prophecies failed.

Jim Wood rubbed his jaw thoughtfully. Then he pointed his thumb back over his shoulder at the lake and quoted the Ethiopian in Acts 8:36, "Here is water; what doth hinder me to be baptized?"

There was nothing to hinder, so right then and there he was baptized in the name of the Lord Jesus Christ.

IN MAY OF 1957, William Branham traveled north to Saskatoon, Canada. This was his first major healing campaign without any Pentecostal churches sponsoring him. Instead, his support came from Presbyterians, Anglicans, Baptists, and other denominations. The Pentecostal churches in Saskatoon flatly refused to cooperate, but that did not hinder God. Several thousand people filled the ice arena to hear Bill speak. When it came time for a prayer-line, God's Spirit moved as smoothly and elegantly as a figure skater on ice. On the first night of this campaign, a blind woman miraculously received her sight; a spastic boy instantly regained his coordination; another boy, who had never heard or uttered a sound in his life, suddenly heard the organist playing "Only Believe." The boy screamed, which was the only way he could praise his healer, Jesus Christ.

One night a hunchbacked boy came through the prayer-line. Bill put his arms around the lad and prayed for him. Then he said, "When you go home tonight, have your mommy pull a string around your chest and over the hump. Have her cut the string off for a measurement. Tomorrow morning if that hump hasn't shrunk by three inches, then I'm a false prophet. Bring the string back here tomorrow night and show these people."

The next night this boy came up to the front and showed everyone the string his mother had used to measure his chest. His hump had indeed shrunk three inches. Even more amazing was the fact that now he could raise his arms above his head, a feat that is normally impossible for hunchbacks because of deformities in their arm sockets.

While people were lining up for prayer, Bill said, "I'm going to tie two Scriptures together now. When Jesus told Nathanael where he was before he came to the meeting, what did Nathanael say? He said, 'Rabbi, Thou art the Son of God. Thou art the King of Israel.' That is what a Jew thought when he saw the sign of discernment done. When that Samaritan woman heard the discernment, she said, 'Sir, I perceive Thou art a prophet. We Samaritans know that when the Messiah cometh, He will do these things.' Jesus said, 'I am He who speaks to you.' And upon that sign, she left her water pot and went to tell the villagers, 'Come; see a man who told me the things I have done. Isn't this the very Messiah?'[165]

"If that was the sign of the Messiah in their day, then it's the sign of the Messiah today. Take all your denominational 'isms' out of it now, and just look at the truth of it in the Word. Jesus Christ is raised from the dead."

After this introduction, an usher brought forward the first person in that night's prayer-line. When the vision came, Bill said, "I know this woman is a Christian because her spirit is saying welcome. Lady, you are a preacher's wife, and you're suffering with a tumor in your breast. You're not from this city. I see the West Coast, and a big city where there's a big park. Vancouver, British Columbia—that's where it is. Is that the truth?" She said it

---

[165] John 1:44-51; 4:5-29

was true. Bill laid a hand on her shoulder and prayed, "Almighty God, in the name of the Lord Jesus Christ, I bless this woman and ask for her healing in Christ's name. Amen."

Next in line stood a man who said, "I am a pastor and that woman you just prayed for is my wife. Everything you told her is true and I can vouch that we are both strangers to you."

"Thank you, my brother. You have something wrong with your shoulder. You had a motorcycle accident and your shoulder never went back to its place just right. It's over now. You can go on your road rejoicing and be well. God bless you. Amen."

To the next woman in line he said, "Believe with all your heart that Jesus Christ is the Son of God, and I am His prophet, or His servant. Now, if the audience can still hear my voice, I see the woman is nervous about something. I see her going into a little room—it's a bathroom—and there she fell and bruised her chest about a year ago. She hasn't gone to a doctor about it. She's trusted God. That is the truth. Isn't that right, lady? All right. Go to your seat and be well then, in the name of the Lord Jesus Christ."

All over the building, bits of doubt were falling off Christians like ice falls from frosty trees when the sunshine warms their branches. Bill said to the next woman in line, "Lady, I don't know you. We're strangers to each other." Suddenly he turned his head and stared into the audience, watching the light of the angel. "Something happened in the audience—somebody somewhere believed." Intensely he studied the crowd. Then he pointed. "It's that little black-headed lady sitting there looking over another lady's shoulder. She suffers with headaches. She was praying, 'Lord, have him call me.' You've been having tremendous headaches. If that's right, raise your hand." Her hand went up. "All right. It's over now. You can go on your road, and rejoice, and be made well, in Christ's name." The angel was not yet through with that spot; the vision spilled over… "The lady sitting behind you has arthritis, and she's been wanting to be healed. That's right, isn't it, lady? That's right." Bill staggered from the strain of the visions that were draining him. "See, you couldn't hide your life if you had to. None of you could. Amen. Oh, I'm happy that He's raised from the dead—Jesus Christ is the same yesterday, today, and forever!"

He turned back to the woman waiting on the platform beside him. "Lady, you're not here for yourself. You're here because you have a mentally retarded son." She gasped. Then he prayed for her son.

The next patient was an elderly woman who had a large growth on her nose. The vision revealed her history. Bill said, "There is more than one growth. They fall off and they come back again somewhere else. You've got one now on your chest. You're not from this city. You come from the west. You're from Edmonton, Alberta. Your name is Pearl Lennox. Miss Pearl Lennox, if you'll believe with all your heart, you'll get well."

So it went—person after person, vision after vision, night after night, always perfect. On his last night in Saskatoon, that woman who had been blind on the first night of this campaign, now walked up to the podium and handed Bill a letter containing her testimony—a letter she had typed herself.

AFTER his faith-healing campaign in Saskatoon, William Branham held his next long campaign in Indianapolis, Indiana, June 10-14, 1957. He returned from Indianapolis aching with weariness. Besides the 15 to 20 visions he saw nightly in the prayer services, he also saw 20 to 30 visions a day during private interviews which he granted in his hotel room. The strain of all these visions had siphoned off most of his energy. He had 14 days to rest before starting his next campaign in Chicago on June 29, so he asked Banks and Lyle Wood if they wanted to go fishing with him. They did.

The evening before their fishing trip, Bill and Banks walked out to Banks' garden to dig up some worms to use for bait. While they were digging, eleven-year-old Rebekah ran over to the garden, but not to see the worms. Her lower lip quivered like she was about to cry. "Daddy, I found a poor old kitty-cat that has eaten some poison and now she's all swollen and going to die. Would you let me keep her until she dies?"

Bill didn't like cats very much and seldom allowed them around the house; but when Rebekah looked at him with those sad, pleading eyes, he softened. "Well, if it's going to die soon, I guess we could keep it for a while. Let me see it."

Rebekah ran away and soon returned with the sick cat in a cardboard box. Remembering what happened when her father had prayed for that dying opossum, Rebekah said, "Daddy, will you pray for this kitty?"

Bill took one look at the cat and knew what was going to happen. He told Rebekah to put the animal in the shed for the night. Early the next morning Rebekah ran out to the shed to check on her kitty. Looking in the box, she squealed with delight. The cat was nursing a dozen kittens.

While Bill was loading Banks' car with camping equipment, two-year-old Joseph toddled from the shed holding one of the newborn kittens by its neck. "Joseph, don't hold the kitty like that," Bill scolded. Startled, Joseph squeezed the kitten hard before dropping it. Bill took the kitten back to the shed and laid it beside its mother. The kitten squirmed like it might be badly hurt. Bill thought, "Poor little thing, it can't help being a cat. I hope it's all right."

Banks, Lyle, and Bill headed for Dale Hollow, the same place in Kentucky where they had fished with Jim Wood last month.

When they reached Wolf Creek Dam, Bill borrowed a boat from his relatives. Once out on the lake, the three men baited their hooks with worms and soon caught several dozen little sunfish, which they cut into pieces and used to bait their trout lines. Then they settled back to wait for the big ones.

A light bluish haze covered the green slopes of the Appalachian Mountains around them. The lake smelled of seaweed, algae, fish, gas, and two-cycle engine oil. Sunshine warmed Bill's shirt even as a gentle breeze cooled his face. After just a few minutes in their boat, Bill felt his weariness drift away like ducks floating on the waves.

While their little boat trolled lazily along the shoreline, the three men talked about the Bible. They discussed the time Peter, James, and John saw Jesus talking to Moses and Elijah. Jesus began to shine like the sun. When Peter wrote about this experience, he said, "We...were eyewitnesses of His majesty. For He received from God the Father honor and glory when such a voice came to Him from the Excellent Glory: 'This is My beloved Son, in whom I am well pleased.' And we heard this voice which came from heaven when we were with Him on the holy mountain."[166]

"You know," Banks said, "that is sort of the way I feel because I've been privileged to spend so much time with a holy man like you, Brother Bill."

"Oh, Brother Banks, don't say that," Bill answered. "I'm not a holy man. There is no such thing as a holy man; it's just a holy God dwelling in a man. And there isn't a holy mountain either, just a holy God who visits the mountain. I think that is what Peter is saying."

They discussed how a holy God could dwell in His people. Banks mentioned an elderly woman he knew who had the Spirit of God dwelling in her. When Banks and Lyle were boys, this

---

[166] 2 Peter 1:16-18

lady often invited them into her home, where she fed them freshly baked bread and told them about the love of Jesus. They took the bread, but left Jesus behind. Banks said, "That lady must be over 90 years old by now. You know, Lyle, she lives close to here. Wouldn't it be nice if we stopped by her house and told her that we're both Christians now?"

When Banks said this, Bill felt the Spirit of God splash over him like the cool spray from a waterspout. In a flash of inspiration, he said, "Thus saith the Lord, 'Soon you will see the glory of God, for there is a little animal that will be raised from the dead.'"

When he came back to his senses, he saw Banks and Lyle staring at him in amazement. Banks said, "Brother Bill, did you really mean that the way it sounded?"

"What did I say?" Bill asked, honestly not knowing. After Banks repeated the prophecy, Bill assured him, "It will happen just the way it was spoken. It has to, because it wasn't me that said that. It was the Holy Ghost."

"What do you think that animal will be?" asked Lyle.

"I don't know, but I could guess. This morning my little boy squeezed a kitten too hard. It wasn't dead when we left, but maybe it will die; and then, when we get home, God will give it back its life."

They fished throughout the day without success. The big fish didn't bite until later that evening; but when they did, in a matter of minutes each man reeled in a trout. All together these three fish weighed 20 pounds. By then they had run out of bait, so they quit for the day.

In the morning, after a breakfast of pan-fried trout and fried potatoes, they climbed into their little boat, started the outboard engine, and trolled along the reservoir parallel with the shore. They fished for bluegills and sunfish to replenish their supply of bait, but at first they didn't catch anything. Then Bill pointed the bow of their boat into a little cove. When he throttled the motor down, the engine sputtered and died. He let the boat drift in close to shore. Sticking a worm on his hook, he cast his line, and soon felt a fish nibbling on his bait. One jerk hooked a little bluegill.

While they were fishing in this cove, they talked about the power of God. They discussed the time Jesus said to Simon the fisherman, "Launch out into the deep water and let down your nets for a catch." Simon answered, "Master, we have toiled all night and caught nothing; nevertheless, at Your word I will let down my net." As soon as Peter dropped his net into the lake, it filled with so many fish that it started to break. He called for his partners in another boat to come and help him. They pulled up the net and filled both boats with so many fish that the boats began to sink.[167] Bill said he didn't think those fish were in the lake before Jesus spoke. He believed God actually created those fish on the spot.

Winged bugs skittered over the water. The bluegills and sunfish were hungry. Regularly they swam to the surface and snapped their jaws on a bug. Because bluegills are so small, Bill was using a fly rod with a tiny #4 hook. Lyle, on the other hand, was using a large #12, the same hook he used to catch trout. Lyle impaled a worm on the hook's point, and then cast his line. Really he was paying more attention to the conversation between Banks and Bill than he was to his fishing. Feeling a tug on his line, Lyle reeled it in and was surprised to find that a bluegill had swallowed his hook all the way down into its stomach.

"Look at this," Lyle said, holding up his line with a three-inch-long fish dangling on the end. "You can't even see the hook."

Gripping the bluegill in one hand and wrapping his line around his other hand, Lyle pulled. With a tearing sound the

---

[167] Luke 5:17

hook came out, bringing with it the animal's stomach and part of its gills. Lyle whistled in surprise and said, "Little fishy, you've shot your last wad." After working his hook free, he tossed the fish overboard. For a few moments the bluegill thrashed his fins and tail, struggling to swim away. Then it flopped over on its side and died. It floated limp and lifeless, ten feet from the boat, drifting slowly towards the shore, nudged by a gentle breeze and the lapping of waves.

"Lyle, that didn't need to happen," Bill said. "You should use a smaller hook. Then as soon as you feel the bite, jerk your line. That will set the hook in its jaw."

"Aw, I'm just a country boy who hasn't done much fishing," Lyle said, sticking another worm with his #12 hook. "This is the way I've always done it."

Banks and Bill resumed their discussion on the power of God. About 30 minutes later, Bill mentioned a Scripture that had always puzzled him. One morning when Jesus was hungry, He looked for figs on a fig tree. Finding none, He cursed the tree. By that evening all the leaves on the tree had turned brown. When the disciples marveled at how soon the tree had withered, Jesus said, "Have faith in God. For assuredly, I say to you, whosoever says to this mountain, 'Be removed and be cast into the sea,' and does not doubt in his heart, but believes that those things he says will be done; he will have whatever he says."[168]

While he talked, Bill watched that little dead fish bobbing not far from the boat. The breeze had pushed it up against some water lilies. There it floated on its side, its entrails bulging from its green mouth, its characteristic blue gills now turned white.

Suddenly Bill heard a strange noise. Looking up, he saw the angel of the Lord burning like a fire on the mountainside. Down the mountain it came in a whirlwind, rushing over the treetops,

---

[168] Mark 11:12-23

heading straight for the boat. Then the angel was beside him, the roar of the whirlwind filling his senses. The angel ordered, "*Stand!*"

Bill stood.

Lyle asked Banks, "What is he doing?"

"Quiet," said Banks. "Something is going to happen."

The angel said, "*Speak to that fish and it will live again.*"

Pointing at the dead bluegill floating by the lilies, Bill said, "Little fish, Jesus Christ gives you back your life."

Immediately the angel vanished. With all three men watching, that bluegill sucked in its stomach, flipped its body upright, and swam down through the water to rejoin its school.

Lyle fell over backwards in the boat. He stuttered, "Uh— Brother Bill—uh—do you think that—uh—that was for me, because I—I said to that fish, 'You shot your last wad'?"

"No, Brother Lyle, God was simply showing His great power, confirming the Scriptures we've just been talking about."

"But why?" asked Banks. "You said yourself you have hundreds of people on your prayer list, including a bunch of spastic children. Why would God use His power to resurrect a little fish?"

"He's God and He can do whatever He wants. That is Scriptural. Think of all the lepers who were in Jerusalem the day Jesus used His power to curse a fig tree. See? It just goes to show that God is concerned about everything. If He is interested enough in a little fish to speak back its life, He certainly will speak eternal life into all of his children."

IN AUGUST William Branham flew north again, this time to Alberta, Canada, for a nine-day faith-healing campaign in the city of Edmonton. The crowds were large but the reception they gave him was cool. By the third night, Bill knew something was wrong. The faith of these Canadians should be rising like the heat from a prairie fire. Instead their attitudes seemed as cold as permafrost.

When Bill finished preaching, he said, "Between here and where that step goes down, do you see that light circling? It just now appeared. I believe that light is the same Pillar of Fire that led the children of Israel in the book of Exodus.[169] Later that Pillar of Fire became flesh and lived among us in the form of the Son of God, Jesus Christ. When He was on earth, Jesus said, 'I come from God and I go back to God.'[170] I believe that when He returned to God, He went back into the form of that light. It is the same light that struck Paul blind on his road to Damascus. Paul asked, 'Who art thou Lord?' and the light replied, '*I am Jesus...*'[171] I believe it is the same light that came to the apostle Peter that night in prison, opened the prison doors and led him out.[172] I truly believe that Almighty God is the Creator of heavens and earth, and Jesus Christ is His Son, who is present with us now.

"He is answering the prayer of that little woman sitting right there." Bill pointed to a dark-haired woman sitting close to the front. "You're suffering with nervous trouble. The man sitting next to you is suffering with back trouble. You are husband and wife. Raise your hands if those things are true." They both raised their hands. "Do you have prayer-cards? You don't? You don't need any. You are both healed. Jesus Christ makes you well. Amen.

"The man sitting right behind them has got gallbladder trouble. Your name is Clarence. You're from a place called Grand Prairie. That's right, isn't it? Your gallbladder trouble has ended, sir. You can go home and be well. Amen.

---

[169] Exodus 13:21
[170] John 16:28
[171] Acts 9:3-5
[172] Acts 12:5-11

"You say, 'Brother Branham, you called that man's name?' Didn't Jesus Christ, when He was here in a body of flesh, tell Simon his name was Simon, and his father's name was Jonas, and he'd be called Peter after that?[173] Jesus is still the same today.

"There hangs that light over a woman. She's suffering with high blood pressure. Her name is Mrs. Fishbrook. Stand to your feet. You're from this city. You live on 125th Street. Your house number is 13104. If that's right, raise your hand. All right, Mrs. Fishbrook, you're healed. Jesus Christ makes you well.

"Do you believe His presence is here? I want every man and woman who is backslidden, or who has just accepted Christ, to come forward so I can ask a blessing over you while the anointing is here."

The organist played a hymn. Although there were thousands of people in the auditorium, no one came forward. Eventually Bill said, "What is the matter with you Canadians? You get so churchy until you leave Christ out. It's good to be conservative, but don't be so starchy that you grieve the Spirit away. You won't have any revival."

At that moment he saw a black wave roll over the audience. He warned, "If I am the prophet of God, I speak in His name. You had better get right with God because the hour is coming when you're going to scream to find this, and you won't find it. That is 'Thus saith the Lord.' If the love of God is not in your heart, you're a sinner and you're on the road to hell. That is 'Thus saith the Lord.' The same God who discerns the spirits and tells people their condition, is speaking right now. I speak in the name of Jesus Christ. Fly to the altar and repent quickly, before God turns the page over on you and you're doomed forever. 'Thus saith the Holy Spirit' that is in the midst of us now."

[173] John 1:40-42

After more pleading and persuading, a few repentant souls straggled up to the front for prayer. Bill felt gravely disappointed because he knew there were many more people in his audience who needed salvation, and that even the Christians there needed revival.

"Friends, I have not seen this happen in years. I have never before had such a feeling as came over me just a few moments ago when I saw that black wave roll through the building. Something struck me. God knows that is the truth. Something is wrong."

When he woke the next morning, he still felt discouraged. What was wrong? Why didn't these Christians in Edmonton recognize the presence of Jesus Christ in their midst, and receive all the blessings that came with that revelation? Bill wondered if it was his fault. Maybe he wasn't presenting the Gospel the best way it could be presented.

Sitting up in bed, he took his Scofield Reference Bible off the nightstand and browsed through the notes he had written on the back flyleaf. He read again about the vision he saw in 1952 on the morning when God had healed him from those deadly amoebas. He remembered how a disembodied hand pointed to Joshua chapter 1, verses 2 through 9, suggesting that these verses applied to Bill's ministry as much as it did to Joshua's.

He closed his Bible, but he didn't lay it down. Instead, he held it upright between his two palms while he sat brooding. Soon he felt the angel of the Lord come into his hotel room. Bill's melancholy changed to fear. He jerked his hands up near his heart and folded them for prayer, expecting God to speak to him at any moment. As soon as he removed his hands from his Bible, the book parted in two. His Bible was well worn from many years of constant use. It could have fallen open to any one of a hundred places that he read often. Now it fell open to Joshua chapter one. Bill read:

There shall not any man be able to stand before thee all the days of thy life: as I was with Moses, so I will be with thee: I will not fail thee, nor forsake thee.

Be strong and of a good courage: for unto this people shalt thou divide for an inheritance the land, which I sware unto their fathers to give them...

Have not I commanded thee? Be strong and of a good courage; be not afraid, neither be thou dismayed: for the LORD *thy God is with thee withersoever thou goest.*[174]

His fear subsided, his depression lifted and his confidence returned. God had called him by an angel and was leading him by His Spirit through visions. Even if every Christian denomination rejected him, it would not change the fact that God had ordained him to do what he was doing. He used to think his only task was to take a gift of divine healing to the world. Then God showed him the three parts to his ministry—the three 'pulls' on that fishing line. The first two pulls represented his healing ministry, but the third pull was different. The third pull would catch the big fish, the trophy fish. The third pull would call those people who are the Bride of Jesus Christ and would divide for them an inheritance in the land which God swore He would give them. Somewhere there had to be people who would hear it, recognize the truth, and act upon it. Jesus said, "*The truth shall make you free.*"[175]

Bill turned to the front of his Scofield Study Bible and found the page that said: "How to use the study references." Picking up his pen, he wrote in the margins:

It has been for some time that this 1st chapter of Joshua opens to me. This morning of August 7, 1957, I have been Branham, William (Bill); and I looked at a vision that was given me, which is wrote on the fly leaf in back

---

[174] Joshua 1:5-6, 9
[175] John 8:32

of this book. Then I opened the Book. Again it turned to this same chapter. Dear Jesus Christ, help me to be courageous for your glory. Bro. Branham.

Flipping the pages back to Joshua chapter one, Bill scrawled at the top of the page:

I promise, by God's help, to be courageous from this day on.
—August 7, 1957.

IN OCTOBER of 1957 Bill organized his usual fall hunting trip to the Corral Peaks Wilderness Area in northern Colorado. They reached their camp site late in the afternoon. While they were setting up their tents, some of the men said they didn't feel well. In the morning it was clear that everyone except Bill had come down with the Asian flu. Aching from fevers, these sick men didn't even feel like eating, let alone hunting. They were so miserable they didn't even take their rifles out of their gun cases. They simply packed up their tents and drove home—with Bill following.

As soon as Bill got home from Colorado he made arrangements for a fishing expedition into central Idaho. A few days later he and some companions drove to Ketchum, Idaho, and then north into the Sawtooth Mountains Wilderness Area. When he looked at the Sawtooth Mountains behind Redfish Lake, Bill knew how they got their name. These tall, jagged peaks did indeed look like the teeth of a giant saw pointing up.

The fishermen rented horses for themselves and packhorses for their supplies; and then they rode way back into the wilderness, setting up their camp in a meadow next to the East Fork of the Salmon River. The Indians and early settlers called this river the River-of-No-Return because it meandered several hundred miles to the west where it joined the Snake River and later the Columbia River before finally emptying into the Pacific Ocean. Since Bill was fishing in the fall of the year near its headwaters, the water level of the Salmon River was quite low in some stretches, but collected in deeper pools wherever the course of the river curved or leveled out. This made for excellent fishing because the largest trout were forced into these pools.

The nights were chilly, but the days were still warm. Snow had not yet fallen. Autumn colors brightened the mountain slopes and the valley floor. Evergreen trees were interspersed with the reddish needles of tamarack trees and the bright orange leaves of shrubs like huckleberry bushes. In the wetter ground next to the Salmon River, aspen and poplar trees flourished, now displaying their orange and yellow leaves. There was a certain smell in the air that brought back memories of his childhood, of hunting in the fall when he was a boy. He grew wistful. Bill felt his pent up tension slowly leaving him. This was the type of country he loved best. Here in this wilderness he could relax, surrounded by breathtaking mountain scenery. Here the demands of civilization could not reach him—or so he thought.

The day after setting up their camp, Bill went fly-fishing by one of those pools where the river made a bend. Standing on a granite boulder, he cast his fly-line as far out into the pool as he could make it go. The light, feathery fly-hook landed on top of the water, but didn't sink. That was by design. Bill pulled it back to shore in short jerks that imitated the movement of a bug skittering over the surface of the river. The pool was crystal clear. Soon he saw a torpedo-like shape swim out from underneath a log that was half in and half out of the river. The trout lunged for what it thought was a bug, and then it was hooked. Now the battle began—the fisherman trying to reel in his prize and the trout fighting desperately to get away. It was a monster of a trout.[176] A less experienced fisherman might easily have pulled too hard too soon and thus broken his line; but Bill knew exactly what to do. In a few minutes he had that trout safely in his pick-up net.

He continued fly-fishing, but it wasn't long until he heard the drone of an airplane approaching. Looking up, he spotted a Piper Cub flying up the valley towards his camp. This small plane was following the river and flying fairly low as if the pilot was searching for something, or someone. As it passed overhead, Bill waved. The pilot must have seen him wave because the plane circled and flew back towards him. When it passed overhead again, a small object attached to a parachute dropped from the plane. While the parachute drifted down into a nearby meadow, the airplane flew back down the valley and was soon out of sight. Walking over to investigate the parachute, Bill discovered it was connected to a canister with a screw-on top. Bill unscrewed the lid. There was a folded piece of paper inside. He unfolded it and was surprised to find it was a message for him. His brother Howard had just died and the family wanted Bill to speak at Howard's funeral.

The next morning Bill and his companions loaded their camping gear onto their packhorses and rode back towards the demands of civilization.

AFTER HOWARD'S FUNERAL, William Branham left Jeffersonville for a short campaign in Lakeport, a city in northern California. The Full Gospel Business Men's Fellowship had arranged for these meetings to be held in a large building at the fairgrounds. Several thousand people sat on folding metal chairs. One night Bill preached on a Scripture that was haunting him lately.

---

[176]   This fish turned out to be the largest rainbow trout on record to that date. Bill had a taxidermist mount it on a plaque.

> *And Jesus answering saith unto them, Have faith in God.*
>
> *For verily I say unto you, That whosoever shall say unto this mountain, Be thou removed, and be thou cast into the sea; and shall not doubt in his heart, but shall believe that those things which he saith shall come to pass; he shall have whatsoever he saith.*
>
> *Therefore I say unto you, What things soever ye desire, when ye pray, believe that ye receive them, and ye shall have them.*[177]

Mark 11:23 called to him. He couldn't get away from it. Something lay hidden there, something powerful that he didn't quite understand. However, on this night in Lakeport he emphasized verse 24, where Jesus encouraged his followers to have faith when they prayed.

Near the end of his sermon, a photographer on his right side snapped a couple of pictures. When this photographer developed his color film, the first picture looked normal, showing the right side of William Branham standing behind a podium, making a gesture while preaching. A wicker basket full of lilies decorated the right side of the podium, next to a single microphone fixed to the top of a floor-length stand. Behind him, hanging from the ceiling, was the square metal box of an electric heater. Two men sat on folding metal chairs at the back of the stage. Beside these men hung a curtain, swooping down from a single point above, and fanning out below, either for decoration or to hide something that could not be easily moved.

In the next photograph the stage looked like a surreal painting, blazing with licks of fire and blotchy with patches of amber-colored mist. The angel of the Lord stood on Bill's right side, looking like a cloud about six feet tall. He stood between the evangelist and the people who had formed into a prayer-line on the far side of the

---

[177] Mark 11:22-24

building. (Bill always had the people in the prayer-line approach him from his right side so they would have to stop and stand in the presence of that angel.) In this picture, the angel was not the only astonishing form that was visible. Directly behind Bill was the profile of Jesus (face, beard, neck) with his arms extended and tongues of fire flying from his hands—seven distinct strands of fire, marching like messengers, rushing toward the man who was preaching. Bill's body seemed to be absorbed into the glow from that supernatural fire. (When Bill looked at this photograph later, he said it reminded him of scenes the prophets had described in Ezekiel 1 and Revelation 4:5.)

In such an atmosphere miracles were bound to happen, which was fortunate for the blind woman who someone led through the prayer-line that night in Lakeport. She was an American Indian. Her eyes looked completely white—not like her irises and pupils were covered with a film; her irises simply weren't there. Bill talked with her a minute until he contacted her spirit. Then by vision he said, "Nine years ago a blood clot in your brain temporarily

Photo 1—Lakeport, California

Photo 2—Lakeport, California

paralyzed you. Mostly you recovered, but that stroke pulled your eyes up into your skull and you've been blind ever since, suffering constantly, day and night, with no peace at all."

Bill felt an extra burden of compassion for this woman because she reminded him of his mother, who was half Cherokee Indian. When he prayed for her in Jesus' name, the same one who supplied the vision now reached out and touched this woman. Her eyes rolled back into their correct positions and she could again see the world, such as it was, blurred with tears of joy. Refusing help from the person who led her there, she walked away from the podium on her own.

That miracle ignited the faith of an elderly Lutheran gentleman sitting on the platform behind Bill. This man's wife suffered from a bleeding ulcer that had steadily grown worse in the last four years. Now his wife could not eat solid food, and she had become so anemic that her doctor wanted to give her a blood transfusion and operate on her in a week. The old Lutheran gentleman prayed silently, "Lord, if You will let Brother Branham call out my wife's problem, and if You will heal her tonight, I'll take the $500 I set aside for her operation and I'll give it to that Lutheran church they're building in Ukiah."

Instantly Bill whirled around, pointed at the Lutheran and said, "You, sir—you just prayed that if God would heal your wife, you would donate the $500 for her operation to help build a Lutheran church."

The old man felt faint, but he managed to say, "Friends, that is the truth."

"God doesn't want your money," Bill said, "but he does want your faith. Sir, your wife is healed. That is 'Thus saith the Lord'!"

The next morning this man and his 80-year-old wife attended a Christian Businessmen's breakfast. Bill watched her eat ham and eggs with the zest a woman half her age.

AS SOON AS William Branham got home from California, Mrs. Bosworth called from Florida to say that her husband was dying. Bill told her he would come right down. While Meda repacked his suitcase with clean clothes, Bill got the car ready and soon he was racing southeast to Florida. When he entered the hospital room, Fred Bosworth raised his bald head off of his pillow and held out his bony arms. Bill hugged his old friend and cried, "My father, my father, the chariot of Israel, and the horsemen thereof!" quoting Elisha's last words to Elijah.[178]

Fred Bosworth said weakly, "Son, always remember your mission. You are preaching the real Gospel."

---

[178]　2 Kings 2:12

Plopping back into a chair, Bill held his friend's hand. He said, "Brother Bosworth, I'm 48 years old and I'm so tired. Maybe my ministry is about over."

"Nonsense. You're young. Your ministry hasn't even begun to be what it will be in the future. Stay on the field. Don't let these Pentecostal preachers muddy the water with their fanaticism. Go on with the genuine Gospel that you've got. I believe you are an apostle and a prophet of the Lord our God."

"Brother Bosworth, you were preaching the Gospel before I was born. Out of all those years, when was the greatest moment of your life?"

Fred Bosworth didn't hesitate. "The greatest moment of my life is right now. Soon the one who I've preached about all these years, the one who I love—soon He will come through that door and I'll go out with Him."

Bill felt like he was looking at the equal of Abraham, Isaac, or Jacob. "Brother Bosworth, we both believe the same thing. By the grace of God I will preach the Gospel until the last breath leaves my body. I will not compromise when it comes to the Word of God. I will stay as true as I can to Jesus Christ. Someday I will meet you in a better land where we'll both be young forever."

Bosworth smiled weakly. "You'll be there, Brother Branham. Don't worry."

A month later Fred Bosworth lapsed into a coma for two days. Then suddenly he opened his eyes and sat up in bed. Extending his right arm, he shook the air like he was shaking someone's hand. "Brother Jim, I haven't seen you since you died. You were one of my converts to the Lord at my meeting in Joliet, Illinois. Sister Julie, I led you to the Lord at my Winnipeg meeting." For two hours he greeted people (in the room?) who had come to the Lord through his ministry but had died before him. Finally he laid his head back on his pillow and fell asleep in the arms of Jesus. Fred Bosworth was 84 years young, on his way to eternity.

Chapter 78
Disappointed at Waterloo
1958

THE FIRST TIME Gene Norman heard William Branham preach was in Minneapolis, Minnesota, in July 1950. Of course the discernment and miracles impressed him, but from the first he suspected that William Branham's ministry harbored a deeper purpose. Gene took a vacation from his job so that he and his wife, Mary, could attend the next Branham campaign in Cleveland, Ohio.[179] When the Cleveland meetings ended in August, Gene drove home to Minnesota and ordered *The Voice of Healing* magazine, which printed the schedule of William Branham's meetings and reported on the outcome of his campaigns. Gene also ordered William Branham's tape-recorded sermons from the Branham Campaigns' office in Jeffersonville, Indiana.

In 1953 Gene Norman moved his family to Parkersburg, Iowa. He continued to get William Branham's recorded sermons from Fred Sothmann, who was now handling the distribution of these tapes. Through their letters, Gene Norman and Fred Sothmann became friends. Fred Sothmann was originally from Saskatchewan, Canada. In 1956, Sothmann arranged a Branham

---

[179] This was the same faith-healing campaign where David Wood had his crippled leg straightened.

campaign in Prince Albert, Saskatchewan. Gene Norman attended these meetings. After the campaign ended, Fred Sothmann took William Branham on a three-day fishing trip and he invited Gene Norman to go along. Amid the conifer forests and glacier-gouged lakes of Saskatchewan, Bill and Gene bonded.

Eventually, the Normans became convinced that William Branham was a prophet of God. In 1957, Gene Norman decided to sponsor a Branham campaign in Waterloo, Iowa, a nearby metropolitan area of over 100,000 people. He called Lee Vayle, who was currently acting as the Branham Campaigns manager. Lee Vayle talked to Bill and then called Gene Norman with the dates that Bill was available—Saturday, January 25 through Sunday, February 2, 1958. Immediately Gene contacted all the Christian ministers in Waterloo, trying to organize support for this Branham faith-healing campaign. Then he rented a large auditorium called the Hippodrome and began to advertise.

During the last week of January 1958, a snowstorm blew across Iowa, making every road dangerously slick. For the first two nights of this Waterloo campaign Bill blamed this snowstorm for the disappointing turnout at his meetings. Both nights the crowds didn't even fill the Hippodrome half full with people. Then one night on his way to the meeting he passed a high school that was hosting a basketball game. Judging by the number of parked cars, it looked like the school gymnasium was filled to capacity. That is when he realized it was not the freezing weather and slick roads that was keeping people away from his meetings. Something had changed in the attitude of people towards divine healing—and that included Christians.

Even among the several thousand people who did attend this evangelistic campaign, their general attitude seemed as cold as the ice on the sidewalk outside. Nor did an abundance of miracles do much to warm their spirits. At the end of the Tuesday night service, Bill did not call for a prayer-line. Instead he did something he had never done before. He asked his audience to bow their heads and repeat after him: "Almighty God... Creator of heavens and earth... Author of everlasting life... Giver of every good gift... Be merciful to me... Forgive my unbelief... I believe the Gospel... I believe that You are now performing Your word in my body... Open the channels... I empty out my unbelief... I receive Your Spirit... I believe that You are in me now... I believe my sickness will vanish... I accept You now as my Healer."

When the audience finished this universal confession, Bill asked them to keep their heads bowed while he prayed for them. He said, "I will pray with all my heart that the Holy Spirit will witness to you that the work is finished."

He prayed, "God, my Father, I come in Jesus' name to pray for this people who have now honestly and sincerely confessed their wrongs. Blessed God, may this be a night they will never forget. May the Holy Spirit come into every heart just now and move out all sickness from their bodies." With his head still bowed and his eyes still closed, he said, "I now challenge the devil to a debate. Satan, you are aware that you are whipped. You have no legal rights. Jesus Christ, my Lord stripped away your authority when He died at Calvary to take away sin and sickness. Satan, you are nothing but a bluff and we are calling your bluff. After our Lord withered that fig tree with a curse, He urged His disciples to have faith in God. He said that if any believer tells this mountain to be moved, and doesn't doubt in his heart that it would happen, he could have whatever he says. That same promise is for us today. Satan, you know the Scriptures on that. I just taught this people that God is in them. So if God is in them and they say to a disease, 'Leave me,' and don't doubt in their hearts, right then every disease has got to move, because Christ said so. For it is not them that speak; it is the Father that dwells in them that is speaking. I say this as God's servant, by a message from an angel, who anointed me and has proven to this people that Jesus is here and the message is right. Satan, I adjure you to leave every sick person here and go into outer darkness, in the name of the Lord Jesus Christ."

A strange noise followed this prayer. It sounded like an organist had mashed down ten discordant keys of a pipe organ all at once. But there wasn't any organ in the Hippodrome. Suddenly a gust of wind blew through the building from one end to the other, sounding like a whirlwind rattling corrugated metal. But the Hippodrome was built out of concrete blocks and wood. Since no doors were open, the wind had to have started inside the building. Bill felt this supernatural wind blow across the platform, fanning the fabric of his suit as it passed. Before he took two more breaths, it was gone.

The crowd seemed unable to grasp what had happened. Bill explained that the Holy Spirit had passed through the building like a wind, confirming His Word. Something similar had happened when Peter preached on the day of Pentecost.[180] When Bill asked how many people in the audience had heard or felt the wind, around 500 people raised their hands, including Gene Norman and Lee Vayle. Yet, even this supernatural phenomenon did not raise the level of faith very high in the meetings that followed.

On Saturday morning Gene Norman had scheduled a ministerial breakfast so that Bill and the local pastors could fellowship together and get better acquainted. When everyone finished eating, Bill stood to give a short message. He took his text from Paul's testimony to King Agrippa:

---

[180] Acts 2:2

At midday, O king, I saw in the way a light from heaven, above the brightness of the sun, shining round about me and them which journeyed with me.

And when we were all fallen to the earth, I heard a voice speaking unto me, and saying in the Hebrew tongue, Saul, Saul, why persecutest thou me? it is hard for thee to kick against the pricks.

And I said, Who art thou, Lord? And he said, I am Jesus whom thou persecutest.

But rise, and stand upon thy feet: for I have appeared unto thee for this purpose, to make thee a minister and a witness both of these things which thou hast seen, and of those things in the which I will appear unto thee;

Delivering thee from the people, and from the Gentiles, unto whom now I send thee,

To open their eyes, and to turn them from darkness to light, and from the power of Satan unto God, that they may receive forgiveness of sins, and inheritance among them which are sanctified by faith that is in me.

Whereupon, O king Agrippa, I was not disobedient unto the heavenly vision. [181]

Using this story as a precedent, Bill shared his own testimony about baptizing people in the Ohio River in 1933, when that supernatural light appeared and a voice said, *"As John the Baptist was sent to forerun the first coming of Jesus Christ, so are you sent with a message to forerun His second coming."* Then he told about the night in 1946 when an angel had appeared to him and told him he was ordained to take a gift of healing to the peoples of the world. Like Paul of old, Bill declared, "I have not been disobedient to the heavenly vision."

While Bill was still speaking, a minister pushed his chair away from his table, grabbed his coat, and walked out. Then another minister did the same thing—then another, and another and

---

[181] Acts 26:13-19

another, until ten pastors had donned their coats and walked out into the cold. Gene Norman cringed with embarrassment.

He felt even more uncomfortable as he drove Bill back to the motel. His guest rode along in weighty silence. Gene said, "Brother Branham, I want to apologize for the rudeness of those ten men."

Bill turned and said, "Brother Gene, do you love me?"

Surprised by this question, Gene answered, "Do you want me to prove it, Brother Branham?"

"Brother Gene, if I were you, I'd leave here and move west. This place is under judgment."

Bill had one more meeting in Waterloo, Iowa. On Sunday, February 2, 1958, he talked to his audience about the supernatural wind that had blown through the Hippodrome on Tuesday night. Although God had come to him in the form of a whirlwind many times in his life, only one other time had he heard that supernatural wind roar like it did last Tuesday night. Then Bill told them about his fishing trip with Banks and Lyle Wood, when the Spirit of God rushed down from the mountains like a mighty wind, inspiring him to speak life back into that little dead fish.

He said to this crowd, "I do believe that the next step in my ministry is approaching, which will be far beyond this now. Is there anybody here who remembers the beginning of my ministry, when I put my hand on people and could feel the vibrations of germ-caused diseases? The Lord promised back then, if I'd be sincere I would someday know the secrets of their hearts. Today everyone can see that has happened. Now I'm telling you, there is something else coming up which is going to be still greater."

Then he read Luke 17:26-30:

> And as it was in the days of Noe [Noah], *so shall it be also in the days of the Son of man.*

They did eat, they drank, they married wives, they were given in marriage, until the day that Noe [Noah] entered into the ark, and the flood came, and destroyed them all.

Likewise also as it was in the days of Lot; they did eat, they drank, they bought, they sold, they planted, they builded;

But the same day that Lot went out of Sodom it rained fire and brimstone from heaven, and destroyed them all.

Even thus shall it be in the day when the Son of man is revealed.

From these verses, he extracted three important lessons. First, Lot came *out* of Sodom; second, Noah went *into* the ark. These two men typified the need of people today, who must come *out* of the world systems and go *into* the safety of Christ. For his third lesson Bill went back to the days of Lot, pointing out that just before Sodom burned, Abraham (who was Lot's uncle) had an unusual visitor.[182]

Bill said, "A Man came up. It was an Angel, none other than Almighty God manifested in the form of a man. Abraham called Him Lord, *Elohim*. He was the Almighty Jehovah dressed in the clothes of a man. This Man sat with His back to the tent and said to Abraham, 'I'm going to visit you next year and Sarah is going to have a son.'

"Sarah was 90 years old. When she heard what this Man said, she laughed—not out loud, but in her heart. The Angel, with His back to the tent, said to Abraham, 'Why did Sarah laugh?'

"What kind of mental telepathy was that? Aren't you people here in Waterloo ashamed of yourselves? That same Angel of mercy comes to this building each night and performs the same thing. It is happening again before fire and destruction shall burn this earth. *As it was in the days of Lot...Even thus shall it be in the*

---
[182] Genesis 18:1-15

day when the Son of man is revealed.[183] In Lot's day an Angel came to Abraham with a message; and that Angel could discern what was going on in Sarah's heart, even with her standing behind Him and inside a tent.

"Can't you people see the nature of that Spirit? It was none other than the Spirit of Christ. Later, when he was on earth in the form of the Lord Jesus, He performed the same sign to prove who He was. The same one is here today, performing the same sign before fire and destruction consumes this world."

This was the first time on record Bill used Luke 17:30 as a text. It would become a major theme for him in the last years of his life.

The next morning Bill and Billy Paul packed their clothes into Bill's pickup truck and headed back to Jeffersonville. The stormy weather had passed and the temperature had risen slightly. Iowa state snowplows had plowed and salted the highways. Billy Paul drove so that his father, exhausted from preaching and praying for the sick, could nap.

Tired as he was, Bill couldn't sleep. He sat quietly, watching mile after mile of snow-covered fields go by. Presently he felt that unseen presence of the angel beside him. It stiffened his spine and numbed his hands. Suddenly his pickup vanished. Bill found himself sitting behind the steering wheel of his car, turning into the driveway in front of his house. He had to stop in the street because a mess of large stones blocked his driveway. Wooden surveyor stakes jutted from the ground along the edge of his property parallel to the street. Road graders and scrapers rumbled up and down Ewing Lane. Some of the trees on both sides of the road had been cut down and their stumps uprooted.

A young man was driving a bulldozer through Bill's yard, pulling on the steering brakes, making one track rotate while the other track paused, turning the machine this way and that,

---
[183] Luke 17:28, 30

tearing up Bill's lawn far outside the line marked by the surveyor's stakes. When Bill got out of his car, he noticed a wooden stake hammered into the ground by his feet. The top of this stake was painted orange.

Bill motioned for the driver of the bulldozer to come talk with him. The young man climbed down from his machine and walked over to the driveway. Bill asked, "What are you doing? Don't come this far in. You're ruining my yard."

The young man shoved him backwards and sneered, "That's the way it is with you preachers. You're always telling people what to do."

The aggressiveness of this man surprised Bill. "I only asked you why you are doing this. You are coming too far into my yard."

The young man shoved him again. Then he tried to slap Bill in the face. Bill's old boxing reflexes flared and he drew his head back so quickly that the man's swing missed. Without thinking, Bill punched the young man hard enough to knock him to the ground. When the man got up, Bill knocked him down again. The man got up a second time, and Bill knocked him down a third time.

Now the angel of the Lord appeared behind him and to his right. *"Don't do that,"* the angel said. *"You are a minister."*

Bill felt ashamed of himself. He hadn't hit anyone since his days as a professional boxer, before he was a Christian. Picking the young man off the ground, he dusted him off and said, "I'm not angry with you. I just want you to know you can't talk to me like that."

The angel said, *"Bypass this."*

"How?" Bill asked.

"When you see that stake driven down in your front yard by your gate, then go west."

Turning towards the west, Bill saw a team of horses hitched to a covered wagon—the kind of wagon American pioneers called a prairie schooner. His wife sat on the front seat, a pioneer-style bonnet on her head. Their children sat in the back, looking out from beneath the wagon's cover. Bill climbed up and sat beside his wife. Picking up the reins, he said, "Meda, I've stood all I can stand." Then he turned the team of horses westward and snapped the reins. When he did, the horses vanished and the covered wagon changed into an automobile—his Ford station wagon.

Suddenly he was back in his pickup, sitting on the passenger side, looking out the window, watching the snow-covered fields of Iowa rush by him at 60 miles per hour. At his first opportunity he wrote this vision in his vision book. It would prove to be significant.

Gene Norman took seriously Bill's suggestion to move west. Within six months he sold his home and his business, and moved his family to Tucson, Arizona. Eventually his move would play a part in William Branham's own move out to the American West.

Chapter 79
The Knowledge of Good and Evil Explained
1958

THROUGH the spring and summer of 1958, William Branham held faith-healing campaigns from Chattanooga, Tennessee, to Bangor, Maine. Although most of his sermons still focused on building faith for healing, he touched on other subjects as well. At least seven times in 1958 he preached about the Queen of Sheba, using Matthew 12:42 as his text: "*The queen of the south shall rise up in the judgment with this generation, and shall condemn it: for she came from the uttermost parts of the earth to hear the wisdom of Solomon; and, behold, a greater than Solomon is here.*" Jesus was, of course, referring to Himself as the person who was greater than Solomon. Bill explained how the same Jesus Christ was there in his meetings each night, discerning the secrets of the heart, healing the sick, and performing other miracles, just like he did when he walked the earth nearly 2000 years ago.

Although faith-healing campaigns kept him busy, he still found time in 1958 to preach over a dozen times at Branham Tabernacle. On the last weekend of September he preached several sermons that stirred more controversy than any other messages he had preached up to that time. On Saturday night, September 27, he preached, "Why Are We Not a Denomination?"

He pointed out that Jesus never started a school or formed a denomination. Christian organizations began in the year 325 AD when the Roman emperor Constantine organized the Roman Catholic Church. Revelation chapter 17 speaks about the great whore, mother of harlots, who rules the world from atop seven hills. Rome was founded on seven hills. The Catholic Church, headquartered in Rome, is the only institution that fits this description. But the Roman Catholic Church isn't alone in her errors. Bill stressed how the Bible says she was the mother of harlots. The first Christian organization was the mother, and that mother had daughters. Those daughters are the other Christian denominations, all of which adopted, in some form or another, the rigidity of their mother's organizational system.

The basic flaw in every denomination is rigidity, which creates barriers. As soon as a group writes down their creeds, bylaws and articles of faith, they freeze God's Spirit of revelation. The Bible is perfect, but man's understanding of the Bible is not. If God gives someone deeper understanding, people who are bound to a denominational creed can't accept it. The hierarchy of leadership inside each denomination resists the spirit of revelation, as each man seeks to preserve his own position within the hierarchy and the comfortable, overall status quo.

The next morning he preached on the "Baptism of the Holy Spirit." He approached this subject differently than most of his contemporaries. He read Ephesians 1:4-6:

> *According as He* [God] *hath chosen us in Him before the foundation of the world, that we should be holy and without blame before Him in love:*
>
> *Having predestinated us unto the adoption of children by Jesus Christ to Himself, according to the good pleasure of His will,*
>
> *To the praise of the glory of His grace, wherein He hath made us accepted in the Beloved.*

From here Bill's preaching rose to eloquence. "Who did it? He did! Before the foundation of the world, He made me acceptable in the presence of His grace. I didn't have one thing to do with it. I was a sinner, born into a family of drunkards. I grew up sitting on a barrel of whisky, and yet the Holy Ghost came to me when I was seven years old and said, 'Don't you touch a drop of it, and don't smoke a cigarette, or chew tobacco, or fool around with girls.' What was it? The Father's good will before the foundation of the world was to send me to preach His Gospel and lead His sheep. God bless forever His great name. I'll stay by His Bible, swim or drown, popular or unpopular, whether anybody loves me or not.

"If the Methodists and Baptists turn me down, it doesn't matter. I want to do that which pleases Him. Even the Pentecostals are turning me down, because I don't believe their doctrine that speaking in tongues is the initial evidence of the Holy Ghost baptism. I don't believe that speaking with tongues makes you filled with the Holy Ghost, no more that I believe that living in a king's palace makes you a king. It doesn't. You could be a servant. See? I believe that you receive the Holy Ghost by an experience; not by an intellectual conception of the Scriptures, but by an experience that you alone know. If you want to know whether it was the Holy Ghost or not, watch the pattern of your life afterwards. That will tell you what kind of a spirit came into you."

On Sunday evening, September 28, 1958, Bill preached a sermon he called "The Serpent's Seed." This short message sowed the seed for one of his most enlightening and controversial doctrines. He took his text from Genesis chapter 3:

> *Now the serpent was more subtil* [subtle] *than any beast of the field which the LORD God had made. And he said unto the woman, Yea, hath God said, Ye shall not eat of every tree of the garden?*

And the woman said unto the serpent, We may eat of the fruit of the trees of the garden:

But of the fruit of the tree which is in the midst of the garden, God hath said, Ye shall not eat of it, neither shall ye touch it, lest yet die.

And the serpent said unto the woman, Ye shall not surely die:

For God doth know that in the day ye eat thereof, then your eyes shall be opened, and ye shall be as gods, knowing good and evil.

And when the woman saw that the tree was good for food, and that it was pleasant to the eyes, and a tree to be desired to make one wise, she took of the fruit thereof, and did eat, and gave also unto her husband with her; and he did eat.

And the eyes of them both were opened, and they knew that they were naked; and they sewed fig leaves together, and made themselves aprons.

Bill taught that in the beginning the serpent was not a reptile at all; rather, it was a mammal. The Bible calls it a beast. The serpent walked upright like a man, and was physically built like a man. He was so close to a human being in intelligence that he could talk. The word *subtle* means "having a true knowledge of the principles of life." In Hebrew, the words *crafty*, *smart*, *subtle*, and *naked* all come from the same root word. The forbidden fruit in the midst of the garden was the carnal knowledge of human sexuality. The word *midst* means the middle. When Eve and Adam "ate" this "fruit" they suddenly knew they were naked. What actually happened in the Garden of Eden was that Eve committed adultery with the serpent and became pregnant by him. Then she showed Adam what she had learned and she immediately became pregnant with a second child by Adam. Nine months later she gave birth to twins: Cain, who was the seed of the serpent; and Abel, who was the seed of Adam.

Although this explanation is a radical departure from Christian tradition, it is not a departure from the Bible, or even from common sense. Suddenly mankind's first sin is lifted out of the category of myth and legend, and placed firmly in the reality of human genetics. According to this interpretation of events, the fall of man was not based on something as arbitrary as biting into an apple from a single apple tree among hundreds of other apple trees; it was based on adultery, an act that has never ceased to be a sin in God's eyes. That is why God told Eve, "*I will greatly multiply thy sorrow and thy conception; in sorrow thou shalt bring forth children...*"[184] The judgment that God placed upon Eve was directly related to her sin. Bill said, "If eating an apple will cause a woman to know she is naked, we had better start passing around apples."

When God punished the serpent for his part in man's fall, God said, "*Thou art cursed above all cattle, and above every beast of the field; upon thy belly shalt thou go, and dust shalt thou eat all the days of thy life.*"[185] If the serpent was cursed to slither on its belly after Adam's fall, how did it move before the fall? It moved on legs like a man. Notice that God mentioned cattle when He cursed the serpent? God was classifying the serpent with other mammals, like cows, lions, and apes. Then He changed the serpent from a mammal with legs, to a reptile without legs. That is why anthropologists will never find the "missing link" between man and monkey. The original serpent is that "missing link," but God changed the species so completely that it can no longer be structurally linked to man. Still, the nature of the beast lingers in mankind, since those original genes are now part of the human genome through Eve's sin.

---

[184] Genesis 3:16
[185] Genesis 3:14

Then God said to the serpent, "*I will put enmity between thee and the woman, and between **thy seed** and **her seed***."[186] The serpent had a physical seed or offspring, and that seed was Cain and his descendents. Look at Cain's attributes. He was just as religious as his brother Abel. Both men built altars so they could worship God. Cain, who lacked a revelation of the true nature of sin, offered fruit on his altar; whereas Abel, who had a revelation of the true nature of sin, offered blood. God accepted Abel's offering, but rejected Cain's. That made Cain so angry he killed his brother. Murder is not an attribute of God, but an attribute of the devil. That is how Satan injected evil into God's plan. Evil was genetically introduced into man's nature by combining the genes of the first woman with the genes of a beast, the original serpent. The resulting beastly nature of their offspring multiplied down through history, mixing with and diluting Adam's genes, spreading envy, hatred, bigotry, and every other hurtful characteristic known to mankind, and bringing countless sorrows upon the earth.

Bill stressed that God had a purpose in allowing all this to happen. Before the universe appeared, there existed the "I AM." He was not yet God, because God is an object of worship and there was nothing alive to worship this great eternal being. The "I AM" possessed certain attributes that He wanted to express. For example, He was a Savior, but there was nothing lost for Him to save. Since His nature was totally good, He could not directly create evil. Therefore, when He created the world, He gave the first man and woman the ability to choose their own path, knowing they would fall. Then He could express Himself as a Savior, which He did in the form of Jesus Christ. Bill asked rhetorically, "Who came first, the Savior or the sinner? The Savior came first. Who is more powerful, the Savior or the sinner? If a Savior can take away the sin, He is more powerful."

---

[186] Genesis 3:15

At the end of this sermon, he said, "You ministers and brethren, please don't feel offended because of the way I drive this in just as hard as I can. This is our tabernacle and this is what we stand for, and we want to lay it right on that Word and shake people with it. Then, if you ever get out of line, we are going to come back and say, 'You knew better. Here it is on tape.'

"We have a whole lot more to share, which we'll get to after awhile. We believe in baptism in the name of the Lord Jesus Christ. We believe in foot washing. We believe in Communion. We believe in the second coming of Christ—not just a spiritual coming, but the visible, corporal body of the Lord Jesus, coming again in glory. We believe in the physical resurrection of the dead to receive a new body. We believe in the immortality of the soul. We believe there is only one form of eternal life and that's the life that you receive from Christ Jesus; therefore, we do not believe in eternal punishment. We believe in a literal hell, burning with fire and brimstone, but we don't believe people suffer there eternally. They may suffer for a million years, I don't know, but they can't burn eternally. If they did, they would have eternal life. So you see, there are many things yet to be taught that we'll get to later. The Lord bless you."

IN NOVEMBER OF 1958, William Branham packed his station wagon and headed for California. Meda and three-and-a-half-year-old Joseph went with him. Miner Arganbright (who lived in La Crescenta, California, near Los Angeles) had arranged for Bill to preach one night in several different churches in the Los Angeles area. But Arganbright was not in southern California waiting for him. He had flown to Tulsa, Oklahoma, to attend a Full Gospel Business Men's Fellowship (FGBMF) convention. Bill was supposed to meet his friend in Oklahoma, so they could ride out to California together.

Bill arrived in Tulsa on Saturday afternoon and checked into a hotel. Miner invited him to the FGBMF dinner banquet later that evening. Bill went because he wanted to hear Oral Roberts speak. Before dinner Oral Roberts preached on the abundant life that Jesus promised to give the believer. When Jesus told the fishermen to let down their nets, they caught so many fish that their nets could not hold them all.[187] Roberts said, "There is plenty of everything for everybody in Jesus Christ."

After dinner Demos Shakarian, president of the FGBMF, said, "I feel led to ask William Branham to bring the final message for the evening." This announcement caught Bill unprepared. Before dinner, Miner had introduced him to many of these people. Bill knew that most of them were millionaires, and many were even multimillionaires. What could he add to their lives? In his simple, humble way he preached the barebones Gospel with such conviction that dozens of people gave their lives to Jesus Christ. Then Demos Shakarian asked him to pray for the sick. Most of life's problems afflict rich people the same as everyone else. George Gardner earned his fortune selling Oldsmobiles. He flew an airplane as a hobby and had crashed once, breaking his legs and damaging his knees so that he walked stiffly. After Bill prayed for him in Jesus' name, Gardner could walk as smoothly as he had before his accident. Meanwhile, a woman with severe arthritis sat with her back hunched over and her upper arms bound to her torso. She felt her back straighten and her arms come unbound. Dropping to her knees, she clapped her hands and praised God so exuberantly that everyone around her couldn't help but notice. That night a smattering of millionaires learned what true riches are. The greatest wealth of all is found in the Gospel of Jesus Christ.

---

[187] John 10:10; Luke 5:1-11, respectively

As Bill was leaving this banquet, a richly dressed woman grabbed his hand and said, "Brother Branham, your sermon moved my heart greatly. I thought I was a Christian before, but now I see what I was lacking. From now on, I will serve the Lord Jesus."

"Thank you," Bill said, feeling very humble.

From Tulsa, Oklahoma, Bill drove to southern California. When he arrived in La Crescenta, instead of staying in a motel, he and his wife stayed in Miner Arganbright's home. Each night Bill preached at a different church in the Los Angeles area.

One night he preached for Pastor Smith at the Pisgah Bible Church. Pisgah's large auditorium was full, and several hundred people stood outside, listening through open windows. After Bill's sermon, Pastor Smith led the congregation in a few hymns so Bill could rest before he prayed for the sick. On this night two things happened that Bill had never experienced before. Several thousand people sang in the congregation, but Bill could hear another choir singing from somewhere higher. Curious, he climbed the stairs to see who was singing in the choir loft. There was no choir assembled, just the overflow from the congregation. The voices he heard seemed to be coming from higher still. Bill listened carefully. Yes, he could definitely hear two choirs. The voices of one choir rose from below him, composed of several thousand people sitting in pews, male and female voices, some on key and some off key. The voices of the second choir drifted down from the high-arched rafters. It sounded like a hundred thousand sopranos singing in perfect harmony. It was the loveliest music he had ever heard in his life.

Exhilarated, Bill walked down the stairs to the main floor. The congregation ended their hymn with a melodious "Amen." During the hush that followed, a man in the back of the building spoke half a dozen words in an unknown tongue. Although Bill had never before interpreted an unknown tongue, suddenly he knew that this one meant, "The pastor shall pray the prayer of faith," but he was afraid to say it out loud. A minute later that strange wave of inspiration swept over him again, this time so strongly that he had to hold his mouth shut to keep from speaking. It didn't matter. Even without the interpretation, Pastor Smith began praying for the sick. Bill gladly stepped back and let the pastor pray the prayer of faith. Both inside and outside the Pisgah church, hundreds of people received a blessing from God that night. Bill was one of them.

One morning several days later, Bill heard Arganbright's telephone ring. Miner was not in the room at the moment, so Bill answered the phone.

A voice with a Mexican accent said, "Hello, Señor. Could you tell me if Brother Branham is staying here?"

"I am Brother Branham."

"Thanks be to God! I'm Brother Duponsta and I'm a missionary to Mexico, although I live here in La Crescenta. I have a four-month-old son who has cancer in his jaw. A surgeon tried to remove it, but now the cancer has moved over to his tongue. Ricky can't swallow. My doctor says it's hopeless. Brother Branham, I know it's not customary for you to visit a hospital and pray for someone when you're traveling, but could you have mercy on me and do it just this one time?"

"Stay on the line. I'll get Brother Arganbright so you can give him directions to the hospital."

When Bill met Señor Duponsta, it surprised him to see a Mexican man whose skin was no darker than his own. His wife was also light-skinned, but that was to be expected, since she was a blue-eyed, blond woman who came from Finland. Bill followed them into Ricky's hospital room. He had seen lots of disturbing things during his years of praying for sick and afflicted people, but the condition of this baby was one of the most pathetic sights he had ever seen. Ricky lay on his back, naked except for a diaper. A blue scar followed the contour of his jaw from one side of his throat to the other, where the surgeon had tried to remove the cancer. His black tongue had swollen so big that it blocked his air passages and he was now breathing through a hole in his throat. The metal insert that was his new airway whistled slightly with each breath. A nurse regularly suctioned this hole to keep mucus from clogging it. The doctor had bound Ricky's arms in splints to keep him from tearing away this metal tube poked into his trachea.

Señor Duponsta leaned over the crib, patted Ricky's stomach, and said, "Daddy's little boy." Recognizing his father's voice, Ricky tried to lift his splint-bound arms. "Ricky, Daddy has brought Brother Branham to pray for you."

Bill's heart melted into a puddle inside his chest. He thought, "If this sight makes me sad, what must it do to Almighty God, who is the source of sympathy and compassion? Lord Jesus, if You were standing here, what would You do?"

At that moment something spiritual happened. Bill didn't hear an audible voice, but inside his head (or his soul) he heard the Holy Spirit say, "*You preached on Mark 11:23, 'say to this mountain—' I gave My authority to My church. Now I'm waiting to see what you will do about it.*"

Gently holding one of Ricky's little hands, Bill said, "Lord Jesus, hear the prayer of your servant. By faith I place the blood of Jesus Christ between this demon of cancer and the baby's life." For some reason, he couldn't think of anything else to say.

As Bill walked away from the room, Ricky's father ran after him and stopped him in the hall. "Brother Branham, the Lord put it on my heart to give you some tithe money." He offered Bill an envelope.

"Oh, brother, no," Bill said, shaking his head. "I can't take your money. Use it to pay your son's hospital expenses."

"It's only $50, and it needs to go to a minister. Please take it."

"Well, since I'm a minister and you're a minister, consider it received by me and I turn around and give it back to you."

Reluctantly, Duponsta put the money back in his pocket.

Although Bill had only prayed a brief prayer for Ricky Duponsta, it was enough. A few hours after Bill left the hospital, Ricky's tongue shrank back to its normal size. The next day his doctor removed the metal hole from his throat. At the same time his doctor performed a biopsy, which later confirmed that no cancerous cells remained in Ricky's mouth. Of course, Ricky's father called Bill to tell him about this miracle. But that distant thank you was not good enough for Señor Duponsta. He and his wife drove to Arganbright's house to thank Bill in person.

Bill was packing his Ford station wagon for his trip back home when the Mexican missionary arrived. Señor Duponsta flung open his car door, scrambled out of his seat, and ran to Bill as though he thought Bill might leave before he got there. Jerking his hat from his head, he said, "Brother Branham, Ricky is coming home from the hospital today."

"I'm grateful for that," Bill said. "God is so merciful."

"Here is the tithe money the Lord told me to give you."

"Brother Duponsta, I told you to put that money toward your hospital expenses."

"I did—I mean I tried to. The doctor said I didn't owe him a penny because he didn't have anything to do with Ricky's recovery. He said it was just an unexplainable phenomenon, a quirk of nature. You and I know different. So, please, Brother Branham, take my tithing." He held the $50 forward.

Bill thought, "Oh, I can't. Lord, I don't feel like taking it." Then he remembered how Jesus let a widow woman put her last coin into the synagogue's collection box.[188] Reluctantly, he took the money.

When he returned to Jeffersonville and told his congregation about the miracle of Ricky Duponsta, he said, "I have the man's tithing now. I don't know exactly what I'll do with it, but I do know I'll give it to someone who is working for the glory of God."

Then he said, "The shadows are falling. Christ is appearing. That's why signs and wonders are appearing. The church (like that great satellite, the moon) is reflecting the light of the Morning Star as it comes over the horizon with 'healing in His wings.'[189] If He will bring healing from the reflection of His presence, what will He do when He comes in person? These corruptible bodies of ours will be changed and made like His glorious body.[190] Until that day, we are thankful for the sunlight of His presence. As do the stars, I climb the ramparts of glory and sit there waiting to hail His coming in this dark hour."

---

[188] Luke 21:1-4; Mark 12:41-44
[189] 2 Peter 1:19, Malachi 4:2, respectively (See endnotes.)
[190] Philippians 3:21

Chapter 80
The Word of Life
1959

IN THE SPRING of 1959, while conducting another faith-healing campaign in Chicago, William Branham's ministry changed again. One night, as usual, he called for a prayer-line to form on his right. One... two... three people came before him, each pulling a vision from his gift, and some of his strength along with the vision. The fourth person to stand before him that night was a young woman with shoulder-length black hair. She wore a brown suit coat with a matching brown skirt, and she held a baby wrapped in a pink blanket. Bill thought, "It seems like I ought to know this woman. She looks so familiar." Studying the baby's face, he could tell by its hollow cheeks and pasty skin that it was very sick. A vision revealed much more. He said to this mother, "Your baby is six months old and she weighs only three pounds. You can't get her to eat. Everything you put down her comes right back up. You have taken her to many doctors, but none of them can help her. They don't know what is wrong. You know your baby is dying. You're a member of the Swedish Covenant Church and your pastor advised you to bring the baby to me for prayer."

"That's right," she whispered with trembling lips.

The scene in the vision shifted. Bill saw this baby laughing and playing. He said, "Sister, Thus saith the Lord, 'Your baby is healed.'"

The young mother left the platform weeping with relief.

Bill thought, "There's something strange about her." Then he remembered. Four years earlier, while he was praying in the desert outside of Phoenix, Arizona, God had showed him a vision of this very moment, saying. *"When you see this come to pass, your ministry will change."* This was the woman in the brown dress he had seen in that vision. Here was his sign that he would receive more strength to pray for the sick.

Starting with the next person in line, he felt less of a strain from each vision he saw during his prayer services. Although he had never been able to control the flow of visions, he had learned how to position himself so that visions were likely to appear. First he talked to his audience until he felt the presence of the angel of the Lord. Then he talked with the first person in line until he contacted that person's spirit. A vision always followed. After the first vision happened, the next visions came easily. His problem had never been getting into the spirit of discernment; his problem had always been getting out. Previously, the visions had always controlled him during his prayer services, pulling him along until he was exhausted. Some nights it took hours for him to recover after the prayer service ended; sometimes it took days, or even weeks for him to recover his strength. Tonight that changed. Now he was able to snap out of a vision as easily as he had slipped into it. This ability let him conserve his energy and make a conscious decision of how many people to pray for before he quit. The visions still tired him, but not as severely as they had in former years.

Returning home from this Chicago campaign, Bill learned that Linda Kelly Smith was hospitalized with a life-threatening condition.[191] The Kelly family used to attend Branham Tabernacle, but they had drifted back into the world and had not come to church for years. Mrs. Kelly called Bill to ask if he would come to the hospital and pray for her daughter.

When he arrived at the hospital, he found Linda Smith lying in bed under an oxygen tent, surrounded by her parents, her husband, her husband's parents, and several other family members. Linda was five months pregnant with her third baby, but sadly the baby had already died in her womb. To make matters worse, her doctor could not surgically remove the dead baby because Linda had developed uremia, a condition where her blood was retaining substances that were ordinarily eliminated in her urine. An operation under such conditions would almost certainly kill her, yet the dead baby had to be removed or it would eventually be fatal to the mother. Linda's predicament looked hopeless. Bill raised the flap of her oxygen tent and said, "Linda, this is Brother Bill. Do you remember me?"

Her voice sounded weak, but her mind was clear. "Yes, Brother Bill, I remember you."

"Do you understand how sick you are?"

"Yes, that's why I asked mother to call you."

"Linda, how is it between you and the Lord?"

Her forehead creased with sadness. "Brother Bill, I'm not ready to go."

Kneeling beside her bed and holding her hand under the oxygen tent, Bill prayed with her. Linda told Jesus she was sorry for her sins and promised Him she would love Him and serve Him from that day forward. When she finished repenting, Bill prayed for God to heal her in Jesus' name.

---

[191] This is not her real name. (See endnotes.)

The next morning when her doctor tested her blood, he was surprised to find her uremia was gone. Encouraged by this unexpected turn in her condition, he scheduled an operation for the following day. If her blood stayed clean for 24 hours, her doctor could safely remove the dead baby. When Linda's family heard this good news, many of them also repented of their sins and promised God they would serve Him the rest of their lives. Bill felt deeply gratified.

That night Linda could not sleep. About midnight she said to her mother, "I'm so happy now that I'm at peace with God. Mother, I'm going home."

Mrs. Kelly patted her daughter's arm. "Yes, Linda, in the morning the doctor will remove the baby. Then, in a few days you can go home to your husband and children, and you can live for God."

"No, Mother, you don't understand. I mean I'm going to my heavenly home. This is the end of my earthly journey." A few minutes later Linda quietly died.

The news of Linda's death stunned Bill. Then it bothered him. In a moment of weakness he said, "Lord God, You owe me an explanation. After I prayed for her and You healed her of uremia, and after many of her family members came back to Christ because of that miracle... and then You took her life? I think You owe me an explanation."

The explanation he wanted didn't come right away. After a few days of pouting, Bill forgot about his rash demand. But God didn't forget. Four months later while Bill was fishing, he saw a vision that showed him the reason. He saw Linda and her family having a picnic by a creek. He saw Linda jumping from rock to rock along the edge of the creek. Then he saw her slip and fall into the water; he saw her legs become tangled among the reeds and water lilies. Her family didn't notice she was missing until it was almost too late. By the time her husband pulled her from the creek, her skin had turned blue from oxygen deprivation. Frantically, her husband blew air into her lungs and she revived. The angel of the Lord said to Bill, *"Go to her mother and say, 'Did not Linda almost drown in a creek on a picnic last year? She should have died at that time, but she was not ready to go. God had to wait until her soul was ready.' That is why all this happened, and why you went to that hospital to pray for her."*

When the vision left him, Bill threw aside his fishing pole and buried his face in the grass, crying, "Lord Jesus, forgive me for my stupidity. I should have never said, 'You owe me an explanation.' You don't owe Your children anything. We are indebted to You for everything."

Returning to Jeffersonville, he drove to the Kellys' house on Market Street and knocked on their door. Mrs. Kelly answered. "Brother Bill, what brings you here?"

"Sister Kelly, I want to ask you something. Didn't Linda almost drown at a picnic last year?"

"Yes, Brother Bill. She fell into a creek when no one was looking. Her husband pulled her out and probably saved her life with mouth-to-mouth resuscitation. How did you know that?"

"The Lord showed me a vision of it. Sister Kelly, the day of that picnic was Linda's time to go, but God in His mercy spared her life until her soul was ready."

ALTHOUGH his campaigns no longer exhausted him, other burdens weighed on William Branham during 1959. No doubt the heaviest of these burdens was his continuing struggle with the Internal Revenue Service. The government's investigation of his campaign financing had started back in 1955. Over the past four years they had audited his financial records several times, but they could not find any improprieties, certainly nothing on which to accuse him of mishandling funds. So the IRS agents changed their tactics. They said that any check with William Branham's name on the front was his personal income, even though the money went directly into the Branham Tabernacle bank account. When people donated money to his campaigns, they usually wrote the checks to William Branham, instead of to William Branham Campaigns. The IRS said he owed income tax on every penny of this. Calculating back over ten years, and including interest and penalties, they said he owed the United States government $355,000.

One day the government lawyers asked Bill to meet with them again at their Louisville office. Bill groaned at the thought, because these meetings seemed to go nowhere. The lawyers asked him the same questions repeatedly, and then they took his answers and twisted them into things he did not mean to say. These interrogations frustrated him, but since he didn't have much choice in this matter, he agreed to see them.

Roy Roberson went with him. Roberson was not only Bill's friend, but he was also on the board of trustees for Branham Tabernacle. Several IRS attorneys sat on one side of a long table. Bill, Roy Roberson, and Mr. Orbison (Bill's attorney) sat on the other side. An IRS lawyer said, "Mr. Branham, we still have a few questions about some of your expenditures. Because we have all of Branham Tabernacle's canceled checks, we know where every penny of it went. We question whether some of this money was spent on legitimate church expenses. For example, at one meeting in Alberta, Canada, you received an offering of $3,000. The next Sunday you gave the money to a church in the next town."

"They needed a new roof on their church building."

"Hmmm. Here are some checks to a woman in New Albany—one check to pay off her $300 grocery bill, and the other to cover her rent. Isn't $500 steep for rent?"

"She is an 80-year-old widow and she lives with her two children who are both afflicted with rheumatoid arthritis. She has very little income and her landlord was going to put her out of her house in the middle of winter. I paid off her back rent, then paid her rent up until June."

"Hmmm. Here is another check we question. You gave $1500 to one man to help him build a house."

"The man's old house burned down. What would you do if you saw a father with five children living in a tent in December, snow on the ground, and the temperature below freezing? Do you think I could sit comfortably in my warm house knowing that those children were shivering, and me having access to enough money to help them?"

"Hmmm. Did the trustees know you gave this money away?"

"No, sir, they didn't."

"Why didn't you tell them?"

"Because Jesus said, 'Don't let your left hand know what your right hand is doing.' There is no higher law than the law of God. It just wasn't necessary for the trustees to know."

"We think you should have told them. According to your records, you have given tens of thousands of dollars to individuals over the years—most of it without your trustees knowing where the money went."

"Are you calling me dishonest?"

"No, Mr. Branham, we think you're honest. What we are saying is that you didn't know how to properly handle the money for income tax purposes. When you signed those checks, the money became yours before it went into the church account, even if you had it for less than one minute. Therefore, you owe income tax on that money."

"Of course my signature is on the back of each check. I am the treasurer of Branham Tabernacle."

"Most of the checks were made out to William Branham, not Branham Tabernacle. We are not taxing Branham Tabernacle, because that is a church, and churches are exempt from paying income tax. This money was your personal money before it went into the church account."

"But it was an IRS agent who told me I could sign those checks like that."

"That man is no longer with the government."

"The men who wrote the Constitution are no longer with the government either. Does the Constitution stand?" Bill was tired of arguing the same point repeatedly. He said, "When I was a young man, and my wife got sick and died, I owed thousands of dollars in medical bills. I worked hard and paid every bit of it off. I'm not a young man anymore, but if I owe the money, I'll pay it. What makes me sad is to think that all those people I gave money to will have to pay income tax on it, like that poor 80-year-old widow woman."

"Oh, you're mistaken, Mr. Branham. They won't have to pay income tax on it because they received the money as a gift, and unsolicited gifts are not taxed."

"Really? Then I don't owe the government anything, because all the money I deposited came as unsolicited gifts. I have never taken up an offering in my life."

The government attorneys looked at each other in surprise. One asked, "Can you prove that, Mr. Branham?"

"If you want, I can have a million people send letters to your office saying it is true. I have never in my life asked anyone for money. The prayer cloths that we send out are free of charge. I have even fired a couple of campaign managers because they wanted to pull for donations. Whenever people gave money to my campaigns, they did it by their own choice."

This information unsettled the government lawyers. They whispered furiously among themselves for a few minutes, and then ended the meeting for that day. Bill left their office feeling like he had won.

But the government's case against him was far from over. During the last week of July 1959, attorneys from the IRS questioned Bill at their office five days in a row. After the Friday morning session, Bill came home weary, his head dizzy from answering the same questions repeatedly. He felt nervous from the pressure of the audit, frustrated because it was keeping him from scheduling meetings, and anxious because he had so many sick people asking for prayer, and had no time to pray for them. At least this afternoon he could make a few sick calls, because the IRS attorneys said they were done with him for the week. On top of his list of people to visit was a man waiting in a motel who had driven 400 miles to Jeffersonville with his sick baby.

Meda fixed him a sandwich for lunch. "How did it go this morning?" she asked.

"Honey, the way those attorneys question me, it makes me dizzy. After a while I feel like my head is going to fall off."

He had just sat down to eat when the telephone rang. Meda answered it, then put her hand over the phone, and whispered, "Billy, it's our attorney. He says the IRS attorneys want to see you again this afternoon."

"Oh, no. I can't stand another afternoon of that stuff. Tell him I'm not in right now." He got up from the table and walked outside into the backyard.

Meda frowned, but she did what her husband told her to do. When she hung up the phone, Bill came back in the house, sat down at the table, and poured himself a glass of orange juice. Meda asked, "Was that just exactly right?"

"Sure," he rationalized. "I wasn't in when you said it."

"But you were in here when he called."

"Honey, just forget about it. It's all right." Deep inside he knew it wasn't.

After lunch he drove to the motel where the man with the sick baby was waiting. When he was about to pray for the baby, a pang of guilt smote him. He thought, "I'm a hypocrite. How can I pray for this baby when I just lied and had my wife tell a lie?" He said, "Mister, I'm not worthy to pray for your baby now. I did something wrong and my heart is condemning me. If you will just be patient, I'll pray for your baby later. Right now I have to go make something right."

First he went home and apologized to his wife. Then he drove to his attorney's office.

Mr. Orbison was working at his desk when Bill entered his office. "Mr. Branham?" he said with an upward lift of his brows. "I thought you weren't home."

"I had only stepped outside the house." Then he confessed what he had done, and apologized.

Mr. Orbison walked around his desk and shook Bill's hand. "Mr. Branham, I have always had confidence in you, but now I have more than ever."

Bill felt a little better, but he still had one more apology to make. Saturday morning he drove out to the Tunnel Mill area and hiked through the woods to his secret cave. He prayed from seven in the morning until late in the afternoon, crying out his repentance to God. As the sun was finishing its arc, he came out of his cave and climbed on top of a big rock where he could watch the shadows lengthen across the valley. The forest was quiet and the air was humid, without any wind to stir the deciduous leaves about him. Bill raised his arms over his head and praised God for making such a beautiful world. Dropping his arms, he said, "Lord, one day You hid Moses in the cleft of a rock and passed by him so that he could see Your backside. If You have forgiven me for my sin, would You pass by me so I can know my iniquity is gone; so I can pray for Your sick children again?"

As soon as he finished this prayer, a whirlwind rustled through a nearby bush and swirled along the trail toward the rock where he stood. It brushed against him with enough force to make him grip his hat and shut his eyes until it had passed. Bill raised both of his arms again and said, "I love You, Lord, with all my heart. I'm so glad that You are a prayer-answering God, and You forgive those who will turn to You with all their hearts and repent."

Now that his confidence had returned, Bill hiked the trail that took him to his car; and that car took him down the highway; and that highway took him to a motel in Jeffersonville, Indiana, where he confidently prayed for a stranger's suffering baby. Through the power of a merciful Jesus Christ, that baby was healed.

ON THURSDAY, October 8, 1959, William Branham, Banks Wood, and Fred Sothmann set aside three days to go squirrel hunting near Salem, Indiana, about 40 miles north of Jeffersonville. Each morning they rose at four o'clock so they could be in the woods by daybreak, hoping to surprise some sleepy-eyed squirrels as they foraged for their breakfast. They weren't successful. It was late in the season, and an overabundance of hunters had thinned the squirrel population considerably. After two days of hunting, the three men didn't even have one squirrel to show for their efforts.

Early Saturday morning Bill dropped Fred and Banks off at one patch of woods, and then he drove further along the road to another patch of woods. It was not a good day for squirrel hunting. Frost, wind, and gravity had stripped the trees bare and carpeted the ground with a crunchy layer of brittle leaves. Besides this handicap, the cold wind was probably keeping most squirrels snuggled in their nests. Bill prowled the woods for several hours without seeing one bushy red tail.

He walked down a hill into a dry creek bottom, and then walked up the hill on the other side. Soon he came to a hillside overlooking a field where several farmers were harvesting corn. This hillside was covered with sycamore and locust trees. Having hunted these woods since he was a boy, he knew squirrels avoided locust trees because of their spiny branches, and they disliked sycamores because these trees had buttonball seeds they could not eat. They preferred beech, walnut, and oak trees. A few walnut trees dotted the hillside, but these were devoid of leaves and nuts—nothing there to attract a squirrel.

Although Bill knew there would be nothing to shoot at here, he was tired and needed to rest, so he stretched out on the ground between two sycamore trees to get out of the wind and let the sun warm him. One of the trees reminded him of a compass, because it had four main branches pointing due north, south, east, and west. Leaning back against the trunk of this "compass" tree, he considered taking a nap, but decided not to. It was already 9:30 a.m. and he was supposed to pick up his hunting buddies in an hour. If he fell asleep, he might not wake in time.

As he watched the farmers work, he thought about the Scripture that for the past two years had been frequently on his mind. Jesus said, "Whoever says to this mountain, 'Be removed and be cast into the sea,' and does not doubt in his heart, but believes that those things he says will be done, he will have whatever he says."

That Scripture puzzled him. Why did Jesus word it the way he did? Jesus didn't say, "If *I* say to this mountain, 'Be removed...'" Jesus said, "If *you* say to this mountain..." There wasn't even a prayer involved. How could that be? Bill wondered if it was an isolated promise that Jesus gave strictly to His disciples before the atonement.

"As far as I know," Bill thought, "all the promises of power to the church were released by the atonement Jesus made on the cross; and they were instituted when he gave the church His Holy Spirit on the day of Pentecost. So, if I'm ever asked about Mark 11:23, I'll say Jesus gave His disciples that power before the atonement, just like He gave His prophets special powers before the atonement."

From somewhere in the branches above him, a voice said, *"Do you think it was the prophets talking when they predicted the future? Didn't you just preach on how the prophets were so anointed by the Holy Spirit that it wasn't them speaking, it was God speaking through them?"*

Bill thought, "Yes, Lord, that's true."

The voice continued, *"That was included in the atonement too. If any man at any time can surrender himself so completely to God that God can use his voice, then it isn't the man speaking, it is God using him. How do you see those visions during the prayer-lines? Do you think it is your own wisdom that tells people their histories and what will happen next? Do you think it is your wisdom that gives you insight when you are preaching? What do you think happens when one Christian speaks in an unknown tongue and another interprets it?"*

"I see," Bill said aloud. "Wrapped in the atoning blood of Jesus Christ, it's possible for a man to surrender himself so completely to the Spirit that it's no longer him speaking, it's God. But how does that explain Mark 11:23?"

"That Scripture is true, just like every other Scripture is true. If you are anointed by the Holy Spirit to say it, whatever you say will happen."

Suddenly Bill felt something sweep over him with such force that he scrambled to his feet, scared. "Who said that?" he demanded, his eyes scanning the hillside. "Who am I talking to?" There was nobody there. The only sounds he heard were those made by the wind rustling dry leaves and the farmers harvesting in the distance. "Lord, is that You? Usually I see that light when You're talking to me, but there's no light here."

The voice spoke again, very close to him. Bill heard it more clearly than he heard the farmers working in the cornfield. The voice commanded, *"Say what you will, and it will be given to you."*

He thought, "What is going on? Am I losing my mind? I don't want to be a fanatic and go off the deep end somewhere." He bit his finger until it hurt. "I'm not asleep, so this can't be a dream. It doesn't seem like a vision either. Usually when the anointing comes deeply, a vision follows. I'll just wait here a bit and see if a vision comes."

His body felt strangely numb, so he walked around in a little circle, stretching his arms. Presently a deep anointing poured over him like honey. Again that voice commanded, *"Say what you will, and it shall be given unto you."*

Trembling, Bill asked, "Lord, is this the change in my ministry that You've been telling me would come? Is this somehow connected with that little house under the tent that you showed me in a vision a few years ago?"

The voice answered, *"I am confirming the things I will do. Say what you will, and it shall be."*

"There aren't any sick people out here. What shall I ask for?"

"You're hunting and you need squirrels, just like Abraham one time needed a ram."

"That's right, I could get a mess of—" His tongue stopped, and he thought, "Lord, if I'm doing something wrong, please forgive me; but I'm going to find out if this is really You or not." Aloud he said, "Today I'm going to shoot three young red squirrels."

"From which direction wSupernatural Experiencesill they come?"

Bill took a deep breath, thinking, "I've gone this far, so I might as well finish it. But I'm going to pick something impossible." Looking around, he noticed a locust tree 50 yards away that had several dead limbs. It was standing on the edge of a thicket, near where the farmers were harvesting corn. Knowing that he would never find a squirrel among those thorny locust branches, he pointed at a specific spot and said, "There will be a red squirrel on the end of that naked limb, and I'll shoot him from here."

As soon as he lowered his pointing finger, there sat the squirrel, looking at him. Bill raised his gun to his shoulder and leaned against a sycamore to steady his aim. At the crack of his .22 caliber rifle, the squirrel fell. Bill walked over and looked at the dead animal. He had shot it right through its eye and blood was oozing from its head onto the dry yellow leaves. He picked it up. It felt warm. Putting the dead animal in his game bag, he thought, "Visions don't bleed, so I know this is a real squirrel. Maybe it just happened that way. Lord, if this was You, let it happen again so the devil won't have any room to say it was a coincidence."

Once again, that super anointing swept over him with staggering force. He looked around the woods until he saw another unlikely place to find a squirrel. Fifty yards away stood a dead locust tree that had poison ivy vines climbing up its trunk. Squirrels avoid poison ivy as much as people do. Bill pointed at a particular branch on that tree and said, "There shall be another red squirrel sitting on that limb." When he lowered his finger, there it stood! Bill rubbed his eyes and looked again. It was still there. Leveling his rifle, he fired. The squirrel dropped from the limb and hit the ground with a *thud*. Walking over to the spot, Bill pushed back the vines with his boot, picked up the dead squirrel, and stuffed it in his game bag.

"Lord, that *was* You," he said happily. "Now I think I understand what Mark 11:23 is all about. Thank You, Lord, for confirming Your Word. I can hardly wait to tell the others about this."

He started walking back toward the road. The voice came again. "*You said three squirrels.*"

Bill stopped. That was right, he *had* said three. He looked around for another place to put a squirrel. He thought, "This time I'm going to make it really radical." On the edge of the cornfield stood an old stump, bleached white by the sun, with one slick branch still attached. Bill said, "There will come a red squirrel out of this thicket, run down to that old snag, go out on that limb, and look over there at that farmer."

Nothing happened. He waited ten minutes and still no squirrel appeared. It was getting close to 10:30. He stood up and stretched. "Father, You said in the mouth of two or three witnesses let every word be established. I have two witnesses here in my bag, so I'm content. Thank You, Lord, for these two squirrels. Now, I've got to go meet Banks and Fred." Tossing his game bag over his shoulder, he took a few steps in the direction of the road.

"*But you have already spoken it,*" the voice reminded him. "*The Scripture says, 'If you don't doubt in your heart, but believe that those things you say will be done, it will happen.' Are you doubting?*"

Bill turned back. "No, Lord, I'm not doubting Your Word."

At that moment a squirrel dashed out of the locust thicket, ran down to the cornfield, scrambled up the stump and out on that single limb, where it stopped and looked towards the farmers.

Bill shouldered his rifle, lined up the crosshairs of his scope, and squeezed the trigger. The bullet smacked this squirrel in the head.

While he was putting it in his bag, he heard another voice whisper inside his head, "You know what, the woods are full of squirrels right now. This was all just a coincidence."

Bill answered, "Satan, we'll see about that." Walking back up the hill to those two sycamore trees, Bill settled himself down to watch. He waited until noon before he finally left and picked up his companions. In all that time he did not see the slightest flurry of another squirrel, or even hear a squirrel bark.

ALTHOUGH squirrel season in Indiana closed on October 13, 1959, the season in Kentucky stayed open several weeks longer. During the first week of November, William Branham, Banks Wood, and Tony Zabel drove over to Elkhorn City, Kentucky, to spend several days hunting with Charlie Cox, the brother-in-law of Banks Wood.

Elkhorn is a small town in eastern Kentucky on the edge of the Appalachian Mountains. This wooded area hid some of the best hunting and fishing in the world, and Bill often went there to escape the pressures of his ministry. Charlie and Nellie Cox always made him feel welcome at their home in the country.

The weather that week in November definitely favored the squirrels over the squirrel hunters. A chilly wind blew every day. Mostly the squirrels stayed curled up in their dens. Any brave squirrel that did venture out was forewarned of danger by the crunch of the hunters' boots tramping through dry leaves. After hunting two days, Charlie was the only one in their group who had shot some squirrels, and he had used a shotgun. Bill still trusted his .22 caliber rifle, but it looked like he might not get a chance to use it.

On Friday, November 6, he fared no better. Late in the afternoon he came to a familiar dip between the hills. He called this place Sportsman's Hollow because one time he saw 16 squirrels there, all of them sitting in one tree; and he shot his limit only, letting the rest of them go, which was the sportsmanlike thing to do. Now he stood on the eastern hill above the hollow and studied the foliage below him for signs of life. He watched for a long time, but nothing moved. The trees here lacked squirrels the same as elsewhere in the woods. Standing in one spot made him shiver. The chilly air stung his nose, cheeks, and ears. The tips of his fingers smarted from the cold despite his gloves; even his toes tingled from the cold. He decided he had hunted enough for one day. He would try again tomorrow. Turning to go, he had only taken a step or two when he heard a deep voice like the purr of a lion. The voice said, *"How many squirrels do you want today?"*

Rubbing his chin, Bill mused, "Charlie is going to let me take home those three squirrels he shot; and six squirrels will make a meal for my family; so if I could just get three more..."

Suddenly a supernatural anointing struck him with such force that he had to lean against a tree to keep from falling over. That same voice said with authority, *"Speak what you will, don't doubt, and you shall have whatever you say."*

Bill said, "I shall have my three squirrels."

"Where will they come from?"

"One will come from the west, one from the south, and one from the north."

He studied the woods. After a few minutes he saw something move on the ridge on the other side of the hollow. Bringing his rifle up to his shoulder, he spotted a gray squirrel through his scope. It was at least 90 yards away, which was a long shot for someone who sighted his gun in at 50 yards. Bill raised the muzzle slightly over his target to compensate for the distance. When he squeezed the trigger, the squirrel dropped dead.

"There's one. I might as well face south because that's where the next one will come from."

For a long time he sat on a fallen log facing south, thinking "Surely it will happen because I spoke it under the anointing. If that was the Holy Spirit talking to me, then it will have to be just like I said it would be."

After about 15 minutes he saw a squirrel scamper around the base of a beech tree directly south of where he sat. It was an easy shot, about 50 yards. He hit the squirrel right in one eye. At the sound of his rifle, another squirrel in the same direction darted from a thicket, running down the hill, stopping in front of a log about 40 yards southwest of Bill.

"There's the third squirrel," he thought, swinging the barrel of his rifle a mere 45 degrees until it pointed southwest. He aimed for the squirrel's ear because its head was turned sideways to him. When he pulled the trigger, he missed. The squirrel jumped in surprise and ran down to the other end of the log, where it stopped to gnaw on a hickory nut.

"I must be shivering so much I can't aim," he thought, "but I was just as cold when I shot that other squirrel." Leaning against the tree to steady his aim, he tried again. This time his bullet struck four inches above the squirrel's head, splintering the log behind it. The squirrel ran about ten feet, and then stopped to look around nervously.

"I must have knocked my scope out of line," he thought, as he bolted another shell into the chamber. If possible, Bill avoided shooting a squirrel in the chest, because that is where the meat was. He liked to shoot his squirrels in the head, preferably in the eye. Now he lined up the crosshairs of his scope over the squirrel's chest. His third shot scattered leaves a foot in front of the animal.

This time the frightened squirrel disappeared into a thicket of scrub brush.

For a minute Bill was puzzled. Out of the 119 times he had shot at squirrels that year, he had only missed five shots; and here he had just missed three shots in a row! How could that be? Then he realized why. He had said the next squirrel would come from the north. God would not let him kill this squirrel that had run southwest of him.

Facing north, he waited 15 minutes without anything happening. The sun was settling; the forest was darkening. At four o'clock he decided to go pick up the two squirrels he had already shot before it got too dark to find them. When he came back to the original spot from where he had shot the two squirrels, he decided to keep walking, figuring it was too dark to shoot another squirrel that day. Before he had walked ten more steps, that deep voice rumbled, *"Go back and get your third squirrel. You've already said it would happen."*

Turning back to his original shooting spot, he said, "Lord, I won't doubt You a bit." Just then he saw his third squirrel run up a white oak tree about 60 yards due north. By now it was so dark that even though he used his scope to search up and down the tree, he couldn't see the squirrel. Finally he spotted a dark lump high in the branches and decided to take a chance. After he fired, he heard the noise of little claws scrambling along tree bark. Then something landed on the ground, scattering the leaves. A moment later a squirrel ran up a tree 20 feet farther east. Bill assumed it was the same squirrel. He must have missed it in the white oak, so it scampered over to this other tree. Aiming at a dark spot on the trunk where the squirrel had stopped, Bill squeezed his trigger. This time he scored an obvious kill; the squirrel plummeted straight to the ground.

Just to be sure, Bill checked the base of the white oak tree first. There lay his third squirrel, straight north from where he had been when he said it would happen. "This is wonderful," he thought. "I asked for three squirrels, and the Lord gave me another one for good measure." But when he walked over to get the fourth squirrel, it wasn't there. "That's strange. I know I killed it." He searched all around through the dry leaves, but couldn't find it. Then he noticed a hole between the roots at the base of the tree. His hand wouldn't fit into the narrow opening, so he poked a stick down the hole. He could feel something loose inside, but he couldn't get it out with the stick. "That's the squirrel, all right. I can't get it tonight. I'll have to come back and get it tomorrow."

He covered the opening with a rock, then went back to meet his friends at the car. They were impressed when he showed up with three squirrels, since none of them had shot any. Then when he told them the circumstances, they were astonished.

That night before they went to bed, Tony Zabel led them in prayer. Among other things, Tony prayed, "Lord God, tomorrow let Brother Bill find that squirrel in that hole, so we can know he is telling us the truth."

That shocked Bill. Tony was a deacon in his church. When Tony's wife lay dying and her doctors had given up on her, Bill had prayed for her and God had miraculously healed her. How could Tony doubt him?

Saturday morning looked as cold and miserable outside as the rest of the week had been. At the breakfast table, Tony said, "At least we'll get one squirrel today, won't we, Brother Bill."

"Brother Tony, you just didn't understand. When I spoke under the inspiration, I said 'three squirrels.' That fourth one had nothing to do with it."

"Well, it will be there anyhow."

Since they were leaving for Jeffersonville at noon, they only planned to hunt until nine o'clock that morning. Bill spent two hours searching the woods in vain for a patch of gray fur to shoot at. Finally he gave up. He had just enough time to stop by Sportsman's Hollow on his way back to the car. As he neared the hollow, a voice whispered inside his head, "What if that squirrel isn't there? Then your own deacon will think you lied."

Suddenly that super anointing baptized him again. Another voice said, *"Even if it's not there now, say you will find it, and it will be so."*

Bill said, "Lord, Mark 11:23 is Your Word, so I'm taking You at Your Word. I shall find that squirrel."

Reaching the tree, he took the rock off the hole and widened the opening with his hunting knife. When he reached into the hole, instead of finding a dead squirrel, he found a ball of loose roots. He recoiled in surprise. "Oh, my! We're supposed to meet at nine o'clock, and here I am with no squirrel. What will Tony think? What will the rest of them think?" He searched again through the dead leaves around the base of the tree, but he found nothing. "Wait a minute," he thought. "When I said I would find that fourth squirrel, I was under the same anointing that brought the other three. If this is supposed to confirm the beginning of my new ministry, then that fourth squirrel has to be here someplace. So where is it?"

The voice said, *"Look under that piece of bark."*

Bill kicked the slab of bark aside. There was nothing under it but leaves. "Something's funny here," he thought. Looking closer at that spot, he noticed a few gray hairs poking out from under the brown leaves. He dug deeper and there he found it, his fourth gray squirrel. Counting the three red squirrels in Indiana, that made seven squirrels in all—God's number of completion.

ON WEDNESDAY MORNING, November 11, 1959, William Branham, Banks Wood, and David Wood drove to the Wright's farm to get some communion wine for the church. George and Murle Wright made this wine from grapes they had grown in their garden. Bill liked the idea that the wine his church drank during their communion service was made by people who were filled with the Holy Spirit.

As usual, the Wright family welcomed their company cordially and urged them to stay for lunch. Edith (George and Murle Wright's daughter) asked Bill to shoot a rabbit or two so her mother could make rabbit stew. Bill didn't have the heart to turn Edith down. He always felt sorry for her. She was 37 years old and had spent most of her life in a wheelchair. She had been paralyzed since she was a baby. Ironically, it was through Edith's suffering that Bill first came to know the Wright family. Back in October of 1935 he held a revival meeting at Branham Tabernacle. When George Wright heard about this revival, he took his crippled daughter to church for prayer. Edith had been suffering in terrible pain for many years. The first time Bill prayed for her, she wasn't healed of her paralysis, but the pain left her and never returned. Bill appreciated this touch of God's mercy. Still, it always bothered him that Edith was not completely delivered, especially since he had seen many people healed who were in worse condition than her. Over the years he had spent many hours fasting and praying for God to show him a vision of Edith's healing, but there was no way to force a vision. All he could do was ask, knowing that God was sovereign, and His great will and purpose often lay hidden in realms beyond man's feeble ability to understand.

Shelby (George and Murle Wright's son) loaned Banks a .22 caliber rifle (Bill had brought his own) and together Banks and Bill went out to hunt rabbits. A low covering of gray clouds threatened to get them wet, but the rain held off until they returned with their game. While Bill was skinning and cleaning his rabbits behind the tool shed, he heard the chug, chug, chug, of a tractor engine slowly driving along the road, coming closer. Soon Hattie Mosier and her two sons drove into the yard sitting on the seat of an old two-cylinder farm tractor. Hattie lived about a mile away. When she heard that Bill was visiting her parents, she set aside her unfinished chores and came over to enjoy the fellowship.

Bill was glad Hattie came because he had something in his pocket he wanted to give her. Recently she had donated $20 to the Branham Tabernacle building fund. Knowing how poor she was, Bill wanted to give that money back to her. He remembered the day in 1940 when he had married Hattie Wright to Walter Mosier. Walt died in 1955 when a tractor tipped over on him, leaving Hattie to raise her two sons by herself. She worked hard to make a living out of her small, hillside farm, but economically she wasn't very successful. She had once told Bill she netted around $200 a year, so he knew she needed that $20 more than Branham Tabernacle did. When he reached into his pocket to get the money, he felt checked. The Holy Spirit reminded him again that Jesus didn't stop the widow woman from putting her last coin into the collection box. Bill left the money in his pocket, believing that God would reward Hattie Mosier in His own time and in His own way.

Nine people sat at the Wright's kitchen table for lunch: Banks and David Wood; George, Murle, Shelby, and Edith Wright; Orville and Coy Mosier, Hattie's teenage boys; and Bill. Hattie sat on a cane chair next to the kitchen counter. Around one o'clock Bill finished eating a piece of cherry pie smothered with sorghum molasses. Pushing back his plate, he talked for several hours about the things of God. Periodically someone would ask him a Bible question, which he would answer. Mostly he just talked about his ministry—where it had come from, where it was now, and where it might be going. At 4:30 he finally got to Mark 11:23 and the miraculous events of the past few weeks. First he described the creation of three red squirrels in Indiana; then he told them about the four gray squirrels created in Kentucky.

Bill asked, "What could have happened? Brother George, you're well over 70 years old, and you've been hunting squirrels all your life; Brother Shelby, you're an expert squirrel hunter; Brother Banks, so are you. Did any of you ever see a squirrel in a sycamore tree or a locust thicket?"

None of them had.

"Neither have I, and I've hunted squirrels since I was a kid. I've thought a lot about this, and here is what I think it is. In Genesis 22, God told Abraham to take his son Isaac up Mount Moriah and sacrifice him as a burnt offering to the Lord. Abraham obeyed, even though God had already told him that Isaac was going to be his heir. On top of the mountain Abraham built a stone altar and was ready to kill Isaac when the angel of the Lord stopped him, saying, 'Now I know that you fear God, since you have not withheld your son, your only son, from Me.' Of course this drama foreshadowed the greater story of God the Father sacrificing His own Son, Jesus, on Calvary. Abraham still needed a sacrifice on Mount Moriah. When he looked around, he saw a ram caught in some bushes. Now, I want to ask you something. Where did that ram come from? When Abraham was building that altar, he gathered stones from all around the mountaintop, and that ram wasn't there then. How did it get there all of a sudden?"

"Here is what I think," Bill continued, answering his own question. "One of God's attributes is Jehovah-jireh, meaning 'the LORD will provide.' Abraham needed a sacrifice, so God simply spoke that ram into existence. It wasn't a vision. It was real. Abraham killed it and the blood drained over the altar.

"God is the same Jehovah-jireh today. He was trying to explain to me His promise in Mark 11:23. I was having trouble understanding it, so He simply showed me how it works, first in Indiana and then in Kentucky. I needed squirrels, so He created squirrels. They weren't visions. I shot them and ate them. They were real squirrels. If He could speak a ram into existence for Abraham, He can speak squirrels into existence for me, because He is the Creator of both."

All afternoon Hattie Mosier had been sitting off to the edge of the group, listening quietly. After Bill told everyone his conclusion, Hattie said, "Brother Branham, that's nothing but the truth."

Suddenly the Spirit of God swept through the kitchen, bringing Bill to his feet. His body felt charged with the same anointing he had felt in the woods when he said there would be squirrels. Clearly he heard that same voice say, *"Tell Hattie to ask for whatever she wants, then you speak it into existence."*

"Sister Hattie," Bill said, "you have found favor in the sight of the Lord. Because you said the right thing, God told me to tell you: Ask for whatever you want, and He will give it to you."

Hattie flung her hand up against her cheek, astonished and more than a little confused. "Brother Branham, what do you mean?"

"The God of heaven is going to show you that Mark 11:23 is just as true as the rest of His Scriptures. Ask anything your heart desires, and He will produce it right here, right now."

She glanced around nervously. "What should I ask for?"

Bill suggested, "You're poor. You could ask God for enough money to buy a bigger farm or build a new house. You could ask for something to help your parents. They're old. Ask God to renew their youth. Or, what about your sister Edith? She's been crippled for 37 years. Ask for her healing and she'll have it. Ask

God for anything you want, and if it doesn't happen right now, then don't ever believe me again."

Hattie noticed that her two teenage sons, Orville and Coy, were snickering and poking each other in the ribs. That reminded her of what she really wanted. "Brother Branham, the greatest desire of my life is to see the salvation of my two boys."

Without hesitation, Bill declared, "Sister Hattie, by the command of Almighty God, I give you the salvation of your children in the name of Jesus Christ."

Hearing the name of Jesus, both boys leaped from their chairs and ran into their mother's arms, weeping tears of repentance. Hattie screamed so loud that the cows in the barn could hear her—maybe even the cows in their neighbor's barn.

The rain tinkled steadily on the roof. Because Hattie's tractor didn't have a cab, Shelby wanted to drive his sister home in his car. Hattie preferred to ride home with her sons on the tractor. For the rest of that week she felt so good, she felt like she was walking on air. When Sunday came, Orville and Coy Mosier came to Branham Tabernacle and were baptized in the name of the Lord Jesus Christ.

Bill stood behind the pulpit and told his congregation about the seven straight times God created squirrels, and about what happened at the Wright farm. He finished by saying, "So you people might know that I've told you the truth, Sister Hattie, would you stand? There is the little woman that the miracle happened to. God bypassed all the great people of the world and let this happen first to a poor, humble widow woman. The reason He chose her is because He knew she would ask for the right thing.

"Now I want to say something to my little church here, my little flock that's been so faithful and has prayed for me while I have traveled around the world. I believe there is another worldwide shaking coming. These things I have told you about are the truth. At the Day of Judgment, I will face you yonder with the same story, just as true as I'm standing here today.

"I'm sure you can all see what it is; it's the coming of a greater, deeper anointing of the Holy Spirit. I challenge everybody in the name of the Lord, if that Spirit strikes you like It did me, I don't care what you ask for, it shall be granted. How you get into that deeper anointing, I don't know. All I know is that it will take God to put you there, so you just live as sweet and humble and close to God as you can. Don't doubt Him. Just believe that everything is working for your good, and everything will work out all right."

Hattie Wright Mosier with her sons, Orville and Coy

Chapter 81
Beyond the Curtain of Time
1960

BETWEEN FEBRUARY 28 AND MARCH 13, 1960, William Branham preached fourteen sermons in Phoenix, Arizona. On Tuesday night, March 8, he preached a sermon called "Discernment of Spirit." Amidst growing resistance to his ministry, he wanted to make his motives perfectly clear to everyone. He noted that John commanded Christians to test the spirits to see whether or not they are from God. Bill urged Christians to discern the spirit of any ministry by looking at the minister's objectives. What is he trying to accomplish? Is he trying to bring attention to himself, and therefore glorify himself? Is he trying to build up his own organization? Does he want everybody else to get out of the picture so that he and his group can be the picture? That is the wrong spirit.

Jesus didn't glorify Himself, but gave all the glory to His Father. A true minister will always use his gift to build up the body of Christ, and in this way he will glorify God. A true minister will never try to break people apart, but will always try to bring people together—not to a denomination, but to a unity of spirit. A true prophet (a New Testament prophet is a preacher) will always point people away from himself and toward Calvary.

Bill said, "Don't dis-fellowship a man because he doesn't belong to your group. Discern his spirit. If he is working for the same purpose that you are, then you have fellowship. You are working for one great cause—the cause of Christ."

Moses was a true prophet because his only motive was to achieve something for the kingdom of God. He forsook the riches and fame he could have had in Egypt so that he could help God's people fulfill their destiny. Compare Moses with the false prophet Balaam. Balaam had a genuine prophetic gift, but he wanted to use it to get rich and famous. Bill said, "If you see a person with a great gift who is trying to do something to glorify himself, your own discernment of the spirit tells you that is wrong.

"When a man is anointed of the Spirit of God, he will act like God; and the action of God is never to break us up. The action of God is to draw us together, for we are one in Christ Jesus. God's purpose is to bring us together. Love one another. A true prophet, a true teacher, will try to bring the church to a unity of spirit so that people might recognize God. May we have discernment of spirit to discern the spirit that is in the man, to see if it be the Spirit of God or not."

From Phoenix, Bill drove to Tulsa, Oklahoma. Starting on Saturday, March 26, he preached nine times in nine days, finishing in Tulsa on Sunday morning, April 3, with a sermon called "As the Eagle Stirreth Her Nest." He told how a mother eagle pads her nest with fur to make it comfortable for her young eaglets. When it is time for them to learn to fly, she removes the fur and the nest becomes uncomfortable. Likewise, God sometimes makes life uncomfortable for his children because He wants them to learn something new and to move to a higher level.

On Sunday afternoon he received a message from his old acquaintance, Oral Roberts, who lived in Tulsa. Roberts had fallen and hurt his leg, and he wanted Bill to come to his house and pray for him. When Bill arrived at Roberts' large, beautiful home, he found Roberts in bed, his knee swollen so badly that he could not bend it. While Bill was praying for Jesus to heal him, the blood vessels in Roberts' knee formed a V-pattern and the swelling went down. In a few minutes, Oral Roberts was able to get out of bed and walk with Bill to the front door.

While they were saying good-bye, Roberts asked, "Have you seen my new office building yet?"

"No, Brother Roberts. I'm going to visit Tommy Osborn in the morning. I'll swing by and see your place after that."

"Good. You'll be impressed. Just remember that you played a part in building my organization. You inspired me when I was young and just starting my ministry."

On Monday he visited the headquarters of Tommy Osborn's worldwide missionary organization. Bill spoke at their morning chapel hour, where the office personnel met to worship and pray before they began their daily duties. Then Tommy Osborn gave him a tour of his building. A map of the world covered one wall of Osborn's office. Hundreds of pins pushed into that map indicated the spots where Osborn supported Christian missionaries. He said, "Brother Branham, I am just one of your students. You are the one who sent me out to do this." Then he gave Bill a memento—a statuette of an African native with a block of wood in his mouth. Osborn said, "Think of how many thousands of people we have delivered from that."

Afterwards, Bill drove to Oral Roberts' new office building, which covered nearly a city block and cost several million dollars to build. Mr. Fisher took Bill on a tour. They entered through glass doors into a foyer lined with imported marble. Mirrors, paintings and sculptures decorated the large room. Even the ceiling was a work of art, composed of intricately woven aluminum wires. This was just the beginning of marvels. Bill saw the sound studio where Roberts produced his radio and television programs, the printing press that printed his monthly magazine, *Healing Waters*, and many offices filled with managers, accountants, secretaries, clerks, and hundreds of electric IBM machines processing mail. When they finished this tour and were walking back to the foyer, a policeman warned, "Mr. Branham, you're going to have a hard time getting out of here. There must be 50 people waiting for you by the front door."

"Is there another way out?" Bill asked.

"Yes," said Mr. Fisher. "Go back along this corridor to a door marked 'Exit.' That will open into the employees' parking lot. If you give me your car keys, I'll drive around and pick you up."

Following these directions, Bill was soon standing outside, admiring the exterior architecture, and thanking God for everything this one man had achieved. It was gratifying to think that he had once inspired Oral Roberts to begin his faith-healing ministry.

Then, like the backward swing of a pendulum, his emotions swung the other direction. In five days he would be 51 years old. What had he accomplished of any lasting significance? Since 1933 he had preached directly to millions of people around the world, seen thousands of visions, prayed for hundreds of thousands of people, and seen hundreds of thousands of healings and miracles. What on earth did he have to show for it? When he compared Tommy Osborn's ministry and Oral Roberts' ministry to his own, the achievements of these students seemed to overshadow those of their teacher. He would be ashamed to show Osborn and Roberts his own office building—an old trailer-house where a part-time secretary answered his mail on a secondhand, manual typewriter. As for his financial position, right now his bank account had less than $150 in it.

"Dear God," he thought sadly, "I guess you can't trust me with money and responsibility like you can these other brothers."

Just then, as clearly as he had ever heard any sound in his life, Bill heard a voice say, "*I AM your portion.*"

The pendulum stopped its melancholy swing in mid-arc, and swung back toward peace and joy. Bill said, "Thank You, Lord. I'm happy to have You as my portion." Mr. Fisher came around the corner of the building with the car. Bill thought, "At the end of my road, after I've preached my last sermon and prayed my last prayer, maybe God will give me a little portion of Himself over there on the other side." That was the most gratifying thought of all.

While Bill was driving home, he thought about the three meetings he was scheduled to preach in Kentucky over the next ten days. When three of his friends had asked him to preach one night in their home towns in Kentucky, Bill had felt a faint check in his heart, like the Holy Ghost was telling him no; but he said yes anyway. Each friend promptly rented his local National Guard Armory building and advertised the meeting. Unfortunately, Bill must have picked up a virus in Tulsa because as soon as he got home, his sinuses became plugged and his throat tightened. The next day his fever rose to 105 degrees and he developed laryngitis so bad that he could barely whisper. For nine days he couldn't talk above a raspy whisper. Earnestly he prayed for God to heal him so he could fulfill his commitments to his three friends, but the days for his Kentucky meetings passed and still his fever kept him in bed.

On Monday morning, April 11, 1960, he tried to get up, but he felt so weak he quickly sat back on the bed. Meda brought him a glass of orange juice and a slice of buttered toast. He motioned for her to sit beside him, and then whispered, "Meda, I wonder what's the matter. Why would those meetings be scheduled in

Kentucky and God let me lay here sick like this? Sometimes I wonder if He even called me."

"Bill, aren't you ashamed of yourself?" Meda chided sweetly. "God knows what He's doing with you. Just be quiet, sit back, and eat your breakfast. I'm going to go get you some clean sheets."

As soon as she walked out, the room disappeared. Bill seemed to be standing in a parking lot next to an armory building. A lightning bolt struck the armory and blew it into pieces. A man and three women walked up to the rubble carrying nail-guns. The man picked up two pieces of plywood, held them together and said, "Brother Branham, we'll help you rebuild this armory. If you will hold these pieces together like this, I'll nail them."

"All right," said Bill, taking the two sheets of plywood and balancing them one beside the other.

"*Don't do it!*" the angel of the Lord commanded. Bill dropped the plywood sheets. The angel continued, "*They are on the road right now to get you to reschedule those meetings in Kentucky. They sincerely believe they have 'Thus saith the Lord,' but they are wrong. Don't do it.*"

The vision left him. About an hour later, Fred Sothmann stopped by his house to see how he was feeling. In a hoarse whisper, Bill told him about the vision he had just seen. Presently Meda came in and said, "Bill, you have some visitors from Kentucky."

Bill whispered, "There are three women and a man, right?"

"Yes."

"They say they have 'Thus saith the Lord' for me, right?"

"That's what they say."

Motioning for Fred Sothmann to come closer, Bill whispered, "Brother Freddie, go tell them I can't do it. They are fine people, but they're sincerely wrong."

After all of his visitors left, he wondered again, "Why is this happening? Why can't I talk? Why can't I preach for my friends in Kentucky? God told me He was going to change my ministry, but I don't know what to do next. What if I make a mistake? Moses made a mistake when he struck that rock instead of speaking to it. Elisha made a mistake when he cursed those children who made fun of his baldhead. I don't want to go presuming, and make a mistake like they did."

Meda brought him another glass of orange juice and set it on the stand beside his bed. As he watched her leave, he noticed a flicker of light on the wall. Turning his head to see what it was, he saw the paint on the wall dissolve until the whole wall became transparent. Soon he was looking at a giant Bible hanging in the sky. This huge Bible blocked the sun, causing sunbeams to radiate from behind it in every direction. Out of that heavenly Bible came a golden cross, and out of that cross came the Lord Jesus. He walked down from the sky, stepped through the wall, and stood in the air above Bill's bed. The light from that heavenly Bible illuminated Jesus' face and cast His shadow across the room. That face embodied every good characteristic to its fullest potential— love and compassion, knowledge and wisdom, peace and justice, authority and power, all of this and more radiated from the Lord. No artist had ever captured on canvas the depth of His visage, but the closest painting Bill had ever seen was Heinrich Hofmann's *Christ at 33*. Bill had seen the face of Jesus twice before in visions, and he saw His character whenever he read his Bible…but to see Jesus here in his bedroom now—that overwhelmed him.

Jesus said, *"You are waiting for your new ministry to be confirmed to you. I have already confirmed it. You just have to accept it."*

Instantly Bill understood. So many times he had told people, "Jesus already saved you and healed you when He died on the cross, but it won't do you any good unless you accept it"? That same principle applied to his new ministry. The Bible said, "Without faith it is impossible to please Him..." Maybe he didn't understand everything God wanted him to do, but he knew enough to take one more step in faith, trusting God to show him the next step when the time came.

Jesus added, *"You are walking with too many people. To walk with Me, you will have to walk alone."*

That statement Bill also understood. He must still be catering too much to other people's suggestions, which only confused him when he tried to listen to the Holy Spirit. His new ministry lay before him; the third pull was at hand. It was time for him to shrug off the opinions of others and listen only to the still small voice of the Holy Spirit leading him. That was the lesson God wanted him to learn from those three canceled meetings in Kentucky.

As the vision faded, Bill said, "Amen, Lord!" The words burst from his lips with tone and volume. His throat felt different. Suddenly his sinuses dried and his fever left him. Jumping out of bed, he hollered, "Meda!"

She ran back into the bedroom. "Bill, you've got your voice back!"

"More than that—I've got my strength back. The Lord just healed me."

TWO WEEKS LATER—Saturday morning, May 7, 1960— William Branham dreamed that Joseph was coughing. Picking up his five-year-old son, Bill held him close to his chest, pressing Joseph's temple against his own cheek. Joseph was burning with a fever. Bill woke with his heart pounding like an alarm clock. He breathed deeply with relief when he realized it was just a dream.

Then he wondered if it meant something. Perhaps Joseph was going to get sick.

As he lay on his bed considering the dream, he stared idly out his bedroom window. The shades were drawn, but he could still see a little through the slats. Outside it looked like a typical spring morning for Indiana: cloudy, breezy, and chilly. He heard a dog barking in the distance. A truck rumbled by on Ewing Lane, briefly drowning out the barking dog.

He was just about to get up when he saw a little brown shadow moving across the floor of his room. The shadow had nothing in front of it to block the light, so there was no apparent reason for it to exist. Yet there it was. Its shape looked strangely familiar. Suddenly Bill realized the shadow resembled him. Then he saw a white shadow come along behind the brown shadow, pushing the brown shadow forward. The white shadow reminded him of the Lord Jesus.

Bill looked over to see if his wife was awake so he could show her the vision. Meda was still sleeping. He sighed. "I'm sorry, Lord, but that's the way it's been my whole life. Anything good I've ever done, You've had to push me into it. If You could only lead me."

At that moment the white shadow seemed to step ahead of the brown one. It looked like the white shadow reached back and took the brown shadow's hand as though it was going to lead. The head of the white shadow turned toward the bed and, for the briefest moment, it solidified. As the vision faded, Bill glimpsed the prettiest face he had ever seen on a man.

The next morning—Sunday, May 8, 1960—Bill dreamed he was out in the West. Around him lay a dry land dotted with creosote bushes and desert grasses. In this dream he and his wife were walking home from fishing. Bill had his fishing pole in one hand and a string of trout in the other. He stopped to open a gate in a barbwire fence. "The sky is so clear out here in the West," he said. "It doesn't have that blue haze we see back in Jeffersonville. Meda, we should have moved out here a long time ago."

"Yes, Billy, for the children's sake we should have."

Bill woke. It was seven o'clock. "I've been dreaming so much lately," he thought. "I wonder why?" Raising himself on one elbow, he looked at his wife and asked, "Are you awake, honey?" She didn't stir. Flipping over on his back, he scooted up on his pillow until his head almost touched the headboard. Then he tucked his hands behind his head and thought, "I'm glad I'm not preaching this morning. It will be good just to sit and listen to Brother Neville preach for a change."

His thoughts drifted back to his dream. It had painted such a heavenly picture of the American West that it made him think about what lay beyond this life. What would it be like to die? He knew he would instantly enter his theophany, but he wasn't sure what that celestial body would be like. Would he have a form at all? He knew he would have a solid body when Jesus returned to earth to set up His millennial kingdom. But what if he died before the next coming of Christ? What would he be like while he waited for the Millennium? Would he be a spirit, like a cloud floating around, unable to talk to his friends or to shake their hands? That didn't sound very appealing.

"I hope I don't have to go through that," he thought. "I'd rather just stay a man until the Rapture. I wonder how much time I have left. I'm 51 years old now, so at best, over half my time on earth is gone, and probably more than that. Dad died at 52. Of course he drank himself to death. Still, I have no guarantee I'll live longer than he did. If I'm going to do anything more for God, I had better do it soon."

From somewhere indefinite, a voice said, *"You're just starting. Press the battle."*

Shaking his head, Bill thought, "I probably just imagined that."

The voice said again, "*Press the battle. Keep going.*"

"Maybe I said that," Bill thought. He put his hand over his mouth to make sure his lips weren't moving.

For the third time that voice repeated, "*Your reward is coming. Just keep pressing the battle. If you only knew what was at the end of the road…*"

Faintly, Bill heard a choir singing an old church hymn:

> I'm homesick and blue, and I want to see Jesus;
> I would like to hear those sweet harbor bells chime;
> It would brighten my path and would vanish all fears;
> Lord, let me look past the curtain of time.

The voice asked, "*Would you like to see just beyond the curtain of time?*"

"It would help me so much," Bill answered.

What happened next he could not explain. One moment he was lying on his bed, and the next moment he was standing on a hillside overlooking a wide, grassy plain. Thousands of people were running toward him across this plain, screaming, "Our precious brother!" He could only guess how many thousands, but they could number in the millions, all of them running towards him from every direction. They all looked young, perhaps in their early twenties—men and women in the bloom of youth, eyes twinkling like stars, teeth glistening like pearls. They ran barefooted, their white robes fluttering with each bounding step. The men had hair down to their shoulders; the women's hair fell all the way to their waists.

If this was a vision, it was different from any vision he had ever experienced. He could feel the soft grass beneath his bare feet and a gentle breeze on his face. Even stranger, he could still see his bedroom 20 feet away, slanting at a 45 degree angle to the place where he now stood. There hung his shirt on the bedpost and there lay his wife asleep. Strangest of all, he could still see his own body lying next to his wife on the bed. His eyes were closed like he was sleeping—or dead. How strange it felt to look at himself on that bed, to see himself as other people saw him—his body now a half-century old, with its bald forehead, thinning gray hair and wrinkled skin. Skin? He looked down at his hands. Here (wherever *here* was) his skin looked soft and tight. Reaching up to his forehead, he slid his fingers into a thick mat of curly hair.

"I don't understand this," he said. "Maybe I had a heart attack and died? But who are all these people running towards me?"

The voice said to him, "*Don't you remember, it is written in the Bible that the prophets were gathered with their people?*"

"Yes, I remember that. But surely there aren't this many Branhams."

"*These are not Branhams. These people are your converts to the Lord.*"

A lovely young woman reached him first. She threw her arms around him and cried out in joy, "Oh, my precious brother!" Her embrace was as solid as any hug he had ever shared with his wife on earth, but here he did not feel the same sensation.

The voice said, "*Don't you recognize her?*"

"No, I don't."

"*When you led her to the Lord, she was more than 90 years old.*"

Bill held the young woman at arm's length so he could get a good look at her face. She was one of the most beautiful women he had ever seen, yet he could not recall having seen her before. It was hard to imagine her as a wrinkled old lady. No wonder she was so excited to see him now.

Although he didn't recognize the first woman, he recognized the next one. It was Hope, his first wife. She looked as radiantly beautiful as the day he married her. When Hope threw her arms around him, she didn't say, "My precious husband." Instead, she cried, "My precious brother!" Then she turned and hugged the first woman, both of them shouting, "My precious sister!"

Bill felt the love inside of him expanding like the universe. There could be no jealousy here. This place resounded with perfection. No, it was beyond perfection; it was sublime. No, it was beyond sublime, it was... He searched for the right descriptive word, but couldn't find one that would fit. Every grand concept in the dictionary fell short of this reality.

"I don't understand this," he said.

The voice explained, *"This is what you preached was the Holy Ghost. This is perfect love. Nothing can enter here without it."*

By now the throng had surrounded him. Young men picked him up and carried him on their shoulders to the top of the hill. Setting him down, they stepped back and shouted, "Our precious brother!" The multitude surrounded this hill and joined the refrain—hundreds of thousands of young men and women, all of them shouting, "Oh, our precious brother!"

Bill raised one hand, palm out, to silence the excited crowd. When at last they could hear him speak, he said, "I shouldn't be up here. I'm nobody special."

The voice said, *"You were called to be a leader."*

The multitude cried out, "If you had not gone forth with the Gospel, we wouldn't be here!"

"Where is 'here'?" Bill asked. "Where am I?"

The voice replied, *"This is the place the Scripture called 'souls under the altar.'"*

"If I have passed beyond the curtain of time, then I want to see Jesus."

"He is just a little higher. Your people are waiting here for Jesus to come again. When He does, He will come to you first. Then you and your people will be judged according to the Gospel you preached."

"Does every leader have to stand this judgment? How about Paul?"

"Yes."

"Then I'll be all right, because I preached what Paul preached. Where he baptized in the name of the Lord Jesus Christ, I did too. Where he taught the baptism of the Holy Spirit, I did too. Whatever Paul taught, I taught it the same way."

"We are resting on that!" shouted the multitude. "We are rich with assurance. You will present us to Jesus Christ our Savior, and then we will all go back to earth to live forever."

Just then Bill felt something nudge his back. Turning, he saw the horse he had ridden when he was a boy. "Prince! I knew you'd be here." Prince laid his muzzle across Bill's shoulder and nickered. Then Bill felt something licking his hand. Looking down, he saw his dearest childhood friend—his mongrel coon dog. "Fritz, I knew you'd be here too."

The voice said, *"All you have ever loved, and all who ever loved you, God has given them to you here."*

The scene around him faded, and at the same time his bedroom looked more substantial. Bill asked, "Do I have to go back to that old carcass?"

"Yes. You must keep pressing the battle."

His next breath took him back into his old body. But there was a difference. Something had changed inside of him—all fear of death was gone. Now he knew exactly what Paul meant when he wrote, *"For we know that if our earthly house of this tabernacle were dissolved, we have a building of God, an house not made with hands, eternal in the heavens."*

He sat up and put his legs over the side of the bed. "Meda, are you awake?" he asked. She didn't answer. Bill knelt by the side of the bed and prayed, "Dear God, help me to never compromise with Your Word. Let me preach it exactly the way Paul did. I don't care what troubles come, or what anyone else does, let me stay true to Your Word and press on to that place."

The next Sunday morning, after telling this experience to his church, Bill said, "Imagine somewhere out in space a block of perfect love one hundred billion miles square. Now imagine that it narrows with each step as it comes closer to earth until it reaches the point where we are here. That point is the love we feel now, and it's just the shadow of what is out there. Oh, my precious friends, my darlings of the Gospel, my begotten children unto God, listen to me, your pastor. I wish there was some way I could explain it to you, but there aren't any words to do it. Just beyond this last breath is the most glorious thing. Whatever you do, friends, don't miss it. Lay aside everything else until you get perfect love. Get to a spot where you can love everybody, even your enemies.

"That one visit has changed me. I can never be the same Brother Branham that I was before. Whether the plane is rocking, or lightning is flashing, or whether someone has a gun on me, whatever it is, it doesn't matter. By the grace of God I'm going to keep pressing the battle. I'm going to preach the Gospel to every person I can, persuading them to accept Jesus Christ as their Savior so they can enter that beautiful land yonder."

Endnotes and Sources

My endnotes list the source material for most of the stories in each chapter. Many of the details in this biography come from the personal testimony of Wm. Branham as recorded in his 1,100+ sermons between 1947 and 1965. In these endnotes, these source sermons are listed by the year, month and day he preached them, and then by the page number (or paragraph number) within that sermon. The year will be in the form YY-MMDD. (For example: March 11, 1962 will be listed as 62-0311.) Morning and evening sermons are identified by "M" or "E" at the end of the date. If I show a page (or paragraph) number separated by a dash, it means I consulted all the material between those two numbers.

All of Wm. Branham's sermons have been transcribed and put into a searchable computer program called the Message Software Package, or the Message Search Program (which is part of "The Table", a multi-media package). This program can be accessed for free at Branham.org; or it can be purchased at the same website, or order by phone by calling their office at 812-256-1177.

If a sermon was not in print when the Message Search Program was put together, the program developers (Eagle Computing) numbered groupings of paragraphs. To set these arbitrary quotation identifiers apart from straight page or paragraph numbers, Eagle Computing placed a capital "E" in front of the quotation number.

I benefited greatly from all of George Smith's and Rebekah Branham Smith's research that they published in Only Believe magazine. You can read many of these out-of-print issues on-line at Onlybelieve.com.

"Author's Preface"

Wm. Branham is quoted from his sermon 53-1130, E44-E45, edited.

"Chapter 53: Miracles in Black and White"

Biographical details of William Upshaw come from the book "Members of Congress Since 1789," 3rd Edition, published by Congressional Quarterly

Inc., 1984. William Upshaw hears about Shoemaker's healing and reads about Miss Shirlaw's healing. Message source: 54-0320, E43.

Wm. Branham's feelings about ministers on the platform behind him when he is praying for the sick. Message source: 51-0714, E56-E58.

The healing of William Upshaw. Message sources: 51-0501, E31; 51-0505, E39-E41; 51-0719, E3-E7; 51-0929, E54-E55; 53-0902, E87; 53-1111, E103; 53-1130, E29-E41; 54-0724, E30-E35; 54-0620E, E20; 54-0217, E20-E29. Other Sources: William Upshaw's personal testimony in The Voice of Healing magazine, April-May 1951, pgs. 23; Only Believe magazine, Vol. 6, No. 1, March 1993, pgs. 10-11, available on the Internet at www.onlybelieve.com. Note: Wm. Branham sometimes says William Upshaw came into the meeting on crutches and sometimes he says he was in a wheelchair. William Upshaw in Voice of Healing magazine says he walked into the meeting on his crutches.

The healing of the paralyzed black girl. Message sources: 54-0724, E32-E34; 53-1130, E34-E37

"Chapter 54: Looking Back From 1951"

Recollections by his old school. Message sources: 50-0200, E22-E26; 50-0820A, E38, E46-E54; 51-0722A, E37-E40; 52-0720A, E40-E49. Note: In 50-0200 he says this incident took place after a campaign in Texas, placing it in the spring of 1949. In 52-0720A he says it happened after his 1946 Jonesboro campaign. No doubt something like this happened many times over the years. I use this incident here to illustrate the crowds that often gathered at his home preventing him from resting between faith-healing campaigns.

"Chapter 55: The Hall Paradox"

The healing of William Hall. Message sources: 53-0506, E38-E44; 53-0829, E14-E30; 54-0217, E31-E39; 59-1227E, 140-148.

The healing of Mrs. Shane. Message sources: 52-0224, 36-45; 53-0506, E35-E37; 53-0905, E9-E25; 53-1107, E37-E47; 53-1206, E36-E53; 54-0217, E43-E52; 54-0902, E21-E35; 54-1206, E18-E34.

"Chapter 56: Life in a Shabby Café"

The healing line at the beginning of Chapter 56 has been edited from Wm. Branham's sermon 51-0721, E27-E42.

The story around the vision of the blood of Jesus surrounding the world. Message sources: 53-0609, 217-240; 53-0902, E3-E10; 54-0329, 171-185; 54–1203, E46-E56; 55-0222, E65-E70; 55-0606, E18-E23; 56-0916, E21-E24; 57-0419, E55-E77; 59-0419E, E45-E52; 60-0330, E6-E11; 60-0805, E56-E61; 61-0125, E8-E20; 61-0415E, E7-E18.

The healing line from Wm. Branham's New York campaign comes from his sermon 51-0928, E45-E65, edited.

The story around the vision of his infant Sarah's healing. Message source: 51-0929, E1, E33-E35.

"Chapter 57: Tremors in Africa"

Sidney Jackson's dream and subsequent experience meeting Wm. Branham. Source: Only Believe magazine, Vol. 4, No. 2, June 1991, pages 11-15, available at www.onlybelieve.com.

Trouble at the New York airport. Message sources: 53-1109, E11; 54-0718E, E3.

Wm. Branham confuses Durban, South Africa with Southern Rhodesia. Message sources: 52-0717, E23-E24, and other places in his sermons.

Miracles in Johannesburg meetings. Message sources: 52-0725, E4-E8; 53-1109, E13-E21; 54-0902, E38-E41; 59-0510E, E30-E33. Other sources: Book, A Prophet Visits South Africa, by Julius Stadsklev, pgs. 70-83.

An angel's hand supernaturally burns an imprint into a man's shirt. Message sources: 52-0725, E10-E12; 53-1109, E27-E28. Other sources: Book, A Prophet Visits South Africa, by Julius Stadsklev, page 79.

The healing of Reverend Schoeman's daughter. Message source: 53-1109, E18-E21.

"Chapter 58: Satan Springs His Trap"

Trouble in Kimberly, causing F. F. Bosworth to rent a stadium. Message sources: 52-0725, E40; 52-0816, E20; 53-1109, E51.

Wm. Branham's disagreement with National Committee ministers between Johannesburg and Klerksdorp, South Africa. Message sources: 52-0713a, E43-E52; 52-0725, E14-E39; 52-0816, E3-E23; 53-1109, E22-E49; 54-0902, E41-E49. Other sources: Book, A Prophet Visits South Africa, by Julius Stadsklev, pg. 84-85.

"Chapter 59: Durban at Last"

Details of the Kimberly, Bloemfontein, and Capetown meetings. Sources: Book, A Prophet Visits South Africa, by Julius Stadsklev, pgs. 93-116.

Wm. Branham prays for a native woman in a hut. Source: Book, A Prophet Visits South Africa, by Julius Stadsklev, pg. 114.

Wm. Branham talks to a native Christian with an idol. Message sources: 54-0307A, E9-E10; 57-0611, E54.

A native woman gives birth in the Durban meeting. Message source: 54-0304, E11.

A Hindu woman is converted and healed in the Durban prayer-line. Message sources: 53-0508, E50-E51; 54-0307A, E11-E13; 57-0611, E55-E56; 59-0814, E4; 61-0515, E28-E32. Note: Wm. Branham often says this woman was a Mohammedan. He mistakenly confused Hindu with Mohammedan (Moslem). This is evident because it is Hindu women who put a red dot between their eyes and because the other Indians in the audience began to holler "Krishna," which is an earthly form of the Hindu god, Vishnu. Wm. Branham corrects this mistake when he tells this story in 59-0814, E4.

In the Durban prayer-line: a woman dies; a cross-eyed boy is healed; a doctor is saved; a mentally retarded, hunchbacked man is healed. Message sources: 53-0508, E51-E60; 54-0217, E19; 54-0307A, E14-E27; 57-0323, E67-E68; 57-0611, E56-E65; 58-1004, E46-E48; 61-0515, E32-E43; 62-0521, E14-E17. Other sources: Only Believe magazine, Vol. 4, No. 2, page 12, available at www.onlybelieve.com.

A blind Jewish woman is converted and healed in the last Johannesburg meeting. Source: Book, A Prophet Visits South Africa, by Julius Stadsklev, pg. 147.

Estimating the results of Wm. Branham's South African campaigns. Message Sources: 52-0817, E17; 54-0307A, E27. Other sources: Book, A Prophet Visits South Africa, by Julius Stadsklev, pgs. 70-71.

Wm. Branham's parting conversation with F. F. Bosworth. Source: 53-1109, E54-E55.

"Chapter 60: The Angel's Prognosis / Chapter 61: Three Witnesses"

The story surrounding Wm. Branham's healing from invasive amebiasis (amebas). Message sources: 52-0224, 14-17, 31; 52-0713A, E51-E62; 52-0715, E14-18; 52-0725, E41-E54; 53-0329, 17-43; 53-1109, E51-E66; 54-0307E, E27-E29; 54-0620E, E5-E9; 54-0902, E49-E58. Other sources: Facts on Invasive amebiasis came from the article, "Mystery Amoeba: Parasitologists struggle to decipher a puzzling microbe's true identity," Science News, Vol. 136, pages 216-217, Sept. 30, 1989; also I discussed this subject on the telephone with Billy Paul Branham. That is where I learned that the amebas didn't leave his father, but miraculously went dormant.

Wm. Branham's conversations with an agnostic doctor. Message sources: 52-0715, E5-E9; 55-0228, E29. Note: Although Wm. Branham only mentions Moslems when he tells this, in my text I added Hindu because it is the women in the Hindu culture who wear a red dot between their eyes. People of both religions would have been present in his Durban campaign.

"Chapter 62: Left Turn at Lake Michigan"

The story surrounding Wm. Branham's vision of the submarine turning left in Lake Michigan and his test at Battle Creek. Message sources: 52-0720E, E3-E6; 52-0816, E25-E49; 54-0306, E6-E8.

Note: Wm. Branham's sermon 52-0816 is a poor quality recording. "Message Software Package's" transcription of this tape differs from my personal transcription in several places. Since these places supply noticeable details to Chapter 62, I point them out here. In quotation E29, they transcribed: "I took my wife and them, and went down, and took my mother to the ... ?..." When I listen to the tape, I hear him say he took his wife and mother to the "planetarium." In quotation E31, they transcribed: "I dreamed I seen a great, big muddy road a coming, and struck a little...?" When I listen to the tape, I hear him say, "I dreamed I seen a great, big muddy wave a coming, and struck a little...?" Also, in quotation E40, they transcribed him as saying, "It switched and come to Brother ...?..." I hear him saying, "It switched and come to Brother Floyd."

The two prayer-lines described in Chapter 62 come from Wm. Branham's sermons 52-0713E, E55-E62, and 52-0715, E48-E58. Both prayer-lines are edited. The fast prayer-line where he prayed for 78 people and then collapsed is referenced in 52-0717, E35-E72, and 52-0718, E3-E11.

Note: After nearly dying from amebiasis, Wm. Branham resumed his ministry in Hammond, Indiana, on July 13, 1952, which is the day the author of this biography was born.

"Chapter 63: When Love Projects"

The story of the little girl with one blind eye who was healed. Message source: 53-0212, E2-E3.

Wm. Branham is pestered at home. Message sources: 53-0829, E12; 53-1206, E36; 54-1206, E3.

Wm. Branham accidentally disturbs a nest of hornets. Message sources: 54-0216, E40; 54-0724, E50-E53; 550-610, E42-E43; 55-1009, E31-E33; 55-1110, E49-E50; 56-0121, E100; 56-0218B, E17-E18; and many other places.

When Wm. Branham's wife and two daughters are crying, he changes the atmosphere. Message sources: 54-0216, E35; 54-0228A, E59-61; 55-0610, E34-E36. Note: This incident probably didn't happen on the same day as the hornet incident, but it would have occurred near that time.

A minister offers radio listeners $1000 for proof of divine healing. Message sources: 54-0301, E55; 54-0620E, E30; 56-0225, E54-E55; 63-0707, 502 to 513.

The story about Doctor Reedhead receiving the Holy Spirit. Message sources: 53-0729, 42181 to 50237; 53-0830A, E68; 53-1106, E2; 53-1129E, E55-E58; 53-1212, E51-E55; and many other places.

The story surrounding the filming of the documentary film Twentieth Century Prophet. Message sources: 53-1130, E11-E13. Other sources: Movie, Twentieth Century Prophet, a documentary filmed in Jeffersonville, Indiana and Chicago, Illinois in 1953. It is transcribed "Message Software Package" as 53-0800, but you can also obtain VHS video recordings of this documentary from Bible Believers (see Bibliography).

Arrangements for Wm. Branham's trip to Palestine. Message sources: 54-0718A, E49; 60-1211M, 128-129; 61-0217, E49; 64-0726M, 209-215.

"Chapter 64: Anointing for Life"

Both healings of Billy Paul Branham. Message sources: 53-1213E, E51-E57; 55-0123A, E21-E30. Other sources: Billy Paul Branham's personal testimony recorded in 1989 at Cloverdale Bible Way, Surrey, B.C., Canada.

The healing of George Wright. Message sources: 54-0103M, 608 to 6112; 54-0307E, E34-E47; 54-1219E, 10-25; 60-0911M, 282-298.

The healing of Mrs. Baker's daughter and the healing of Charlie McDowell's mother. Message sources: 54-0307E, E36-E46; 55-0119, E23-E28.

Wm. Branham is prevented from speaking at the December 1953 Voice of Healing convention in Chicago. Message sources: 53-1213, E7-E18; 54-0404, E157.

"Chapter 65: Called out of Egypt"

Wm. Branham's vision of an East Indian man in his doorway. Message sources: 54-0307E, E48; 54-0620E, E12.

Wm. Branham's vision of F. F. Bosworth collapsing in South Africa. Message sources: 53-0512, E37; 54-0721, E13-E17; 54-1206, E4-E7; 55-0610, E36-E38.

Wm. Branham in Vatican City. Message sources: 54-0513, 270; 54-0515, 175-Q-33; 54-1003M, E12; 55-0220A, E33-E36; 57-0309B, E30; 57-1006, 327-738; 60-1209, 38-42; 63-0318, 167-5 to 168-2, (342-346).

God speaks to Wm. Branham in Cairo, Egypt. Message sources: 57-0811A, E18-E19; 57-0925, 61-63; 58-0127, E60-E62; 58-0510, E48-E51; 60-1211M, 128-137; 61-0217, E50; 61-0730M, 153-159; 61-0806, 152-156; 62-0318E, 10-71; 63-0323, 4225 to 4234 (215-220); 64-0726M, 209-215. Note: For the reason I explain the five comings of Elijah's spirit at this point in the biography, see 64-0726M, 212-215 and 64-0719M, 424 to 445. If Wm.

Branham had understood the five comings of Elijah before this point in his life, he wouldn't have allowed them to set up a meeting for him in Israel. After this point, he understood that His ministry was only to the Gentiles.

"Chapter 66: A Showdown in India"

Note: Based on Wm. Branham's testimony, it is unclear how long he was in India. In 54-1003M, 80, he says "five nights"; but in 57-0126B, E53, he says three days, and in 63-0605, E9, he says two days. Perhaps he was in India five days, but could only preach two or three nights. He did have opposition from denominational church leaders that prevented him from staying as long as he wanted. (57-0126B, E36-E38, E43) However, it is clear that the blind beggar was healed on the last night he was in India (55-1113, E71; 57-0126B, E84.) He left for America the next day, which was Saturday, September 26, 1954 (54-1003M, 29.)

The Methodist Archbishop of India's comment. Message source: 58-0309E, E34; 60-0221, 111; and other places.

Wm. Branham's dinner with Prime Minister Nehru. Message sources: 53-0513, E6; 54-0620E, E10-E11; 54-1003M, 32, 39, 86-89.

The healing of a deaf-and-dumb boy. Message source: 54-1003M, 50-68.

Wm. Branham challenges India's religious leaders and the healing of a blind beggar. Message sources: 54-1003M, 69–79; 54-1006, 161; 55-0220A, E29-E57; 55-1113, E65-E71; 57-0126B, E36-E84; 57-0326, E95-E101; 58-0315, E56-E58; 59-0613, E5-E14; 60-0709, E8-E18; 61-0119E, E7-E11; 61-0211, E6-E9; 62-1231, E20-E28; 63-0605, E7-E17; 63-0627, 39-51; and other places.

"Chapter 67: Something Haunting Him"

Wm. Branham spends 5 days in bed with nervous exhaustion. Message source: 54-1003M, 29, 122.

Riding a horse through a burn-over: Message sources: 53-0612, E48-49; 53-0830A, E58-59; 53-1122, E64-68, and others.

Vision of American Indian woman holding socks and necktie. Message source: 55-0227A, E5-E20.

Wm. Branham quoted in Chapter 67. Message sources, respectively: 54-1024, 218-220; 54-1219M, 28-31; 54-1231, 55-58; edited.

"Chapter 68: His Teaching Ministry Begins"

Five hundred thousand saved through his preaching in the first seven years of his national ministry. Message sources: 53-0326, 8; 53-0506, E3; 54-1024, 266; 54-1231, E58.

Wm. Branham's testimony and the following discernments have been edited from his sermon "How the Angel Came to Me," 55-0117.

The vision about how a woman wearing a brown suit coat and skirt, and holding a sick baby, would signal a change in his ministry. Message sources: 55-1115, E11; 57-0309e, E52; 59-0406, E12-E20; 59-0612, E42-E50.

While preaching, Wm. Branham saw a vision of the first Adam and the Second Adam. Message sources: 55-0223, E66-E69; 55-0224, E1. The quotation as it appears in my text has been edited (slightly) for clarity.

Quotation beginning, "Tonight, how many people in the building have prayer-cards?" Message source: 55-0225, E8.

Miracles occur at the San Carlos Indian Reservation. Message sources: 55-0227a, E3-E9, E20; 55-0403, 24-30.

Quotation beginning, "Some of you thought I said Adam hadn't sinned. Adam did sin…" Message source: 55-0227a, E12-E15.

"Chapter 69: A Solemn Warning"

Wm Branham sees a vision of buzzards in Los Angeles. Message Source: 55-0311, E48-E53.

Wm. Branham's sermon is condensed from "The Seal of the Antichrist," preached March 11, 1955, in Los Angeles, California. Message source: 55-0311, E23-E57.

Story of a Pentecostal man who tried in vain to cast a devil out of his Lutheran wife. Message source: 56-0101, 293.

He hears about a mixed-up preacher who said a woman had three colored devils in her. Message source: 56-0101, 298.

Under the anointing, he could tell if a person in the prayer-line was a Christian by his or her spirit of welcome. Message source: 51-0505, E58 and E60; 510-506, E31; and many more places. Search using keywords "welcome" and "spirit."

Wm. Branham saw demons as dark clouds. Message source: 54-0216, E60.

He saw the demon of suicide as a black fog. Message source: 53-1108e, E51-E52.

He saw people near death as having a dark cloud or "shadow" surrounding their heads. Message sources: 56-0401, E79; and many other places. Search using the keywords "shadowed" and "death."

A dark streak between sick people meant similar demons were calling to each other for help. Message sources: 55-0807e, E62-E63; 61-0412, E121; and many other places. Search using the keywords "dark" and "streak."

He saw a white light around people who were healed. Message sources: 50-0827e, E38; 53-0511, E34; 54-0314, E82; 55-0220e, E80; 56-0414, E67; and many other places. Search the keywords "light around."

He saw faith as a milky mist over the audience. Message sources: 50-0405, E63; 51-0505, E73; 53-0829, E77; and many other places. Search the keyword "milky."

Story of the woman who thought she had seven devils, minus two. Message source: 55-0224, E13.

Story of the man who read the note, "Where will you spend Eternity?" Message sources: 55-0311, E26-E31; 58-0316a, E68-E71.

"Chapter 70: True and False Vines"

Events surrounding the birth of Joseph Branham. Message sources: 55-0522, 2-15; 55-0724, 23; 55-1006e, E4-E5; 56-0212, E22-E23; 57-0127a, E3-E9; 57-0728, E8-E14; 58-0127, E2; 58-0316e, E15-E16; 62-0629, E26; and 65-1126, 239-287.

Miner Arganbright asks Wm. Branham to go with him to Switzerland. Message sources: 55-1120, E3; 56-0200, E2.

Wm. Branham said the anointing to preach is different than the anointing to see visions. Message sources: 50-0716, E9; 54-0228e, E11; 55-0606, E1; 56-0225, E23; 58-0208, E7; 63-0627, 27.

Wm. Branham's sermon is condensed from "The True and the False Vine," preached in Macon, Georgia, June 7, 1955. Message source: 55-0607.

Willard Collins tells his personal experiences during Wm. Branham's faith-healing campaign in Macon, Georgia, June 1955. Source: Only Believe magazine, Vol. 2, No. 1, pgs. 12-16.

"Chapter 71: Controversy in Switzerland"

Some details about this Switzerland campaign came from Dr. Guggenbuhl's report in The Herald of Faith magazine, November 1955.

He sees a vision of a German eagle watching an English horseman ride across Africa. Message source: 62-1223, 6.

Sermon excerpts and prayer-line excerpts come from his Monday afternoon and Tuesday afternoon Zurich meetings. Message sources: 55-0620 and 55-0621.

Billy Graham and Wm. Branham are both criticized in Zurich. Message sources: 55-0911, 4; 55-1003, E16-E17; 57-0114, E26.

Wm. Branham sees 50,000 conversions during his Zurich campaign. Message sources: 55-0806, E7; 57-0303e, E45.

Wm. Branham is led by the Spirit to the shore of lake Zurich to meet an old man from Russia who has an unusual request. Message source: 55-0731, 7-19.

"Chapter 72: Opossum Fever"

Four hundred major cities ask for Wm. Branham to hold faithhealing campaigns for them. Message sources: 55-0607, E3; 55-0621, E11; 55-0807e, E4.

Vision and subsequent healing of a boy with pneumonia and an old man in a wheelchair, both in Denver, Colorado. Message source: 56-0816, E21-E28.

Wm. Branham prays for a mortally wounded mother opossum. Message sources: 55-0731, 194-213; 55-0807e, E40-E45; 55-1006e, E48-E58; 56-0121, E102-E108; 56-0726, E50-E60; and many other places. Search the Message Software Package using the keyword "opossum."

Quotation that begins: "If God is concerned enough to take pity on an ignorant opossum, think of how much more He cares about His sons and daughters who are in need." Message source: 56-0121, E108, edited and combined with, "The power of Satan is limited. The power of God is unlimited." Message source: 55-1006e, E58. Both statements were made after he told about the mother opossum incident.

"Chapter 73: The Angel Photographed in Switzerland"

Wm. Branham's description of his 1955 German campaign and his second Switzerland campaign. Message sources: 55-0911, 768 (this was his initial account given soon after he came home); 55-1003, E17-E21; 55-1120, E85; 56-0108, E25; 56-0122, E15-E21; 56-0224, E8-E11; 56-1209a, E14; 56-1215, E45; 57-0602; E69-E71; 57-0623, E41; 60-0709, E20-E21. Other sources: Fred Bosworth's report in The Herald of Faith magazine, November 1955 issue (Vol. 22, No. 11); Only Believe magazine, Vol. 2, No. 3, Issue 6, pgs. 14-16. (This article contains pictures of Wm. Branham's 1955 Germany campaign.) Also, some details came from Helene Frank, (who is the translator of this biography into German.) Mrs. Frank sent me a copy of an article written by Albert Goetz called "William Branham in Karlsruhe: An eyewitness report."

When the blind German girl was healed, the vision showed her like a shadow stepping away from her solid body and walking above the crowd. Message source: 56-0129, E61-E63.

Quotation that begins, "Not long ago a woman in America said to me, 'Brother Branham, you brag too much on Jesus…'" Message source: 55-0826, E8-E11 (edited).

"Chapter 74: The Angel Teaches Him How to Fish"

Wm. Branham's sermon is condensed from "Where I Think Pentecost Failed," preached in San Fernando, California, November 11, 1955. The quotation that begins, "The Pillar of Fire is moving out again…" is found in that sermon. Message source: 55-1111, E37.

If Wm. Branham had accepted one-hundredth of the money people offered him personally, he would have been a multimillionaire; but he always refused to make a personal profit from his ministry. Message sources: 55-0120, E13; 56-0429, E4; 57-0106, E3.

Wm. Branham considers impersonators he had seen. Message source: 53-0612, E11-E16.

Wm. Branham's vision of the mysteriously canceled meeting, his attempt to lace a baby shoe, his fishing lesson, and the mysterious room in the giant tent or cathedral—these parts and the events leading up to this vision are told in detail in three places. Message sources: 56-0101, pgs. 27; 56-0219, E7-E25; 56-0403, E16-17; 56-0408a, pgs. 12-19. After this vision, he mentions the first, second, and third pull many times, especially the third pull.

Quotation that begins, "Christian friends, when I leave this world, that secret will still be in my bosom…" Message source: 56-0408a, 186 (edited).

"Chapter 75: Mexico: Mystery and Miracles"

Wm. Branham preaches to his wife until midnight and the quotation that immediately follows: Message source: 56-0101, 101 through 105 (edited).

The sermon called "Why Are People So Tossed About?" was originally printed with the title "Inner Veil." Wm. Branham preached it on January 1, 1956 in Jeffersonville, Indiana. This is the sermon where he first tells about the tent vision and the three pulls of his ministry.

Quotation that begins, "Yet men and women can live good lives…" Message source: 56-0101, 17-19, and 26.

His first Mexican campaign was prematurely and mysteriously dismissed. Message source: 56-0408a, 194 through 204; 56-0403, E16-E20.

Note: The general who helped get Wm. Branham into Mexico is named Narciso Medina Estrada. This information comes from The Voice of Healing magazine, September 1956 issue, pg. 6. However, the Message Software Package transcribes his name as General Valdena, instead of Medina, an honest mistake when listening and transcribing.

He sees a vision of the dead fish. Message source: 56-0408a, 205.

Miracles that happened during the first night of the Mexico campaign. Sources: Juan Fco. Olguín Sánchez, of Mexico, sent me a lot of information on Wm. Branham's 1956 Mexico campaign, including eyewitness accounts of these meetings.

The miracle of the old blind Mexican receiving his sight and the young Mexican mother whose dead baby was resurrected. Message sources: 56-0218b, E8; 56-0617, 36-39; 56-0726, 39-41; 57-0126e, E30-E32; 57-0519e, E28-E32; 57-0610, E16-E19; 59-0424e, E11-E16; and many other places.

Wm. Branham is interviewed by a Catholic newspaper reporter in Mexico: Message Sources: 58-0928e, 315 through 321; 62-0422, 63 through 82; 62-0624, E50-E52.

"Chapter 76: America like Israel at KadeshBarnea"

Wm. Branham declares that 1956 was America's year of decision. Message sources: 56-0115, E59-E60; 56-0212, E12; 56-0304, E12; 56-0408a, 221 through 226; 60-1113, 306; 61-0211, E55; 61-0312, E74; 62-0708, 165.

Wm. Branham's sermon is condensed from "Junction of Time," preached in Jeffersonville, Indiana, Sunday January 15, 1956. The quotations from this sermon are edited. Message source: 56-0115, E4, E5, E7, E37, E38, E52; not necessarily quoted in this order.

Quotation that begins, "Many professing Christians are always having a hard time…" Message source: 56-0121, E20-E21.

Quotation that begins, "The Revelation of Jesus Christ, which God gave unto him, to shew unto his servants things which must shortly come to pass…" Message source: 56-0617, 74-78.

Quotation that begins, "This is a beautiful type which can be applied today…" Message source: 56-0916, E7.

Quotation that begins, "This is not an easy subject to speak on…" Message source: 56-1125E, E5 (edited).

Quotation that begins, "If the Holy Spirit is in me, you had better get right by that stuff before Judgment Day…" Message source: 56-1005, E23, E27, and E29 (edited).

Quotation that begins, "Brother Cox, I have determined in my heart to preach against sin…" Message source: 57-0120m, E5.

Wm. Branham's conversation with a Canadian minister and his experience while riding to church, hearing a voice say, "What is that to thee? Follow thou me." Message Source: 57-0120m, E7-E14.

Wm. Branham preaches that the Father, Son, and Holy Ghost are three offices of one God. Message sources: 57-0309b, E31-E32; 57-0821, 18-118; 57-0901e, 141-124; 57-1002, 288-484. Note: These are some of his 1957 statements. More will be said on this subject in later years.

Wm. Branham has a conversation with Dr. Roy Weed. Message sources: 57-0120m, E2; 57-0306, E24-E25; 57-0324, E28.

Wm. Branham preaches against fanaticism, specifically against the man who said he had the literal blood of Jesus on his hands. Message sources: 57-0306 E19-E34; 57-0407m, E38; 57-0414, E40-E42.

Mentions 30 calls in less than two hours. Message source: 57-0306, E31.

Quoting Wm. Branham in his sermon "God Keeps His Word, No. 1." Message source: 57-0306, E19-E34 (edited).

Quotation that begins, "If you say, 'Oh, hallelujah, I spoke with tongues,' that doesn't mean any more than if you played a tune on a guitar…" Message source: 57-0901m, 9442 through 9544.

"Chapter 77: Dividing an Inheritance"

Pentecostal churches did not support his 1957 Saskatoon, Canada campaign. Message source: 57-0602, E61.

The prayer-line in Saskatoon, Canada. Message sources: 57-0516, E50-E59; 57-0602, E61-E62 (edited).

Because Bill often connected the stories surrounding the Wood family, I list them all here together: The healing of Ruby Wood's tumor and of David Wood's polio; the vision about Lyle Wood and his subsequent conversion; the vision of the fishing trip that led to Jim Wood's conversion; and finally, the resurrection of a little fish that Lyle Wood killed. Message sources: 57-0623, E44-E63; 57-1215, E17-E25; 58-0202, E3-E6; 59-1115, E21-E24; 59-1123, E18-E29; 61-0415b, E16-E22; 62-0624, E10-E17; 65-1127e, 11-22.

Excerpts from the prayer-line in Edmonton, Canada in 1957, the black wave Wm. Branham sees above the audience, and his urgent appeal to the people. Message source: 57-0806, E48-E52 and E58-E60 (edited).

Wm. Branham writes in the margin of his Scofield Reference Bible during the Edmonton campaign. Message source: 60-0911m, 7. Other sources: a photograph of these two pages of his Scofield Study Bible are included in the book Footprints on the Sands of Time, an autobiography of Wm. Branham.

Wm. Branham's attempts to vacation in fall of 1957 are spoiled first by the flu, then by the death of his brother Howard. Message source: 57-1211, E4-E5.

Lakeport, California, campaign—photograph of the angel and tongues of fire and lilies when Wm. Branham is preaching. Message sources: 58-1130, E61-E62; 61-0101, 162-164. Other sources: Reprints of both pictures.

Wm. Branham takes every spirit under his control. Message sources: 54-0900, E31; 55-0221, E71; 55-0604, E65; 55-0607, E81; 56-0415, E70; 56-1206, E101; 64-0207, 135; and other places. I use this here to show the reason for the first picture looking normal and the second picture showing supernatural manifestations. Something supernatural and very real happened between the preaching and the prayer portion of the service. It always did.

The healing of the blind American Indian woman and the Lutheran woman with a bleeding ulcer: Message source: 57-1212, E55-E59.

Wm. Branham visits Fred Bosworth before Fred dies. Message sources: 58-0125, E7-E8; 59-0510E, E18-E19; 60-0518, 220-227.

"Chapter 78: Disappointed at Waterloo"

Details on Gene Norman's part in the Waterloo, Iowa, meetings come from his personal testimony in Only Believe magazine, Vol. 5, No. 1, pg. 11.

Quoting Wm. Branham's prayer in Waterloo, Iowa (edited) and the subsequent manifestation of the Holy Spirit rushing through the building like a wind. Message source: 58-0128, pgs. 24-27.

During his last sermon in Waterloo, Wm. Branham speaks on Luke 17:30, connecting it with the day God visited Abraham and revealed the secret that was in Sarah's heart. Wm. Branham suggests a parallel between these Scriptures and his own ministry. Message source: 58-0202, E10-E37 (edited). Note: He refers to the local basketball game in E37 of the same tape.

Wm. Branham sees a vision of a stake driven into the ground in front of his house, which will be a sign for him to move west. Message sources: 62-1230e, 13-2 through 13-9 and 21-4 through 22-1; 65-0219, 22-6; 65-0725e, 120-125. Other sources: The Acts of the Prophet by Pearry Green, pgs. 128-129.

"Chapter 79: The Knowledge of Good and Evil Explained"

I have given only a brief summary of his sermons: "Why Are We Not A Denomination?" (58-0927) and "The Serpent's Seed" (58-0928E). The quotation that begins, "Who did it? He did! Before the foundation of the world, He made me acceptable in the presence of His grace." Message source: 58-0928m, 158-160 (edited). The quotation that begins, "You ministers and brethren, please don't feel offended because of the way I drive this in just as hard as I can." Message source: 58-0928e, 42-3 through 43-1.

Wm. Branham preaches to millionaires at the Full Gospel Business Men's Fellowship (FGBMF) convention in Tulsa, Oklahoma. Message source: 58-1130, E53-E64.

Wm. Branham hears an angelic choir and interprets an unknown tongue. Message source: 58-1130, E42-E47. Related: 62-1123, E110.

The miracle of Ricky Duponsta: Message sources: 58-1130, E65-E74; 58-1221m, 10-33; 59-0406, E22-E32; 59-0409, E2-E3. Note: In 59-0406, E31, Wm. Branham spells Ricky's last name letter-by-letter, Duponsta. The Message Software Package transcribes his name in 59-0409, E2, as DePompa. This is actually how Wm. Branham pronounced it, probably because Duponsta is harder to pronounce.

The last quotation in this chapter that begins, "I have the man's tithing now…" Message source: 58-1130, E73-E74. Note: When I edit something that Wm. Branham said, I tighten the sentence structure, delete superfluous words, and sometimes rephrase a statement to enhance the reader's understanding, always being careful not to change his meaning. In this particular quotation there is a possibility I have changed his meaning, so I want you to know about it. Wm. Branham actually said, "It's that great satellite reflecting off of the morning stars with healing in His wings." I wrote this as, "The Church (like that great satellite, the moon) is reflecting the light of the Morning Star as it comes over the horizon with 'healing in His wings.'" In context, I think this is what he means. But if you listen to the tape, it sounds like he says "morning stars,"(plural) in which case he might be referring to the Bride of Christ hearing from their theophanies. I doubt this is the case because it doesn't match the context. If you are curious about this point, you should listen to the tape and draw your own conclusion.

"Chapter 80: 'Let There Be Life!'"

A woman with a brown suit and skirt signifies a change in Wm. Branham's ministry. Message sources: 57-0309e, E52; 59-0406, E12-E19; 63-0714e, 23-27.

Wm. Branham sees a vision that explains why a young mother died. Message source: 63-0724, 135-152. Notice that Wm. Branham leaves these people nameless. I named them for convenience in writing and ease of reading and understanding.

These references discuss Wm. Branham's tax case in general, and two of them refer specifically to Wm. Branham's interview with the IRS attorneys, and the details surrounding that interview. Message sources: 58-0720m, E9-E10; 58-0928m, 6674; 59-0609 E44; 59-0706, E33-E35; 59-0712, 59-73; 59-0810, E4-E9; 60-0304, E48; 60-1211m, 75-83; 61-0112, 596-541; 62-1124e, E12-E19; 62-1223, 24; 62-1230m, 26; 62-1230e, 162; 63-0114, E8-E10; 63-0126, E93; 63-0728, 61 through 63; 63-1128m, 35-37. Other sources: Only Believe magazine, Vol. 3, No. 1 and Vol. 3, No. 2.

These three stories—the three red squirrels created in Indiana, the four gray squirrels created in Kentucky, and Hattie Mosier saying the right thing—all deal with the same theme, so Wm. Branham often told them together. Message sources: 59-1115, E29-E66 and E75-E79; 59-1123, E33-E59; 65-1127e, 127-166; 64-0500, E65-E82. Other sources: Hattie Wright Mosier's testimony in Only Believe magazine, Vol. 2, No. 2; and Charlie Cox's testimony in Only Believe magazine, Vol. 1, No. 2.

The quotation that begins, "Now I want to say something to my little church here…" comes from Wm. Branham's sermon "New Ministry," preached in Jeffersonville, Indiana, November 15, 1959. Message Source: 59-1115, E73 (edited).

Chapter 81: Beyond the Curtain of Time

Wm. Branham prays for Oral Roberts' knee, and then tours his office building. Message sources: 60-0417s, 31-33; 60-0611b, E10-12; 60-0804, E6870; 61-0411, E6-E10; 62-0701, E8-E15; 62-0719b, E23-E26; 62-0725, E58-E62.

Wm. Branham sees a vision of an armory building exploding, sees a vision of Jesus, and then he is healed of laryngitis and a fever. Message source: 60-0417m, 138-160.

Wm. Branham is taken beyond the curtain of time. Message sources: 60-0402, 192 through 242; 60-0515M, 19-1 through 24-1; 60-0803, E27-E40; 61-0305, E17-E25; 63-0115, E8-E16; 63-0322, 376-5 {347} to 384-5 {429}; 65-1128m, 21-36; 65-1205, 117-129.

Note: Concerning the explanation Wm. Branham received beyond the curtain of time, the voice said, "This is the place the Scripture called 'souls under the altar,'" referring, of course, to Revelation 6:9. Notice that the voice did not say it was the same group of people referred to in Revelation 6:9. It said this was the same place. In other words, it is the same dimension. In his sermon "Countdown" (preached November 25, 1962) Wm. Branham taught there are seven dimensions. He mentioned the four dimensions which science has identified: length, width, height, and time. The fifth dimension he called the Region of the Lost, where Satan and his demons dwell, as well as those people who die without knowing Jesus Christ and are waiting for the Day of Judgment. The sixth dimension is Paradise, the Region of the Blessed, where those who die in Christ live in their theophanies (spiritual bodies), not needing to eat, drink, or sleep. They are waiting for the second coming of Christ, at which time they will get new bodies—glorified bodies—and return to inhabit the earth after the Great Tribulation. The seventh dimension is the dwelling place of God Himself. Wm. Branham also mentions this on March 22, 1963 when he preached "The Fifth Seal." Message sources: 62-0908, 19-22; 621125e, E19-E21; 63-0322, 389 (revised format edition).

The quotation that begins, "Imagine somewhere out there a block of perfect love one hundred billion miles square," comes from Wm. Branham's sermon "The Rejected King," preached in Jeffersonville, Indiana, on May 15, 1960. Message source: 60-0515m, 23-6 through 24-2 (edited).

Bibliography

Acts of the Prophet, by Pearry Green, 1969. Covers the high points of Wm. Branham's life, along with Pearry Green's personal experiences with Wm. Branham. 207 pages. Available from Tucson Tabernacle, 2555 North Stone Avenue, Tucson, Arizona 85705, USA.

All Things Are Possible: The Healing and Charismatic Revivals in Modern America, by David Harrell, Jr., 1975. Shows how Wm. Branham's ministry started the boom in other healing/revival ministries in the 1950's. 304 pages. Available from Indiana University Press, 601 North Morton Street, Bloomington, Indiana 47404, USA.

Only Believe magazine, Rebekah Branham Smith, editor. This magazine features articles about Wm. Branham's life and ministry. Available on the Internet at www.onlybelieve.com.

Sermons of Wm. Branham are available from the following:

Voice of God Recordings, Inc., P.O. Box 950, Jeffersonville, Indiana 47131, USA, has the sermons on audiocassettes and audio CDs, printed sermons, a sermon index, and the Message Software Package which has all of the sermons in a searchable database. You can also hear or print sermons via the Internet at www.branham.org

Bible Believers, 18603-60th Avenue, Surrey, BC V3S-7P4, Canada. You can hear or print sermons via the Internet at www.bibleway.org.

End Time Message Tabernacle, 9200 - 156 Street, Edmonton, Alberta T5R1Z1, Canada, has several printed sermons.

The Word Publications, P.O. Box 10008, Glendale, Arizona 85318, USA, has several printed sermons.

William Branham, A Man Sent From God, by Gordon Lindsay (in collaboration with Wm. Branham), 1950. Covers Wm. Branham's life up to 1950, with chapters contributed by Jack Moore, Gordon Lindsay, and Fred Bosworth. 216 pages. Available from The William Branham Evangelistic Association, P.O. Box 325, Jeffersonville, Indiana 47131, USA.

William Branham, A Prophet Visits South Africa, by Julius Stadsklev, 1952. Detailed account of Wm. Branham's 1951 trip to South Africa. 195 pages. Available from The William Branham Evangelistic Association, P.O. Box 325, Jeffersonville, Indiana 47131, USA.

Index

Read or Listen to all Six Books of "Supernatural: the Life of Willam Branham"

VOLUME I
  BOOK 1: The Boy and His Deprivation
  BOOK 2: The Young Man and his Desperation
  BOOK 3: The Man and His Commission

VOLUME II
  BOOK 4: The Evangelist and His Acclamation
  BOOK 5: The Teacher and His Rejection

VOLUME III
  BOOK 6: The Prophet and His Revelation

Audio Edition of these books available for purchase in mp3 disk format or digital download

Available from:
  BC Christian Fellowship, on the web at bcfellowship.org,
  Supernatural Christian Books, at supernaturalchristianbooks.com
  Amazon.com and other online distributors

Announcing!
**The Supernatural Christian Books free audio book project
at supernaturalchristianbooks.com**

**FREE DOWNLOAD of some wonderful public domain biographies and
other Christian works read by volunteers.**

Also you can VOLUNTEER to read for others!

Details at supernaturalchristianbooks.com